PRAISE FOR *THE BOMB*

Editors' Choice, *The New York Times Book Review*
A Best Book of the Week, *Financial Times*
Starred Review, *Kirkus Reviews*

"[A] rich and surprisingly entertaining history of how nuclear weapons have shaped the United States military and the country's foreign policy . . . Kaplan has a gift for elucidating abstract concepts, cutting through national security jargon and showing how leaders confront (or avoid) dilemmas."
—Justin Vogt, *The New York Times Book Review*

"Kaplan brings fresh detail and nuance to the most important narrative of our time."
—*Air Mail*

"Kaplan is a leader in this field . . . Those who are relatively unfamiliar with the period will learn an enormous amount, and even experts will find nuggets, twists and turns, and important themes . . . Fascinating and important."
—Robert Jervis, *H-Diplo*

"*The Bomb* is both timely and classic, a joy to read, and rich in information."
—Paige Cone, *RealClearDefense*

"Brilliantly chronicled."
—Jessica T. Mathews, *The New York Review of Books*

"In *The Bomb*, Fred Kaplan has delivered a timely, lively, highly readable account of how presidents from Truman to Trump have prepared for nuclear war—a history that is as deeply informed as it is utterly alarming."
—Steve Coll, author of *Ghost Wars* and *Directorate S*

"*The Bomb* is like the Pentagon Papers for US nuclear strategy. Kaplan has the insider stories of an investigative journalist, the analytic rigor of a political scientist, and the longer-term perspective of a historian. Insightful and important."
—Scott Sagan, professor of political science at Stanford University and chairman of the American Academy of Arts and Sciences' Committee on International Security Studies

"Fred Kaplan is the world's preeminent Dr. Strangelove whisperer, and *The Bomb* is the smartest, most riveting and up-to-date history of how US leaders, military and civilian, have thought the unthinkable."

—Timothy Naftali, author of *George H. W. Bush* and
coauthor of *Khrushchev's Cold War*

"With powerful anecdotes and a wealth of historical detail, Fred Kaplan tells the story of the men and women who found themselves appalled and entranced by the fearful, mad logic of nuclear war from the aftermath of Hiroshima to the present day. *The Bomb* is a frightening but necessary read."

—Rosa Brooks, author of *How Everything Became War*
and the Military Became Everything

"Fascinating insights . . . Kaplan writes well, engaging the reader even when describing arcane bureaucratic battles."

—Lawrence Freedman, *Foreign Affairs*

"Kaplan has done an admirable job of unraveling the minutiae and esoterica and writing a lucid, absorbing narrative . . . Fine, impressively researched . . . Terrifying."

—Howard Schneider, *National Review*

"An authoritative and highly readable history of the Damocles Sword that has hung over humanity for some seventy years."

—Walter Clemens, *New York Journal of Books*

"If you loved Kaplan's earlier work, *The Wizards of Armageddon*, or if you're a history/international relations buff, this is the book for you."

—*Literary Hub*

"Fascinating and sometimes harrowing."

—*Shelf Awareness*

"A taut, detailed history . . . Compulsively readable . . . Will keep military history and Cold War buffs up past their bedtime."

—*Library Journal*

"Rich in detail . . . Meticulous and frightening."

—Associated Press

"Jaw-dropping."

—George Will, *The Washington Post*

"Read *The Bomb* by Fred Kaplan! It is just an awesome book!"

—Malcolm Nance

Presidents,
Generals,
and the
Secret History
of
Nuclear War

THE
BOMB

FRED KAPLAN

Simon & Schuster Paperbacks
New York   London   Toronto   Sydney   New Delhi

Simon & Schuster Paperbacks
1230 Avenue of the Americas
New York, NY 10020

First Simon & Schuster paperback edition February 2021

SIMON & SCHUSTER PAPERBACKS and colophon are registered
trademarks of Simon & Schuster, Inc.

For information about special discounts for bulk purchases,
please contact Simon & Schuster Special Sales at 1-866-506-1949
or business@simonandschuster.com.

The Simon & Schuster Speakers Bureau can bring authors to your
live event. For more information or to book an event, contact
the Simon & Schuster Speakers Bureau at 1-866-248-3049
or visit our website at www.simonspeakers.com.

Interior design by Lewelin Polanco

3 5 7 9 10 8 6 4

Library of Congress Cataloging-in-Publication Data
has been applied for.

ISBN 978-1-9821-0729-1
ISBN 978-1-9821-0730-7 (pbk)
ISBN 978-1-9821-0731-4 (ebook)

In memory of R.C. Davis and V. Lanphier
And, as always, for Brooke

CONTENTS

Introduction

For thirty years after the Cold War ended, almost no one thought, much less worried, about nuclear war. Now almost everyone is fearful. But the fear takes the form of a vaguely paralyzed anxiety. Because of the long reprieve from the bomb's shadow, few people know how to grasp its dimensions; they've forgotten, if they ever knew.

The holiday from history ended on August 8, 2017, when President Donald Trump, barely six months in office, told reporters at his golf resort in Bedminster, New Jersey, that if the North Koreans kept threatening the United States with harsh rhetoric and missile tests, "they will be met with fire and fury like the world has never seen."

Even to those who didn't remember President Harry Truman's similar description, seventy-two years earlier, of the atomic bomb that destroyed Hiroshima ("a rain of ruin from the air, the like of which has never been seen on this earth"), it was clear that, in language more bellicose than any president's since the end of World War II, Trump was talking about launching nuclear weapons at North Korea—not if its leader, Kim Jong-un, first attacked the United States, but merely if he developed the ability to do so.

Then, six months later, Trump signed and released his administration's Nuclear Posture Review, a seventy-four-page document that called for building new types of nuclear weapons and integrating them with the military's conventional war plans—in short, for treating nuclear weapons as normal. The red lights flashed, the alarm bells rang furiously.

Yet here is what few recognized: none of these notions were new. The president himself seemed a departure from the norm, his character—erratic, eruptive, thin-skinned, willfully uninformed—a combustive mix for a world leader with his "finger on the button." But the button and everything around it were the same. In those decades when most of us chose to forget about the bomb—as global tensions calmed and fallout shelters crumbled and we turned our gaze to other problems and pleasures—the nuclear war machine continued to rumble forth in the beyond-Top-Secret chambers of the Pentagon, the Strategic Command headquarters in Omaha, the weapons labs in various parts of the country, and the think tanks whose denizens never stopped thinking about the unthinkable.

They all kept at their singular tasks, wrestling with the dilemmas posed by the bomb's existence: how to deter nuclear war; how to fight a nuclear war, if it cannot be deterred; how to win it, if such a thing is possible. This is the nature of the nuclear era, and the era never drifted into suspension, even if our attention did. Trump snapped us out of our slumber: reminded those who were old enough to know, and informed those who weren't, that the bomb is still here.

In public, over the years, officers and officials have described America's nuclear policy as second-strike deterrence: if an enemy strikes us with nuclear weapons, we will retaliate in kind; this retaliatory power is what deters the enemy from attacking us. In reality, though, American policy has always been to strike first preemptively, or in response to a conventional invasion of allied territory, or to a biological or large-scale cyber attack: in any case, not *just* as an answer to a nuclear attack. All of these options envision firing nuclear weapons at military targets for military ends; they envision the bomb as a weapon of war, writ large. This vision has been enshrined in the American military's doctrines, drills, and exercises from the onset of the nuclear era through all its phases. Most presidents have been skeptical of this vision—morally, strategically, practically—but none of them have rejected it. Some have threatened to launch nuclear weapons first as a way of settling a crisis. The few who considered adopting a "no first use" policy, in the end, decided against it.

There are rationales for these doctrines, drills, and exercises and for the retention of the first-use option. They are driven by politics, personalities, and bureaucratic rivalries, but also by a logic, which, once its premises are accepted, hurls its adherents—and the rest of us—into a rabbit hole of increasingly bizarre scenarios that seem increasingly, if strangely, rational the deeper they're probed.

Understanding the nuclear era—the era of our lifetime—means understanding the rabbit hole: who dug it and how we got stuck inside. It means tracing the maze of its tunnels, which is to say, the arc of its history: a story enmeshed in secrecy, some of it still secret, much of it now illuminated—by declassified documents and interviews with key actors—though never fully told.

How did we get to this second coming of nuclear panic? How did we wind up with thousands of nuclear weapons, far more than any war aims could justify? What propelled the nuclear arms race during the decades-long Cold War? And what happened to the weapons and their guardians after the Cold War ended? How and why did any of this persist?

CHAPTER 1

"Killing a Nation"

In the spring of 1945, General Henry "Hap" Arnold, commander of the U.S. Army Air Forces, asked his top bombardier, Major General Curtis LeMay, when the war would be over. Nazi Germany had recently surrendered to the Allies, but the Japanese kept fighting, despite the pummeling of their cities by LeMay's firebombing raids.

LeMay took the question to his staff officers. They calculated how many Japanese cities hadn't yet been hit, how many more bombs were needed to hit them, and how long it would take for the men of his XXI Bomber Command to deliver and drop them. LeMay came back with the answer.

"The war will be over by the first of September," he told Arnold with his trademark gruff confidence. That, he explained, was when his men would run out of targets to hit—when every square mile of Japan would be incinerated.

This was LeMay's philosophy of how to win modern wars: *bomb everything.*

In fact, the war ended a few weeks earlier, on August 6, when a B-29 Superfortress aircraft, nicknamed *Enola Gay*, dropped a new kind of weapon—an atomic bomb—on Hiroshima. The level of destruction was astonishing. LeMay's air raids had been terrifying enough: his most intense attack, five months earlier, had amassed 334 B-29s to drop incendiary bombs over Tokyo, burning to a crisp nearly sixteen square miles of the city and killing 84,000 residents. A single A-bomb, dropped by a single airplane over Hiroshima, obliterated almost five square miles and killed 150,000 people. On August 9, another B-29, called *Bockscar*, dropped an atom bomb on Nagasaki. Six days later, the Japanese emperor surrendered. The war was over, but warfare had been transformed.

The generation of Army airmen who came of age in the 1930s, LeMay included, were enthralled by the theories of the Italian and American generals, Giulio Douhet and Billy Mitchell, visionaries who saw air power as the decisive force in wars of the future, transcending the brutal skirmishes on the ground, striking directly at the enemy's industrial strength and civilian morale, without which its leaders could no longer wage war. The present war, the Second World War, the first war in which air power played a major role, hadn't yet clinched the case, especially in the European theater, where the clash of armies still dominated. But at the end of the war, this new weapon, it was thought, might make the airmen's dream come true.

In 1947, in recognition of its impact on the recent victory, the Army Air Forces were declared a separate service, coequal with the Army and the Navy. This was a significant move. As long as they were a unit within the Army, the air forces would support the Army's policies and missions, mainly by providing air support to troops on the battlefield. Even LeMay's bombing raids were initially intended to degrade Japan's military machine and thus pave the way for the Army's impending invasion of the mainland. But as a separate service, the U.S. Air Force, as it was now called, could set its own missions and strategies. (LeMay was already accustomed to this: toward the end of the war, when thick clouds over Japan prevented him from hitting specific targets, he started dropping firebombs on populated *areas*—because areas were all he could hit—on his own initiative.)

In 1948, LeMay was placed in charge of a unit within the Air Force known as SAC, the Strategic Air Command, which planned the missions for the planes that would drop atomic bombs in the next war. Under LeMay's tight, aggressive leadership, SAC came to dominate not only the Air Force but the entire military establishment: its thinking, its culture, its war plans, its budgets.

At first, President Harry Truman resisted this juggernaut. Soon after Hiroshima, as he realized the full extent of the new weapon's devastation, Truman decided not to build any more A-bombs, in case the United Nations banned them. When it became clear that this wasn't going to happen and that the Russians were getting aggressive in Berlin, he cranked up the program. But even then, he kept the bomb under civilian control. For several years, the Air Force had to go through the Atomic Energy Commission even to load the weapons onto their planes.

On July 21, 1948, at a meeting with David Lilienthal, the AEC commissioner, and a few of the top generals, Truman explained his reasoning: "I don't think we ought to use this thing unless we absolutely have to. It is a terrible thing to order the use of something that"—and here, Truman looked down at his desk reflexively—"that this is so terribly destructive, destructive beyond anything we have ever had." He continued:

> You have got to understand that this isn't a military weapon. It is used to wipe out women and children and unarmed people, and not for military uses. So we have got to treat this thing differently from rifles and cannons and ordinary things like that.

Much of the history of the bomb over the subsequent seventy years, and doubtless beyond, is the story of the generals—and many civilian strategists, as well—trying to make it a "military weapon" after all.

At first, the Army and the Navy tried to halt history too. In 1949, when the Defense Department cut the budget for ships in order to buy more bombers, the Navy's top echelon of admirals staged an unprecedented revolt. Several of them condemned the A-bomb on moral grounds. At a congressional hearing, Rear Admiral Ralph Ofstie—who had served on the U.S. Strategic Bombing Survey, a postwar panel of officers and economists that downplayed the role of air power in the Allied victory—condemned Air Force–style city-bombing as "random mass slaughter," "ruthless and barbaric," and "contrary to our fundamental ideals."

Other officers criticized the A-bomb as militarily ineffective. One unfortunate Navy commander named Eugene Tatom testified that you could stand at one end of Washington National Airport, set off an atom bomb on the other end, and walk away "without serious injury."

The admirals' revolt soon collapsed from its own incoherence. The contradiction between Ofstie's testimony and Tatom's was risible: the A-bomb couldn't be both barbaric and toothless. It became all too clear that the admirals' main problem with the bomb was that the Air Force had it and the Navy did not. The admirals relented and then, after something less than a decent interval, embraced the bomb with a convert's fervor.

Besides, the bomb was, by and large, popular. Tensions between the United States and its largest wartime ally, the Soviet Union, had been brewing since their joint victory. The war had ended with their troops facing one another across the border demarking the two new German states—a U.S.-occupied West Germany and a Soviet-controlled East Germany. Since then, the United States had demobilized much of its vast army; life on the home front was settling into normalcy. If the Cold War heated up to a shooting war, as seemed likely, better, many believed, to win it quickly by slamming the Communists with A-bombs than to send millions of American boys back to the grueling battlefields of Europe from which they'd only recently departed.

By 1952, a mere three years after the admirals' revolt, all of the Navy's new combat planes were designed to carry nuclear weapons. The Army and even the Marine Corps were equipping their battalions and brigades with short-range nuclear missiles and even nuclear artillery shells to help repel an invasion.

In that same year, the Los Alamos laboratory built and tested a hydrogen bomb. While the blast of an A-bomb was measured in kilotons (the equivalent of thousands of tons of TNT), the H-bomb released the power of megatons (millions of tons). Some of the scientists who'd helped build the atom bomb questioned whether this new weapon—at first called the Super—was more destructive than any war aim could justify. But by this time, the Cold War was in full force; if American scientists could build an H-bomb, Soviet scientists could someday do so too. Just months later, in fact, the Soviets did test a bomb that came close to matching the explosive power of the H-bomb. And so the project zoomed forth, and super-bombs were cranked out in vast quantity.

The American military wove the new weapons into its war plans with no hesitation. In March 1954, the Joint Chiefs of Staff—the top officers of all the branches of the armed forces—declared in a Top Secret document, "In a general war, regardless of the manner of initiation, atomic weapons will be used at the outset." The term "general war" was defined as an armed conflict that pitted American and Soviet forces directly against one another. In other words, a war between the world's two new superpowers would be, from the first salvos, a nuclear war. This would be the case "regardless of the manner of initiation." Any armed Soviet incursion into territory deemed vital to U.S. interests—even a tentative crossing of the East-West German border—would spark an instant, all-out nuclear response.

This wasn't exclusively the military's position. The JCS document that set forth this policy was attached to a policy paper titled "U.S. Objectives in the Event of General War with the Soviet Bloc," drafted by the National Security Council and signed by President Dwight Eisenhower.

Eisenhower was a retired Army general—a five-star general, the Supreme Allied Commander in Europe during World War II, and the Army chief of staff soon after. Yet, like most of the citizens who elected him president by an overwhelming margin in 1952, he had no hunger for another land war. His most popular campaign pledge had been to end the war in Korea, a bitter stalemate that had gone on since 1950, killing more than 35,000 American troops. He ended the war, so it seemed, by threatening to drop nuclear bombs on the Soviet Union—which, along with the new Communist government of China, had backed North Korea in its invasion of South Korea. An armistice was signed six months after he took office.*

It wasn't that Eisenhower was itching to use nuclear weapons; he abhorred their destructive power and understood that a nuclear war would herald catastrophe. But for that reason, he thought that threatening to use them would deter the Kremlin and any other foe from aggression.

He came to this view in the weeks leading up to his inauguration. After winning the election, he traveled to Korea and visited the troops, then flew to Guam and Pearl Harbor, where he met his entourage of top advisers, who joined him on board the cruiser USS *Helena*, to steam back to the United States.

The group included his designated secretaries of state and defense, John Foster Dulles and Charles Wilson; his incoming treasury secretary and budget director; and Admiral Arthur Radford, commander of the Pacific Fleet, whom Eisenhower wanted to size up as a possible chairman of the Joint Chiefs of Staff. (Radford passed the audition.)

In the relaxed setting of a boat ride in the Pacific, they talked about how to solve what Eisenhower called the "great equation"—how to protect the nation without wrecking the economy. Eisenhower was a penny-pincher. Throughout his presidency, in speeches, diary entries, and private conversations with aides, he worried that weakening the U.S. economy would weaken its defenses—and that a rising federal

---

* It remains a dispute how much this threat affected Moscow's actions; Josef Stalin's death in March 1953, three months before an armistice was signed, may also have had an impact. But Eisenhower and many others viewed the threat as decisive.

budget, even if much of it was spent on troops and weapons, would hurl the nation's economy and thus its defenses into a tailspin.

So the solution that Eisenhower and his group devised—the essence of the great equation—was to rely a lot more on the nuclear bomb.

Almost immediately after taking office, Eisenhower directed his cabinet secretaries to flesh out the idea. A little more than a year later, in March 1954, the NSC and JCS signed the documents declaring that atomic weapons would be used at the outset of a general war. Two months before then, in order to close off further debate and to make the new policy public, Eisenhower told John Foster Dulles to deliver a speech on the subject to the august Council on Foreign Relations.

Titled "The Strategy of Massive Retaliation," the speech portrayed an enemy—the Sino-Soviet bloc—bent on exploiting weaknesses in every crevice of the Free World. If we played the enemy's game, Dulles said, we would wind up sending troops to shore up defenses everywhere, thinning our forces, straining our alliances, and going bankrupt in the process. Instead, he announced, the United States would now pursue "maximum protection at a bearable cost"—meaning it would "depend primarily upon a great capacity to retaliate, instantly, by means and at places of our own choosing." In other words, it would retaliate, at the start of a war, with nuclear weapons.

Through the next few years, battles continued to rage within the Pentagon over the degree to which the nation should rely on nuclear weapons for its defense. On one side, Army generals and Navy admirals argued that the military should at least try to push back a Soviet or Chinese invasion with conventional forces in the first rounds of battle—a strategy that would mean, among other things, larger budgets for their services. The JCS policy paper of March 1954 reflected this balanced approach to some degree, stating: "It is the policy of the United States that atomic weapons will be integrated with other weapons in the arsenal of the United States." In other words, atomic weapons would be "used at the outset," but in tandem with conventional weapons, as part of a campaign that "integrated" nuclear and nonnuclear forces.

On the other side of this interservice rivalry, Air Force generals pushed for the pure Mitchell-Douhet vision: relying entirely on nuclear weapons and winning the war by annihilating Russia. At one closed Senate hearing, General LeMay derided any other form of armed strength, and any other strategy, as obsolete. An aide to Lyndon B. Johnson, the Senate's top Democrat, wrote in a memo after the hearing that LeMay "is not just calling for more bombers and more H bombs. He is calling for nothing but heavy bombers and H bombs."

Late in 1955, the JCS chairman, Admiral Radford who just a few years earlier had been a ringleader in the revolt against the growing dominance of the A-bomb, switched sides and joined the Air Force in its unabashed advocacy. The Army chief of staff, General Matthew Ridgway, remained a dissident. A decorated officer in World War II and commander of the Eighth Army in Korea, Ridgway resigned in protest. His successor, General Maxwell Taylor, another commander in those wars, roused his staff to mount one more round of resistance.

In a draft of the following year's JCS war plan, known as the Joint Strategic Capabilities Plan, Taylor tried to insert language suggesting that the military might refrain from using nuclear weapons in wars that were smaller and more geographically confined than general war. When Radford found out about Taylor's maneuver, he fired off a memo to all the Chiefs, calling the proposal "a radical departure from the present approved policy," which "clearly states" that "atomic weapons will be used not only in general war but in local war"—including small, distant wars that didn't necessarily involve vital interests—"if the situation dictates."

Radford met with Eisenhower on May 14 to complain about Taylor's recalcitrance. Eisenhower said that, on one level, he agreed with Taylor: a really small war, one involving a few Army or Marine battalions, might be fought with only conventional weapons. But beyond that, especially if the fighting grew to the magnitude of the Korean War, we would have to bring in nuclear bombs.

The admiral had no problem with that distinction, but he added that if we ever got involved in, say, Vietnam, we wouldn't send large numbers of soldiers, as the French had done with disastrous results. Instead, Radford said, we'd drop nuclear bombs there too. Eisenhower didn't disagree.

Ten days later, in a final appeal, Taylor asked for a meeting in the Oval Office with Eisenhower and Radford to make his case against this all-but-total reliance on the Air Force and nuclear weapons. Eisenhower calmly reminded his old Army friend that it was official U.S. policy to base all military planning on the use of nuclear weapons, without restriction, at the outset of any war with the Soviet Union. True, some NSC staffers had advocated using conventional weapons and escalating step by step if possible. But, Eisenhower said, he personally thought that atomic bombs would be dropped at once and in full force; he saw no basis for thinking otherwise; it was "fatuous" to believe the United States and the Soviet Union would be "locked in a life and death struggle" *without* using atomic weapons.

Eisenhower did not concede, as he had in his earlier one-on-one meeting with Radford, that he might refrain from going nuclear in a very small war. Instead, he now told Taylor that, even in those kinds of wars, commanders should plan on using "tactical" atomic weapons—short-range missiles and munitions—against strictly military targets.

Taylor argued that even the use of small nuclear weapons would trigger escalation to general war. Eisenhower waved away the concern, saying that they were no more likely to do so than setting off "twenty-ton blockbusters."

Then came a remark that Eisenhower intended as reassurance, but that left Taylor puzzled and angry. Don't worry, the retired Army five-star general told the current Army chief of staff, you won't be rendered obsolete: if nuclear war comes, the Army will be vital for maintaining law and order on the home front.

Still, for all his calm confidence, Eisenhower was conflicted about the nuclear era. By this time, the Soviets had built their own atomic arsenal and a fleet of aircraft with the range to drop bombs on American soil. On July 1, seven weeks after his meeting with Radford and Taylor, the president and his senior national security advisers heard a Top Secret briefing on the consequences of a nuclear war between the United States and the Soviet Union. The briefing was delivered by a retired Air Force general named Harold Lee George, the staff director of the Net Evaluation Subcommittee, a secret unit—its very existence was highly classified—inside the National Security Council. The unit's task was to take data and intelligence about Soviet and American nuclear arsenals, encode the data in a computer program that simulated mutual attacks, and calculate the results.

The results were grim, for both sides. An attack by the United States destroyed the USSR as a society. But an attack by the Soviet Union hardly left America unscathed: the federal government would be wiped out; the economy would undergo near-total collapse, with no recovery of any sort for at least six months; two thirds of the population would require medical care, and most of them would have no way to obtain it.

Eisenhower was visibly shaken by the briefing. That night, he wrote in his diary, "The only possible way of reducing these losses would be for us to take the initiative" and to "launch a surprise attack against the Soviets." But that option, he continued, was "impossible." It would go "against our traditions," and, in any case, Congress wouldn't allow it.

The only way to keep the nation secure, he concluded, was to maintain a powerful deterrent—and that meant a mighty nuclear arsenal. If deterrence failed, if the Soviets doubted our resolve and mounted an attack, Eisenhower was stumped on how to respond. For that, he relied on General LeMay.

LeMay wasn't the first leader of the Strategic Air Command. When SAC was formed in 1946, a year before the Air Force became independent, General George Kenney was put in charge. Kenney had run the air campaign in the Southwest Pacific toward the end of World War II, but he had never been involved in strategic bombing, nor was he a remarkable organizer.

When LeMay succeeded him in 1948, he found a command in shambles. LeMay ordered a drill: every B-36 bomber, from every SAC base across the country, would launch a full-scale mock attack on Dayton, Ohio. The results were devastating: not a single pilot finished the mission, not a single navigator found his assigned target, not a single gunner managed to simulate the procedures of dropping a bomb.

Over the next three years, through relentless drilling, unforgiving discipline, and shrewd lobbying for more money from Washington (for more planes, personnel, and bombs), LeMay whipped SAC into shape, transforming it, in the words of his admirers, from a "hollow shell" to a "cocked pistol." His intensely loyal subordinates gave him a variety of doting nicknames: "Old Iron Pants," "The Big Cigar," "The Demon," and "Bombs Away LeMay."

When LeMay had been a colonel, placed in charge of an air division in Europe in the early years of World War II, he heard reports that many pilots were aborting their missions in the face of heavy fire from German fighter planes or antiair batteries. Upon taking command, he told his airmen that he would ride in the lead plane on every bombing run, and if any plane behind him veered away from battle, its entire crew would be court-martialed. The abort rate plummeted overnight.

Now at SAC, as commander of the most powerful armada of planes in the history of the world, LeMay's mystique only deepened. The culture of SAC was the cult of LeMay.

On paper, LeMay answered to higher powers, specifically to the Air Force chief of staff, General Hoyt Vandenberg, who subscribed to a more traditional concept of warfare. While LeMay was firebombing cities in Japan, Vandenberg was commander of the Ninth Air Force, providing close air support to Army soldiers fighting in France. So, when he and his aides in the Pentagon devised plans for a nuclear war, they focused on tactical objectives—defeating the Soviet Union's armed forces, not just obliterating it as a country.

Vandenberg described his plan as "killing a nation," but he parsed the campaign into three categories of targets, which he labeled "Delta-Bravo-Romeo." Delta stood for "the disruption of the vital elements of the Soviet war-making capacity." Bravo called for "the blunting of Soviet capabilities to deliver an atomic offensive against the United States and its allies." Romeo stood for "the retarding of Soviet advances into Europe." In this scheme, destroying all three sets of targets would destroy the Soviet Union as a war-making power.

LeMay thought this was abstract nonsense. The quickest way to destroy the Soviet war machine was to destroy the Soviet Union—especially its large cities, where the political leaders and military commanders and factory workers lived. This concept had worked for LeMay in Japan; and now that A-bombs and H-bombs were in the arsenal, the idea of going after small, discrete targets—a ball-bearing plant here, an electrical plant there—struck him as the height of inefficiency. It was also impractical. Nobody quite knew where a lot of these targets were; SAC's pilots would have to go searching for them while flying over enemy territory. This was the opposite of planning, and LeMay was a stickler for rigid plans. (On this point, the Joint Chiefs' intelligence branch shared LeMay's skepticism.)

Besides, LeMay had already written his own orders. Labeled SAC Emergency War Plan 1-49, it called for slamming the Soviet Union with "the entire stockpile of atomic bombs" in "a single massive attack," dropping 133 A-bombs on seventy cities within thirty days.

SAC headquarters was located at Offutt Air Force Base, just outside Omaha, Nebraska, more than a thousand miles west of Washington, D.C., and the Pentagon. This remoteness from the center of political power would have put many commanders at a disadvantage, but LeMay turned isolation into a strength. It allowed him to ignore orders when they contradicted his ideas about modern warfare. So he ignored Vandenberg's nuclear war plan and continued to work on his own.

In preparation for LeMay's plan, his staff drew up a list of roughly 100 targets to hit, mainly the largest Soviet cities. As SAC's budget swelled, and as the labs churned out more bombs, LeMay's intelligence officers came up with more targets. The work took on a self-serving circular logic: more weapons drove the need to find more targets; more targets propelled a need to buy more weapons.

From 1949, the year of SAC's first war plan, to the spring of 1955, the list of targets grew fourteen-fold—and continued to grow each year through the end of the decade.

Over the same time span, the Navy also expanded its arsenal of nuclear weapons, most of them strapped under the wings of combat planes, which, in a war, would take off from supersized aircraft carriers as they steamed near Soviet and Chinese shorelines. Some of these planes would hit the same targets as SAC bombers. To LeMay, this was a nuisance, but not much more than that.

In the mid-1950s, though, the Navy launched a new project, a new kind of weapon, which posed—and was explicitly designed as—a threat to SAC's survival.

Since the collapse of their revolt at the start of the decade, the Navy's admirals had never stopped resenting the Air Force for usurping the defense budget—nor had they stopped looking for a path to regain their own dominance.

In 1956, Admiral Arleigh Burke, the newly named chief of naval operations, thought he found it. Burke, the commander of a carrier task force in the Second World War, had been a keen supporter of a controversial program in the late 1940s to build a nuclear-powered submarine. Now, as the Navy's top admiral, he jump-started funding for a similar, more modern sub capable of carrying sixteen long-range ballistic missiles, each tipped with a half-megaton nuclear warhead. The missile would be called the Polaris.

Around this time, several defense analysts, in the Pentagon and in outside consulting firms, were warning that, as the Soviets built more nuclear weapons, the Air Force's bombers, sitting on airfields—and its intercontinental ballistic missiles, which were scheduled for production in the next few years—would be vulnerable to an attack.

The Polaris subs didn't have that problem. They could roam beneath the ocean's surface, undetectable and therefore invulnerable. The Polaris missiles were proving in tests to be inaccurate, but that didn't matter much: a half-megaton blast would flatten buildings across a radius of five miles, meaning each missile would demolish a large city, even if it veered a bit off course.

In short, the Polaris could do what SAC's bombers would do—and without the bombers' vulnerability, which practically invited the Soviets to launch a preemptive attack. The implication was clear: the Navy could soon supplant the Air Force as the main proprietor of the bomb.

Just a year before the Polaris project got under way, the Navy formed a team of technical specialists called the Naval Warfare Analysis Group. And the analysts of NAVWAG, as the group's name was abbreviated, devised a strategic doctrine—a new way of looking at nuclear weapons and nuclear war—that provided a rationale for the Polaris and a critique of SAC's weapons and war plan.

NAVWAG's main thesis was that, once the Soviets had their own nuclear arsenal, the notion of winning a nuclear war was absurd and any plan to launch an American first strike was suicidal. Therefore, the only sensible purpose of nuclear weapons was to deter an enemy attack. The only way to deter an enemy attack was to develop a nuclear arsenal that could answer an enemy attack with a devastating counterblow to the enemy's cities. The best way to do that was to maintain an invulnerable second-strike force. And the most invulnerable force imaginable was a fleet of missile-carrying submarines moving undetected beneath the ocean's surface.

Under this doctrine, it didn't matter if the Soviets kept building more and more nuclear weapons. As long as the United States had enough weapons to destroy the Soviets' cities—Burke thought that the missiles in forty submarines, or 640 missiles in all, would be sufficient—and as long as those weapons couldn't be attacked, there was no need for the United States to respond in "an eternal, strength-sapping" numbers contest.

By contrast, the only way to compensate for the vulnerability of SAC's bombers' missiles was to build more bombers and missiles—and to keep building more as the Soviets built more. This approach, the NAVWAG study noted, was "a prescription for an arms race" and "an invitation to the enemy for preventive-war adventurism."

In the summer of 1957, at the annual conference where the service commanders came to the Pentagon and briefed the Joint Chiefs of Staff on their individual slices of the nuclear war plan, one of the NAVWAG analysts outlined this new view of how many weapons were really needed. LeMay was in the room, as commander of SAC, and as he listened to the briefing, his tongue started shoving his cigar from one side of his mouth to the other and back again. It was well known that LeMay's emotional state could be gauged by the intensity of his cigar's lateral movements. By the end of the NAVWAG briefing, he'd nearly chewed it down to a stub.

The Air Force chief of staff, General Thomas White, was also worried. Eisenhower had military aides from each service working for him in the White House. The Air Force aide had been writing memos, warning White that his Navy counterpart was making serious "inroads" in selling Polaris to the president.

Burke and his fellow admirals were waging war on the Air Force, and the NAVWAG report—which Burke circulated to all active and retired Navy officers—was the lance of the charge. White and LeMay knew they had to come up with their own doctrine—a strategic concept that only the Air Force could execute—and to spread the word at least as widely.

The first step, White felt, was for the Air Force to come clean on a crucial piece of its strategy for nuclear warfare. The NAVWAG report, and Burke's whole concept for the Polaris, rested on the premise that a "second-strike" deterrent was enough to keep the nation secure. The Air Force had contributed to this notion, White wrote in a memo to all of its commanders, "through the over-use of the term 'retaliation.'" It was time to emphasize, up front, that in a confrontation with today's enemy, the nation needed to "take the initiative." The ability to *respond* to a Soviet nuclear attack was necessary but insufficient. We also needed the ability to *preempt* that attack before it happened—to destroy the Soviet missiles and bombers before they were launched, before they inflicted catastrophic damage on American soil.

At the same time, White knew that he needed something more than "take the initiative" to sink the Polaris. A preemptive strike might take out a large part of the Soviets' nuclear arsenal, but probably not all of it; if the Soviets retaliated with the weapons that survived, they could still kill millions of Americans.

The Air Force had its own think tank, the RAND Corporation. Unlike NAVWAG, which was a unit of the Navy, RAND was nominally independent, but it received most of its funding from the Air Force and was frequently called upon to support or rationalize Air Force doctrine and weapons.

By coincidence, a new analyst at RAND named William Kaufmann, a former political science professor at Princeton, had come up with an idea that fit the bill. A few years earlier, Kaufmann had written an influential critique of John Foster Dulles's "massive retaliation" speech, arguing that it was tantamount to suicide in an age when both the United States and the Soviet Union possessed nuclear arsenals. Kaufmann's main point was that Dulles's doctrine lacked credibility: the Kremlin wouldn't believe that an American president would attack the Soviet Union with nuclear weapons in response to an incursion in Asia or even an invasion of West Germany—because the Soviets would respond by launching a nuclear attack on the United States. Kaufmann recommended, instead, a strong buildup of U.S. conventional forces to deter and repel a Soviet invasion on the Kremlin's own terms. Army officers, including General Maxwell Taylor, loved Kaufmann's article and distributed it widely, though it made no inroads in Eisenhower's White House.

At RAND, enmeshed in debates over nuclear strategy, Kaufmann figured out a way to apply his thesis to his new sponsor's agenda, especially in its fight with the Navy. (He titled one of his memos on the subject "The Puzzle of Polaris.") He called his idea the "counterforce" strategy. It stemmed from the same premise as his critique of Dulles: in an era when both sides have nuclear weapons, it would be suicidal to launch a nuclear first strike on the other side's cities. But, he observed, there were other kinds of targets, even for nuclear bombs. For instance, if the Soviets invaded West Germany, and if we were unable to mount a conventional defense, we could launch a small number of nuclear weapons against the USSR's military forces, especially its nuclear bomber bases and missile sites—deliberately leaving its cities untouched. Then, the American president could tell the Soviet premier: Stop your invasion, or I'll launch my remaining nuclear weapons against your cities.

Neither White nor LeMay was keen on the notion of a "limited" nuclear attack; it rubbed against what they saw as the main appeal of nuclear bombs—the immensity of their destructiveness. SAC was aiming some of its bombs at specific Soviet military sites. Since the early 1950s, U.S. intelligence had made strides—thanks to Air Force and CIA reconnaissance planes, communications intercepts by the National Security Agency, and the recruitment of well-placed spies—in discovering where some of the sites were located. Still, SAC's officers drew the target circles on the map in such a way that the bomb's blast would destroy the military site *and* a large chunk of a nearby city. In this view, the resulting civilian damage—the number of urban factories destroyed and people killed—wasn't something to avoid; to the contrary, it was touted as a "bonus."

Yet Kaufmann's counterforce strategy contained a kernel of appeal to Air Force officers: SAC bombers—and only SAC bombers—were accurate enough to hit Soviet military targets without doing much damage to nearby cities. By contrast, the missiles on Polaris submarines would veer too far off target to pull off this feat.

And so, even though they didn't quite buy its principles, the top officers of the Air Force adopted counterforce as their strategy. Before the Polaris challenge, Air Force doctrine had referred to city bombing as SAC's "Primary Undertaking" and the destruction of military targets as the "Alternate Undertaking." White now realized that this fell into the Navy's trap. The label "Primary Undertaking" would be cited by many as proof that SAC agreed with the Navy's emphasis on attacking cities as "the most important segment" of nuclear strategy. This inference, White wrote in a memo, would be invoked not only "as further justification of Polaris" but also as a strong argument—which the Navy was already making—to "eliminate virtually any strategic requirement other than Polaris" and thus to eliminate SAC. He had to switch the priorities, even if, behind the scenes, the actual policy remained the same.

By this time LeMay was stationed in the Pentagon, having been promoted to Air Force vice chief of staff. He understood what White was up to. But his successor at SAC, General Thomas Power, vigorously protested the doctrinal shift. Power had been LeMay's chief of staff during the firebombing of Tokyo, and he took on the task with such enthusiasm that LeMay made him deputy when he took over SAC. Now, as his successor, Power emulated his former boss with a disciple's zeal.

There was a cruelty to Power's zest for bombing cities. Even LeMay privately referred to his protégé as a "sadist." When Bill Kaufmann briefed him on the counterforce strategy at SAC headquarters, Power reacted with fury. "Why do you want us to *restrain* ourselves?" he screamed. "Why are you so concerned with saving *their* lives? The whole idea is to *kill the bastards*!" After a bit more of this tirade, Power said, "Look. At the end of the war, if there are two Americans and one Russian, we win!"

Kaufmann snapped back, "You'd better make sure that they're a man and a woman." Power stormed out of the room.

Afterward, Power cabled White to make sure Kaufmann's briefing didn't reflect Air Force policy. White wrote back, assuring him that, while the briefing made a convincing case for "a wider range of options in the future," official doctrine would still call for attacking "a mix of vital military and important urban-industrial targets." In short, SAC would still get its way.

Embracing counterforce provided the Air Force some intellectual heft in the fight against the Navy, but that wouldn't be enough to win the bureaucratic war, especially since the Navy's concept of deterrence resonated with President Eisenhower's policy of massive retaliation. The harder, crucial task would be to crush the Polaris—if not to kill the program, then to place its operations under SAC's control.

———— ∞∞∞ ————

LeMay had been pushing for some time to consolidate all the nation's nuclear weapons under his command. To officials outside the Air Force, he stressed the need to eliminate redundancies. The Joint Chiefs of Staff calculated that, in a general war, at least 200 targets inside the Soviet Union and China would be hit by Air Force bombers and Navy attack planes. (The Army and Marine stockpiles of short-range nuclear missiles and artillery shells didn't pose a problem, as they would be fired at tactical targets on the battlefield.)

LeMay had a case, but by early 1960 General White concluded that a unified command was a pipe dream: the admirals and the Army generals were implacably opposed, and for good reason. So White devised what he described in private memos as a "fallback position." He proposed the creation of a new organization called the Joint Strategic Target Planning Staff. It would consist of officers, from all the services, who would combine their individual nuclear war plans—their lists of what weapons would be fired at what targets—into a Single Integrated Operational Plan. Sitting on top of all these creations—which soon became known by their acronyms, the JSTPS and the SIOP—would be the Director of Strategic Targeting.

The catch was that the JSTPS would be located inside SAC

headquarters, and the Director of Strategic Targeting would be the same four-star Air Force general who served as SAC commander. In short, the SIOP would be a multiservice war plan, but SAC would plan the war.

White put forth a seemingly innocuous rationale for this arrangement: when it came to performing the bomb-damage calculations, charting the logistics, scheduling the precise times when hundreds of bombers and missiles would fly over hundreds of targets halfway across the globe, SAC was the only entity that had the experience, and SAC headquarters was the only place stocked with enough computers, to crunch the necessary data. Clearly, this was a case for a power grab within the military, but it was also true: no other service could do what SAC had learned to do—what SAC had invented as an activity—over the previous dozen years.

On June 14, Secretary of Defense Thomas Gates flew to SAC headquarters in Omaha to hear General Power brief the concept, which carried the title "Unity in the Strategic Offensive." White and his staff had written the briefing, along with strict instructions to Power on how to present it; but they figured that Gates—who had been at the Pentagon for just six months—would be more impressed if he heard it inside the belly of the nuclear war machine, with the banks of computers churning in the background.

Gates was sold. On July 6, he endorsed the idea in a meeting with the president. Eisenhower needed no persuading. General Nathan Twining, the former Air Force chief of staff who was now chairman of the Joint Chiefs of Staff, had been complaining for months about the Navy's refusal to cooperate in any way with SAC. Nearly a year earlier, in August 1959, Twining had sent a memo to all the service chiefs, asking them eighteen basic questions about nuclear targeting. The chiefs had failed to reach consensus on any of them. Eisenhower, who had just over six months remaining in his presidency, approved White's plan.

On August 16, Gates formally anointed the SAC commander as the Joint Chiefs' agent on all matters relating to the planning and waging of nuclear war. Control of the bomb was thus transferred from the Pentagon to Omaha.

Burke and Taylor acceded to the directive—they knew when they were outgunned—but Burke, in particular, was livid. He recognized the JSTPS and the SIOP for what they were: the tools of a takeover.

A matchless brawler when it came to internecine conflicts, Burke hated the Air Force with a passion. "This is just like Communism being here in the country," he grumbled to a few of his aides after realizing the implications of White's scheme. "It needn't have happened," he mused at another meeting, "that Lumumba can take over a country or that Castro, with a very few people and no following at the beginning, can take over a country, with a well-disciplined force, small but well-disciplined. It doesn't have to happen that way. It just does." To Burke's mind, the Air Force was doing to national security what Patrice Lumumba had done in the Congo and what Fidel Castro had done in Cuba.

One of Burke's aides tried to calm down the boss during one of his diatribes. "They think they are doing the best thing they know how for the country," he said of the Air Force brass.

"You're more generous than I am," Burke replied. "They're dishonest. They're dishonest, and they know it. They have no feeling at all that they are responsible for anything but the Air Force. They will wreck the United States."*

⎯⎯⎯⎯⎯ ⋘⋙ ⎯⎯⎯⎯⎯

General Tommy Power and his crew at SAC took no time to set up the new machinery. Within two weeks of Gates's directive, they presented an organizational chart for the Joint Strategic Target Planning Staff. More than half of its officer corps—140 out of 269 slots—would come

---

* Burke secretly tape-recorded many conversations, including this one, which comes from a transcript typed by his secretary.

from SAC, with another eight representing its parent service, the Air Force. (This did not include the 1,300 SAC officers who worked in the same building.) Just twenty-nine officers on the JSTPS would come from the Navy, ten from the Army, and three from the Marines.

As Burke predicted, the SAC-heavy staff proceeded to design a war plan—called SIOP-62, because it would take effect in Fiscal Year 1962—that emphasized SAC weapons, made a case for buying more SAC weapons, and relegated the Navy's Polaris missiles to a secondary mission.

Burke well understood that whichever service drew up the list of targets, and set the rules for how much damage to inflict on those targets, would also be the service that decided which weapons would be aimed at those targets, how many of those weapons were needed to do the necessary damage, and therefore how many more weapons the nation needed to build—in short, how much more money the Pentagon and Congress needed to give the service that built those weapons.

At the first SIOP Planning Conference, chaired by General Power on August 24, the main topic on the agenda was the creation of a National Strategic Target List, abbreviated as the NSTL.

The Navy officers at the meeting tried to cap how many targets the United States needed to hit with nuclear weapons in the event of war. But Power noted that the NSTL wasn't about military requirements. The point was simply to list all the objects, all the possible targets in the USSR, the Warsaw Pact nations, and China that had some strategic value—air bases, naval ports, missile sites, radar stations, command-control facilities, military factories, civilian factories. It didn't necessarily mean that the SIOP would call for all those targets to be attacked. The Navy backed down.

As it turned out, the list identified about 4,000 points on the map as "targets." All told, the Air Force and Navy combined had 3,423 nuclear weapons with the range to hit those targets. It was no coincidence that those two numbers weren't far apart—or that the number of targets slightly exceeded the number of weapons. If anyone argued that SAC had too many nuclear weapons, General Power could respond that, to the contrary, he didn't have enough weapons to hit all of the enemy's targets. The NSTL became a device to justify the arsenal's expansion.

Because SAC's philosophy of war required more weapons, and the Navy's did not, the two quarreled over how many targets the U.S. military had to hit—and how many weapons it needed to hit them.

SAC's intelligence officers predicted that, by 1962, the Soviets would have 700 intercontinental ballistic missiles. The Navy's intelligence branch predicted they would have just 200. SAC officers vastly outnumbered Navy officers on the JSTPS, so SAC won the argument. That meant 500 extra targets, requiring 500 extra weapons to hit them—or actually, as Power and his staff worked the numbers, way more than 500 extra weapons.

Even before the JSTPS held its first meeting, Power had convinced the Joint Chiefs to sign a document called the National Strategic Target and Attack Plan, which set the basic rules for the SIOP. The N-Stap, as it was called, required that certain targets—for instance, Soviet and Chinese bomber bases, missile sites, and other crucial military facilities—had to be destroyed with a probability of "at least" 75 percent.

The key phrase was "at least." In the first round of bureaucratic negotiations, SAC officers argued that there were 200 extremely important targets that each had to be destroyed with a probability of 97 percent—and another 400 targets that needed to be destroyed with 93 percent assurance. Under Navy pressure, SAC relaxed these demands. Still, the final draft of the SIOP specified seven targets that had to be destroyed with 97 percent assurance, 213 targets with 95 percent confidence, 592 targets with a 90 percent chance, and 715 targets with 80 percent.

These rules dramatically inflated the number of nuclear weapons that would be "required" for an attack. A fair number of bombs and missiles would veer widely off course; some of them wouldn't explode; some bomber planes would be shot down en route to their targets. As a result, it was imprudent to assume that one bomb or missile would destroy a target with anything close to 90 percent certainty. Thus, for each target that had to be destroyed with a high degree of certainty, SAC would have to launch more than one weapon. And there were hundreds of such targets.

Burke's fears were vindicated; and, as his men in Omaha took a closer look at the war plan's details, they realized the game was more rigged than even he had predicted. The SIOP, it turned out, laid down nine nuclear weapons on four targets in Leningrad, twenty-three weapons on six target complexes in Moscow, and eighteen weapons on seven target areas in Kaliningrad.

Calculating the ratios across the board, they saw that the SIOP assigned an average of 2.2 nuclear weapons—each unleashing an explosive force of several megatons—to each and every target across the Soviet Union, China, and Eastern Europe. And, in keeping with LeMay's philosophy of modern war, these weapons would be launched in waves as massive and rapid as possible.

If a war started with short notice, the SIOP called for firing 1,459 nuclear weapons—all of the weapons that were on day-to-day alert, ranging in power from 10 kilotons to 23 megatons, totaling 2,164 megatons in all—against 654 targets.

If the United States had time to prepare a first strike, which most SAC officers assumed would be the case (they assumed no president would sit back and let the Soviets or Chinese get in the opening salvo), the plan called for launching 3,423 nuclear weapons—a total of 7,847 megatons—against 1,043 targets.

The objective, either way, was to disable the Sino-Soviet bloc's nuclear weapons, destroy its military and governmental centers, and cripple its economy to the point where it could no longer sustain a war.

No one disagreed with this objective—the Joint Chiefs had endorsed it ahead of time—but the Navy officers on the targeting staff regarded all of SAC's rules, assumptions, and calculations as excessive. As a result, they argued, SIOP-62 would inflict way more damage than the objective required.

At one point, the SAC planners were asked how many Russian, Chinese, and Eastern European people would die in the all-out version of SIOP-62's attack. The answer came back: at least 275 million. Who ever heard of such a number? What kind of war, what plausible strategic goal, required killing so many civilians?

On December 1, Secretary Gates, the Joint Chiefs of Staff, the chiefs of the various combatant commands, and their top aides— thirty-two officers and officials in all—gathered at SAC headquarters to hear General Power brief them on the finished SIOP.

In the discussion that followed, Rear Admiral John Hyland, a decorated war pilot who had commanded an air group on the USS *Intrepid* in the Pacific Fleet and who now served in the Pentagon's strategic plans office, spoke up on behalf of the Navy. He particularly criticized the SIOP's "requirement" to destroy so many targets with a probability of 90 percent. The number was not only excessive, Hyland said, but impractical. In the fog of war, nobody could hit these targets with such high confidence; nor was there any way, after the bombs were dropped and the missiles were launched, to assess whether the targets had been truly destroyed, merely damaged, or hit at all.

Finally, Hyland noted, the plan took into account only the damage caused by the bombs' blast. Ignored were the other effects of a nuclear explosion: heat, fire, smoke, and the radioactive fallout that would contaminate an area, making it impassable for months, if not longer.

SAC's targeting staff had an explanation for this omission: there was plenty of data, from studies of conventional bombing in World War II, on the effects of blast, but almost nothing on the other effects. And those effects were, to some degree, unpredictable, influenced by weather, wind, and other factors. Still, to wave the effects away, simply because they couldn't be precisely calculated, greatly understated the damage wreaked by a nuclear attack. There was no reason to kill as many people or to destroy as much territory as SIOP-62 called for. And even if there were, the damage could be done with far fewer weapons.

Hyland knew that others in high places had expressed the same concerns and horror. One of them was President Eisenhower's chief science adviser, George Kistiakowsky, a chemist who'd headed the Explosives Branch of the Manhattan Project, which built the first A-bomb. At Eisenhower's request, Kistiakowsky had traveled to Omaha for a private SIOP briefing, taking along one of his aides, a fellow weapons scientist named George Rathjens. Before the trip, Rathjens asked a CIA liaison for the name of the Soviet city that most resembled Hiroshima in size and industrial concentration. When he got to SAC headquarters, he asked a staff officer how many weapons the SIOP laid down on that city. The answer: one 4.5-megaton bomb, followed by three 1.1-megaton bombs, in case the first one was a dud. The A-bomb that destroyed one third of Hiroshima, at the end of World War II, had released an explosive force of 12.5 *kilotons*.

In other words, SIOP-62 would hit that Soviet town with more than six hundred times the blast power of the Hiroshima bomb.

One other senior officer protested the war plan's excess at General Power's December briefing—General David Shoup, commandant of the Marine Corps (and, later, an outspoken critic of the Vietnam War). The Marines had little interest in nuclear weapons. They had only three officers on the JSTPS, which fairly reflected the Corps' small atomic arsenal—fewer than 200 short-range artillery rockets. Still, Shoup was bothered by one of the briefing's charts, showing that tens of millions of Chinese would die as a result of the U.S. attack.

"Do we have any options, so that we don't have to hit China?" Shoup asked.

"Well, yeah, we could do that," Power replied, squirming in his front-row seat, "but I hope nobody thinks of it because it would really screw up the plan."

The next day, December 2, Gates and the Joint Chiefs held a meeting on whether to approve SIOP-62. Gates asked if anyone had a comment. General Shoup stood and said, "Sir, any plan that kills millions of Chinese, when it isn't even their war, is not a good plan. This is not the American way."

Nonetheless, the plan was approved with no revisions. It would go into effect the following April.

By this time, Maxwell Taylor had resigned from the Army and written a book condemning the policy of massive retaliation. Burke and Shoup had made their protests known and saw no point in resisting further. Eisenhower's time in office was nearly up. A new president, a Democrat, John F. Kennedy, would enter the White House in a couple of months. The fight could be taken up again soon.

Meanwhile, the template was set for the policies and politics on nuclear weapons and nuclear war through the decades to come, into the next century.

CHAPTER 2

The Race Begins

Whoever won the 1960 presidential election, his term would mark the onset of the nuclear arms race as we still know it more than a half-century later. The 1960s were when the two superpowers would build and deploy nuclear weapons in large numbers, and when other, smaller but ambitious powers would join the game. Many, soon most, of these weapons would be missiles—nuclear-tipped rockets that could be launched from underground silos or undersea vessels, then streak across the heavens and plunge back down to the other side of the earth, exploding with monstrous waves of energy, heat, and toxins, all in a mere half-hour from blast-off to touch-down. There would be no time to deliberate, no time to hide. From this moment on, the shadow of the bomb would loom forever present.

When the election's winner, John Fitzgerald Kennedy, took the oath of office on January 20, 1961, he carried away the dubious prize of getting first crack at handling the new era's threats and challenges. His presidency seemed to offer promising prospects for all factions of the United States armed forces. Kennedy had campaigned on warnings of a "missile gap," echoing intelligence estimates that the Soviets were far ahead in the race to build long-range nuclear missiles and that, therefore, the U.S. Air Force needed more money and more missiles to catch up. He had also absorbed the studies showing the growing vulnerability of land-based missiles and bomber bases, and thus championed the Navy's Polaris missiles. And, like many of the Democratic Party's national security experts, he'd criticized John Foster Dulles's massive-retaliation policy and called for more conventional weapons and troops for the Army; he even brought General Maxwell Taylor out of retirement to serve as his special military adviser.

Finally, Kennedy touted himself as a man of "vigor," boasting not only his youth—at forty-three, he was the youngest man ever elected president, succeeding Eisenhower, who, at seventy, was stepping down as the oldest—but also his eagerness for military action, pledging in his Inaugural Address to "pay any price" and "oppose any foe" in the pursuit of liberty's survival. At his first meeting with the Joint Chiefs, five days later, he assured the nation's top officers that he valued their advice and would solicit it routinely.

Kennedy's secretary of defense was another matter. Robert Strange McNamara was just one year older than Kennedy (he too was the youngest man ever to take his job) and no less vigorous, though in ways that the Chiefs found unsettling. During the Second World War, McNamara had worked in the Statistical Control Office of the Army Air Forces, as part of a group recruited from the Harvard Business School to apply new management techniques to the planning of bombing raids over Europe and Japan.

Toward the end of the war, the group's revamping of fueling routes gave the B-29s in Curtis LeMay's XXI Bomber Command 30 percent more mission flight-hours, which is to say, 30 percent more time to bomb targets. The feat bolstered McNamara's sense that the generals didn't know everything about their business—that a numbers-smart civilian, like him, could help in ways that the high brass hadn't been trained to comprehend.

After the war, he and his teammates sold themselves as a group to Ford Motor Company, where they rationalized production practices, swept the firm's finances clean of debt, and earned for themselves the nickname "whiz kids." McNamara had risen to the top of Ford Motor, as the company's youngest president ever, before coming to work for Kennedy, and now he hired a new set of whiz kids to overhaul the Pentagon.

He found them at the RAND Corporation, the Air Force–funded think tank in Santa Monica: young economists mainly, who had written books and monographs on how to analyze defense budgets, weapons systems, and war plans rationally—assessing, for example, how to pick the right weapon, and discard the wrong ones, by calculating which of them would destroy the most targets for the same amount of money (or destroy the same number of targets for the least amount of money). These were the sorts of calculations that McNamara had performed during the war, but the RAND analysts were applying them across the gamut of national security issues. From a cursory flip through the Pentagon budget, McNamara saw a lot of redundancy. The Air Force had three bombers in production or development; the Air Force and Navy, between them, planned to produce four different types of cruise missiles; the Army, which had lost the ICBM competition to the Air Force, was developing two different models of anti-ballistic-missile systems. Certainly some of these projects were expendable.

Previous defense secretaries had set limits on how much the generals and admirals could spend, but none had restricted what the top brass could buy; no previous secretary had thought it proper to question their professional military judgment, to tell them which weapons they could build and which they'd have to give up. McNamara was determined—he was keyed up—to assert his wisdom over theirs: to force big changes. And the whiz kids from RAND would help him figure out how.

Two weeks into Kennedy's presidency, seized in this frame of mind, McNamara flew to Omaha, then took the ride to SAC headquarters, to hear General Tommy Power brief him on the nuclear war plan.

He came away as shocked and appalled as he'd ever felt in his life.

It was the briefing for SIOP-62, the same stem-winder that Power's staff had delivered to McNamara's predecessor and a roomful of officers and aides two months earlier. But McNamara, the supreme numbers cruncher, saw through the glossy graphs and complicated charts; he instantly discerned the connection between the high "damage-expectancy" curves (the hundreds of targets that needed to be hit with a probability of more than 90 percent) and the "requirement" for more weapons.

He told Power that the plan seemed excessive: the number of targets struck him as staggeringly high; and hitting hundreds of them with two, three, in some cases four nuclear weapons would kick up "fantastic" levels of radioactive fallout.

The Navy's notion of deterrence held that we needed only enough weapons to destroy the largest cities in the Sino-Soviet bloc. But in the SIOP, just 200 of the 4,000 targets were "urban industrial" complexes. The rest were military targets. Three hundred of those were air defense sites, most of them in the USSR's "satellite" nations of Eastern Europe, which needed to be destroyed with nuclear weapons in order to plow a "corridor," allowing Air Force bombers to fly toward their targets inside Russia without getting shot down along the way. McNamara was already close to concluding that ballistic missiles were better than bombers, precisely because they couldn't be shot down and were, therefore, more reliable as deterrents. Now he saw another benefit of cutting the number of bombers: it would mean he could cut the number of targets and, in the event of war, inflict less damage on Eastern Europe, whose populations despised their Soviet overlords and certainly bore no responsibility for the Kremlin's actions.

If the briefing's substance jolted McNamara out of his customary cool, Power's style, especially his vulgar jokes, sent him over the top. One of SIOP-62's targets was a huge air defense radar in Albania. The bomb sent to hit it would release several megatons of explosive power, enough to kill hundreds of thousands of Albanians, even though the tiny country was politically independent of Moscow.

"Mr. Secretary," General Power said with a chuckle, "I hope you don't have any friends or relations in Albania, because we're going to have to wipe it out."

McNamara fumed with contempt.

Back at the Pentagon, McNamara recited the horrors of Omaha to some of his top aides, including a couple of the RAND whiz kids. They told him about their colleague Bill Kaufmann and his counterforce study. McNamara told them to have Kaufmann come brief him.

The briefing took place on February 10, one week after the debacle at SAC. McNamara was fascinated by Kaufmann's concept: limiting the initial attack to the Soviets' military targets, holding back a secure reserve force to threaten their cities, and brandishing the force as a bargaining chip to persuade the Kremlin to halt the aggression that prompted our attack in the first place. Any idea that seemed to rationalize conflict would have appealed to McNamara; counterforce held a special allure, as a saner alternative to SAC's war plan.

McNamara expressed two qualms about Kaufmann's idea. First, he didn't quite see how this war ended. What if the Soviets didn't get the signal that we were sending with the small dose of destruction and the threat of more to come? What if they simply weren't inclined to play by the rules we were trying to lay down and, instead, retaliated with full force?

Kaufmann said that he'd mulled over the same concern and, frankly, didn't have a lot of confidence that the strategy *would* work; it was quite possible that, once nuclear weapons were used, escalation to all-out war would prove inevitable. But, he reasoned, if there was even a small chance of controlling the spiral, it was a chance worth pursuing. Meanwhile, if the Soviets retaliated anyway, the fact that we'd destroyed a large portion of their missiles and bombers would mean their attack on us would wreak less damage.

McNamara's second qualm was that he didn't see how this strategy would help him put a cap on SAC's voracious appetite for more missiles and bombers. The Navy's notion of attacking only Soviet cities had its strategic drawbacks, but at least it set a cut-off point on how many weapons were needed. Counterforce seemed to have no cut-off point: if we targeted only Soviet military sites, we would have to keep buying more weapons, as long as the Soviets kept buying more weapons.

Kaufmann had no answer to this one. Neither, for the moment, did McNamara.

On March 1, McNamara issued a thirteen-page memo, asking ninety-six questions, each one assigned to a specific group or individual—some to the Joint Chiefs, some to an assistant secretary of defense or to one of the service secretaries—with unreasonably tight deadlines. Some of the colonels and generals had taken to calling the whiz kids "McNamara's Band," so they called this memo the "96 Trombones," a play on "76 Trombones," the title of a song in a hit Broadway show called *The Music Man* about a charlatan bandleader. (McNamara later cut the number of questions to ninety-two, but the label stuck.)

The first two questions on McNamara's list were direct follow-ups to Kaufmann's briefing. The first: "Prepare a draft memorandum revising the basic national security policies and assumptions, including the assumptions relating to 'counterforce' strikes." The second: "Prepare a 'doctrine' which, if it is accepted, would permit controlled response and negotiating pauses in the event of thermonuclear attack."

Project No. 1, due May 1, was directed to the chairman of the Joint Chiefs of Staff, Army General Lyman Lemnitzer, and the assistant secretary of defense for international security affairs, Paul Nitze. Project No. 2, due April 17, was assigned only to Lemnitzer.

Nitze delegated the first assignment to his deputy, Henry Rowen, one of the RAND whiz kids that McNamara had brought on board. Rowen, in turn, handed it to a RAND colleague, now working for him as a consultant, named Daniel Ellsberg. The previous year, Ellsberg had conducted a highly classified study of the military's nuclear command-control network. He was one of the very few civilians ever to immerse himself in the nuts and bolts of the nuclear war-making machinery, and he emerged from his probe with deep alarm over the rigidity of the system: not only how easily a small conflict could escalate into all-out nuclear war, but how the system had been designed to *ensure* escalation.

It was only logical that Ellsberg would find much to like in his colleague Bill Kaufmann's counterforce briefing. A decade later, Ellsberg would transform himself into an antiwar activist and win fame (or, in the eyes of his former colleagues, infamy) for leaking the Pentagon Papers, the Defense Department's Top Secret history of America's intervention in Vietnam. But for now, he was a Cold War hawk; he thought that war with the Russians was not just possible but likely. A few years earlier, he'd decided not to enroll in RAND's quite generous retirement plan, because he didn't think he'd live long enough to reap its benefits—he'd be killed in a nuclear war, along with millions of others, well before the plan came due. Counterforce struck him not only as a more credible deterrent than SAC's current war plan, but also as a possible way out of total annihilation.

Ellsberg's response to McNamara's question, which he finished on April 7, his thirtieth birthday, drew heavily on Kaufmann's briefing. He noted the suicidal consequences of SIOP-62's "spasm" attack, "in which we fire off everything we can" all at once. He proposed instead a "doctrine of controlled response" to Communist aggression, giving the president the option of hitting only Soviet or Chinese military targets, refraining from hitting Soviet cities—refraining from hitting China altogether if that country wasn't involved in the war—and holding back a secure "reserve" of nuclear weapons, which the president could *threaten* to launch against Soviet cities if the Kremlin didn't back down. The explicit goal here was not merely to end the war quickly, before it spiraled out of control, but to end it in a way that didn't leave the U.S. military inferior to the Soviet military after the first volley of attacks: to give the United States a means of "prevailing"—not just surviving but, in some meaningful sense, winning—a nuclear war. To Ellsberg, and to many of his colleagues, counterforce was both a more humane approach to nuclear war and a shrewder strategy.

The Joint Chiefs' response was skeptical, bordering on hostile. The Chiefs were coming to view McNamara's whole approach as a violation of their space and a danger to national security. They accepted that the president and his cabinet had the right to make broad policy on war and peace—that's what civilian control of the military was about—but the details of tactics and strategy should be left to the professionals: should be left to *them.* And the whiz kids, with their incessant intrusiveness, did little to mollify their anxiety. Alain Enthoven, the chief whiz kid, a thirty-one-year-old from RAND with the appointed rank of deputy assistant secretary of defense, particularly annoyed them. Once, Enthoven ended an argument with a three-star over the nuclear war plan by bellowing, "General, I have fought just as many nuclear wars as you have."

In this light, the Chiefs saw the "96 Trombones" exercise as another annoyance. And the first two of McNamara's ninety-six questions, they saw as a stab at the heart of the war plans—of their province.

General Lemnitzer replied with a brief memo, speaking on behalf of all the Chiefs, dismissing the whole notion of "controlled responses" and "negotiating pauses" in a nuclear war. First, he argued, it was impractical. U.S. nuclear forces were too vulnerable to risk holding back a large number of them once a war had begun; a Soviet strike would disable this so-called reserve force, so, as a practical matter, we had to use it or lose it. Second, there was a conceptual problem. The alleged advantages of "limiting" our attack were plausible only if the Soviets cooperated—that is, if they limited their attack too—and that premise, he wrote, "does not now appear realistic."*

Finally, Lemnitzer argued, the act of even advocating this "controlled response" doctrine "could gravely weaken the current deterrent posture." Though he didn't bother to elaborate, his point was clear: to

---

* There was another vulnerability, of which McNamara seemed only dimly aware: if the weapons themselves survived a first strike, the communications links between the president and the weapons—the links allowing him to order a launch—might be severed. This was a grave concern to SAC officers: it was one reason, quite aside from the cult of LeMay, that many of them saw little alternative, in the event of nuclear war, to firing as many weapons as quickly as possible.

the Chiefs, and to SAC, the appeal of nuclear weapons—the crux of their power to keep the enemy at bay—was precisely their massive destructiveness. Talking about restraining this power, much less touting restraint as a new "doctrine," might tempt our enemies to flex their muscles without fear of a devastating counterpunch.

Still, Lemnitzer—who had briefly replaced Maxwell Taylor as Army chief of staff in the final year of Eisenhower's presidency, before his subsequent promotion to chairman—had witnessed the internecine warfare sparked by SIOP-62, and he was well aware of that plan's excessive "requirements" for weapons and damage. In the final lines of his memo to McNamara, he acknowledged that it was "desirable" to examine the possibility of adjusting the SIOP, so it could respond proportionately to a "less than large-scale" attack, and he told McNamara that he had ordered a strategic council within the JCS to analyze the idea "as a matter of priority."

With that concession, McNamara felt that he'd wedged his foot in the door—that he'd won a say in the planning of nuclear war.

In fact, though, he was kidding himself.

By the summer, the Joint Chiefs of Staff worked up the guidance for a new war plan—SIOP-63—based, in part, on McNamara's desire for more options and restraints. But crucial details of this guidance were couched in deliberately ambiguous language, which had the effect of blunting, in some cases reversing, McNamara's reforms.

The guidance for SIOP-63 was written by a few of McNamara's whiz kids and the strategic plans division of the Joint Staff, the large cadre of colonels and generals in the Pentagon who do the spade work for the Chiefs on specialized issues. The guidance split the SIOP's existing list of targets into three categories: Soviet and Chinese nuclear weapons and their infrastructure; other Soviet and Chinese military targets that were located outside cities; and military, industrial, and governmental buildings that were inside cities.

It then outlined five discrete U.S. "attack options." Under Option 1, the president would attack the first types of targets—the Sino-Soviet nuclear arsenal. This would involve launching only some of America's nuclear weapons, holding back the rest, and threatening to use them against other targets if necessary—a clear reflection of Kaufmann's counterforce idea, as embodied in Ellsberg's response to McNamara's "96 Trombones."

Under Option 2, the president would attack the first and second types of targets, still refraining from hitting cities. Options 1 and 2 were both explicitly preemptive attacks: the United States would launch a nuclear first strike in response either to a Communist invasion of allied territory or to intelligence reports that the Soviets were about to launch a nuclear attack against the United States.

Options 3 and 4 assumed that the Soviets had already launched a nuclear first strike and that the president responded with the same "controlled" attacks described in Options 1 and 2.

Finally, Option 5 was the all-out attack, launched either preemptively or in response to an attack—the unloading of the entire U.S. nuclear arsenal against every target in Russia, China, and Eastern Europe.

Curtis LeMay was now in the Pentagon, serving as the Air Force chief of staff. He tore into this guidance, intent on blocking even the slightest modifications of SAC's total-destruction philosophy. Any substantial reduction in "our strategic nuclear offensive operations," he wrote in a memo to his fellow chiefs, would incur an "unacceptable risk" not only to a credible deterrence strategy but also to "the survival of this Nation."

To LeMay, all the options except Option 5—the all-out attack—would leave too many crucial targets untouched. As an example, he noted that the other four options all called for nuclear attacks on Soviet air bases, including their repair depots, but that they held back from attacking the factories supplying those depots with spare parts because the factories were in nearby cities. This omission, LeMay wrote, "would permit the enemy to reconstitute significant portions" of his nuclear forces "in a minimum period of time" and thus "enable him to continue his attacks on the U.S. and its allies."

The landscape evoked by LeMay's critique was astonishing even by the Chiefs' standards. Hundreds of nuclear warheads would have exploded across Russian and Chinese territory, destroying every air base, missile site, naval port, and dozens of other garrisons and facilities—yet, to LeMay, this attack would inflict too little damage, to the point where the very survival of the United States would be imperiled, because a spare parts factory was left standing, as a result of which the Soviet and Chinese air forces might be up and flying in next to no time.

General Lemnitzer overrode LeMay's protest; the five options were allowed to stay. But LeMay objected, above all, to the fact that the plan imposed restraints of any sort on SAC's freedom of action—that it took seriously McNamara's demand for "controlled responses" and "negotiating pauses." And the other Chiefs, including Lemnitzer, sympathized with LeMay on that point.

Over the next several months, SAC and the Joint Strategic Target Planning Staff drew up a new SIOP that incorporated the five options. When Power and his staff briefed McNamara on the results, he thanked the commander for a job well done—just what he and the whiz kids had ordered.

But, perhaps because he heard so many of his own buzz words in the briefer's presentation, McNamara didn't scrutinize the fine print or ask as many probing questions as he had at his briefing on the first SIOP. Had he displayed the same critical curiosity, he might have learned that no one, either in the Joint Chiefs or at SAC, took Options 3 or 4 at all seriously. In their minds, if the enemy had already launched a nuclear attack, it would make no sense for the United States to hold back; any weapons held in "reserve" would probably be destroyed before SAC had a chance to launch them. The only "option" would be to use them or lose them, and given that choice, the military would always choose "use them." The idea behind Option 3 in particular—attacking only Soviet and Chinese nuclear weapons sites after a first strike against us—struck SAC officers as so preposterous, they didn't bother rehearsing it.

In other words, SIOP-63, like SIOP-62, was, basically, a nuclear first-strike war plan.

Even the first two options—the ones that called for attacking only military targets, sparing Communist cities from destruction—wound up, in SAC's hands, departing drastically from McNamara's principles. The final draft of the guidance noted that damage to Soviet and Chinese civilians would be minimized "to the extent that military necessity permits." Similarly U.S. nuclear responses would be controlled, enemy cities would be excluded from an attack, and a secure reserve of weapons would be retained "to the degree practicable."

What "military necessity" permitted, or what was deemed "practicable," were matters to be decided by SAC and the Joint Strategic Target Planning Staff, not by McNamara and his whiz kids or even by the Joint Chiefs of Staff. And they decided that these notions were not remotely practicable or consistent with military necessities.

Finally, the "damage-expectancy" numbers—the requirement that certain targets be damaged with 90 or 95 or even 97 percent probability, which provoked such agitation in the debates over the first nuclear war plan—remained the same in this revised plan.

As in the first war plan, the Navy's delegates to SAC led the protest against these requirements. The plan, they said, called for too much damage against too many targets, "far in excess" of the Joint Chiefs' requirement. For all practical purposes, they concluded, SIOP-63 was not much different from SIOP-62. It was still, by and large, a Single Integrated Operational Plan—an only slightly less rigid blueprint for an all-out nuclear first strike that would kill hundreds of millions of people.

———— ✕✕✕ ————

McNamara was more prone to compromise with the Chiefs than his stiff bearing might have suggested. He and his whiz kids canceled nuclear weapons that were clearly redundant or outmoded, but when it came to the military's core programs, he met them much more than halfway.

This was particularly true of the new Minuteman intercontinental ballistic missile. First tested soon after Kennedy entered office, the Minuteman was powered by a solid-fuel rocket, meaning it could be launched straight out of its underground silo, carrying a 1-megaton warhead from the continental United States to any target in the Communist world in thirty minutes. The Air Force wanted to build 2,300 of these missiles over the next six years; McNamara sliced the request to 1,000. This may have seemed a drastic cut—it certainly was in General LeMay's eyes—but several officials in the White House urged Kennedy to cut the number further to 600 ICBMs.

Kennedy's national security adviser, McGeorge Bundy, a former professor and dean at Harvard as well as an eminent figure at the Council on Foreign Relations, had assembled in the West Wing of the White House a staff of fellow intellectuals—economists, political scientists, and physicists—who he'd hoped would form the nucleus of critical thinking on national security issues. But McNamara insisted on controlling that sphere from the Pentagon, and Kennedy, who believed in giving his cabinet officers a wide lane, assented to the wishes of the defense secretary. Still, Bundy didn't come to Washington to serve as a mere bureaucratic coordinator and note-taker, which is how most of his predecessors had defined the job; he was keen to set and engage in the debates.

His deputy, Carl Kaysen, who'd been a colleague of Bundy's at Harvard, wrote two memos—the first for Bundy, then a more concise rewrite for Kennedy—arguing that McNamara's proposal was excessive and could provoke a nuclear arms race. The notion that the United States needed 1,000 ICBMs, Kaysen wrote, seemed to be based on "the old estimate of the probable development of Russian missile strength." If we look at "the newer estimates," he went on, "we find we can accept a significantly smaller force."

Kaysen was referring to the fact—awkward to discuss but enormously pertinent all the same—that, in the first few weeks of the new administration, the "missile gap" proved to be a myth. It was an awkward fact because Kennedy had built much of his election campaign on the charge, which he drew from Air Force Intelligence estimates, that there was a missile gap—that the Soviets were outbuilding us in ICBMs and that, as a result, a moment of "maximum danger" would soon come when they could launch a first strike with such devastation that we could not effectively retaliate.

In August 1960, three months before Kennedy's election victory, the Eisenhower administration launched the first photoreconnaissance satellite, called the Discoverer. The camera on board the Discoverer took pictures of such high resolution that a skilled analyst could identify objects as small as one meter in diameter. The first photos were dropped down to earth and processed in November. The satellite had traversed the entire length of the Soviet Union, along every road and railroad track—any passageway that could support a gigantic missile and its launching gear. Before this, Air Force Intelligence had claimed that the Soviets had 200 ICBMs; Army and Navy Intelligence had put the number at 50. In fact, the Discoverer photos revealed that they possessed just four long-range missiles.

McNamara learned about the pictures during his first week in office. He and his deputy, Roswell Gilpatric, a former undersecretary of the Air Force and a true believer in the missile gap, walked up to the Air Force Intelligence photo shop on the fourth floor of the Pentagon and spent hours gazing at the images with the analysts, who explained what they were seeing and its implications. There *was* a missile gap—but, they said, the gap was very much in *America's* favor.

No one inferred from this that the Russians would now sit still. But the intelligence agencies scaled back their projections for the future. Before Discoverer, they'd estimated that, by 1965, the Soviets would have 750 ICBMs and, by 1967 they'd have 1,000. After Discoverer, they cut the estimates in half—to 340 and 525, respectively.

And yet, in calculating how many ICBMs the United States needed to build, McNamara was still assuming the old intelligence numbers. If the Soviets were going to possess half as many missiles, Kaysen argued, the United States could get by with half as many too. This would be the case, he wrote, whether the goal was "a survivable second-strike capability" (as the Navy proposed) or an ability to attack the Soviet nuclear force while retaining "a reserve force . . . capable of threatening Soviet cities" (as the counterforce strategy required).

But the main issue, as Kaysen saw it, wasn't merely one of waste. In setting the size of our nuclear arsenal, he wrote, "we must always consider the possibility of interaction" with the Soviets. If we built many more missiles than we needed for deterrence, the Russians might take that as a sign that we were striving for "a full first-strike capability"—and, in response, they might order a crash buildup of their own, setting off an arms race.

To Kaysen and some of his colleagues in the White House, this was a pivotal moment. The debunking of the missile gap meant not only that the Soviets had no ability to launch a first strike but also, perhaps, that they had no such desire. General Lemnitzer had recently told President Kennedy, in reply to a query, that the Soviets could not pull off a successful strike against U.S. nuclear forces for at least the next few years. The CIA had observed, in a recent report, that the Soviets seemed to have adopted a "finite deterrence" posture, possessing just enough weapons to deter a nuclear attack, not to instigate one. If McNamara's proposal for a "large increase" were approved, Kaysen asked, "how great is the risk that we will push the Russians over to another strategic concept?"

At a meeting with Bundy and Kaysen, McNamara acknowledged that this analysis was sound. But, he said, he couldn't recommend any fewer than 1,000 Minutemen without provoking a rebellion from the Chiefs. He reminded the two White House officials that the Air Force had wanted 2,300 missiles; he'd managed to cut that request by more than half.

McNamara's air of triumph on this point too would be short-lived, as the Air Force figured out a way to maneuver around him. For now, though, the president sided with McNamara. Again, it came down to

Kennedy's preference for giving the secretary of defense the leeway to run his own department.

⸺⊷∞⊶⸺

There was one question that Kennedy knew he couldn't delegate. It was the ultimate question, which only he as commander-in-chief could answer—what would he do in the event of "general war"? Would he actually push the nuclear button?

Ten days into his presidency, Bundy wrote a memo, laying out the decisions that Kennedy would soon have to make on issues spanning "the whole spectrum from thermonuclear weapons systems to guerrilla action and political infiltration." On the question of nuclear war, he would need to decide whether to emphasize "strike first" "counter-force" strategies or a "second strike" "deterrent" posture. "The matter is of literally life-and-death importance," Bundy wrote, "and it also has plenty of political dynamite in it."

The same day, David Bell, the budget director, wrote a memo noting that the three military services disagreed on these strategies. The Air Force advocated "counterforce deterrent," requiring more heavy bombers and ICBMs; the Navy touted "finite deterrent," accomplished by a limited number of submarines; and the Army coined the phrase "credible deterrent," defined as more conventional forces—tanks, troops, artillery, and so forth—to minimize the chance that a small conflict might escalate to nuclear war in the first place. The implications were twofold: first, disputes over nuclear strategy would spawn battles over budgets; second, the military services, in this sense, seemed no different from other government bureaucracies—their vested interests drove their policy preferences, their top officers weren't necessarily founts of ultimate wisdom.

In his first substantive meeting with the Joint Chiefs, on February 6, Kennedy asked about the nuclear war plan. Three days earlier, General Lemnitzer had flown with McNamara and a few of his aides to Omaha for General Power's briefing on SIOP-62. If we launched the first strike, Kennedy asked, would that wipe out the Soviets' ability to strike back?

Lemnitzer replied that it would not. At least a few of the Soviets' missiles or bombers would survive the attack, and they could hit back hard.

That told Kennedy a lot about his so-called "options" in a nuclear war. There was no silver bullet, no magic escape valve from catastrophe.

Within a few months, Kennedy found himself embroiled in a crisis that could easily boil over into nuclear war. It involved a face-off over the Cold War's most volatile hot spot, a patch of vital land that the Soviets had been threatening for years and were now threatening more ominously than before—a threat that, Kennedy's advisers were saying, could be met only with nuclear weapons. And in the middle of this crisis came an idea, which morphed into a detailed alternative war plan, suggesting that there might be a silver bullet after all—that the United States might be able to pull off a disarming nuclear first strike against the Soviets if the Kremlin made a move. For several weeks in the summer and fall of 1961, it seemed that such a strike might be the only alternative to losing West Berlin.

CHAPTER 3

The Crises

The Berlin crisis began before John Kennedy took office. On January 6, two weeks prior to the inauguration, Soviet premier Nikita Khrushchev delivered a speech to Moscow's leading ideological institutes, vowing that the policy of "peaceful coexistence," which he had forged with President Eisenhower, would not interfere with the political and economic struggles between East and West. Much of the speech focused on the "wars of national liberation," which he affirmed were "sacred," to be supported by Communists "wholeheartedly and without reservation." It was these passages that triggered Kennedy's keen interest in counterinsurgency operations. But there was another section of the speech that stirred deeper alarm: Khrushchev's threat to annex the city of West Berlin.

Berlin had been the centerpiece of struggle throughout the Cold War. It was where the Second World War ended, the Allied armies meshing into one another as they occupied Nazi Germany—the United States, Britain, and France from the west, the Soviet Union from the east, carving out the separate zones of West and East Berlin. Soon after, Germany itself would split into East and West, and the border between the two hardened into the dividing line between Soviet-controlled Eastern Europe and a democratic capitalist Western Europe. West Berlin emerged as an anomaly—a tiny landlocked island, stuck a hundred miles inside East German territory but claimed and protected by the Western powers. In 1948, Josef Stalin imposed a blockade, cutting Berlin off from its Western suppliers. The United States responded with an airlift (managed by Curtis LeMay, who was commander of U.S. Air Force Europe, the success of which spurred his promotion to run SAC), keeping the zone supplied for eighteen months—at its peak, 500 flights a day, bringing in 1.5 million tons of food, coal, and medical supplies—before access was formally restored. Ten years later, Khrushchev again threatened to place West Berlin under East German sovereignty—an act that he characterized as ending World War II—but backed off after a harmonious meeting at Camp David with President Eisenhower.

Eisenhower had stressed to Khrushchev that West Berlin stood as a beacon of freedom, and a home to two million people, which the United States was committed to defend at all cost. As Kennedy took office, there was no debate on this point; it was accepted as a key premise of Cold War policy.

During his presidential campaign, Kennedy had predicted that, in the coming year, Berlin would pose "a test of our nerve and our will." On June 3 and 4, he met with Khrushchev at a summit in Vienna. It proved disastrous. Kennedy had hoped to calm tensions and avoid a crisis. Khrushchev, twenty-three years older than Kennedy, berated him repeatedly, vowed to sever Berlin's Western ties by the end of the year, and warned that the Soviet army would go to war if the West tried to maintain its access. Boarding the plane back to Washington, Kennedy mumbled to an aide, "It will be a cold winter."

In late April, just weeks before the Vienna summit, Kennedy had asked McNamara for a report on the status of military planning in case of a crisis over Berlin. On May 5, McNamara replied, citing a national policy guidance signed by the National Security Council in February 1958. The United States, it said, "will be prepared to go immediately to general war"—that is, to all-out nuclear war—"after using only limited military force to attempt to reopen access to Berlin." McNamara added

that this policy was "inconsistent with current thinking." But the fact
was, West Berlin could not now be defended with conventional forces
alone.

After returning from Vienna, Kennedy asked Dean Acheson to
write a report, laying out the stakes and the options. Acheson, sixty-
eight years old, was the ultimate elder statesman: he'd been Harry
Truman's secretary of state, the cofounder of NATO, one of the architects of the Marshall Plan. He later wrote a memoir titled *Present at the
Creation*, and the claim was not hyperbole.

On June 28, Acheson sent Kennedy a thirty-three-page paper, and
the next day he recited its conclusions at a meeting of the National
Security Council. Acheson's main point was that the stakes were much
larger than the mere fate of one city. Rather, he wrote, "the whole position of the United States is in the balance." Khrushchev believes he
would prevail in a confrontation because we "will not do what is necessary to stop him." The real question, then, was "how to restore the
credibility of the nuclear deterrent"—that is, how to "make Khrushchev revise his appraisal that the United States was unwilling to resort
to nuclear war." The essential task, he continued, was "to make an early
decision on accepting the hazard" of nuclear war "and preparing for it"
with "all its grimness and cost," a task requiring "steady nerves."

<hr />

Around this time, the U.S. intelligence agencies were revising their estimates of the Soviet nuclear arsenal, acknowledging, in the wake of the
photos from the Discoverer satellite, that there never had been a missile gap. Among the most avid readers of these new estimates was Bill
Kaufmann, who, like many of his RAND colleagues, was now working
as a consultant in the Pentagon.

The CIA was releasing highly detailed intelligence not only on
the number of the Soviet Union's missiles but also on the strengths
and weaknesses—mainly the weaknesses—of its bomber fleet, its air
defense networks, its command-control facilities, and more. Not only

was the Soviet arsenal much smaller than previously believed, but its missiles weren't loaded with warheads, the bombers weren't on alert, and the early warning network was riddled with gaps, which would make it hard to detect a U.S. bombing raid, especially if the pilots flew in at low altitudes.

To Kaufmann, the implications were stunning. The notion of a disarming U.S. first strike against the Soviet Union—a small nuclear attack that destroyed all, or very nearly all, of the Kremlin's nuclear weapons—suddenly seemed plausible: a realistic way to deter or push back Soviet aggression and honor U.S. nuclear commitments, without triggering a catastrophe. In short, his counterforce idea might be the solution to the crisis over Berlin.

Kaufmann took his conclusions to Henry Rowen, his RAND colleague, who was now deputy assistant secretary of defense. Rowen brought Kaufmann to the White House to meet with Carl Kaysen, Bundy's deputy. On June 29, the same day that Acheson briefed the NSC on his report, Rowen and Kaysen met with Henry Kissinger, a noted Harvard professor who was serving as a consultant in the White House, to discuss the military's official contingency plan, which the Joint Chiefs had recently briefed to McNamara, and Kaufmann's suggested alternative. This Chiefs' plan was essentially the all-out nuclear attack laid out in SAC's SIOP-62, which had recently gone into effect. (The guidance for SIOP-63, McNamara's revised war plan, was still in its early stages.)

On July 3, in a memo to Bundy, Kaysen wrote, "The planning for several alternative limited target lists, which might be relevant to the Berlin crisis, has not yet begun. Rowen is drafting a request for such planning," which "should be considered as an urgent matter at higher levels."

Four days later, Kissinger wrote Bundy a similar memo, dissenting somewhat from Acheson's grandiosity. The president, Kissinger wrote, "should not be asked to make a decision about going to nuclear war in the abstract. It seems to me that before he makes the decision he has to know what is meant by nuclear war." The Pentagon, he suggested, "might be asked to prepare recommendations about graduated nuclear actions" and "to submit a plan for graduated nuclear responses." He added, "I've discussed this with Kaysen and Rowen."

Bundy acted on the suggestion at once, writing Kennedy that he, Kissinger, Kaysen, and Rowen "all agree that the current strategic war plan is dangerously rigid and, if continued without amendment, may leave you with very little choice as to how you face the moment of thermonuclear truth." The current plan, he noted, "calls for shooting off everything we have in one shot, and it is so constructed as to make any more flexible course very difficult." He suggested that the president ask McNamara to conduct a prompt review and to come up with new orders.

On July 13, Kennedy chaired an NSC meeting on the crisis. The day before, in a memo briefing him on the issues, Bundy stressed the need "to prepare war plans which would permit a discriminating use of nuclear weapons," adding, "It is not believed that such plans now exist." Maxwell Taylor wrote Kennedy a similar memo, urging him to ask his advisers to outline "the various steps of escalation toward general war which might have to be considered."

Twelve days later, President Kennedy delivered a televised address, announcing that he was mobilizing six ground divisions to Europe, asking Congress for $3.2 billion to buy more tanks and other conventional forces, postponing the deactivation of the B-47 bomber (one of the Air Force planes that McNamara had earlier decided to mothball), and—in case of the worst—boosting funds for nationwide fallout shelters.

Then, on August 13, shortly after midnight, East German soldiers started laying the first bricks and wires of what became the Berlin Wall. At first, Kennedy saw this as signaling the end of the crisis. Khrushchev was so determined to take over West Berlin, in part, because the city had long been used as a transit by East German citizens to flee to Western Europe. By the start of the year, the exodus had swelled to 10,000 a month, many of them highly educated youth. But the Wall—its sheer brutality and the speed of its construction—stirred alarm across Europe; Khrushchev continued to rattle his saber. The crisis persisted.

Rowen and Kaysen spent all of August working on their alternative attack plan, Rowen doing most of the analysis with the assistance of a few officers in the Pentagon's Air Staff, Kaysen writing it up. On September 5, Kaysen sent copies of the final draft to Taylor, Bundy, and Rowen. On the cover note to Rowen's copy, he wrote, "Here is what I made of Bill Kaufmann's efforts."

It was a thirty-three-page document, part memo, part highly detailed war plan, a blueprint for a counterforce first strike. The paper began with a critique of SIOP-62, which, Kaysen noted, would kill 54 percent of the Soviet Union's population and destroy 82 percent of its industrial buildings. "Is this really an appropriate next step after the repulse of a three-division attack across the zonal border between East and West Germany?" he asked. "Would the President be ready to take it?" Soviet retaliation would be "inevitable," and it would probably be "directed against our cities and those of our European allies." Kaysen then proposed "something quite different":

> We should be prepared to initiate general war by our own first strike, but one planned for this occasion rather than planned to implement a strategy of massive retaliation. We should seek the smallest possible list of targets, focusing on the long-range striking capacity of the Soviets, and avoiding, as much as possible, casualties and damage to Soviet civil society. We should maintain in reserve a considerable fraction of our own strategic striking power; this will deter the Soviets from using their surviving forces against our cities; our efforts to minimize Soviet civilian damage will also make such abstention more attractive to them, as well as minimizing the force of their irrational urge for revenge.

It was a concept straight out of Kaufmann's counterforce briefing, played out not on a game board at RAND but in a real geopolitical crisis.

The intelligence since the Discoverer flights revealed that the Soviets had only a few crucial targets to hit. They included forty-six bases for the Soviet air force's nuclear-armed bombers, twenty-six staging bases (where Soviet planes would stop for refueling on their way to the United States), and sixteen Soviet ICBM sites (with two "aim points" for each site, to maximize the chance of destroying them), for a total of eighty-eight targets in all.

Even this overstated the number of American weapons needed for the attack. On close inspection, it turned out that half of the targets were located a fairly short distance from one another; a lot of the U.S. bombers—about one third of them—could drop an H-bomb on one target, then fly on (for twenty minutes, at most) and drop another H-bomb on the next target. In all, the attack could be pulled off by just forty-one bombers. The CIA had recently concluded that Soviet air defenses were almost useless against planes flying at low altitudes. Nonetheless, for safety's sake, the Air Force liked to assume that a quarter of the bombers would fail, for one reason or another, before reaching their target. So Rowen and Kaysen upped the estimate to fifty-five bombers—still a relatively small attack.

The memo concluded that, with those fifty-five planes destroying eighty-eight targets, "we will have eliminated or paralyzed the nuclear threat to the United States sufficiently to permit follow-on attacks for mop-up purposes or for the elimination of other targets."

Kaysen acknowledged the need for exercises to test the study's assumptions. "But," he added, "there are numerous reasons for believing that the assumptions are reasonable, that we have the wherewithal to execute the raid, and that, while a wide range of outcomes is possible, we have a fair probability of achieving a substantial measure of success."

In a four-page summary of the report, Maxwell Taylor's staff officer agreed that the study's "assumptions are reasonable." However, other readers homed in on Kaysen's caveats—the admissions of "a wide range of outcomes" and "a fair probability" of "a substantial measure" of success.

Kaysen fully acknowledged the risks in his paper. For instance, he wrote, "Given the location of the targets," some of them near cities, the Soviet death toll "might be less than 1,000,000 and probably not much more than 500,000." He had written, earlier in the report, that one reason for sparing Soviet cities from a direct attack was to minimize the Kremlin leaders' "irrational urge for revenge" and thus heighten the chance that, if they did retaliate with their surviving weapons, they'd spare American cities from attack as well. The tacit assumption here was that no Soviet leader would be moved to seek revenge if the American raid killed more than a half million of his citizens. Kaysen also acknowledged that even this figure assumed "no gross errors in the bombing." If a bomb or two went astray, he implied, the death toll could rise higher.

Finally, Kaysen wrote, if some Soviet bombers and missiles survived the attack, and if the Kremlin did retaliate against the United States, they could do a fair bit of damage. Again, the range of possibilities was "very wide," depending on whether the weapons were aimed at cities or at military targets, whether they were designed to explode in the air or on the ground (the latter would kick up more radioactive fallout), and whether or not American citizens hid in fallout shelters.

Kaysen reproduced two charts, labeled "Prompt Deaths from Alternative Bombing Attacks (Deaths Due to Blast and Prompt Radiation)" and "Deaths from Alternative Attacks on US Cities (Blast and Fallout, All Weapons Ground Burst)." Depending on the assumptions, American fatalities would range from negligible in the best case to 70 percent of the population in the worst. "In thermonuclear war," Kaysen wrote, "people are easy to kill."

He then brought the focus back to the study's context—the Berlin crisis, the real possibility that nuclear weapons will have to be used, and the fact that SAC's current war plan would by design kill hundreds of millions of people. "The choice," he wrote, "may not be between 'go' and 'no-go.' It may be between 'go' and SIOP-62. Compared with SIOP-62, this small-scale minimum-warning attack" had "distinct advantages."

Kaysen told a few White House officials about the study, which was classified Top Secret—Sensitive. Those with some background in nuclear issues were skeptical, warning that Khrushchev might not read our signals the way Kaysen and Rowen hoped—might not regard any kind of nuclear attack on his soil as "limited"—and, therefore, might retaliate accordingly. But those who hadn't immersed themselves in the intricacies of strategy were appalled. Ted Sorensen, President Kennedy's longtime speechwriter, told Kaysen, "You're crazy! We shouldn't let guys like you around here." Marcus Raskin, a friend of Kaysen's and a former foreign policy adviser to a few liberal Democratic senators, who'd been hired by Bundy as the NSC staff's token leftist, was horrified that such a study even existed. "How does this make us any better than those who measured the gas ovens or the engineers who built the tracks for the death trains in Nazi Germany?" Raskin asked him. The two men never spoke again.

President Kennedy found the paper intriguing. This was mainly because, around the same time, he heard two briefings—one on the consequences of a hypothetical nuclear war, the other on the details of SIOP-62, the actual U.S. war plan.

The first briefing took place on July 20, with Kennedy and forty-three officials and officers hearing the results of the latest study by the NSC's Net Evaluation Subcommittee. This was the Top Secret group whose analysis of the world after an all-out nuclear exchange shocked and depressed President Eisenhower, the former war hero, back in 1956. Its update, five years later, for Kennedy, was no less gloomy: tens of millions dead in the United States, the Soviet Union, and China; millions more sick and left with "hopelessly inadequate" medical care;

half of all factories and residences ruined; the "shattering" of "the political, military and economic structure of the country."

After the briefing, the room was stunned into silence. Turning to Secretary of State Dean Rusk, who was sitting beside him, Kennedy said, "And we call ourselves the human race." He instructed everyone in the room not to tell anybody else about even the subject of the meeting.

The second briefing, on SIOP-62, took place September 13. Lemnitzer delivered it in the White House residence to Kennedy, McNamara, Taylor, Kaysen, and Walt Rostow, another one of Bundy's deputies. (Bundy was out of town.) Kennedy had heard from various aides and officials—McNamara, Taylor, and Bundy in particular—that the SIOP was atrocious and inflexible, and it lived up to its reputation. Hardly a war plan in the traditional sense, it would unleash the same global catastrophe as predicted by the Net Evaluation Subcommittee.

"General," Kennedy asked at one point during the briefing, "why are we hitting all those targets in China? As I understand this scenario, this war didn't start there."

"They're in the plan, Mr. President," Lemnitzer matter-of-factly replied.

Kennedy had a habit, well known to those in his circle, of tapping his teeth when he was irritated. In response to Lemnitzer's answer, Kennedy tapped his teeth with particular vigor.

One week later, on September 20, Kennedy held a meeting with Taylor, Lemnitzer, and General Power, the commander of SAC, to discuss the alternative war plan by Kaysen and Rowen.

The day before, the president sent Taylor a list of thirteen questions that he wanted Power to answer. First, he stated the premise: "Berlin developments may confront us with a situation where we may desire to take the initiative in the escalation of conflict from the local to the general war level." Then came the questions. Among them:

> Is it possible to get some alternatives into the plan? . . . Is it possible to exclude urban areas or governmental controls, or both,

from attack? . . . How would you plan an attack that would use a minimum-sized force against a Soviet long-range striking power only? . . . Would it be possible to achieve surprise with such a plan during a period of high tensions? . . . Would not an alternative first strike plan, even if only partially success- ful when implemented, leave us in a better position than we would be if we had to respond to an enemy first strike? . . . Is this idea of a first strike against the Soviets' long-range striking power a feasible one?

Kennedy also posed some questions about risks that Kaysen had not considered. "I am concerned over my ability to control our military effort once a war begins," he wrote.

I assume I can stop this strategic attack at any time, should I receive word that the enemy has capitulated. Is this cor- rect? . . . Although one nuclear weapon will achieve the de- sired results, I understand that, to be assured of success, more than one weapon is programmed for each target. If the first weapon succeeds, can you prevent additional weapons from inflicting redundant destruction?

The question suggested that Kennedy may well have written this memo on his own; anyone familiar with nuclear war plans, including Taylor, would have known that the answer to both of these questions was "No" and would have hesitated even asking it, for fear of being judged naive.

Power spent most of the next day's meeting railing away at the as- sumptions behind the notion of a pure counterforce strike. The So- viets, he claimed, had hidden away "many times more" missiles than the CIA's spy satellites detected—a claim that Lemnitzer and Taylor quickly disputed. Power then warned the president that "the time of our greatest danger of a Soviet surprise attack is now" and that "if a general atomic war is inevitable, the US should strike first"—leading Bundy to wonder, in a later, sarcastic memo, how we could launch a first strike if we didn't know where all the targets were.

Kennedy ignored the general's rant, returning to the main topic—whether he could really launch a sneak attack without provoking catastrophic retaliation. He didn't get a firm answer.

On October 3, Kennedy met with more than a dozen of his top advisers to discuss the status of planning in Berlin. He knew that McNamara had been quarreling with General Lauris Norstad, the commander of NATO, and he wanted the two men to air their differences in front of the group. McNamara had been advocating a rapid buildup of conventional forces in Europe, to push back a Soviet cutoff of access to Berlin. Norstad, who had been an Army Air Forces operations officer in World War II and had aligned himself afterward with LeMay's school of thinking, viewed this proposal as not only futile but counterproductive.

Norstad stressed that he favored a "balanced" NATO force with strong conventional and nuclear weapons. But, he said, once major combat got under way, U.S. commanders had to use whatever force was necessary, and, at some point, that would mean nuclear force. He thought that McNamara's favorite words—"graduation," "calculation," and "pause"—were unrealistic and misleading. They suggested a progression in which we could easily move, step by step, from one stage of combat to another—when, in fact, escalation was likely to be "explosive," erupting all at once.

"This is not a matter which we can control," Norstad emphasized. "The Soviets have at least an equal voice in the matter." Once an armored division rolled across the border, general war—nuclear war—was probably inevitable. And from his view, it was dangerous to skirt that fact. Deterrence, he said, has no meaning except in the context of a willingness to use nuclear weapons. The allies in Europe, especially the Germans, were nervous about this. They'd asked him repeatedly whether the American president would really use nuclear weapons to defend them.

Kennedy interrupted to say that, in his judgment, official statements weren't the issue. He'd personally assured the allies on this point time and again. The source of uncertainty wasn't anything that the United States did or didn't say. It was, rather, the developing balance of power between East and West—the growing relative strength of the Soviet Union and "the increasingly terrible character" of what a general war would be.

Norstad replied that the president could allay the Europeans' anxieties if he and McNamara stopped talking about spending more—and demanding that the Europeans spend more—on conventional weapons. By emphasizing improved conventional capabilities, they were casting doubt on whether they'd use nuclear weapons.

Kennedy said that using nuclear weapons would be like "pulling the house down." Clearly we wouldn't do that unless there was no other choice. Norstad agreed, but said that once serious combat got under way, we couldn't afford to get thrown back. The Soviets outgunned us conventionally in Europe; we would almost certainly get thrown back; so we would have to escalate to general war—to nuclear weapons.

The president asked him whether *tactical* nuclear weapons, used on a limited zone of the battlefield, might push back a Soviet assault. Norstad said it "was not impossible" that a small number of low-yield nuclear weapons, precisely delivered on specific targets, might provide one more chance to stave off a general war; certainly it would be a "sensible course" under certain circumstances; but he doubted that the situation could be controlled in such a fine-tuned manner.

Kennedy mused that as soon as somebody gets killed in these sorts of conflicts, the danger of major involvement grows very large.

Secretary of State Dean Rusk, a veteran diplomat of reticent bearing, then spoke up. The Western world, he said, was not ready to make decisions that would pave a clear path to general war; there needed to be many options for action—economic sanctions, naval blockades, airlifts—before going nuclear.

Norstad replied that the European allies *wanted* a nuclear response. Rusk said that he doubted that. Norstad said that maybe we should find out. Paul Nitze, the assistant secretary of defense for international security affairs, who had been Dean Acheson's chief policy aide in the early days of the Cold War and the Korean War, remarked that it might be dangerous to find out; the answer might box everybody in.

Kennedy sided with Rusk, saying he doubted the Europeans want to rush to general war. But he also said that he would not accept defeat and, on this point, he was just as adamant as the Europeans. In the meantime, he asked his advisers to draw up contingency plans on how to respond if the crisis turned violent.

One week later, at a late-night meeting on October 10, Kennedy and the advisers met in the Cabinet Room to discuss a contingency plan that Rusk, McNamara, and the Joint Chiefs had agreed on. The plan, which they called "Preferred Sequence of Military Actions in a Berlin Conflict," laid out four phases of escalation:

PHASE 1. If the Soviets blocked Western access to Berlin, the United States and NATO would send out a platoon.

PHASE 2. If the Soviets didn't back off, we would mobilize reinforcements and, at the same time, impose an economic embargo against the Soviet Union, harass Soviet ships at sea, and rally the United Nations Security Council to condemn the cutoff.

PHASE 3. If the Soviets still didn't budge, we would take one or more of the following actions: a naval blockade, an expansion of air operations over Berlin (without, as yet, dropping bombs), and moving troops into East Germany. The memo noted that this would be "a politically oriented military operation." NATO would not be able to overpower Soviet troops on East German turf, but Phase 3 would "display to the Soviets the approaching danger of possibly irreversible escalation" and thus, perhaps, bring them to their senses.

PHASE 4. If none of these steps worked, we would use nuclear weapons.

Within this phase, there were three sub-options:

A. "Selective nuclear attacks"—dropping a very small number of bombs, it didn't matter where—"for the primary purpose of demonstrating the will to use nuclear weapons."

B. "Limited tactical employment of nuclear weapons on the battlefield," to push back or annihilate Soviet troops on the ground.

C. "General nuclear war."

Kennedy asked whether there was much chance that 4-A or 4-B could be undertaken without escalation to 4-C—that is, whether nuclear weapons could be used in small doses without triggering all-out nuclear war.

McNamara, who'd had a deeper exposure to the SIOP than anyone else in the room, replied that the consequences of 4-C—all-out war—were so grave, we should at least give the limited options a chance.

Nitze disagreed, saying that the smaller nuclear attacks would tempt the Soviets to launch their own first strike against the United States, so it would be better to move straight to the all-out option. Nitze added that, in this scenario, we could "in some real sense be victorious," whereas if we let the Soviets launch the first big strike, we "might lose."

McNamara argued back that neither side could be sure of winning by striking first and that, in any case, both sides would suffer devastating damage.

Rusk jumped into the debate, pointing out that the first side to use nuclear weapons would carry a very grave responsibility and endure heavy opprobrium from the rest of the world.

Kennedy ended the meeting on that note, asking the advisers to draw up a more detailed document for General Norstad in Europe.

Over the next ten days, the players fired memos back and forth, the disputes sharpening with each volley. As Bundy summarized the fray in a memo to Kennedy, the civilians wanted to delay action for as long as possible, while the military officers wanted to use force right away. Complicating matters, within the military, most of the Chiefs preferred beginning the confrontation with conventional forces, but the Air Force—as personified by the chief of staff, General LeMay—wanted to go nuclear from the get-go.

The debate came to a head on October 20, at another meeting with Kennedy and his advisers. Though General Norstad wasn't present, Bundy described his position (accurately) as insisting that a conventional buildup was not only irrelevant—since the conflict would rapidly escalate to nuclear war—but dangerous, as it might convince Khrushchev that we weren't willing to use nuclear weapons and, therefore, might degrade our deterrent.

Then Dean Acheson, who had been invited to attend, spoke up and at great length. At the first meeting on the Berlin crisis, three months earlier, Acheson had stressed the importance of conveying the will to use nuclear weapons. But now he tempered that view, taking issue with Norstad's opposition to all other forms of military force. It was not the case, Acheson said, that a conventional buildup would mislead Khrushchev into thinking that he would have to deal only with our ground troops. On the contrary, he stated, any serious military movement by the United States is "an ominous thing."

Kennedy signed off on the four-phase contingency plan, but left the questions concerning Phase 4—precisely how to use nuclear weapons—unresolved.

By this time, Kennedy had decided to pursue another way out of the crisis. The upshot of the meetings and the memos was clear: none of the military options were good options. NATO's conventional forces couldn't overpower the Soviet army on its own turf; SAC's SIOP-62 would destroy civilization; the Kaysen-Rowen plan, though less horrendous, might, by the authors' own estimate, still kill millions, including, possibly, millions of Americans.

So Kennedy decided instead to call Khrushchev's bluff. Roswell Gilpatric, the deputy secretary of defense, was scheduled to give a speech at a convention of the Business Council in Hot Springs, Virginia. Kennedy asked him to use it as an occasion to implode the myth of the missile gap more fully than anyone had done in public. Through the late 1950s, Khrushchev had played on the inflated estimates of the U.S. intelligence agencies, boasting that his factories were churning out ICBMs "like sausages." Back then, he had tried to pressure Eisenhower into ceding West Berlin or face the wrath of the Soviet strategic rocket forces. If Khrushchev thought Kennedy might fold on the same hollow threat, Kennedy wanted to let him know that we now knew his hand was empty.

The speech was scheduled for October 21, the day after the meeting where Acheson spoke of the "ominous thing." It had been in the works for weeks, in parallel with the flurry of meetings and memos on Berlin. Bundy had a hand in writing it, as did McNamara and Rusk; Kennedy signed off on the final draft. It was meant not just as a major policy address but as a spear in the war of words with Khrushchev, a warning to back off.

Its key passage was this: "While the Soviets use rigid security as a military weapon, their Iron Curtain"—the phrase that Winston Churchill had coined fifteen years earlier to describe the barrier separating the eastern, Soviet-occupied half of Europe from the West—"is not so impenetrable as to force us to accept at face value the Kremlin's boasts."

Gilpatric recited the number of nuclear weapons that the United States possessed, stressed that this arsenal would remain second to none even after a Soviet first strike, and concluded that, despite Khrushchev's "bluster and threats of rocket attacks against the free world," it was the United States, not the Soviet Union, that enjoyed "nuclear superiority."

The speech came in the middle of the Communist Party Congress in Moscow, and Khrushchev felt he had to respond. The next day, he proceeded with plans to detonate a 30-megaton hydrogen bomb, the largest ever tested. (The authors of Gilpatric's speech, anticipating this event, wrote that the United States too could build a bomb that big, but decided it served no military purpose.)

That night, as the ranking U.S. diplomat drove to an opera in East Berlin, East German border guards blocked his way. Over the next few days, the confrontation intensified, climaxing on October 28, when thirty tanks from each side—American and Soviet—faced one another across a checkpoint for sixteen hours from a distance of a hundred yards, well within firing range. But the Gilpatric speech had its desired effect. After some backchannel diplomacy, Khrushchev backed off; the crisis ended.

However, the standoff led directly to another crisis. After October 1961, Khrushchev saw that he needed real military leverage if he was to make another play for Berlin. American military forces surrounded the Soviet Union, and now he knew that Kennedy knew that the Kremlin had very few—really, next to no—weapons with the range to hit U.S. territory in response to an American first strike. Despite the rhetoric about sausages, the Soviet ICBM program was in doldrums. But Khrushchev did have a fair number of medium-range missiles, and the idea struck him that placing some of those missiles in Cuba—the revolutionary island nation that had recently declared itself a Soviet ally and that sat just ninety miles off American shores—would have the same effect as a crash buildup of ICBMs.

On October 14, 1962, almost exactly one year after the Berlin crisis seemed settled, an American U-2 spy plane spotted Soviet medium-range ballistic missiles—each with a range of a thousand miles—being installed in Cuba. President Kennedy assembled an executive committee of the National Security Council to discuss possible responses. The ExComm, as it was called, met daily in the White

House Cabinet Room over the next thirteen days; it included Bundy, McNamara, Rusk, Taylor (whom Kennedy had just weeks earlier promoted to chairman of the Joint Chiefs of Staff), and Robert Kennedy, the president's brother, who was also the attorney general.

On Tuesday, October 16, at the group's first meeting, nearly everyone, including President Kennedy, figured that, at some point, they'd have to take out the missiles with an air strike—followed, perhaps, by an armed invasion of the island.

Two days later, though, the president was backing away from a military option. In the cool tone that he would maintain throughout the crisis, he told his advisers that most of the allies regarded Cuba "as a fixation of the United States and not a serious military threat." If he attacked Cuba, no matter how good the intelligence data, "a lot of people would regard this as a mad act."*

McNamara and a few others ignored this remark and debated whether or not they should issue a warning before the air strike. Kennedy cut them off. The real question, he said, is what the Soviets would do if we gave them a chance to withdraw the missiles from Cuba. For instance, he proposed, we could tell Khrushchev, "If you begin to pull them out, we'll take ours out of Turkey."

This was the first time anyone around the table had mentioned the medium-range nuclear missiles—known as Jupiters—that the United States had recently installed in Turkey, poised on the southern border of the Soviet Union. Kennedy fixed on the idea. Wondering aloud why Khrushchev had taken this wild gamble of putting missiles in Cuba, he figured that they must be part of some diplomatic bargaining scheme

---

* Kennedy secretly tape-recorded all of the ExComm meetings as well as many other conversations dealing with national security. He had asked the Secret Service to set up two taping systems, in the Oval Office and in the Cabinet Room, the previous spring. Kennedy could switch the machines on and off by flicking one of several concealed switches.

and that, to get rid of them, he might have to let Khrushchev save face. "The only offer we would make, it seems to me, that would have any sense of giving him some out," he told the group, "would be our Turkey missiles."

That night, a handful of Kennedy's top advisers met without the president, so they could speak more freely. Mainly at McNamara's initiative, they hammered out an initial U.S. response: a naval blockade of Cuba, which he called a "quarantine," to avoid raising legal issues of whether the United States had just declared war on the Soviet Union. (Under international law, a *blockade* would do just that.) As for trading the missiles in Turkey, nobody so much as mentioned the idea.

The next day, Friday, October 19, Kennedy met in the Oval Office with the Joint Chiefs of Staff. Taylor opened by saying that the Chiefs were unanimously recommending an immediate air strike on Cuba. At the start of his presidency, Kennedy might have kowtowed to this row of combat-decorated four-stars, all of whom had been senior officers during World War II, when he was a mere PT boat commander. But twenty-one months into his term, Kennedy, feeling vindicated by his approach in one superpower crisis, wasted no time taking charge.

"Let me just say a little, first, about what the problem is, from my point of view," he said calmly. If we attack the Soviets' missiles in Cuba, "it gives them a clear line to take Berlin." He went on, "We would be regarded as the trigger-happy Americans who lost Berlin." The Soviets would respond, probably by forcibly taking Berlin. "Which leaves me only one alternative," Kennedy said, "which is to fire nuclear weapons—which is a hell of an alternative."

Taylor gently noted that he and the Chiefs "recognize all these things, Mr. President." But, he added, "Our strength in Berlin, our strength anyplace in the world, is the credibility of our response under certain conditions. And if we don't respond here in Cuba, we think the credibility of our response in Berlin is endangered."

"That's right, that's right," Kennedy said. "So that's why we've got to respond. Now the question is: What kind of response?"

General LeMay then stepped in. LeMay had always distrusted civilians, and Kennedy's behavior so far—his budget cuts to Air Force weapons systems and his refusal to bomb Russia during the Berlin crisis—left him particularly distrustful of this young president.

"I'd emphasize, a little strongly perhaps, that we don't have any choice *but* direct military action," LeMay growled. "I don't share your view that if we knock off Cuba, they're going to knock off Berlin."

"What do you think their reprisal will be?" Kennedy asked.

"I don't think they're going to make any reprisal," LeMay said, "if we tell them that the Berlin situation is just like it's always been—if they make a move, we're gonna *flame 'em*!" The naval blockade, he added, "is almost as bad as the appeasement at Munich."

This was clearly a jab at Kennedy's father, Joseph Kennedy, who, as Franklin D. Roosevelt's ambassador to England in 1940, had supported Prime Minister Neville Chamberlain's policy of appeasing Hitler's invasion of Czechoslovakia. The president let the remark pass and restated his own position: "We've got to assume there's going to be—they can't let us just take out their missiles, kill a lot of Russians, and not do anything."

LeMay doubled down. "We have to do much more than take out their missiles," he said. "If you don't take out their [airplanes] at the same time, you're vulnerable" to retaliation. "You have to take out the air, the radar, the communications, the whole *works*!"

Taylor then noted that the crisis offered an opportunity to grab Cuba, a notion that he assumed would appeal to Kennedy a year and a half after the failed Bay of Pigs invasion. "We can never talk about invading again after they get these missiles," Taylor warned, "because they've got these pointed at our head."

"Well, the logical argument is that we don't really have to invade Cuba," Kennedy replied, no doubt stunning the top brass. "That's just one of those difficulties we live with in life, like we live with the Soviet Union and China." He summed up his case: "The argument for the blockade was that what we want to do is to avoid, if we can, nuclear war by escalation." If we launch an air strike, he added, "a lot of people are just going to move away from us."

At this point, Kennedy left the room, but he kept the hidden tape recorder running. In the president's absence, LeMay threw a fit.

"He finally got around to the word *escalation*," he shouted. LeMay despised the word; it struck him as the civilians' excuse for using too little force or, worse yet, for avoiding a war that we needed to get into all the way. "That's the only goddamn thing that's in the whole trick," he tore on. "When he says *escalation*, that's it. If somebody could keep them from doing the goddamn thing piecemeal—that's our problem! You go in there, friggin' around with the missiles—you're *screwed*! You're *screwed*! *Screwed*! *Screwed*! . . . Goddamn it, if he wants to do it, you can't diddle around with hitting the missile sites and then hitting the SAM [surface-to-air missile] sites. You've got to go in and take out the goddamn thing that's going to stop you from doing your job!"

On one point, Kennedy would have agreed with LeMay. He too had come to realize that there was no such thing as a "surgical strike." A big attack would be needed. But this was precisely why Kennedy disagreed with LeMay on policy. Because of the infeasibility of a limited attack, LeMay wanted an all-out war, while Kennedy wanted to avert one.

LeMay was hardly alone in his view. For the moment, Robert McNamara still favored a blockade. But at the previous day's ExComm meeting, he'd agreed with LeMay and the other Chiefs. If force must be used to take out the Soviet missiles, the defense secretary said, he would "strongly" recommend "nothing short of a full invasion."

On Monday, October 22, Kennedy went on television to tell the world that Khrushchev had placed missiles in Cuba and to announce that the United States was imposing a naval "quarantine" on the island. For the next few days, Soviet supply ships halted at the demarcation line. Some turned around; neither side fired a shot.

Meanwhile, the CIA informed Kennedy that the missiles already in Cuba would soon be operational; once that happened, they would boost by half the nuclear firepower that the Soviets could unleash against the United States.

At the ExComm meeting on Thursday, October 25, McNamara gave up on the blockade. "I don't see any way to get those weapons out of Cuba—never have thought we would get them out of Cuba—without the application of substantial force . . . economic force and military force," he said.

Bobby Kennedy, who had taken a hawkish stance throughout the crisis, wondered out loud whether a Soviet-American confrontation at sea, which the blockade might provoke, was riskier than an air attack. Maybe, he said, we should "strike the missile sites in Cuba as a *first* step."

On Friday, October 26, Khrushchev sent Kennedy a telegram, offering a deal: if the United States pledged never to invade Cuba, he would pull out the missiles. By this time, the CIA was reporting, all twenty-four of the Soviets' medium-range ballistic missiles were fully operational.

Then, the next morning, Saturday the 27th, Khrushchev changed his terms, probably under pressure from Politburo hard-liners to wrangle a better deal. In the new message, which he made public, the Soviet premier said he would withdraw his missiles from Cuba only if the United States removed its missiles from Turkey—which, he noted, threatened the Soviet Union as much as the missiles in Cuba threatened America. Kennedy had been talking up such a trade since the second ExComm meeting. Once Khrushchev put it on the table, he was quick to grab it.

"To any man at the United Nations, any other rational man," Kennedy told his advisers, "it will look a very fair trade."

His advisers tried to knock down the deal as a danger to the Western alliance. "Keep the heat on," McNamara insisted. Nitze warned that the Turks would regard it as "absolutely anathema, as a matter of prestige and politics." Rusk and Bobby Kennedy suggested that the president put out a statement, accepting Khrushchev's proposal from the night before—with the U.S. pledging not to invade Cuba—while ignoring the demand he made that morning.

The president dismissed the idea. "I think we have to be thinking about what our position's going to be on this one, because *this* is the one that's before us and before the world."

After indulging another round of objections from his advisers, Kennedy made his point more firmly. "Now let's not kid ourselves," he said. "Most people think that if you're allowed an even trade, you ought to take advantage of it."

Bundy protested with unusual vigor. "I think we should tell you the universal assessment of everyone in the government who's connected with alliance problems," he said, his voice quivering. "If we appear to be trading the defense of Turkey for the threat in Cuba, we will face a radical decline."

Kennedy asked, "How much negotiation have we had with the Turks?"

Rusk replied, "We haven't talked with the Turks."

The president was floored. "I've talked about it now"—a possible Cuba-for-Turkey missile trade—"for about a week." Yet no one had asked the Turks what they think?

A few minutes later, Kennedy asked how many missiles we had in Turkey anyway. Nobody knew. An aide in the back of the room called out, "We have fifteen Jupiters."

"Fifteen Jupiters in Turkey?" Kennedy said, once again—judging from his tone—astonished, in this case by the willingness of his advisers to risk so much for the sake of so little.

The attack plan, which the Chiefs had drawn up and McNamara had endorsed, called for 500 air sorties, dropping conventional bombs on the Soviet missile sites and air bases and radar and communications ("the *works*," as LeMay had said), followed, seven days later, by a land invasion of Cuba.

President Kennedy said, reflectively, "I'm just thinking about what we're going to have to do in a day or so . . . 500 sorties . . . and possibly an invasion, all because we wouldn't take missiles out of Turkey. And we all know how quickly everybody's courage goes when the blood starts to flow, and that's what's going to happen in NATO." Then the Soviets will "grab Berlin, and everybody's going to say, 'Well, this Khrushchev offer was a pretty good proposition.'"

Just then, Taylor entered the Cabinet Room with a report that a Soviet surface-to-air missile had shot down one of the American U-2 spy planes over Cuba. The plane had crashed, and the pilot was dead.

"This is much of an escalation by them, isn't it?" Kennedy mused.

"Yes, exactly," McNamara replied, picking up steam. "We ought to go in at dawn and take out that SAM site, and we ought to send the surveillance aircraft in tomorrow, and we ought to be prepared to take out more SAM sites."

Four days earlier, Kennedy had agreed to do just that if a U-2 were shot down. But now that it had happened, he decided against it. "I think we should just wait," he said, and turned again to the idea of trading in the Turkish missiles.

McNamara then put forth a byzantine proposal to remove the missiles from Turkey, but only as a prelude to attacking not just the missiles in Cuba but Soviet targets elsewhere in the world.

"We must be prepared to attack Cuba quickly, that's my first proposition," McNamara began in an almost fevered tone. "Now, the second proposition: when we attack Cuba, we're going to have to attack with an all-out attack." His "third proposition": "if we do this and leave those missiles in Turkey, the Soviet Union may—and, I think, probably will—attack the Turkish missiles. Now the fourth proposition is: if the Soviet Union attacks the Turkish missiles, we must respond with conventional weapons . . . against Soviet warships and/or naval bases in the Black Sea area. Now that, to me, is the absolute minimum, and I would say that it is damned dangerous. . . . Now, I'm not sure we can avoid anything like that if we attack Cuba, but I think we should make every effort to avoid it, and one way to avoid it is to defuse the Turkish missiles before we attack Cuba."

President Kennedy reacted with puzzlement. "If we took them out, we'd get the trade the Russians have offered us"—they take their missiles out of Cuba, we take ours out of Turkey. Why attack when we could settle the crisis without risking war?

At this point, one of the advisers joined the president's side of the argument. George Ball, the undersecretary of state (who would emerge, a few years later, as the sole high-ranking dissident on the Vietnam War), endorsed Khrushchev's offer. Several submarines armed with Polaris nuclear missiles were scheduled for deployment to the Mediterranean in a few months; they would provide Turkey with a more secure defense than vulnerable land-based missiles. "These things," Ball said of the Jupiters, "are obsolete anyway."

Bundy didn't like this turn of events. "And what's left of NATO?" he asked glumly.

"I don't think NATO's going to be wrecked," Ball replied, "and if NATO isn't any better than that, it isn't that good to us."

President Kennedy left the room a few minutes later, but not before repeating his main point. "We can't very well invade Cuba with all its toil, and long as it's going to be," he said, "when we could have gotten them out by making a deal on the same missiles in Turkey. If that's part of the record, I don't see how we'll have a very good war."

The advisers kept talking among themselves for a while longer, no one so much as mentioning the Turkey trade, as if the air strikes were going to commence the following Monday, as the Joint Chiefs had planned. After the meeting broke up, McNamara walked over to the president's brother and said, "We need to have two things ready—a government for Cuba, because we're going to need one, and, secondly, plans for how to respond to the Soviet Union in Europe, because, sure as hell, they're going to do something there."

From a few feet away, one of the advisers—it isn't clear who—said, with a mordant mirth, "Suppose we make Bobby mayor of Havana."

Not long after, away from the Cabinet Room, President Kennedy sent his brother to the Soviet embassy with a message for Ambassador

Anatoly Dobrynin: he would accept the trade, but only if it is never publicly revealed. (Kennedy apparently agreed with Bundy that an *open* trade might irritate the NATO allies.) The official announcement, Bobby told Dobrynin on his brother's behalf, must be worded along the lines of Khrushchev's offer Friday night: a withdrawal of the Soviet missiles in exchange for an American promise never to invade Cuba. Kennedy seemed to think this pledge would be enough to let Khrushchev claim victory to his critics in the Kremlin. (It wasn't; Khrushchev was ousted two years later, in part, as his successors put it, for his "hare-brained scheme" in Cuba.)

The next day, Sunday, October 28, Khrushchev announced that he was withdrawing the missiles. Within six months, all the missiles— Soviet and American—were gone from Cuba and Turkey. Decades later, Khrushchev's former advisers would reveal that 43,000 Soviet soldiers had been hiding on the island to defend the missiles in case of an invasion. Kennedy was right: if the United States had attacked, he would have been at war with the Soviet Union.

Kennedy told just six advisers about the secret missile trade: McNamara, Bundy, George Ball, Ted Sorensen, Roswell Gilpatric, and Llewellyn Thompson, the State Department's leading Soviet expert. Kennedy called them into the Oval Office after Saturday's ExComm session to tell them what he'd ordered his brother to do. He also told them to keep the deal secret. If anyone found out that he'd compromised with the Russians, he'd be denounced as an appeaser and might be defeated in the next election. (In a phone conversation after the crisis was settled, Dwight Eisenhower, the former president and retired five-star general, asked Kennedy if he'd made a backroom deal. Kennedy said he hadn't; he lied about this even to Eisenhower.)

Thirteen months later, after President Kennedy was assassinated in Dallas, Robert Kennedy and the six advisers agreed to keep the secret. In his 1965 biography of his longtime boss, Sorensen perpetuated the myth, writing that the president rejected Khrushchev's missile-trade offer as "propaganda" and, instead, accepted the offer that Khrushchev had made on Friday, ignoring the one made on Saturday. (This was the gambit that, in fact, Rusk and Robert Kennedy proposed and that the president rejected.) The other palace historians picked up on the same myth—as did the anti-Kennedy revisionist historians, who would cite Kennedy's alleged rejection of the trade as an example of his dangerous machismo.

A quarter-century after the crisis, McGeorge Bundy admitted in his memoir that hushing up the missile trade produced pernicious consequences. "We misled our colleagues, our countrymen, our successors, and our allies" into believing "that it had been enough to stand firm on that Saturday." Among the misled advisers was Kennedy's vice president, Lyndon Johnson, who was never told the true story about the trade and who followed the false lesson of the Cuban missile crisis—stand firm, never negotiate—in his decision to escalate the war in Vietnam.

Meanwhile, in the autumn of 1962, Kennedy came away from his tangle in two near-catastrophic crises with the conviction that he had to find a way out of the nuclear trap—and, if possible, out of the whole Cold War.

CHAPTER 4

"This Goddamn Poker Game"

On December 5, 1962, five and a half weeks after the end of the Cuban missile crisis, President Kennedy met with Robert McNamara and General Maxwell Taylor to discuss the upcoming year's defense budget. But Kennedy was consumed with a broader question: Why were his secretary of defense and his handpicked chairman of the Joint Chiefs of Staff requesting more money for nuclear weapons?

"It seems to me," he said, "we have an awful lot of megatonnage to put on the Soviets." By this time, Kennedy had learned, from mulling the grim options in the Berlin and Cuban crises, that he couldn't use these missiles as first-strike weapons. "They're only good for deterring"—and deterrence didn't require many weapons. "You get forty missiles that you could get through, and you're aiming them at the forty largest population centers of the Soviet Union—it ought to deter them from an awful lot," Kennedy said. "It wouldn't make them surrender, but it would certainly not make them adventurous."

Taylor at first agreed with the president's perspective, as he usually did before disagreeing. "As you know," he said, "in the past, I've always said we probably have too much, and I think if we were starting from scratch, I would still take that position. But sir," he went on, "I would recommend staying with the program essentially as it is. There are too many imponderables for us to back away and go back to a very small force."

Kennedy wasn't convinced. "What is it that will deter them?" he countered. "Even what they had in Cuba alone"—he said, referring to the two dozen missiles that the Soviets installed on the island at the start of the crisis—"would have been a substantial deterrent to me."

McNamara sided with Taylor, saying, "I think that there are many uncertainties in all these estimates" of how much is enough for deterrence. My advice, he said, is to take "what any reasonable person would say is required" and "double it." That would be "money well spent."

It was a dumbfounding statement from the man who had cultivated the image of a thinking machine, making judgments entirely on the bedrock of rational analysis.

But then, McNamara offered a different argument for keeping a larger arsenal than mere deterrence might require. If we cut back on nuclear weapons, he said, the military—especially the Air Force—would claim that we were "changing the basic military strategy of this country," abandoning the ability to destroy the Soviet Union's nuclear arsenal. Doing that, he said, would "seriously weaken our position within this country and with our allies."

At this point, Kennedy weighed the other side of the argument. If there were a nuclear war, he allowed, "the only targets, it seems to me, that really make any sense are their missiles." He'd go after their missiles, in order to reduce "the amount of megatonnage that the United States receives," adding, "That makes some sense." We needed to make the Soviets believe that "we'd fire at their cities if we have to, because that will deter them." But, he went on, "as a practical matter, if the deterrent fails and they attack, what we want to do is be firing at their missile sites." And that, he recognized, would mean "maybe buying a lot of missiles"—certainly more than forty.

With that, Kennedy summarized the basic dilemma of nuclear strategy: a minimal arsenal of city-busting weapons might be adequate to deter a nuclear attack—this was the Navy's strategic rationale for the Polaris—but, "if the deterrent fails," if the threat had to be carried out, no president would want to attack Soviet cities, kill millions of their people. On the other hand, the alternative—destroying the Soviet missile sites, the essence of the counterforce strategy—would require matching the Soviet buildup, which might spur them to build more weapons still, which would require another buildup to match that buildup, and onward and upward the spiral would go.

In short, the logic of counterforce sparked the dynamics of an arms race.

McNamara had been wrestling with this dilemma since his first few weeks in office, when he heard Bill Kaufmann's counterforce briefing and asked how the strategy would help him cap the military's appetite for more missiles and bombers. Kaufmann didn't have an answer, and in the subsequent two years McNamara hadn't devised one either.

The intervening crises had, in one sense, deepened McNamara's attachment to counterforce, in part as an alternative to the instant holocaust of SAC's nuclear war plan, but also as a way of keeping the NATO allies in line. Several European leaders and diplomats had expressed doubts that an American president really would launch nuclear weapons at the Soviet Union if the Kremlin annexed West Berlin or invaded Western Europe—whether he would honor the pledge of America's deterrence policy—given that the Kremlin could retaliate by firing its nuclear weapons at the United States. An existential question entered the lexicon of transatlantic discourse: Would the president risk New York for Paris?

Even after the Berlin crisis settled, the question persisted. French president Charles de Gaulle wanted to resolve the uncertainty by building his own independent nuclear arsenal, which Kennedy and his advisers feared might prompt West Germany to build its own bomb, which would trigger mayhem on both sides of the Iron Curtain, given widespread fears of a revanchist West Germany. (Not quite two decades had passed since the end of World War II, and West Germany's ministries were still rife with ex-Nazis.)

So McNamara decided to invoke the counterforce strategy as a balm to European anxieties. You don't have to wonder whether the president would risk New York for Paris, he told them, because if the Soviets grabbed West Berlin or invaded Western Europe, the president would retaliate with nuclear weapons—but not against Soviet cities. And if he didn't hit Moscow, maybe the Soviets wouldn't hit New York. Whether he'd risk New York for Paris didn't enter into the calculation.

McNamara laid out this argument in a Top Secret speech at a conference of NATO foreign and defense ministers in Athens, Greece, in May 1962. He gave the job of writing the speech to Harry Rowen, who had worked with Carl Kaysen on the first-strike plan during the Berlin crisis. Rowen passed the assignment to Bill Kaufmann, the author of the counterforce briefing that had impressed McNamara from the beginning.

A few minutes into his recitation, McNamara put forth the main thesis:

> The U.S. has come to the conclusion that, to the extent feasible, basic military strategy in general nuclear war should be approached in much the same way that more conventional military operations have been regarded in the past. That is to say, our principal military objectives, in the event of a nuclear war stemming from a major attack on the Alliance, should be the destruction of the enemy's military forces, while attempting to preserve the fabric as well as the integrity of Allied society. Specifically, our studies indicate that a strategy which targets nuclear forces only against cities, or against a mixture of civil and military targets, has serious limitations for the purpose of deterrence and for the conduct of general nuclear war.

Conversely, McNamara continued, if deterrence failed and if the U.S. engaged "in a controlled and flexible nuclear response," the Soviets would have "very strong incentives . . . to adopt similar strategies and

programs," thus saving tens or hundreds of millions of lives and bringing the war to a rapid conclusion.

Kennedy had approved the speech, though he implored Mc-
Namara to "repeat to the point of boredom" the absolute assurance
that the United States would use nuclear weapons only in response to
a major attack against the United States or its allies. McNamara took
care to do so.

It was the first time that the Europeans had heard the counterforce
idea spelled out in detail, and many found it engrossing, though only
to a point. When Paul Nitze, the assistant secretary of defense, was in
Paris a few months earlier, de Gaulle had told him, in a private meeting, that the whole notion of "nuclear strategy" was absurd: nuclear
bombs were weapons of mass destruction; you couldn't rationally fight
a war with them; they could be used only to deter war. Many Europeans agreed with this sentiment; and while they admired McNamara's
logic and appreciated his intentions, his speech didn't persuade them
otherwise.

McNamara, on the other hand, was so pleased with his reception in
Athens that he decided to deliver a trimmed-down and declassified version of the speech as the forthcoming commencement address, which
he'd agreed to deliver, at the University of Michigan in Ann Arbor.
McNamara's special assistant, Adam Yarmolinsky, wrote the first draft;
Kaufmann and Dan Ellsberg cleaned it up and toned it down, though
they worked on it reluctantly. Neither believed that nuclear strategy
should be discussed much in public; it would sound too macabre to the
untrained ear. But McNamara insisted, and so the speech was written
and read out loud to the puzzlement of the graduating students and
their parents.

The Ann Arbor speech set off a firestorm of controversy. The Soviet press denounced McNamara as a militaristic madman who was trying to write rules for the holocaust. Disarmament activists predicted
that the policy would set off an ever-spiraling arms race and spur incentives for a preemptive first strike.

But the response that most concerned McNamara came from the Joint Chiefs of Staff, who felt emboldened by the speech to advocate more overtly for a nuclear first-strike strategy—and to push for the larger nuclear arsenal that they would need to carry it out.

McNamara was wavering on the whole issue when he met with Taylor and President Kennedy on December 5 to discuss the defense budget and how many nuclear weapons the United States really needed. For some time he had been managing a delicate, at times deceptive, balancing act on nuclear matters. He endorsed counterforce as an alternative to the horrors of SIOP-62 and as a gambit to soothe the anxieties of NATO allies; but he was also determined to restrain the military's—especially the Air Force's—appetite for more nuclear weapons. At some point, though, he couldn't continue to do both; counterforce required more weapons.

Then there was another matter, which McNamara kept largely secret at the time and for the subsequent quarter-century: he deeply opposed the first use of nuclear weapons, and advised Kennedy—as well as, later, President Johnson—never to initiate nuclear war, under any circumstances, not even in response to a Soviet invasion of Western Europe. This was why, from the outset of his tenure in the Pentagon, McNamara had pushed for a buildup of conventional forces in Europe—so that, in case of an invasion, the president would have some means of repelling the assault before resorting to a nuclear strike.

Dan Ellsberg caught a glimpse of McNamara's insistence on this point early on. One day in the summer of 1961, soon after Ellsberg finished the paper on nuclear strategy that was Question No. 1 in the "96 Trombones" exercise, McNamara invited him to lunch. As they sat eating at the secretary's desk, and as the discussion rambled on for an hour longer than scheduled, Ellsberg asked what effect the new strategy on limited nuclear war might have on NATO. McNamara's tone of speech turned unusually emotional. There was no such thing as limited nuclear war in Europe, he said with startling passion. Any use of nuclear weapons would escalate to "total war, total annihilation for the

Europeans" and, from there, to general war between the United States and the Soviet Union.

Afterward, Yarmolinsky, who sat in on the lunch, led Ellsberg to an adjoining room and told him that he had never heard McNamara speak so frankly with anyone else.

"You must tell no one outside this suite what Secretary McNamara has told you," Yarmolinsky said. If the Chiefs or the allies or Congress knew he felt this way, they would panic, and pressure would build for his dismissal. Neither of them had to spell out the reason for discretion. It was the unquestioned premise of Cold War policy that deterrence required persuading the Soviets that the American president would use nuclear weapons first, in response to aggression against U.S. allies. Once that premise was accepted, the logical corollary became hard to resist: to persuade the Kremlin that he would use nuclear weapons first, the president had to develop the *ability* and display the *will* to use them first.

Given the stakes, McNamara had succumbed to this logic, even though it violated his strongly held instincts about nuclear war. But now, the Chiefs were exploiting his concession to make the case for more bombers and missiles and a more open first-strike policy. Mc-Namara was facing a decisive moment—literally: he might have to *decide* which stance to take; the contradictions in his stance would soon be untenable.

A few weeks before his meeting with Kennedy and Taylor, Mc-Namara drafted a memorandum for the president, to clarify the distinction between his view and that of the Chiefs. He particularly criticized the Air Force's desire for a "full first-strike" capability. "We might try to knock out most of the Soviets' strategic nuclear forces while keeping Russian cities intact, and then coerce the Soviets into avoiding our cities (by the threat of controlled reprisal) and accepting our peace terms," McNamara began, reciting the tenets of counterforce. This "coercive strategy," he went on, is "a sensible and desirable option to have in second-strike circumstances in which we are trying to make the best of a bad situation." But, he insisted, "We should stop augmenting our forces for this purpose"—that is, for the purpose of building a first-strike arsenal—"when the extra capability the increments offer is small in relation to the extra costs."

The Chiefs struck back. On November 20, still two weeks before the meeting with Kennedy, Taylor sent McNamara a memo, rebutting his argument:

> The Air Force has never counseled a "full" first-strike capability in the sense of indemnifying the United States completely from serious consequences. The Air Force has rather supported the development of forces which provide the United States a first-strike capability credible to the Soviet Union, as well as to our allies, by virtue of our ability to limit damage to the United States and our Allies to levels acceptable in light of the circumstances and alternatives available.

The word that Taylor homed in on, which he emphasized by placing in quotation marks, was "full." A *full* first strike was defined as a totally disarming first strike—one that would leave the Soviets with no ability to strike back at the United States. Of course, the Air Force had "never counseled" such a policy, mainly because it was infeasible; even with the first-strike plan that Kennedy had contemplated during the Berlin crisis, a few Soviet weapons would have survived the attack and, if Khrushchev had launched them in response, they might have killed millions of Americans. On the other hand, Taylor went on, the Air Force did strongly support a "first-strike capability," which could limit damage to the United States, to levels that were "acceptable in light of the circumstances and alternatives." He did not define "acceptable," but the implication was clear: the resulting death toll would be very high—in the hundreds of thousands or millions—and, to the Chiefs, that would be acceptable, given the "circumstances" (nuclear war) and the "alternatives" (surrender).

Taylor noted that the Chiefs unanimously regarded an "adequate" first-strike capability as "both feasible and desirable," defining "adequate" as a level of strength that would leave the United States and its allies "with a relative power advantage over the Sino-Soviet Bloc" after a nuclear exchange. The implication was that, before the nuclear exchange, the United States needed to maintain superiority—which meant it would need to keep building more nuclear weapons.

As a final riposte to McNamara, Taylor wrote, in his concluding statement: "U.S. strategy is not and should not be based on a purely second-strike capability."

The awkward fact was that Taylor's arguments could easily have been inferred from McNamara's own statements in Athens and Ann Arbor.

McNamara realized that, to escape the trap that he'd laid for himself and to block the Air Force from reviving its long-rejected demands for more nuclear weapons, he would have to drop the counterforce rhetoric altogether. He didn't quite adopt President Kennedy's position that forty missiles would be enough to deter the Soviet Union, but he moved in that direction.

In January 1963, McNamara told his staff that they were no longer to cite counterforce as the official nuclear strategy, and he ordered the Chiefs to stop citing counterforce as a rationale for their weapons "requirements." He was finally confronting the Chiefs not by picking away at the edges of their dispute but by challenging their fundamental premises.

Meanwhile, in the White House, the view began to take hold that the whole nuclear enterprise was absurd. On February 4, at the daily staff meeting, Bundy and Kaysen, who had seriously explored a nuclear first-strike plan during the Berlin crisis, vented their growing disenchantment with the topic. They were discussing the latest diplomatic antics of Charles de Gaulle, an object of mistrust throughout the Kennedy administration, when Bundy suddenly acknowledged that the French president was right about one thing—there was no logic whatever to "nuclear policy." Bundy scoffed at those officers who calculate that we would win a nuclear war if we killed 100 million Russians while the Russians killed only 30 million Americans. They were, he said, "living in total dreamland."

Kennedy had grown steadily more self-confident in his two years as president—and steadily more skeptical about the judgments of those around him. This evolution began a few months into his term, with the Bay of Pigs operation, the CIA's secret plan to invade Cuba, which he'd inherited from Eisenhower. The generals and admirals assured Kennedy that the plan was well conceived—and it ended in disaster. Around the same time, the Chiefs advised him to prop up an unpopular anti-Communist regime in Laos, some of them suggesting that he use nuclear weapons to do so; Kennedy arranged a diplomatic solution instead. The Berlin crisis strengthened his suspicion that the senior-most military officers held no special wisdom on questions of war and peace.

At a meeting with Bundy and Rusk in the summer of 1962, Kennedy complained that the diplomats in the Foreign Service "don't seem to have *cojones*," then said, "Surely the Defense Department looks as if that's all they've got." There were "a lot of Arleigh Burkes" over there, he went on, referring to the Navy's top admiral—"30-Knots Burke," they called him during World War II, when he was one of Lieutenant Kennedy's heroes. Now President Kennedy dismissed Burke as an "admirable, nice figure without any brains."

In the final stage of his evolution, a few months later, after the Cuban missile crisis, Kennedy realized that his top *civilian* advisers—including Bundy, Rusk, and McNamara—had their shortcomings too. If he'd rejected Khrushchev's offer of a Cuba-for-Turkey trade, as they'd advised, World War III may very well have broken out.

Just as Kennedy had found a way out, short of war, in the crises over Laos, Berlin, and Cuba, he now sought a way out of the Cold

War altogether—at least a way out of the aspect of the Cold War that threatened global annihilation. Even more than McNamara, Kennedy believed that, while a conventional defense of Berlin was worth trying, a Soviet incursion across the East-West German border would escalate almost immediately to nuclear war. So he needed to find a way of defusing the tensions that might someday trigger an incursion.

At the moment, Khrushchev struck Kennedy as a plausible partner in this endeavor. On November 19, three weeks after the end of the Cuban missile crisis, Khrushchev had submitted a report to the Central Committee of the Communist Party of the Soviet Union, calling for the curtailment of foreign adventurism in favor of economic reforms at home. In December, he'd written Kennedy a letter, proposing a mutual halt to nuclear testing—an idea that Kennedy picked up on instantly, dispatching diplomats and technicians to negotiate a test ban treaty.

In May, Kennedy told Bundy and Ted Sorensen that he wanted to give a speech incorporating the lessons of his crises and laying out a new vision for future relations with Moscow. The back-and-forth of ideas and drafts was kept inside the White House, for fear that the State Department might water down its sentiments and the Pentagon might leak it to Congress or the press, setting off thunderous orations and editorials against softness and appeasement.

Kennedy delivered the final draft as the commencement address at American University on June 10, 1963. Sorensen was its main scribe, and its phrases flowed with the most flowery prose of any speech he'd composed since Kennedy's Inaugural Address—though those two pieces couldn't have been more different in content: the Inaugural pledging to "pay any price" to fight "any foe"; the AU speech outlining a plan for "world peace." As the new speech put it:

> I speak of peace because of the new face of war. Total war makes no sense in an age when great powers can maintain large and relatively invulnerable nuclear forces and refuse to

surrender without resort to those forces. It makes no sense in an age when a single nuclear weapon contains almost ten times the explosive force delivered by all the allied air forces in the Second World War. It makes no sense in an age when the deadly poisons produced by a nuclear exchange would be carried by wind and water and soil and seed to the far corners of the globe and to generations yet unborn.

Today, the expenditure of billions of dollars every year on weapons acquired for the purpose of making sure we never need to use them is essential to keeping the peace. But surely the acquisition of such idle stockpiles—which can only destroy and never create—is not the only, much less the most efficient, means of assuring peace.

Kennedy emphasized that he was no pacifist or idealist. "I am not referring to the absolute, infinite concept of peace and good will of which some fantasies and fanatics dream," he said. "Let us focus instead on a more practical, more attainable peace—based not on a sudden revolution in human nature but on a gradual evolution in human institutions, on a series of concrete actions and effective agreements which are in the interest of all concerned."

With such a peace, he allowed, "there will still be quarrels and conflicting interests." And he condemned Communism as "profoundly repugnant," a "negation of personal freedom and dignity." But, he said, "we can still hail the Russian people for their many achievements" and recognize our "mutual abhorrence of war," recalling that "no nation in the history of battle ever suffered more than the Soviet Union suffered in the course of the Second World War," and noting, "Almost unique among the major world powers, we have never been at war with each other." Yet both nations were caught up in "a vicious and dangerous cycle in which suspicion on one side breeds suspicion on the other, and new weapons beget counter-weapons." Both sides, then, "have a mutually deep interest in a just and genuine peace and in halting the arms race." So "let us not be blind to our differences—but let us also direct attention to our common interests and to the means by which those differences can be resolved." Or at least, "while defending our own vital interests," both sides "must avert those confrontations which bring an adversary to a choice of either a humiliating retreat or a nuclear war." He concluded, "Confident and unafraid, we labor on—not toward a strategy of annihilation but toward a strategy of peace."

International reaction to the speech, which the White House and the State Department closely monitored, was positive—especially in the most vital places. The Soviet newspapers published a transcript of the speech in its entirety. Censors suspended the jamming of radio signals, so that Russians could listen to the speech on Voice of America. Officials at the Soviet Union's U.N. Mission cabled home that they found the president's remarks "sincere." The CIA reported that other Soviet officials "were favorably surprised" by "the tenor" of the speech and its "broad progressive approach toward solving current problems." These officials, the report continued, "definitely disliked the fact that President Kennedy mentioned the Communists as being sources of world tension." Still, they "feel that the speech has created an excellent atmosphere."

Khrushchev, whom Kennedy had hoped to impress the most, told his staff—and later repeated to Averell Harriman, a former U.S. ambassador to the Soviet Union, who was now an assistant secretary of state—that it was the greatest speech by an American president since Franklin Roosevelt. The speech spurred Khrushchev to take up Kennedy's challenge. On June 20, Soviet and American negotiators agreed to connect a "hotline" between the offices of the two leaders. (During the Cuban missile crisis, they'd had to send each other telegrams, with unavoidable delays.) Six weeks later, the two countries and Great Britain signed a treaty outlawing tests of nuclear weapons in the atmosphere, under the oceans, or in outer space. The U.S. Senate, most of whose members had opposed any limits on nuclear testing before the American University speech, ratified the treaty by a margin of 80 to 19. The treaty wasn't the complete test ban that Khrushchev and Kennedy had discussed, but it seemed like a good start.

The president received another dose of vindication on September 12, when he and two dozen senior officials, officers, and advisers were briefed on the latest report by the Net Evaluation Subcommittee, the highly secret group within the NSC that, each year, gamed a nuclear war between the two superpowers and computed the consequences. Like the group's previous reports, going back to the mid-1950s, the predicted scale of death and destruction was horrifying; but this year's briefing carried a novel twist—the devastation was equal on both sides, no matter who used nuclear weapons first.

Kennedy picked up on this new angle at once. His first question, after the briefing ended, was to ask if he understood the situation correctly—that, even if we attacked the Soviet Union first, the Soviet second strike would inflict losses that no American president would find acceptable. The director of the NESC, an Air Force general named Leon Johnson, replied that the president was correct.

Did this mean, Kennedy asked further, that both countries had reached an era of "nuclear stalemate"? General Johnson replied that they had.

Kennedy then mentioned an article in that day's *Washington Post*, quoting the Air Force Association—a private group that lobbied for the service's interests—as calling for "nuclear superiority." How could we obtain nuclear superiority, Kennedy asked, if we were in a stalemate?

General Johnson replied that the Air Force Association did not have access to the most up-to-date facts, which revealed that there was no way, no matter what we did, to avoid unacceptable damage if nuclear war broke out. In that sense, he agreed, nuclear superiority was an impossible goal.

Kennedy returned to the question that he'd asked McNamara and Taylor the previous December: Why do we need so many nuclear weapons if, as it now appears, we couldn't protect ourselves from the ravages of war even with a first strike?

Seeing where the discussion was headed, General Johnson changed course, saying that he would be disturbed if the president took this report as a rationale for cutting the nuclear arsenal. If we did that, Johnson said, the relative position of the United States and the Soviet Union would become "less in our favor."

Kennedy said he understood that.

Johnson then went further, saying we could break out of the stalemate if we bought more, and more accurate, weapons, so that we could knock out more of the Soviets' missiles.

Kennedy asked if this didn't get us into "the overkill business."

Johnson mentioned calculations suggesting that we could fight a limited nuclear war without fear that the Soviets would respond by going to all-out war.

Kennedy countered that a better way to deal with Soviet aggression in Europe would be to invest in more conventional forces. Then he thanked General Johnson for his "excellent report" and its "valuable conclusion"—that nuclear preemption was a fruitless option, that it would yield no advantage in any conceivable scenario. Johnson agreed, saying that nuclear war was impossible if rational men controlled governments.

Secretary of State Dean Rusk joined the conversation at this point, saying that he wasn't comforted by this assurance because, if both sides believed that neither side would use nuclear weapons, one side might be tempted to act in a way to push the other side beyond its level of tolerance. In other words, even with rational actors, nuclear war was not impossible. Rusk had witnessed this sequence of bluffs and counterbluffs play out all too close to the edge of the abyss, in crises over Berlin and Cuba, and he was growing leery of the whole nuclear enterprise, which he now described as "this Goddamn poker game."

McNamara took the president's side at the Net Evaluation briefing. At one point, when Kennedy wondered why we needed so many nuclear weapons, given the inescapable stalemate, McNamara chimed in, citing Defense Department studies showing that, even if we spent an additional $80 billion on nuclear weapons and, after that, launched a first strike, at least 30 million Americans would die if the Soviets struck back. He stopped short of endorsing the president's preference for fewer nuclear weapons, just as he'd done at the meeting in December, but there was a shift in McNamara's rhetoric. At the earlier meeting, he had given two reasons for sticking with the current program: uncertainty over how many weapons were needed to deter the Soviets (buy "what any reasonable person would say is required" and "double it") and the need to destroy Soviet missiles in case deterrence failed. This time, he cited only the uncertainty factor; he said nothing in support of counterforce.

By the time of the Net Evaluation briefing, McNamara had crafted a new doctrine that would both deter a nuclear attack and clamp down on the Chiefs' demand for more weapons. He turned to the tenets of what the Navy—back when Admiral Burke and his analysts were devising a rationale for the Polaris—called "finite deterrence": build enough nuclear weapons so that, even after a Soviet first strike, the surviving U.S. forces could destroy the USSR's political and military controls as well as a large percentage of its population and industry.

McNamara called the new-old doctrine "Assured Destruction." (A few years later, a pro-counterforce defense analyst named Donald Brennan would dub this concept "Mutual Assured Destruction" so that it formed the acronym "MAD," a deprecating term that would soon be adopted by the doctrine's advocates as well.) To give the term a scientific tinge, McNamara's chief whiz kid, Alain Enthoven, who'd run the secretary's "systems analysis" shop since the start of his tenure in the Pentagon, calculated that the Soviets would be sufficiently deterred if the U.S. retaliatory strike could kill 30 percent of their population and destroy half of their industrial capacity.

This calculation was a bit of a ruse, in two senses. First, it had nothing to do with an assessment of Soviet thinking or ideology or history. Rather, it stemmed from the readout of a computer program revealing that an attack would reach what economists called "diminishing marginal returns" once it killed 30 percent of the Soviet population and half of its industry. In other words, at that point, all the large Soviet cities would be destroyed, so launching a lot more weapons would inflict only a little more damage; the extra destruction—and the extra weapons wreaking the destruction—would not be worth the extra cost.

Second, the Assured Destruction concept was deeply misleading, in that it did not describe how the weapons would actually be used in a war. In both the original SIOP and in McNamara's revision, only a few hundred bombs and warheads—a small portion of SAC's arsenal—were aimed at Soviet and Chinese cities; the rest, in 1963 no less than in 1961, were aimed at military targets. (Some of those military targets were in or near cities, so millions of people would be killed in such an attack, but people were not the intended targets.) McNamara even admitted, in a Top Secret memorandum to the president, that he was calculating "the destructive capacity of our force on the hypothetical assumption all of it is targeted on their cities, even though in fact we would not use our forces in that manner if deterrence failed." This fact—this duplicity—would not change in the subsequent four years of McNamara's tenure in the Pentagon.

Assured Destruction provided cover for two of McNamara's top priorities when it came to nuclear weapons policy: first, to keep Kennedy from ordering drastic cuts to the arsenal (Enthoven would later devise a chart to show that, in a worst-case scenario, the U.S. needed to retain its current number of weapons to inflict the necessary level of destruction); second, and more urgently, to keep the Joint Chiefs of Staff from asking for more.

On November 22, less than two months after the ratification of the Limited Test Ban Treaty and the revelations of the Net Evaluation Subcommittee's report, President Kennedy was assassinated in Dallas.

Not quite two weeks later, on December 5, his vice president, now his successor, Lyndon B. Johnson, chaired his first National Security Council meeting, with Kennedy's top advisers—most of whom would stay on, at least for a while—in attendance. In the 1950s, as the Senate majority leader, Johnson had immersed himself in the workings of the aerospace industry and helped win many contracts for burgeoning companies in his home state of Texas. As vice president, he'd been charged with monitoring the space program and the race to put a man on the moon, one of Kennedy's most impassioned ambitions. But, like most politicians, Johnson had never taken an interest in the intricacies of nuclear strategy. A few hours before Johnson's first NSC meeting, McGeorge Bundy handed him a script of remarks that he might want to make. As the meeting began, Johnson read from the script almost verbatim. A president's "greatest single requirement," the script noted at one point, was "to ensure the survival of civilization in the nuclear age." Johnson read on, "My view is simple: a nuclear war would be the death of all our hopes, and it is our task to see that it does not happen."

The line so impressed the new president that he repeated it at the end of the meeting.

How to ensure nuclear war did not happen was now an issue of bitter contention between McNamara and the Chiefs. At the NSC meeting, after President Johnson's remarks, the CIA director, John McCone, summarized the agency's latest estimate of Soviet nuclear forces. After McCone wrapped up, McNamara jumped in to highlight what he saw as the estimate's main point: that the U.S. enjoyed a nearly three-to-one advantage over the Soviets in first-strike capability, yet even so—here reprising the argument that he'd made at the Net Evaluation briefing with Kennedy the previous September—no one would gain an advantage from launching a first strike; regardless of who went first, each side would suffer 50 to 100 million fatalities.

The next day, McNamara sent Johnson (via Bundy) a memorandum, which he'd originally addressed to Kennedy, on his new Assured Destruction doctrine. In it, he also mentioned a secondary mission, which he called "Damage Limiting" (a euphemism for counterforce), though he emphasized that it should not "provide a basis for buying more missiles."

One month later, McNamara read a detailed study that cemented his growing sense that nuclear weapons were useless for anything but deterring war. The study was called "Damage Limiting: A Summary Study of Strategic Offensive and Defensive Forces of the U.S. and USSR," by an unusual Air Force three-star general named Glenn Kent—a mathematician who had been in charge of military planning in the 1950s, took leave in the early 1960s to study defense policy at Harvard, then returned to the Pentagon, where he was now an assistant to Harold Brown, a physicist who was McNamara's director of research and engineering.

When Kent first came to work for Brown, the Army was testing a new weapon designed to shoot down an enemy's ballistic missiles as they plunged toward their targets in U.S. territory. The Joint Chiefs were about to run a computer simulation to analyze how many of these anti-ballistic-missiles—ABMs, they were called—would be needed, assuming that the Soviets launched a certain number of missiles in a first strike. Kent pointed out that the Chiefs were asking the wrong question. There would probably be some interaction between the two countries: if the U.S. built an ABM system, the USSR would respond by building more offensive missiles. A more useful analysis would display curves on a graph, showing how many ABM interceptors were needed, at what cost, given a wide range of assumptions about how many missiles the Soviets might launch.

Brown asked Kent to write a study on the relationship between a Soviet attack and the full array of "damage-limiting" programs the United States might fund—including ABMs, counterforce weapons, and the fallout shelters of a civil defense program. In January 1964, Kent finished the study: a series of twenty-nine graphs, showing that, no matter what measures the United States took, the Soviets could overwhelm them with only a slight increase in their offensive forces. For each dollar that the Soviets spent on more offense, the U.S. would have to spend at least three dollars on damage-limiting efforts—at which point, the Soviets could overwhelm those measures, forcing the U.S. again to spend three times as much as the Soviets, and on it would go in an arms race that would drain America's resources far more quickly than it would drain the Soviet Union's. And this calculation assumed that the damage-limiting programs actually worked, when, in fact, the ABM systems in particular had a poor test record of actually shooting down targets in space.

The Chiefs were outraged by the study. Curtis LeMay accused Kent of selling out the Air Force. McNamara, on the other hand, was impressed. He sent the study to Bundy, with a cover note outlining how to brief President Johnson on its implications.

Not long after, in a memo to Johnson on the budget for the up-coming year's nuclear weapons programs, McNamara dropped Damage Limiting altogether as a strategic rationale. Assured Destruction was now the only measure of how many nuclear weapons were enough—though he again explained, almost parenthetically, that the weapons weren't actually aimed at people or cities per se. McNamara also took the bolder step of scaling back the Minuteman ICBM program. In his previous three budget memos, he'd wavered between recommending 1,200 to 1,400 missiles by the end of the decade. Now he proposed keeping the total at 1,000.

The Chiefs were apoplectic. They'd always distrusted McNamara; now they saw him as a saboteur. LeMay sometimes asked his colleagues, "Would things be much worse if Khrushchev were secretary of defense?" McNamara was touting a "doctrine" based entirely on threatening to launch U.S. nuclear weapons at Soviet citizens and industrial plants, knowing full well that the actual war plan called for aiming almost all of them at military targets—yet he wasn't giving the Chiefs enough weapons to accomplish the real mission.

McNamara thought he had the Chiefs cornered, but they had one more trick up their sleeves—a new weapon called the MIRV, which stood for Multiple Independently targetable Reentry Vehicle. The nosecone of a missile with MIRVs would carry several warheads, each of which could be aimed at different targets. One MIRV'ed missile carrying six warheads could hit as many targets as six single-warhead missiles.

The weapons labs had been developing this technology since the late 1950s, but its initial incarnation hadn't been quite so elaborate. The first actual model, known as the A-3 modification to the Navy's Polaris missile, fit three warheads into the nosecone, but all three would land in the same area. (They were known simply as MRVs, for Multiple Reentry Vehicles.) The MRV had two rationales. In the first, the warheads could saturate an enemy ABM system, so that even if one of them got shot down, the others would still dart toward the target. In the second rationale, the multiple warheads offered an efficient way to destroy oddly shaped targets, such as Soviet military airbases, some of which were oblong with twists and turns; a single 500-kiloton warhead (the explosive yield of the original Polaris) would destroy some of the airfield as well as a large circle of empty grass and dirt around it, while possibly leaving a far-flung section of the base unscathed. With three well-placed smaller warheads (each Polaris A-3 warhead would explode with the blast of 200 kilotons), the weapon would destroy all of the air base and less of the surrounding land.

In 1962, NASA designed a "post-boost control system," which, when attached to the nosecone of a rocket booster and launched into space, could release several satellites into different orbits. The weapons scientists, especially at the Lawrence Livermore lab, figured they could adapt this system to the military's missiles, thus turning MRVs into MIRVs.

LeMay at first opposed the idea. Breaking down a payload into several warheads meant that each warhead would be smaller. LeMay wanted his nuclear warheads as big and as powerful as possible. But other officers convinced him that the MIRV might be just the trick to maneuver around McNamara's restriction on how many missiles they could buy. One MIRV'ed missile carrying three warheads could hit just as many targets as three single-warhead missiles. Under these circumstances, McNamara's cap of 1,000 ICBMs wasn't much of a cap at all.

As the MIRV project wended its way through the Pentagon's budget process, as a line item in the research and development account, McNamara took notice—and thought it might be the way to get the Air Force to accept his restrictions. By this time, late in 1964, he was immersed in managing the escalation of the war in Vietnam and so was paying less attention to nuclear programs, which he regarded primarily as a waste of money. To that end, he was adamant about enforcing his limit of 1,000 ICBMs. If the MIRV could buy the Chiefs' assent, he was fine with it.

So, on December 3 he sent a Top Secret memo to President Johnson, approving "development of a capability for delivering three MK-12 warheads"—the model number of the MIRV favored by the Air Force—"to geographically separated targets."

In public, McNamara said the MIRV was designed to saturate Soviet ABMs, but this was false; the old MRVs—multiple warheads aimed at the same area—would suffice for that task. Moreover, McNamara *knew* it was false. The MK-12 was less powerful than the warhead on the original Minuteman—170 kilotons versus 1.2 megatons—but, in that same memo to Johnson, McNamara also approved a new inertial guidance system that would greatly improve the Minuteman's accuracy. A missile didn't need such a large warhead if it exploded close to its target, and the new guidance system would get the MK-12 close enough so that its probability of destroying a blast-hardened Soviet ICBM silo "would be," in McNamara's words, "in excess of 90 percent."

In short, the MIRV was explicitly a counterforce weapon.

It was unclear—even his close aides couldn't tell—whether McNamara had been played or whether, confronted with conflicting pressures, he was trying once again to straddle both sides of the issue. In this case, though, the ploy didn't work to his advantage. Despite his avowal of Assured Destruction and his insistence that a Damage Limiting strategy was futile, his approval of the MIRV and a more accurate Minuteman missile restored to the Air Force a first-strike capability.

In 1961, the Air Force had requested 2,300 Minuteman missiles. McNamara cut the number to 1,200, then, two years later, to 1,000. Yet by the time he left the Pentagon in 1968, he'd approved 550 MIRV'ed Minuteman IIIs, carrying a total of 1,650 warheads, as well as 450 single-warhead Minuteman IIs—for a total of just 1,000 missiles but 2,100 warheads: just short of the number of weapons that the Air Force had requested at the outset of McNamara's tenure.

But in their triumph, the Chiefs too were shortsighted. In October 1964, two months before McNamara approved the MIRV, Nikita Khrushchev was deposed as premier of the Soviet Union and chairman of its Communist Party, mainly for what the hardliners saw as his surrender in Cuba and possibly for his less hawkish stance toward the West. His successor, Leonid Brezhnev, was more indulgent of the military, and so the Soviet nuclear arsenal—which had remained static since the Cuban crisis—began to grow. The U.S. Air Force deployed the first MIRV'ed Minuteman IIIs in 1970, and they gave the United States a momentary edge in land-based missiles. But over the next decade, the Soviets built their own MIRVs, on three different ICBMs—the four-warhead SS-17, the six-warhead SS-19, and the very large ten-warhead SS-18. Their generals too were amassing the makings of a first-strike capability.

Of the three types of strategic nuclear launchers—bombers, submarine-launched ballistic missiles, and land-based ICBMs—the ICBMs were at once the most potent and the most vulnerable: that is, their accuracy made them most capable of destroying blast-hardened targets, such as ICBM silos. Yet, by the same token, their fixed positions made them vulnerable to an adversary's accurately guided missiles. MIRVs compounded this precariousness. If both sides had only single-warhead ICBMs, an arms race would be senseless: one side could easily match the other's buildup. But if one side had MIRVs, adding one more missile would mean adding three to ten more warheads—and the ability to destroy, theoretically, three to ten of the other side's missiles. If both sides had MIRVs, they would both have a dramatic edge—and they would both be vulnerable to the other side's dramatic edge. In a crisis, a desperate or risk-prone leader might be tempted to launch a first strike, if just to preempt the other side's leader from launching a first strike.

In short, the very existence of MIRVs created a hair-trigger situation, in which both sides might feel an incentive to strike first.

The 1960s started with a chance to halt the arms race before it got under way, with the discovery that the Soviet Union's alleged superiority in nuclear weapons—the "missile gap," which had rationalized the U.S. military's desire for a nuclear arms buildup—was, in fact, a myth. But the buildup proceeded anyway. The Berlin crisis revealed that, even with superiority in nuclear weapons, a U.S. first strike—an exploitation of that superiority—could wind up killing millions of Americans and was, therefore, an unacceptable option. The Cuban missile crisis reinforced that lesson. The report by the Net Evaluation Subcommittee a year later, in September 1963, confirmed an unalterable stalemate in the nuclear contest between the two superpowers, and both their leaders not only recognized this fact but started carving a path to relax tensions accordingly. But by the end of the decade, with Kennedy killed, Khrushchev overthrown, and new technologies promising to restore an edge in the arms race, the arsenals swelled beyond numbers ever previously imagined, and plans for fighting—and possibly winning—a nuclear war emerged as too tempting to pass up.

CHAPTER 5

Madman Theories

I n March 1968, hounded by opposition to the Vietnam War and his own growing doubts about its wisdom, Lyndon Johnson announced he would not seek reelection. His vice president, Hubert Humphrey, who emerged as the party's nominee, took too long to dissociate himself from Johnson's policies. So, on January 20, 1969, Richard Nixon was sworn in as president of the United States.

Nixon had campaigned on claims that he had a secret plan to end the Vietnam War. In fact, it turned out, he didn't, but the promise was plausible because, throughout his career, first as a senator, then as Eisenhower's vice president, he had engaged in broad aspects of international affairs, and he remained interested, including in the arcana of nuclear strategy. One week after his inauguration, he and his national security adviser, Henry Kissinger, went to the Pentagon for lunch with his new secretary of defense, Melvin Laird, and the chairman of the Joint Chiefs of Staff, General Earle "Bus" Wheeler; then the four of them, along with several staffers, proceeded to a briefing on the SIOP in the first-floor headquarters of the National Military Command Center, which would transmit orders from the president in case of a nuclear war.

The SIOP was basically the same as it had been since Robert McNamara's slight revision seven years earlier, except both sides' arsenals had swelled since then; so, given that the plan's main objective remained to fire every American nuclear weapon at every target in the Soviet Union, the expected level of damage—the number of targets hit, people killed, and territory ravaged—was greater still.

By the time Nixon entered the White House, the SIOP had been modified, a little bit, to allow for three "attack options": Alpha, which would fire a portion of the arsenal at Soviet and Chinese nuclear weapons sites; Bravo, which covered other military facilities and political-control centers located outside of cities; and Charlie, which would destroy all other military sites, regardless of their location, as well as 70 percent of the industrial floor space inside Soviet and Chinese cities. There was also a sub-option to exclude Moscow and Beijing from Alpha and Bravo strikes. Otherwise, the nuclear war plan offered the president no other choices, and the smallest of those choices—Alpha with the Moscow-Beijing exemption—would fire 1,750 nuclear weapons: hardly a "limited" attack.

Nixon was visibly horrified. Kissinger was at least startled. The author of several notable books and articles on nuclear strategy, Kissinger had been among those who had criticized John Foster Dulles's all-or-nothing strategy of "massive retaliation." More pertinently, he had been a White House consultant in the first year and a half of the Kennedy administration. He knew of McNamara's efforts to inject smaller attack options into the SIOP and had played a peripheral role in the early phase of the first-strike plan that Carl Kaysen and Harry Rowen drew up during the Berlin crisis. He assumed that, in the years since, the war planners at Strategic Air Command had made some changes; he was surprised that they hadn't.

Shortly after the briefing, Kissinger phoned McNamara, conveyed the gist of what he'd just heard, and asked, "Is this the best they can do?" Apparently it was.

Two weeks later, Nixon and Kissinger discussed the war plan further at an NSC meeting. David Packard, the deputy secretary of defense, who was chairing a panel on nuclear policy, noted that, because the Soviets had encased their ICBMs in underground, blast-resistant silos and were starting to put some missiles on submarines, the U.S. no longer had a first-strike capability.

Nixon mused that President Kennedy—who had defeated him in the 1960 election and who was still an object of his envy—enjoyed a five-to-one advantage in nuclear weaponry when he faced down Khrushchev over the missiles in Cuba. He wouldn't have that edge, or the confidence it bestowed, in a crisis today. (Like most of the world, Nixon didn't know about the secret missile trade that ended the Cuban missile crisis.)

"We may have reached the balance of terror," Nixon said.

"That is a new situation," Kissinger replied.

It wasn't really new; Kennedy, McNamara, and Bundy recognized the arms race had hit a "stalemate" in 1963, when they learned that the two superpowers would suffer the same damage in a nuclear war, no matter which side fired first. But now the two countries had roughly the same *number* of nuclear armaments; the stalemate—the fact that neither side could strike first without getting attacked in return, with catastrophic consequences—was palpable to even the casual observer.

The Europeans, Kissinger noted, didn't fully understand that the "nuclear umbrella"—the assurance, at the heart of the NATO alliance, that an American president would respond to a Soviet conventional invasion by firing nuclear weapons at the USSR—depended on a first-strike capability; his attack on the USSR, after all, would be a nuclear first strike. That capability—that foundation of assurance—had now crumbled; the Soviets might think they could get away with an act of aggression; in any case, the allies' anxieties were likely to surge.

This anxiety had impelled McNamara to adopt a counterforce strategy and to try infusing it into the SIOP, even after he'd started to question its plausibility. Now Kissinger realized that McNamara's effort had failed: he'd written the guidance for a new SIOP, but the generals at SAC all but ignored it.

"The SIOP is a horror strategy," Kissinger said at a meeting on the defense budget.

Nixon agreed. "The Air Force is a disgrace." Its generals were "still fighting World War II."

Kissinger realized he needed to do over what McNamara had tried to do: he needed to change the SIOP.

———∞∞∞———

For the moment, though, planning for a hypothetical nuclear war with the Soviet Union took a back seat to fighting the very real guerrilla war in Vietnam, and—despite their awareness of the "balance of terror" and the SIOP's "horror strategy"—Nixon and Kissinger went looking for ways to end that war by threatening to drop nuclear bombs.

As early as the 1968 presidential campaign, Nixon laid out his scheme to H.R. Haldeman, his main political confidant, who would soon become his White House chief of staff. "I call it the Madman Theory," Nixon told Haldeman, who transcribed the exchange in his diary. "Bob," he explained, "I want the North Vietnamese to believe I've reached the point where I might do anything to stop the war. We'll just slip the word to them that, 'for God's sake, you know Nixon is obsessed about Communism. We can't restrain him when he's angry—and he has his hand on the nuclear button.'"

Send them that message, Nixon said, and, "in two days," Ho Chi Minh, the leader of North Vietnam and its Communist revolution, would come "begging for peace."

The idea had its roots in Nixon's years as Eisenhower's vice president. Both men believed that North Korea called a truce to its three-year war against U.S. troops in South Korea because Eisenhower threatened to nuke China, its main supplier, if the war didn't end soon. Nixon also believed that nuclear threats played a role in deterring China from attacking Quemoy, in the Taiwan Strait, and in forcing Khrushchev to back off in the 1959 Berlin crisis. In 1955, Nixon himself had warned Chinese officials that the U.S. would respond with nuclear weapons if they mounted any sort of aggression in the Pacific. Nixon told a *Time* magazine reporter, many years later, that Khrushchev was "the most brilliant world leader" he'd ever met, "because he nurtured a reputation for rashness, bellicosity, and stability"—in short, because he behaved like a madman and, so, was able to "scare the hell out of people." Nixon hoped to pull off the same feat.

Kissinger had sometimes held a similar view. A community of nuclear deterrence theorists coalesced in the late 1950s and early 1960s, spinning war scenarios in which one side sends signals with force and the other side, reading the signals, either backs down or escalates the conflict. Kissinger, an active participant at academic conferences and seminars on nuclear war, wrote, in one volume of essays on the subject, that deterrence "is as much a psychological as a military problem" and that a "threat meant as a bluff but taken seriously is more useful for purposes of deterrence than a 'genuine' threat interpreted as a bluff." In some games of "threats and counter-threats," he wrote, a "premium will be placed on irresponsibility," and both sides—Americans and Soviets—will "have to be ready to act like madmen."

After Nixon entered the White House, he put the Madman Theory to a test. On his instructions, Kissinger warned the North Vietnamese delegates at peace talks, which were taking place in Paris, that Nixon had a temper and couldn't be controlled. His counterparts from Hanoi seemed unimpressed.

That summer, Kissinger formed a small, cloistered group within the National Security Council to devise new ideas on how to pressure North Vietnam. "I refuse to believe that a little fourth-rate power does not have a breaking point," he told his aides. The group's task was to examine options for "a savage decisive blow" that would make the North Vietnamese eager for peace.

As his staffers put it in a paper produced on September 13, the goal was "to demonstrate U.S. resolve to apply whatever force is necessary" and thus "achieve maximum political, military, and psychological shock, while reducing North Vietnam's over-all war-making and economic capacity." The range of possible actions in this campaign included the mining of North Vietnam's ports, the bombing of its dikes (which would unleash intense flooding), large cross-border sweeps into Laos and Cambodia, and—toward the end of the list, if all else failed—a "clean nuclear interdiction" of three passageways between North Vietnam and Laos or of two between North Vietnam and China.

Some of the group's members, who'd been told to write the "meanest" memo they could imagine, didn't know whether Kissinger was serious: whether he really wanted to do these things, or wanted to coerce Hanoi by threatening to do them, or just wanted to impress Nixon with how tough he could seem. A few of the aides—notably Anthony Lake, a former consul in the U.S. embassy in South Vietnam who was now Kissinger's special assistant, and Roger Morris, who was brought over from the NSC's Africa desk for a fresh perspective—found the whole business "appalling" and told him so. Kissinger didn't bother to send the September 13 report to Laird, who was known to view the idea of nuclear options for Vietnam as preposterous.

By late October, Nixon realized that the Madman Theory wasn't having any effect on the North Vietnamese and that actually using nuclear weapons would be politically unacceptable.

He and Kissinger were hardly the first to brandish, or consider using, nuclear weapons in Vietnam. In 1954, when the Vietcong surrounded (and ultimately crushed) the French colonial army at Dien Bien Phu, John Foster Dulles offered the French foreign minister two tactical atomic bombs. (The offer was declined.) At the same time, a special study group in the Pentagon concluded that three well-placed tactical A-bombs would "smash" the Vietcong offensive. General Curtis LeMay, the commander of SAC, drew up a detailed plan to do just that.

During the Johnson administration, even McNamara wasn't above engaging in nuclear bluffs. In April 1965, just after a major deployment of U.S. troops to Vietnam, he told reporters, on a not-for-attribution basis, "We are not following a strategy that recognizes any sanctuary or any weapons restriction." We wouldn't drop A-bombs unless all other courses fail, he added, but "inhibitions" on using nuclear weapons were "not overwhelming." A few days later, on the record, he backpedaled, saying, "There is no military requirement for nuclear weapons," nor would there be in the foreseeable future. But, clearly, he had meant to send a message to the Vietcong—and the Vietcong, just as clearly, ignored it.

In early 1968, Walt Rostow, by this time President Johnson's national security adviser, consulted with the war's two top officers—General William Westmoreland, commander of U.S. forces in Vietnam, and Admiral Ulysses Sharp, commander of U.S. naval forces in the Pacific—on whether nuclear weapons could and should be used to repel a siege that the Vietcong were mounting against the Marine compound in Khe Sanh. Discussions were very tightly held. At one point, Westmoreland and Sharp drew up a plan to transfer nuclear weapons to an area near the compound, in case they were needed and a request to use them was approved.

Ultimately, in all of these incidents of bluff and brinkmanship, American political leaders kept the nukes locked up.

Eisenhower may have talked casually about nuclear weapons, saying on one occasion they would be used "exactly as you would use a bullet," but he acted differently when facing a real challenge. He decided not to follow the French into Vietnam with any sort of force, much less with A-bombs. He ordered nuclear-capable fighter-bombers to fly over Quemoy as a demonstration of American power and will; but he also told the Joint Chiefs that, in case of Chinese aggression, they should respond with *conventional* force, at least initially. McNamara privately made clear to one and all that he firmly opposed using nuclear weapons in Vietnam. And when Johnson learned of Westmoreland's nuclear gambit at Khe Sanh, he ordered it halted at once.

Then again, even McNamara allowed that if China invaded Vietnam, he might be moved to change his mind; the spectacle of Chinese troops overwhelming U.S. positions would evoke memories—at the time, not so distant—of the Korean War. More than 35,000 Americans had died in that conflict, and few believed that an American president would get embroiled in another war so deadly without resorting to the ultimate weapon. Still more Americans would wind up dying in Vietnam—but no president dared to cross the nuclear threshold.

———— ∞∞ ————

After Hanoi's negotiators ignored Kissinger's warning that Nixon was insane, the president and his national security adviser pivoted to a variation on the ploy. On the assumption that the North Vietnamese Army and the Vietcong relied on the Soviet Union for supplies, Nixon decided to try out the Madman Theory on the Kremlin.

In July 1969, Leonard Garment, a special consultant to the president, was about to meet with top Soviet officials in Moscow. Kissinger told him to convey the impression that Nixon was "somewhat crazy"— immensely intelligent, organized, experienced, but capable of "barbaric cruelty" to those who challenged him in tests of strength.

In October, Nixon and Kissinger staged an alert of strategic nuclear forces—one of the largest alerts in SAC history. Kissinger's military assistant, Colonel Alexander Haig, wrote to his counterpart in the Pentagon, Colonel Robert Pursley, that the alert should be "unusual and significant"—"discernible to the Soviets" without "threatening" their existence. For more than two weeks, from October 13 to 30, SAC bombers were dispersed, ordered to maintain radio silence, and relieved from routine training drills, as if they were preparing for combat. Tactical spy planes stepped up surveillance of Soviet shipping. Aircraft carriers and submarines carrying nuclear weapons were kept at sea for longer tours; and for a few of those days, all U.S. strategic nuclear forces were placed on a higher alert level.

The intent was to warn the Kremlin's leaders that Nixon was about to take serious military action against North Vietnam, possibly against the Soviet Union—and that, to ward off calamity, they should pressure their allies in Hanoi to submit to his terms at the Paris peace talks.

The alert was kept extremely secret; only a handful of officials in Washington knew what was going on and why. But the Soviets did take notice, and their ambassador, Anatoly Dobrynin, asked for a meeting with Nixon and Kissinger, who took the request as a sign that the stratagem was working. At the meeting, Nixon urged Dobrynin to prod the North Vietnamese into accepting a reasonable peace and threatened stronger action if they refused. Dobrynin replied only in vague and general terms, without so much as mentioning the nuclear alert. Meanwhile, General Wheeler, the chairman of the Joint Chiefs of Staff, reported to the White House that the alert had sparked "no significant reaction" from Soviet military forces.

And so, on October 30, the alert fizzled out, with no follow-up. If the Soviets expected an American attack of some sort, they must have come away from the drill merely puzzled. As with Nixon's earlier and more direct stab at applying the Madman Theory to Vietnam, it had no effect—perhaps because the Soviets and the North Vietnamese knew that Nixon wasn't a madman, perhaps because they didn't quite know what his signals were conveying, perhaps because they didn't care.

Over the next few years, Nixon played Madman a few more times, during various Middle East crises, moving the Sixth Fleet and two extra nuclear-armed aircraft carriers into the Eastern Mediterranean when Iraq and Syria seemed on the verge of invading Jordan, and raising SAC's alert status when the Soviets made noises about intervening in the 1973 Yom Kippur War—all, again, to little or no effect. The Soviet foreign minister, Andrei Gromyko, observed at the time: "Americans put forces on alert so often that it is hard to know what it meant."

In the summer of 1972, Kissinger focused his attention once again on the nuclear war plan. He learned that, earlier in the year, Melvin Laird had formed a panel on the subject and that it had just turned in its report to the Joint Chiefs. The panel was headed by the Defense Department's top research scientist, John S. Foster, Jr., a renowned physicist and former director of the Livermore weapons laboratory.

The Foster Panel, as it was known, had its roots in the final year of the Johnson administration, when a new generation of Air Force officers—who had risen through the ranks mainly as tactical fighter pilots, not as strategic nuclear bombardiers—mounted a challenge to Curtis LeMay's bomb-everything ethos at SAC. Initially, the challenge was purely intellectual and low-key: a study, coordinated with a few analysts at the RAND Corporation, titled NU-OPTS, short for Nuclear Options or Nuclear Operations. Its participants all realized that Bill Kaufmann's counterforce doctrine—which they'd championed a few years earlier—had become obsolete. The idea of counterforce was to keep a nuclear attack limited—aimed strictly at the USSR's military targets, sparing its cities, so that, if the Soviets retaliated, they might spare American cities too. But in the post-Khrushchev era, the Soviets had deployed several hundred ICBMs; to destroy all of them in a counterforce strike, the United States would have to launch more than a thousand nuclear bombs or warheads. That would constitute a massive attack, and the Soviets would retaliate massively.

McNamara had reached the same conclusion and, as a result, had lost interest in all plans for a nuclear first strike. By contrast, the NU-OPTS members took the premise as a springboard to explore new concepts of nuclear warfighting—new ways to make nuclear weapons usable. They were driven by two motives: first, they wanted to keep the deterrent credible in an era of Soviet-American parity; second, and especially prominent in the minds of the officers, they wanted to maintain the bureaucratic preeminence of the Air Force—to make a case for buying more Air Force bombers and missiles.

In December 1968, the group produced a RAND monograph titled *Rationale for NU-OPTS*. It was written by a RAND analyst named James Schlesinger and supervised by Richard Yudkin, an unusual Air Force general—Jewish, bookish, with no experience as any sort of airplane pilot, having earned his three stars entirely as a military strategist. They derived their key insights from Thomas Schelling, a former RAND eminence who had written two books—*The Strategy of Conflict* and *Arms and Influence*—which applied mathematical Game

Theory to modern warfare, depicting combatants as rational actors pursuing a strategy that maximized their interests, given the strategy that their opponent was most likely to pursue. Schelling imagined scenarios involving small-scale nuclear strikes: shots across the bow to demonstrate resolve, pricks of pain to convey a message to an adversary that more pain would follow unless he halted his aggression.

Yudkin and Schlesinger outlined a concept built largely on Schelling's ideas, suggesting that small-scale nuclear strikes should be built around prepackaged slices of the SIOP—a specific slice for one war scenario, a different slice for another scenario—which they labeled "Selective Attack Options."

Over the next several months, a somewhat wider team of Air Force officers and RAND analysts produced a detailed three-volume study, laying out dozens of slices for dozens of scenarios, each jammed with calculations on the optimal targets, the optimal weapons for hitting each target, and the optimal flight routes if the weapons were dropped by bombers. All the scenarios began with a Soviet invasion or land grab—in northern Norway, the Middle East, or Central Europe—followed by a small-scale U.S. nuclear attack against either the invading troops or some vital target inside the USSR, depending on the desired outcome.

The project went on for nearly two years, but to no one's satisfaction. The uncertainties were daunting, the assumptions dubious, slamming into the same analytical obstacles that plagued the architects of the first-strike plan during the Berlin crisis or, for that matter, all the real-life musings on the theory of counterforce: Would the Soviets read the signals correctly? Could they respond in kind, if they wanted to—and would they want to? What if they retaliated with a larger nuclear attack, or with no nuclear attack at all? What would the next move be? How does a president or a commander end the war on favorable terms?

No one knew the answers, or even how to go about finding them.

Yudkin and Schlesinger recognized these obstacles from the outset, yet, despite the dead ends, they kept up the search. They wrote in the RAND memo that the case for Selective Attack Options was "not that they are especially appealing," but rather that they "may be less miserable than the other alternatives under given circumstances." It was like "playing Russian Roulette with three chambers filled, hardly an enticing prospect for decision-making," but preferable to the SIOP, which would pull the trigger of a pistol fully loaded.

The NU-OPTS project eventually ground to a halt, but it had an afterlife. In the early days of the study, at least one official took an interest, a young engineer named Ivan Selin, who was the deputy for strategic affairs in the Pentagon's Office of Systems Analysis, the nerve center of McNamara's whiz kids. When Selin first took the job, he made the obligatory trip to SAC headquarters in Omaha and discovered—as Nixon and Kissinger would a couple of years later—that the SIOP was still basically a doomsday machine, that the most "limited" option would unleash thousands of nuclear weapons against the "Sino-Soviet bloc," and that, while many of those weapons were aimed at military targets, many of those targets were located in large Soviet and Chinese cities: millions of civilians would be killed. Not long after the briefing, Selin learned about the NU-OPTS studies. Like their authors, he didn't find any of the options appealing but, also like them, he thought that, given the existence of nuclear weapons, plans had to be devised in case deterrence failed—and almost any plan would be better than the SIOP. Selin and another systems analyst named Laurence Lynn wrote their own study, in which they tried to calculate how many weapons were needed to deter the Russians and to accomplish some objectives, while avoiding catastrophe, in case deterrence failed.

By this time, McNamara had made his bargain with the Chiefs— they accepted the ceiling of a thousand Minuteman ICBMs and a public doctrine of Assured Destruction, while he approved the MIRV and let them do whatever they wanted with the SIOP—so neither he nor Selin's immediate boss, Alain Enthoven, the assistant secretary of defense for systems analysis, took any interest in this work.

Soon after Nixon was elected, Enthoven resigned, Selin replaced him, and Lynn moved over to the White House to work for Kissinger on the NSC staff. The day after Nixon's inauguration, Lynn wrote a memo, signed by Kissinger and addressed to the secretaries of state and defense, as well as to the director of the CIA, requesting "a study reviewing our military posture and the balance of power." Selin and Lynn had already written the study. They took it through an interagency process, made a few tweaks, and on May 8 turned it in as a National Security Study Memorandum called NSSM-3.

It amounted to a critique of McNamara's Assured Destruction policy—and a reassertion of the "controlled response" doctrine that he had tried to impose in his first few years as defense secretary. "Up to now," the memo read, "the main criterion for evaluating U.S. strategic forces has been their ability to deter the Soviet Union from all-out aggressive attacks on the United States." But a nuclear war might not occur as an exchange of "spasm reactions." Instead, it "may develop as a series of steps in an escalating crisis in which both sides want to avoid attacking cities, neither side can afford unilaterally to stop the exchange, and the situation is dominated by uncertainty."

Selin stayed on in the Pentagon for only the first year of Nixon's presidency, but in that span he drew two of his deputies into the topic—James Martin, who had worked with Selin on the analysis of the SIOP, and Archie Wood, a former Air Force civilian who, as a graduate student in the mid-1960s, had studied nuclear strategy with Bill Kaufmann at MIT. After Selin left, Martin and Wood persuaded his successor, Gardner Tucker, to let them continue the work. Tucker set up a project, called the Strategic Objectives Study, to explore the issues that NU-OPTS and NSSM-3 itemized but didn't solve. However, as the three soon realized, McNamara and Enthoven had so alienated the military that the very term "systems analysis" was radioactive in most corridors of the Pentagon. If a study of this sort were to make any dent on policy, it would have to reside elsewhere. So Gardner persuaded Melvin Laird to set up a higher-level panel to continue the exploration.

To head the panel, Laird appointed the Pentagon's director of research and engineering, Johnny Foster.

The Foster Panel first met in January 1972 and completed an interim report early the following summer. On July 27, Foster briefed Kissinger and his staff on its conclusions. He began by noting that the SIOP hadn't changed much since McNamara's earliest effort at reform in the early 1960s—and not at all since Nixon was briefed on it during his first weeks in office. The plan still called for winning the war quickly by destroying the enemy. Foster's report proposed a different plan, aimed at trying to stop the war quickly while wreaking as little destruction as possible.

His alternative plan borrowed heavily from the Selective Attack Options in the NU-OPTS study. It laid out twelve of these SAOs, as he abbreviated the term—small-scale attacks, involving far fewer than the thousand or so weapons needed to destroy the entire Soviet and Chinese nuclear arsenals. Each option specified distinct categories of targets that would *not* be hit—for instance, targets in Moscow and Beijing, targets in major cities, targets in China (if China had nothing to do with the war), and key national command-control centers (in order to avoid killing the enemy's political or military leaders, so they could control their response to a U.S. strike and negotiate an end to the war). Beyond these selective options, the study called for developing an unspecified number of Limited Nuclear Options (LNOs)—attacks consisting of still fewer nuclear weapons, geared to specific scenarios.

If the LNOs and SAOs failed to make the enemy stop fighting, the plan would allow a president to choose from four Major Attack Options (MAOs). One of these would hit every Soviet military target, nuclear and conventional. Another would hit every Chinese military target. Still another would hit every target in the Soviet Union, including urban factories. The final option would hit every target in China.

However, all of the MAO options contained a twist: the targets would be chosen not with the aim of killing people and destroying factories for their own sake, but rather to impede the enemy's ability to recover—as a military, economic, and political power. That, the plan's authors thought, was what national leaders most valued—and what they would most fear losing.

At a small interagency meeting one month before Foster's briefing, Kissinger had noted that, given the parity in the nuclear balance, the president could no longer assume that the Soviets would back down before a crisis turned violent. Yet, in such a crisis, the president might feel paralyzed if he had no nuclear options short of the SIOP's all-out attack. How, he asked his staff, more in frustration than in hopes of finding a good answer, do you most effectively deter nuclear war? Failing that, how do you limit nuclear war once it broke out—what sorts of targets would you need to hit, and what sorts of weapons would you need to fire?

These were the questions that Kissinger's predecessors had been exploring for the entire quarter-century of the nuclear age. No one had come up with good answers. Maybe Foster's outline of a plan could supply some.

Over the next year, Foster and his staff continued their work, turning their outline into detailed guidance on how to use nuclear weapons in various scenarios. In February 1973, Kissinger ordered an interagency review of the guidance, to be chaired by Foster himself, in order to expedite the process. This was, Kissinger wrote in a memo to Nixon, "an unprecedented opportunity to gain a measure of control over a vital area of national security policy which, for too long, has been unresponsive to Presidential direction."

Four months later, on June 8, the group produced a seventy-six-page document called NSSM-169. It endorsed and elaborated the themes of the Foster Panel report, even asserting that the ability to destroy Soviet and Chinese "political, economic and military targets critical to their post-attack recovery" was "the basis of the U.S. deterrent to nuclear war." But it also acknowledged several caveats. For instance: "There is, of course, no guarantee that escalation can be controlled." Because many Soviet military facilities were located in cities, even a limited attack would "result in substantial fatalities," making such an attack seem less-than-limited to the Soviets. Finally, there was "virtually no indication that the Soviets accept the notion that limited strategic war is feasible." Nonetheless, the study concluded that it "would be in the best interests of the Soviet Union to keep a nuclear war limited," and, therefore, the Kremlin leaders "may decide" to do so.

At a meeting of fifteen officials from the Departments of State and Defense, the Joint Chiefs, the CIA, and the NSC staff, Kissinger complained about the gaps that the Foster report left unfilled.

"We have been discussing this topic for four years," he grumbled, "and have come to no conclusions." The document struck him as jargon. "What," he asked, "does 'control of escalation' mean?"

Jasper Welch, a one-star Air Force general who was working under Foster at the Pentagon, replied that the phrase had several layers of meaning. "Initially," he said, "it was a slogan."

"We're good at that," Kissinger commented.

Welch then dug himself in deeper. The idea, he said, was to make the adversary change his mind and realize that continuing to fight was not in his interest. For instance, he went on, in China, we would strike nuclear facilities, conventional forces, and leadership targets.

Kissinger interrupted him. "What are you talking about?" he asked, fuming. "Is this on paper?" Six months had passed since Nixon's historic trip to China and his summit with Mao Zedong. Kissinger had lined up the trip with his own series of secret visits, to lure China into a strategic partnership, in part to pressure the Soviet Union—and here the Pentagon was still talking about nuking the "Sino-Soviet bloc"?*

To Kissinger, NSSM-169 left a slew of problems unsolved. On the one hand, he said, we want the Soviets to think that a war might get out of hand, in order to deter them from attacking in the first place; on

---

* Even so, China remained in the SIOP until 1983, and it was restored to the target list in 1998.

the other hand, if war did somehow erupt, we would want to persuade them not to let things get out of hand.

"I'm not being judgmental," he said. "I want the President to have an idea of what he can do." Nixon's most recent briefing on the nuclear war plan had taken place four years earlier, "and it didn't fill him with enthusiasm."

Kissinger then made a remarkable statement: "Nixon has heard only the SIOP, and if that's all there is, he won't do it"—he won't push the button, won't use nuclear weapons in a crisis. "To have the only option that of killing 80 million people," he exclaimed, "is the height of immorality."

NSSM-169 met with greater favor in the Pentagon. Laird had resigned as defense secretary in January, at the start of Nixon's second term, as he'd long planned to do. His replacement, Elliot Richardson, lasted just four months before he moved to the Justice Department (where he would, soon after, resign in protest, as part of the budding Watergate scandal). Succeeding Richardson as secretary of defense was James Schlesinger.

Schlesinger had been the author of the RAND memo, *Rationale for NU-OPTS*, and, in his three prior positions in the Nixon administration—chief of the Budget Bureau's national security division, chairman of the Atomic Energy Commission, and director of the CIA—he had taken part in the interagency reviews of the Foster Panel report, which had grown out of the NU-OPTS project. He was well disposed to NSSM-169, its caveats notwithstanding, and ordered work to begin on a National Security Decision Memorandum (the next step up from a study memorandum), which, if signed by the president, would turn its concepts into policy.

Back in the early 1960s, General Tommy White, the Air Force chief of staff, had referred to the whiz kids who'd come out of the RAND Corporation as "pipe-smoking, tree-full-of-owls type of so-called 'defense intellectuals,'" and, though Schlesinger wasn't yet at RAND when White coined the phrase, he fit the bill to a T. Confident in his grasp of grave matters, condescending toward those who didn't share his views, a pipe constantly clenched between his teeth, Schlesinger was the first defense secretary to have emerged from the community of nuclear strategists that was sprouting in think tanks and academia. Kissinger, if anything more arrogant than Schlesinger (though also wittier), was the first national security adviser with roots in the same coterie. So it was almost inevitable that the two would compete for preeminence.

Schlesinger and his staff—which included Bill Kaufmann, architect of the original counterforce strategy, who had come along as his special assistant in all of Schlesinger's government jobs—spent the rest of the year drafting the decision memorandum, which became known as NSDM-242, and the Nuclear Weapons Employment Policy (NUWEP) to go with it. Kissinger's staff kept tossing up obstacles, some for good reason—the caveats cited by NSSM-169 hadn't been resolved—some stemming from internecine politics. Schlesinger tried to break the logjam by going public.

On January 10, 1974, at a lunchtime press conference before the Overseas Writers Association, he announced that he was implementing a "change in targeting strategy," an alternative to the idea of a "suicidal strike against the cities of the other side." In an age of Soviet-American parity, the old policy of Assured Destruction was no longer adequate for deterrence; therefore, we needed "a set of selective options against different sets of targets," including purely military targets, on a more limited scale and with greater flexibility.

His remarks set off a ferocious controversy. Most people—including otherwise informed academics, arms control advocates, and editorialists—had taken McNamara's rhetorical shift seriously, had thought that Mutual Assured Destruction reflected real policy: that if the Soviets launched a nuclear attack, the U.S. would retaliate by destroying their cities; that nuclear deterrence relied on the threat to do so; that threatening to attack military targets, as Schlesinger now said he was doing, would be tantamount to treating nuclear weapons like conventional weapons—nuclear war like a conventional war—and would, therefore, undercut deterrence and make nuclear war more likely. They didn't know that, even under McNamara (and with his consent), the United States had been aiming the vast bulk of its nuclear arsenal at military targets all along. They also didn't know that the new policy, to the extent it was new, had been in the works for a few years, under the purview of the NSC staff in the White House; and so it widely came to be called the Schlesinger Doctrine—much to Kissinger's annoyance.

Still, Schlesinger's ploy worked. One week after his speech, Nixon signed NSDM-242 into policy; two and a half weeks later, Schlesinger signed the NUWEP.

At this point, the Strategic Air Command had to figure out how to translate the guidance into an actual war plan. SAC's commander, General John Meyer, was skeptical about the whole business. He doubted that the Soviets would regard as "limited" any nuclear attack beyond maybe a handful of bombs and that, therefore, whatever the president's intent, they would retaliate full bore.

In August, Meyer was replaced by General Russell Dougherty, who was more sympathetic to the concept, having worked a few years earlier on the NU-OPTS project. Still, even to Dougherty, the puzzle was how to interpret the directive that SAC should aim its nuclear weapons not merely at Soviet and Chinese political, economic, and military targets but, more specifically, at targets that were "essential" to those countries' "post-attack recovery."

To get a grip on the problem, SAC's technical analysts examined their list of targets—the factories, air and missile bases, weapons sites, control centers, and so forth, which the SIOP called for hitting in a nuclear war—and assigned a certain number of points to each target, indicating the extent to which its destruction would delay the enemy's recovery. The higher the total number of points, the "better" the attack plan. Or, to put it another way, the way to "improve" the attack plan was to boost the number of points—and the easiest way to do that was to attack more large Soviet and Chinese factories, which tended to be located in their most heavily populated cities.

The irony was enormous. The idea behind NSDM-242 and the NUWEP was to limit the damage wreaked by a nuclear war. But SAC's application of these directives would heighten the damage to new extremes.

The point system applied only to the Massive Attack Options and the Selective Attack Options. They were not applied to the Limited Nuclear Options—the LNOs—the set of pre-packaged plans to deal with specific scenarios, which called for firing a very small number of weapons.

In the spring of 1974, around the time that Schlesinger signed the NUWEP, Kissinger fashioned a little experiment. He asked the Joint Chiefs to devise an LNO that the president might order in response to a Soviet invasion of Iran, which was then ruled by the Shah Mohammed Reza, a loyal U.S. ally. A few weeks later, two generals briefed their plan to Kissinger and a few aides, including an arms control analyst named David Aaron and a former Pentagon whiz kid, now working on the NSC staff, named Jan Lodal. The plan called for launching nearly 200 nuclear weapons at military targets—air bases, bivouacs, and so forth—in the southern region of the USSR, near the Iranian border.

Kissinger exploded. "Are you out of your minds?" he screamed. "This is a *limited* option?" He told them to go back and come up with a smaller plan.

A few weeks later, the generals returned. There were two roads leading into Iran from the USSR. The revised plan called for exploding an atomic demolition mine on one of the roads and dropping two nuclear bombs on the other.

Kissinger's eyes rolled. "What kind of nuclear attack is this?" he scoffed. The president of the United States takes the horrible risk of firing nuclear arms in anger for the first time since the end of the Second World War—and he uses only three weapons? Kissinger later told Aaron and Lodal that if the president carried out this plan, Brezhnev would think he was "chicken."

It was the dilemma faced by every policymaker trying to make sense of nuclear weapons and Cold War politics: how to plan a nuclear attack that was large enough to terrify the enemy but small enough to be recognized unambiguously as a limited strike, so that, if the enemy retaliated, he'd keep his strike limited too.

Kissinger frequently complained about the Pentagon's obtuseness, telling his aides to press the officers across the river to come up with better ideas. Lodal, who was charged with making these calls, would nod sagely and pick up the phone. But his personal view, which deepened with each exposure to the debates and directives on this subject, was that there was no scenario in which using nuclear weapons would give the United States—or any country—an advantage. This was the conclusion that, thus far, every president of the nuclear age, and most high-level political officials, had also reached.

Yet those presidents and officials also realized, as did Lodal, that they had to act as if they would use nuclear weapons, or else their threats might not be credible in a crisis. And so, the officials and the analysts—the likes of McNamara, Bundy, Kissinger, Schlesinger, the whiz kids at RAND, the targeteers at SAC, and everyone else burdened with making policy of this madness—had to huddle over the problem, again and again, even if there was no solution. No one wanted to be the adviser who steps forward in the middle of a crisis with the Russians and tells the president of the United States, "I'm sorry, but there are no good options in a nuclear war; there is nothing that you can do."

CHAPTER 6

Bargaining Chips

Richard Nixon resigned from office on August 9, 1974, to pre-empt impeachment—which the House of Representatives was about to pass—for his abuses of power and obstructions of justice in the Watergate scandals. His vice president, Gerald Ford, took his place and, soon after, fired James Schlesinger, mainly for his arrogance, and pulled the last Americans out of Vietnam. But he also pardoned Nixon for any and all crimes that he may have committed, and, in part for that reason, lost the 1976 presidential election to Jimmy Carter, the governor of Georgia and a prosperous but frugal peanut farmer who rode an anti-establishment wave to the White House, promising, among other things, never to tell a lie.

Senior military officers eyed Carter with suspicion from the start. A devout Christian, he'd campaigned on a platform to cut the defense budget and to wipe the moral blight of nuclear weapons from the face of the earth. The Air Force distrusted Carter for an additional reason: he had graduated from the Naval Academy and spent several years as a protégé to Admiral Hyman Rickover, the architect of the nuclear submarine program. Like many Navy veterans of this background, Carter thought that nuclear war could be deterred with nothing more than a small number of missile-loaded submarines—that bombers and missiles, the Air Force's stock in trade, were unnecessary at best.

Carter deepened the officers' apprehensions a few days before taking office, when, along with a few senior aides, he sat through a briefing from the Joint Chiefs of Staff on the Soviet-American military balance, clenching his teeth in what some may have seen as a smile but acquaintances knew was anything but. After the final slide, he asked the Chiefs how long it would take to cut the arsenal of land-based intercontinental ballistic missiles down to 200. At the time, the United States had 1,054 ICBM.

The JCS chairman, Air Force General George Brown, didn't quite understand the question. Did the president-elect want to know how long it might take to negotiate a reduction of that scope with the Russians?

No, Carter replied. He wanted to know how long it would take the military to cut down to that small a force unilaterally.

A stunned silence draped the room.

Carter's new secretary of defense, Harold Brown (no relation to the general), wrote a memo to the president soon after the inauguration, explaining why such a drastic cut would be unwise. Brown, a nuclear physicist, had been the Pentagon's director of research and engineering under Robert McNamara; he'd supervised Glenn Kent's study concluding that efforts to "limit damage" in a nuclear war were futile and that, therefore, deterrence—as defined by McNamara's Assured Destruction doctrine—was the only valid purpose of nuclear weapons. Nevertheless, even Brown thought that whittling down the ICBM force to just 200 missiles was extreme. The Soviets—who by this time had more than 1,300 ICBMs, some loaded with multiple warheads—were unlikely to follow suit and, with such a massive edge, they might be tempted, in a crisis, to launch a first strike. Finally, Brown argued, even if an arsenal of 200 ICBMs seemed sufficient to deter the Soviets from attacking the United States, it might not be enough to assure the NATO allies that we had their security covered too.

The last argument persuaded Carter, and he dropped the matter.

Once in the White House, for all his antipathy toward the whole business of nuclear weapons, Carter immersed himself in its intricacies more deeply than any previous president. The Joint Chiefs ran periodic simulations of a Soviet nuclear attack, with assistant secretaries and other aides role-playing their bosses. In the first two of these exercises during his term, Carter played himself, an act that both impressed and unnerved the officers in the room; he soon after learned that he was the first president ever to take part in the exercise, a fact that astonished him. Why, he wondered, wouldn't a president want to rehearse what he would have to go through in the face of the gravest crisis imaginable?

During the simulation, Carter read from a document called the Black Book—literally a black binder, about an inch thick, prepared by the J-3, the operations division of the Joint Staff, laying out the president's options and how to order each one. Carter, who may also have been the first president to leaf through the Black Book, complained that the options were too complex, the language too dense with jargon.

"I'm pretty smart," he said, in his clipped Georgian drawl, "and I don't understand any of this." By the time of the next exercise, the J-3 had simplified the text.

Carter also ordered impromptu drills of the White House Emergency Procedures, the steps to be taken in the event of an attack—where the president and other officials should go, how they should get there, and how quickly. He ordered the first of these drills at nine o'clock on a February night, just weeks after taking office. It did not go well: the helicopter didn't arrive on the White House lawn in time; most of the officials to be evacuated couldn't be located. He repeated the drills, at random hours, with no advance notice; the response times improved. In all these briefings and drills, he took care to involve his vice president, Walter Mondale—another first: remarkably so, given that, in a nuclear war, the president might be killed and the vice would have to step into his shoes immediately.

After the first, disastrous test of the White House Emergency Procedures, Carter's national security adviser, Zbigniew Brzezinski, decided to take a closer look at the broad planning for nuclear war.

Brzezinski was an anomaly in the upper ranks of the Carter administration, an intellectual and a hard-line hawk on foreign and defense policy. Some called him Carter's Kissinger, and there was something to the comparison. Both were immigrants from totalitarian powers: Kissinger, a Jewish exile from Nazi Germany; Brzezinski, the son of a Catholic Polish diplomat who had taken refuge during World War II while posted to Canada. Both were educated at Harvard, where they then taught international relations, rising through the faculty as rivals. At the end of the 1950s, the department had room for just one Central European scholar of a Realpolitik bent, and the tenured slot went to Kissinger. Brzezinski decamped to New York, where he became a star at Columbia University.

He met Jimmy Carter in the early 1970s while setting up the Trilateral Commission, a rival of sorts to the Council on Foreign Relations, which sought to strengthen ties among the democratic, capitalist institutions in North America, Western Europe, and Japan. He wanted two governors to serve on the board, one from the West Coast, the other from the East, but not from any of the predictable northeastern states. He heard that the governor of Georgia had established trade offices in Brussels and Tokyo and figured this was the right man. He later learned that the trade offices had been set up by Carter's predecessor, but no matter: Carter, whose grand ambitions were soon apparent, was eager to join and quick to learn. When he announced that he was running for president, he brought Brzezinski to stand alongside him, a move that lent the unlikely unknown a dash of credibility; and, soon enough, "Zbig"—as friends called him—became his chief foreign policy adviser.

After Carter won the election, his campaign manager, a voluble young southerner named Hamilton Jordan, told the press, "If, after the inauguration, you find Cy Vance as secretary of state and Zbigniew Brzezinski as head of national security, then I would say we failed."

As it happened, Carter nominated precisely those men—emblems of the establishment that he'd pledged to tear down—suggesting that he might be a more complicated, less firebrand politician than some in his entourage imagined.

Brzezinski spent much of his first month in office studying the myriad aspects of nuclear war planning—the SIOP, the evolution of doctrine over the previous decade, the extent to which those doctrines aligned with what SAC was actually doing—and, like his predecessors who'd taken a similarly close look, he came away appalled. During a trip to SAC headquarters, he asked the commander, General Richard Ellis, what he envisioned happening thirty days after the war began. Ellis responded with vague bromides. Clearly there was no plan beyond the unleashing of the SIOP. And he discovered that the SIOP—despite the efforts of McNamara, Kissinger, Schlesinger, and their staffs—hadn't changed much at all over the years.

In a March 31 memo to Carter, he wrote, "The SIOP, as you know, offers retaliatory options short of a full response, but they remain massive in both direct and collateral damage." NSDM-242, the most recent presidential guidance on the subject, signed by Nixon three years earlier, had ordered SAC to devise some "limited nuclear options," but, Brzezinski learned, no one had provided any rationales or procedures for these options—what political or military objectives they were supposed to accomplish—and, therefore, even if SAC had followed the guidance (which it hadn't), the options would serve no purpose.

And so, like a scene in the movie *Groundhog Day*, yet another new administration rolled out yet another new set of documents, slogans, and acronyms in yet another stab at revising the nuclear war plan. In one memo penned by Brzezinski, Carter called for a "comprehensive net assessment" of the nuclear balance; in another, Harold Brown outlined the requirements of maintaining "essential equivalence" between the United States and the Soviet Union; in still others, their staffs explored new angles on nuclear targeting.

In the midst of this, President Carter faced his first international crisis—not a superpower standoff or some threat of nuclear war, but rather a dispute within NATO about new nuclear weapons in Europe.

Over the previous twenty years, the U.S. Army, Air Force, and, to a much lesser extent, the Marines had dotted the European landscape with a steadily swelling stockpile of nuclear weapons—7,000 of them by the time Carter entered office: short-range missiles, 8-inch and 155-millimeter artillery shells, atomic demolition mines, and a couple of hundred atomic bombs strapped to the bellies of FB-111 tactical fighter planes. The missiles and shells were short-range, relatively low-yield weapons, which would explode on the battlefield, killing Soviet soldiers and busting up their armored concentrations, in the event of an invasion across the East-West German border—or forcing those soldiers to disperse ahead of time, which would minimize the damage done by a nuclear explosion but also blunt the force of their offensive, thus further deterring the Kremlin from invading in the first place. President Kennedy and Robert McNamara had spent a lot of money upgrading NATO's conventional defenses, in the hopes of reducing the need to use nuclear weapons in the event of a war in Europe. But under President Johnson, spare parts, ammunition stocks, supplies, and troops were diverted to Vietnam. The nuclear stockpile grew in importance—and in number.

The Soviets had also deployed a substantial number of atomic weapons in Eastern Europe, but in the mid-1970s they fielded something new—the SS-20 missile, which had the range to hit targets in Western Europe from launch pads inside the USSR. An older generation of missiles, the SS-4 and SS-5, could do this too; but the SS-20 was mobile, it was fueled by more reliable solid propellants, and each missile carried three MIRV warheads in its nosecone.

None of the nuclear-armed missiles in Western Europe had the range to strike back at targets in the Soviet Union. American diplomats told the NATO allies not to worry: the "nuclear umbrella" was solid; a

Soviet invasion of West Germany would be answered by a U.S. nuclear strike against the Soviet Union, if necessary.

But de Gaulle's fear, that an American president might not "risk New York for Paris," still haunted some Western European leaders—and this worry intensified with the double whammy of the deployment of the SS-20 and the election of Jimmy Carter.

The Joint Chiefs' concerns about Carter had seeped across the Atlantic and found particularly fertile soil in the mind of West German chancellor Helmut Schmidt. A centrist politician with a background as defense and finance minister, Schmidt straddled a delicate balance on the Cold War's front line. With the Nazis' militarism still a fresh memory, West Germany was constitutionally barred from building a large military; so Schmidt, even more than the other NATO allies, depended on Washington's firm commitment and Moscow's goodwill to keep the peace. But Moscow couldn't be trusted as the sole foundation of security, and Schmidt didn't trust Carter at all.

Schmidt's few personal dealings with the new American president only deepened his worries. He saw Carter as an unworldly hayseed. Carter had pleaded with the chancellor to help solve the West's financial difficulties by inflating his economy, seemingly unaware of the Germans' deep phobia of inflation, dating back to the Weimar era, when hyperinflation helped trigger the rise of Nazism. Schmidt saw Carter waver and finally do nothing about Soviet activities in Ethiopia and Somalia. He heard reports of internal clashes within the administration—disputes among Brzezinski, Cyrus Vance, and the U.S. ambassador to the United Nations, Andrew Young—and of Carter's disinclination to pick one side or the other. Finally, he read press reports—inaccurate, as it happened—about a secret presidential memorandum that advocated surrendering large swaths of West German territory in the event of war with the Soviet Union.

Schmidt decided to go public with his anxieties. On October 28, in a speech before the International Institute for Strategic Studies in London, amid the standard boilerplate about economic interdependence and the scarcity of key resources, Schmidt lit the fuse of a political bomb. The key line was his declaration that the "principle of parity"— equal levels of nuclear armaments between East and West—"must apply to all weapons," not just to those based in the United States and the Soviet Union. He further asserted that the parity in intercontinental strategic arms "magnified the significance of disparities" on the European continent. Therefore, Schmidt urged the United States to deploy a new generation of theater nuclear weapons having the range to hit Soviet targets from inside Western Europe—in short, missiles that matched the capabilities of the Soviet SS-20s.

The implication was not merely that America's nuclear umbrella had leaks, but that it was broken.

Schmidt's speech prompted a series of interagency meetings in the Situation Room in the West Wing of the White House. In the months before the speech, several defense analysts had been pushing for precisely the kind of new weapon that Schmidt was requesting. Most of these analysts were members of the European-American Workshop, a low-key group chaired by Albert Wohlstetter, a charismatic consultant who had written some influential studies in the 1950s at the RAND Corporation. The author of Schmidt's speech, Walter Stützle, director of the German Defense Ministry's planning office, was an active member of the workshop. Other members had contacts inside the American defense bureaucracy.

By the time the interagency review began, a doctrinal rationale for the new missile had come into being. Brzezinski hadn't given the issue much thought, but his deputy, David Aaron, who'd held a similar post under Kissinger, was an ardent advocate. The SS-20s, Aaron said at one meeting, were creating a "gap in the escalation spectrum"—an odd phrase that was circulating in NATO circles as a result of the workshop's influence. The premise behind the concept was that the United States needed to match Soviet deployments at every step along the "escalation ladder," to invoke another metaphor.

Lieutenant General William Y. Smith, assistant to the chairman of the Joint Chiefs of Staff, touted two new weapons under development that would fill the gap: the Ground-Launched Cruise Missile, which could home in on a target with impressive accuracy, exploding just a few feet away; and a ballistic missile, the Pershing II (an upgrade of the Pershing, one of the long-standing nuclear weapons in Europe), nearly as accurate as the cruise missile and much faster. The Chiefs preferred an all–Pershing II force, since the cruise missile was slow and might be shot down by Soviet air defenses, but they were fine with fielding both. (Though Smith didn't say so, their position was driven by the fact that the Pershing II was an Army project and the cruise missile was funded by the Air Force; buying both would avoid interservice tensions.) Either way, Aaron and others on the NSC thought that these weapons would prevent the Soviets from thinking that they could fight a "sanctuary war"—hitting Western Europe with missiles launched from the USSR, with the United States unable (or unwilling) to strike back.

Leslie Gelb, the assistant secretary of state for politico-military affairs, was skeptical. Gelb had been the Pentagon's chief arms control analyst under McNamara, during the Johnson administration, then spent four years as a diplomatic correspondent for the *New York Times*. Immersed in the debates over nuclear weapons and deterrence theory from various angles, he felt uncomfortable with this notion of a gap in the escalation spectrum. On a strategic level, he considered it overly abstract, doubted that it had anything to do with the way real decision makers thought about war and peace. On a geopolitical level, he worried that even talking about the concept, and appearing to take it seriously, would heighten suspicions that America was canceling its NATO obligations altogether—"decoupling" its defense from that of Western Europe.

The technical and strategic debates went on for weeks, at several meetings in the Situation Room, with little sign of resolution. Then came an event that settled the matter.

All that fall, much controversy swirled around another new weapon called the enhanced radiation warhead, popularly known as the neutron bomb. Nuclear explosions released several effects—blast, heat, X-rays, gamma rays, neutron radiation, and radioactive fallout. The ERW was designed to minimize blast and maximize neutrons: specifically, it released about 1 kiloton of blast but the same amount of radiation as an ordinary nuclear bomb ten times as powerful. The military planned to build the weapon in three sizes—as an 8-inch artillery shell, a 155-millimeter shell, and a new warhead for the aging Lance missiles—seeing them as ideal for stopping a Soviet invasion of Western Europe without damaging the surrounding structures. Brzezinski and Harold Brown supported the program, which was classified, as a routine line item in the defense budget.

Then the *Washington Post* ran a story with a blazing headline about this new "killer warhead." Suddenly, critics denounced it as "the ultimate capitalist weapon"—killing people while sparing property. From a more analytical angle, arms control advocates saw it as a destabilizing weapon, blurring the distinction between a conventional and nuclear weapon, thus lowering the threshold between conventional and nuclear war, and thus increasing the chance that some president might actually use it.

The ensuing debate was symptomatic of the schizophrenia induced by thinking about the bomb: on the one hand, you wanted the Soviets to think you'd actually use these things, in order to deter them from aggression; on the other hand, you didn't want to make a weapon too easy or tempting to use if war broke out.

President Carter grasped both sides of the conundrum, though his instinctive revulsion toward nuclear weapons colored his view. The previous spring, he had toured a nuclear submarine with his old mentor, Admiral Rickover, who confided that he wished the atom had never been split. Coming from the man who designed the first nuclear-powered submarine, the remark stiffened Carter's commitment to bring down the number of nuclear weapons, if possible to zero. Carter knew, as he wrote in his diary, that the popular critique of the neutron bomb—that it killed people while protecting property—was a "gross oversimplification." Yet, at the same time, he told Brzezinski he didn't want to go down in history as the president who approved such a monstrosity. He decided that, if the NATO allies wanted it, they would have to ask for it. Schmidt took this as another sign of Carter's insensitivity toward Europe's—especially Germany's—political dilemmas. Finally, though, Schmidt came through and, at the risk of alienating his party's left wing, agreed to ask for the weapons as long as at least one other NATO nation on the continent did so, as well.

Then, on April 7, 1978, Carter canceled the project. Schmidt was furious. And since the Soviets had mounted a propaganda campaign against the neutron bomb throughout Europe, it looked as if Carter was caving in to the Kremlin.

At that point, the interagency debate over the cruise missiles and Pershing II screeched to a halt. Everyone agreed that another "neutron bomb fiasco" must be avoided, that these nuclear weapons programs had to go through. The tough questions were dropped because those who had been asking them feared there might be no answers; without answers, there might not be deployment; and without deployment, America's leadership of NATO would be doubted, might dissolve—and that had to be prevented at all cost.

So, with Brzezinski's approval and Carter's consent, the NSC put forth a plan to build 572 of the new weapons—464 Ground-Launched Cruise Missiles and 108 Pershing IIs. A few European prime ministers—still battered by the neutron-bomb flap—were reluctant to go along unless the plan was coupled to an arms control proposal. The NSC offered two sweeteners to the deal. First, if the allies accepted the 572 medium-range missiles, the United States would immediately remove 1,000 of the 7,000 short-range nuclear weapons in Europe—and dismantle another 572 as the new missiles were installed. Second, the whole program would be canceled if the Soviets agreed to get rid of their SS-20s by 1983, the year when the new American missiles would be fielded.

On December 12, 1979, at a meeting in Brussels, the NATO ministers voted to approve the plan. It marked a rare political victory for Carter, even if its point was to erase the effects of a political near-disaster and even if the missiles in question lacked much military purpose. This wouldn't be the last time Carter was forced to approve nuclear weapons that he abhorred for the sake of politics that he found distasteful.

Six months before the resolution of the NATO crisis, President Carter and Soviet president Leonid Brezhnev signed the Strategic Arms Limitation Treaty—SALT II, as it was known—the culmination of seven years of negotiations, through the previous two presidents, and the most ambitious nuclear arms control treaty to date. Yet to obtain the Joint Chiefs of Staff's endorsement, which was necessary to win the Senate's ratification, Carter had to fund what would be the biggest, most destabilizing missile in the U.S. arsenal.

This political tradeoff—an arms buildup in exchange for an arms treaty—had become standard practice by this time, a built-in feature of the arms control process that the Chiefs had honed to an art. It began under Nixon. At the same time that he and Kissinger were unfurling nuclear threats, they were also crafting a diplomacy of "détente," a complex of forums and agreements to reduce tensions and build trust with the Kremlin—and the Strategic Arms Limitation Talks formed the centerpiece of this effort. It led, on May 26, 1972, to the Anti-Ballistic Missile Treaty, which limited each side to two ABM sites of 100 interceptors per site, and an interim accord on offensive weapons, which froze the number of both sides' long-range missiles and bombers. The ABM Treaty was a significant accomplishment, which, for the next thirty years, blocked what would otherwise have been an unending arms race, with each side building more offensive weapons to penetrate the other side's defenses, then more defensive weapons to block the other side's offense. The interim accord, by contrast, triggered a dynamic in domestic politics that spurred an arms race of its own.

Kissinger publicly said that the purpose of SALT was "to create a vested interest in mutual restraint," but in fact it did the opposite. Secretary of Defense Melvin Laird gave senators a memo headlined "SALT-Related Adjustments to Strategic Programs." But the "adjustments" amounted to requests for more nuclear weapons, not fewer. Among the demands: "Accelerate and complete development of site defense" for an ABM system, "Develop submarine-based cruise missiles," "Develop improved re-entry vehicles [warheads] for ICBMs and SLBMs [submarine-launched ballistic missiles]," and increase spending ten-fold—from $100 million to $1 billion—for an accelerated Trident submarine program. Laird and the Chiefs told the senators that they would oppose the SALT agreements unless these requests were approved.

At a hearing on the accord, Senator John Stennis, chairman of the Armed Services Committee, asked Laird, "Under this agreement, will any of the United States' planned deployment programs for offensive missiles be affected?"

Laird replied, "They are not."

Gerard Smith, the director of the Arms Control and Disarmament Agency, the branch of the State Department that had negotiated the accords, went further, announcing that the United States would soon double its number of MIRVs, since SALT placed limits only on missiles, not on warheads.

Congress approved all of Laird's "adjustments," even though some of the new weapons hadn't yet been tested; the Trident submarine wasn't even fully designed. Some senators suspected they were being taken for a costly ride. "It seems to me," Stuart Symington, a longtime defense hawk, observed "that these SALT talks are being used in an effort to sandbag the Congress into heavy additional arms expenditures when the hope of all of us . . . was that agreements . . . would make it possible for us to reduce armaments, certainly not to increase it."

In 1974, Brezhnev and President Ford signed the Vladivostok Accords, which further constrained ABM deployments—each side was now allowed just one site with 100 interceptors—and limited each side's offensive nuclear arsenal to no more than 2,400 strategic launchers (ICBMs, SLBMs, and bombers), 1,320 of which could be equipped with MIRVs. However, these limits exceeded the number of launchers and weapons that each side possessed at the time. (The United States had 2,200 launchers and 820 MIRV'ed missiles; the Soviets had 2,375 launchers and no MIRVs.)

At a press conference, Ford proclaimed that the accords "put a cap on the arms race." But when asked whether he would build up to the maximum allowed limits, he replied that he had an "obligation" to do so.

With the SALT process, two rationalizations for new weapons systems came into being: the need to maintain the "perception" of power, regardless of how many weapons were really needed; and the need for "bargaining chips," so that U.S. diplomats could "negotiate from strength" in the next round of arms talks. These arguments could be summoned to justify any weapon, and once the weapons came into being, they were rarely bargained away. Kissinger later admitted that he'd pushed for the sea-launched cruise missile, which no admiral had requested, as "a bargaining chip," not realizing that "the Navy would fall in love with it."

Negotiations for SALT II got under way soon after Nixon and Brezhnev signed the interim agreement and the ABM Treaty. Brzezinski was skeptical of Nixon and Kissinger's détente—he distrusted the Russians, thought they were exploiting good relations with Washington as a cover for continued aggression in the Third World—but Carter found support for his enthusiasm in his secretary of state, Cyrus Vance, and his arms control director, Paul Warnke. The talks between Soviet and American diplomats were inherently complex. By this time, the two military establishments had built very different nuclear arsenals: the Americans emphasizing smaller, more accurate missiles, a substantial fleet of submarines, and high-tech adjuncts like cruise missiles; the Soviets placing a premium on larger, more powerful missiles, with the bulk of them based on land, where the commissars could keep them under close watch. It was difficult, even with good intentions, to devise formulas for "parity" when the arsenals were so asymmetrical.

Still, they managed to work out tradeoffs, and, on June 18, 1979, Carter and Brezhnev signed the treaty. It built on the Vladivostok Accords and went further, addressing at least some of each side's concerns about the other. But the Joint Chiefs adamantly refused to endorse it—which would doom the treaty in the Senate, where ratification required a two-thirds majority—unless Carter fully funded a new ICBM called the MX missile.

The MX—for Missile Experimental (it would be called, in a Strangelovian touch, the Peacekeeper, when deployed a few years later)—was conceived by the Air Force back in 1971. It would be a land-based ICBM, armed with ten nuclear warheads, each twice as powerful and twice as accurate as the warheads on the Minuteman III—making it powerful and accurate enough to destroy Soviet ICBMs in their blast-hardened underground silos. That was the explicit mission of the MX: to maintain America's first-strike capability in an era when the Soviets were building more ICBMs.

The Soviets were deploying their own MIRV'ed missiles, matching what the Americans had started fielding five years earlier. And while each Minuteman III carried three warheads, the Soviet models—the SS-17, SS-18, and SS-19—carried between four and ten warheads apiece. Harold Brown's staff calculated that, by 1983, a mere 308 of these missiles would be able to destroy nearly 90 percent of America's one thousand Minuteman missiles.

From that calculation, several defense analysts warned that the early 1980s would open a "window of vulnerability"—a time, reminiscent of what some had called a "year of maximum danger" back in the 1950s amid fears of a looming missile gap—when the Soviets might exploit their momentary edge and launch a first strike.

Chief among those sounding the alarms was Paul Nitze, the protégé of Dean Acheson during the Truman administration and one of the more hawkish senior officials under Kennedy and Johnson. Nitze had been the author of the Gaither Report, which popularized the missile gap and introduced the phrase "the year of maximum danger." A few years earlier, in 1950, he had written NSC-68, the seminal Cold War blueprint that portrayed the Soviet Union as an implacable foe bent on world domination, requiring a massive U.S. military buildup. In 1976, the year before Carter took office, as the Soviets began MIRV'ing, Nitze helped form an organization called the Committee on the Present Danger, which produced articles, pamphlets, and op-ed pieces on what they saw as a growing imbalance of power between the superpowers.

Nitze wrote two highly influential articles around this time, in *Foreign Affairs* and *Foreign Policy*, arguing that the SALT II treaty—which was in negotiation—would not block the Soviets from pursuing "a nuclear superiority" that could give them a "war-winning capability." Nitze laid out a nightmare scenario: the Soviets launch an attack on America's ICBM silos, using only a fraction of their own missiles to do so; the U.S. is left with only its submarine-launched missiles, which lack the accuracy to hit anything except cities; if the president retaliated with those missiles, the Soviets would launch their remaining missiles against American cities; therefore, the president doesn't dare retaliate. The title of Nitze's *Foreign Policy* piece was "Deterring Our Deterrent."

This was the mirror image of the scenario that Bill Kaufmann had run in his counterforce briefing and that Carl Kaysen and Harry Rowen had played out in their first-strike plan during the Berlin crisis—except, in those explorations, it was the United States that was seen as launching the first strike, then threatening to follow up with more strikes, to deter the Soviets' deterrent. Nitze well knew this, having taken part in the internal debates on that briefing and that plan.

But the context of first-strike schemes and threats had changed dramatically in the decade and a half since the original scenarios were hatched. In the Kaysen-Rowen plan of 1961, SAC was seen as having a good chance of disarming the Soviet nuclear arsenal by sending a mere fifty-five bombers to hit eighty-eight targets. For the Soviets to mount the attack that Nitze envisioned in 1976, they would have to launch enough missiles to hit 1,000 American ICBMs. Because they'd have to fire at least two warheads against each missile, to make sure that one hit, this would mean firing 2,000 warheads; and because the ICBMs were in underground, blast-resistant silos, the warheads would have to explode on the ground, not in the air, thus kicking up a lot more radioactive fallout.

Even the fairly pristine American first strike of 1961 would have killed a half-million to a million Russians—more, if some of the bombs went astray. The hope—a dubious one—was that this toll would be low enough for the Kremlin to refrain from seeking revenge by bombing U.S. cities. By contrast, the "collateral damage" of a Soviet first strike, as envisioned by Nitze in 1976, would kill tens of millions of Americans, possibly more than 100 million—and the strike would destroy only the ICBMs, leaving thousands of nuclear weapons on U.S. submarines and whatever bombers had taken off from their runways in time. It was a stretch to assume that a Soviet premier would believe that an American president would simply surrender—would stand down the subs and the bombers and not retaliate at all—after absorbing a death toll unprecedented in human history.

But Nitze's scenario plumbed still wilder improbabilities. In the *Foreign Policy* article, he and his coauthor, an engineer at the Boeing Company named T.K. Jones, produced a series of graphs showing that after a Soviet counterforce first strike and an American counterforce second strike, the Soviets would end up with more missiles, warheads, megatonnage, and throw-weight than the United States—and could, therefore, declare victory. The implication was that the American president would—and could—tote up the numbers of weapons left on both sides, see that the U.S. was behind, and accept defeat.

Nitze's articles scaled new heights of abstraction in strategic thinking, yet they served—and were intended—as ammunition in the election year campaign to brush aside Kissingerian détente and revive Cold War rearmament.

Around the time his articles were published, Jimmy Carter was emerging as the unlikely front-runner in the Democratic primaries. Nitze had hopped aboard his campaign early on, even before his victory in the Iowa caucuses. He sent Carter several of his speeches and articles. When the two first met in Washington, Carter said that he'd read them all as well as several more that Nitze hadn't sent him. Nitze and his wife each contributed $750, the maximum legal amount, to the Carter campaign. When Carter won the general election in November, Nitze joined the transition team. But then, when Carter took office, Nitze was shut out, offered no job. More demeaning, those who did get plum posts held views diametrically opposed to his. Cyrus Vance, Paul Warnke, Harold Brown—all men whom Nitze had known for years—were doves, skeptics of counterforce, adherents of minimum deterrence, with more sanguine views about Soviet intentions than he felt was responsible. Nitze came to loathe Jimmy Carter. He felt personally betrayed. And so, he fought back.

When Carter submitted SALT II to the Senate for ratification, Nitze billed himself as the star witness for the opposition. The treaty's advocates portrayed it as a modest but significant achievement: it limited how large Soviet ICBMs could be and how many warheads they could carry; it constrained the size of their nuclear arsenal overall while barring no weapons that the United States was planning to build. But to Nitze, SALT II was a disaster because it left the Soviet missiles with superior megatonnage and throw-weight, creating an imbalance and endangering the Minuteman. Nitze, remarkably energetic at age seventy-two, lambasted the treaty in congressional hearings, speeches, debates, and on TV talk shows.

In private, the Air Force generals didn't much care that the Minuteman ICBMs might be vulnerable to a first strike; they figured, as did their brethren going back to the days of LeMay, that, if the Soviets did launch an attack, the SAC commander would launch his missiles on warning, before the Soviet warheads landed.* But many members of Congress were convinced that the numerical imbalances posed an imminent danger. As the MX entered full-scale development, the Senate passed an amendment, refusing to fund the missiles unless they were placed on some sort of mobile platform (the specifics of which could be determined later). So, in public, the generals went along, testifying that they too were concerned about the impending "window of vulnerability," and even pretended that the vulnerability of America's ICBMs—not their own desire to keep *Soviet* ICBMs vulnerable—was the rationale for the MX.

The White House pretended too. In response to letters from several lawmakers, scholars, and arms control advocates, protesting that the MX would destabilize the nuclear balance, Brzezinski replied, "I do not share your conclusions," adding, "The MX will not give us a first strike capability nor is that our strategy." He wrote this, even as the authors of a major Pentagon review of nuclear targeting plans, which Brzezinski was closely following, wrote, "We don't have prompt hard-target-kill capability"—the vernacular for an ability to destroy blast-hardened targets, such as Soviet ICBM silos, with the speed of a ballistic missile—"but MX and Trident II will give it to us." (The Trident II was a new submarine launched missile, about to be deployed, which also had the explosive power and accuracy to destroy hardened targets; the Navy too was now shifting to a counterforce strategy.)

Carter despised the whole charade. In his diary, he described the MX as "nauseating" and a "gross waste of money." Harold Brown noted in a memo that the vulnerability of the ICBMs was "not synonymous

---

* By this time, LeMay's influence, even within Air Force circles, had otherwise diminished. He retired from the military in 1965, campaigned as the running mate of segregationist candidate George Wallace in the 1968 presidential election, and, at one rally, promised to bomb North Vietnam "back to the Stone Age." LeMay died in 1990 at the age of eighty-three.

with the vulnerability of the United States" nor with the loss of our ability to deter a nuclear attack. But, he added, it did create a problem "in the perception of the military balance."

From the outset of his term, Carter had relied on a crew of national security advisers who rarely agreed, and often clashed, with one another. Sometimes he went with one faction, sometimes with the other; sometimes he'd play one side off the other and split the difference. Les Gelb, the State Department's assistant secretary for politico-military affairs, worried that this time Carter would side with Cy Vance, his boss, in favor of SALT II and against the MX missile, skirting the plain fact that he needed the latter to get the former. Gelb wasn't keen on the MX either, but he understood that it was necessary to pass SALT II, which he considered vital to the peace. Gelb was friendly with Lieutenant General Willie Y. Smith, assistant to General David Jones, the chairman of the Joint Chiefs of Staff. He and Smith put together a meeting—the two of them, along with Vance and Jones—to hammer out a deal: the Chiefs would support SALT II, and the State Department would support the MX. They knew that Carter wouldn't overrule both State and the JCS. And, in fact, he did wind up approving the missile as the price for the arms control treaty.

Then on Christmas Eve 1979, Soviet paratroopers landed in Kabul, the capital of Afghanistan, on the USSR's southern border, followed in the coming days by a full-blown invasion. President Carter denounced it as "the greatest threat to world peace since World War II." In a New Year's Eve interview on ABC News, he admitted, "My opinion of the Russians has changed more drastically in the last week" than in his entire time as president. Across Washington, and much of the world, détente was declared dead. Carter canceled wheat sales to Russia, barred U.S. athletes from competing in the Olympics (which were about to take place in Moscow), and—in what he later described as "the worst disappointment to me personally"—withdrew SALT II from the Senate's ratification process (though both countries would continue to abide by the treaty's terms).

In the intramural clashes of the national security bureaucracy, Brzezinski, the hard-line Russophobe, felt triumphant. He seized the moment to renew his campaign to revise the nuclear war plan.

Senior and midlevel White House and Pentagon officials had been working on the war plan all along. Back in September 1977, Walter Slocombe, the deputy assistant secretary of defense for international security affairs, wrote a memo, on behalf of Harold Brown, calling for a Nuclear Targeting Policy Review (later abbreviated as the NTPR), including an assessment of the need for a hard-target-kill capability.

Slocombe, who'd been immersed in nuclear issues since the start of the Nixon administration, when he was a twenty-seven-year-old NSC staffer, ran the review along with Andrew Marshall, a former RAND strategist dating back to the 1950s, who'd come to the Pentagon when Jim Schlesinger was defense secretary. Schlesinger created a job specifically for him—the director of net assessment, a job that, with his mastery of bureaucratic politics, Marshall would hold through eight presidents, until 2015, when he retired at the age of ninety-three.

The NTPR was Brzezinski's initiative. His predecessors, dating back to John Kennedy's time, had all concluded that the president needed more options and flexibility than the nuclear war plan offered, but they'd barely nudged SAC in that direction. The problem, Brzezinski thought, was a failure to think through the issues strategically. The key question, he told Slocombe, was what did the Soviet leaders most value—what assets or capabilities would they dread losing most? Threaten those assets, and that would deter them more than threatening to burn their cities and military garrisons. The Nixon-Kissinger-Schlesinger doctrine, NSDM-242, which grew out of the Foster Panel and RAND's NU-OPTS study, had asked a similar question, but Brzezinski didn't buy their answer. Slowing down the Soviet Union's recovery as an economic and military power may have seemed well grounded, but on scrutiny, it didn't mean much: SAC's officers didn't know how to translate the goal into a set of targets that were any different from the targets they'd hit if their orders were simply to blow up factories and cities; it was, in effect, massive retaliation under a fancier name.

Slocombe and Marshall commissioned a RAND analyst named Leon Sloss to write a paper outlining different goals. His conclusion seemed conceptually elegant: to deter the Soviet leaders, he suggested threatening not just their tools of military power—their nuclear arsenal, command centers, and so forth—but also the leaders themselves and the things they personally cherished. But this raised a slew of other questions. If the whole idea was to launch a limited strike that had a chance of ending the war early, with minimal destructiveness, wouldn't you want the Soviet leaders to survive, so that they could negotiate a cease-fire and make sure their subordinates obeyed it? The dilemmas were discussed at length, inside the Pentagon and at interagency meetings in the White House. Sloss, Slocombe, and others finessed the issue by proposing an option that would let the president withhold attacks on *senior* political and military leaders, if he wanted.

They also put some flesh on Schlesinger's concept of "limited nuclear options," to give the options political purpose. For instance, it was becoming obvious that the Kremlin's leaders feared rebellion from the ethnic nationalities in some of the Soviet republics; so they proposed an option to attack the political centers that controlled those republics. Tensions were also building between Moscow and Beijing; so another option called for launching some nuclear missiles at Soviet military garrisons on the USSR's eastern border, leaving a huge swath of territory open to incursions by China. Other limited options were studied: for example, the possibility that the Soviets might be sufficiently deterred by threats to destroy a key handful of oil refineries or the transmission centers of their electrical power grids.

Finally, there was a new technical feature to consider. Thanks to digital transmissions, which had replaced parachuted photo packets, the images from spy satellites could now be viewed in real time. This raised the possibility of attacking targets on the move—for instance, Soviet armored battalions as they invaded Western Europe. The idea of fighting a war with nuclear weapons—of erasing the distinction between nuclear and conventional warfare—took on an air of plausibility.

Brzezinski's military assistant, an Army colonel named William Odom, was particularly intrigued, even obsessed, with this idea. Odom was a longtime intelligence officer, with a specialty in Soviet affairs, who had earned a PhD from Columbia, where he'd studied under Brzezinski and formed an intellectual bond with the man who would later be his boss, both of them deeply hostile to Communism and suspicious of détente. Even more than Brzezinski, Odom found SAC's war plan, with its premium on destroying Russian cities, not only horrifying but puzzling. If the Soviets invaded Western Europe, a better use of nuclear weapons, Odom argued, would be to deal with the direct threat—to destroy the Red Army on the battlefield—and this new digital technology presented a chance to do that. Odom took part in the Nuclear Targeting Policy Review with an intense verve. One of his ideas was to scuttle the SIOP, with its rigid preplanned attack options, and to turn SAC into an improvising organization, adapting to scenarios as they developed in a real battle, in real time, and using nuclear weapons in the same way that the Army used artillery or the Air Force amassed tactical fighters for air support of troops on the ground.

Odom's ideas attracted interest but no following. Other military officers, especially those with SAC experience, explained that nuclear planning was a complex business: bomber runs had to be carefully timed, an attack's expected damage and collateral damage couldn't be calculated so easily, missiles couldn't be retargeted on a moment's notice—the process took days (a few years earlier, it had taken weeks). Then there was the strategic question: Where did *deterrence* enter into Odom's picture? Was it such a good idea to turn the nuclear bomb—the ultimate weapon—into a mere tactical adjunct of a conventional defense? Even those who endorsed a shift away from a pure deterrence policy thought Odom was going too far.

On April 4, 1979, Brzezinski convened a meeting of senior officials to discuss the NTPR. Brown outlined the conclusions of Leon Sloss's study: its focus on hitting leadership targets and mobile tank columns on the battlefield; some of the ideas for limited nuclear options, such as disrupting Soviet troops on the Chinese border; and, another new element, the idea of "endurance" as a strategic goal—nuclear forces (and especially command-control networks) that could survive and continue functioning through days, even weeks, of back-and-forth attacks.

At the same time, Brown made clear that he didn't quite believe any of this. He had traveled some distance from his view, when he first joined the Carter administration, that deterrence was the sole purpose of nuclear weapons; he now accepted the need for limited options and controlled escalation, in case deterrence failed. But, he said, he still thought that, if there were a nuclear war, it would probably escalate to all-out war very quickly.

Brzezinski disagreed, saying that the most important aspect of the new policy was its shift from a policy of "spasm war." Brown conceded the point, but added that spasm war was the most likely possibility, given the unlikely possibility of nuclear war in the first place. Brzezinski replied that spasm war was more likely to happen if that was the only option we had.

At this point, Stansfield Turner, the CIA director, interjected to ask the officials around the table a fundamental question: What did they think deterred the Soviets the most?

Brzezinski replied, "Threats to the population." Vance agreed. In context, it was an extraordinary response: the senior national security officials were discussing nuclear war in a baroquely intricate fashion, parsing which limited options would most dampen the Soviet leaders' incentive to go to war—yet, pressed on the matter, the most insistent advocate of these options acknowledged that the most potent dampener was the most basic: an all-out attack on their largest cities.

More than a year passed before the Pentagon and the NSC pieced together a new presidential directive on nuclear targeting—which became known as PD-59—and the Nuclear Weapons Employment Policy that spelled out its principles in greater detail. Both documents incorporated most of the ideas in the Nuclear Targeting Policy Review from nearly two years earlier: the emphasis on hitting targets important to the Soviet leaders, an enduring nuclear warfighting capability, more tailored nuclear options. But Brown managed to weave in some of his own skepticism. There was no talk of "winning" or even "prevailing" in a nuclear war, as in similar documents of the past. Instead, he wrote, the best outcome was to "terminate the war on acceptable terms that are as favorable as practical." And the main goal was to make the likelihood of nuclear war "even more remote" by remaining capable, in all scenarios, of fighting successfully so that the adversary would perceive that, if he engaged in "military adventurism," he could not achieve his objectives and would suffer "unacceptable" losses.

Still, the contradictions between deterrence and warfighting remained unresolved: such phrases as "acceptable terms" and "as favorable as practical" remained undefined; and the officers at SAC and the Joint Strategic Target Planning Staff were at a loss for how to translate such concepts as "leadership targets" and "endurance" into actual procedures and attack plans.

By this time, President Carter's interest in nuclear strategy had dwindled, his attention subsumed by the more pressing matters of a hostage crisis in Iran, a covert war in Afghanistan, and a campaign to win a second term in the White House—all of which were going badly. He didn't even attend the final NSC meeting on PD-59, settling instead for a debriefing by Brzezinski. Still, on July 25, he signed the directive, satisfied that, if a nuclear war ever happened, the resulting new plan would lay more weapons down on Soviet military targets and fewer on Soviet cities.

Yet, as with similar documents signed by Kennedy, Nixon, McNamara, Kissinger, and Schlesinger, PD-59 and the Pentagon's related Nuclear Weapons Employment Policy made only a slight dent on the vast chambers at SAC where the wars were planned. As Odom later acknowledged in a memoir of his time in office, the changes outlined in PD-59 were "only on paper"; they were never implemented in actual policy or doctrine.

There was one exception, though no one outside Strategic Air Command headquarters, in Omaha, knew it at the time. By the end of Carter's presidency, SAC controlled nearly 11,000 strategic nuclear warheads and bombs. The war planners in the Joint Strategic Target Planning Staff, also at SAC headquarters, were always seeking more weapons to hit targets—and more targets to justify weapons. PD-59 had called for hitting "leadership" targets; in response, JSTPS revised the SIOP so that hundreds of nuclear weapons were aimed at the headquarters of every government ministry—even the homes and vacation dachas of every government minister—not just on the national level but in every oblast throughout the Soviet Union. Although these weapons would not be aimed at "population per se" (a phrase often invoked in nuclear-targeting documents), those targets were in or near large towns or cities, and so many more hundreds of thousands of people would be killed.

Even here, in this unintended consequence of an attempt to reduce the ravages of nuclear war, Jimmy Carter's dreams were thwarted.

CHAPTER 7

"A Super Idea"

P resident Carter approached the 1980 election with the odds stacked against him. By some measures, he had built up American military power—increasing the defense budget by 3 percent per year, establishing a Rapid Deployment Force to stave off Soviet incursions in the Persian Gulf, and, eventually, against his better judgment, approving new weapons for all three legs of the nuclear Triad. But the Soviet invasion of Afghanistan, the surge in Soviet missile production, the alienation of the NATO allies, the taking of American hostages by the Iranian revolutionary regime and the botched attempt to rescue them—all made it easy for Republicans to lambast him as a weak president. He was beat in a landslide by Ronald Reagan, a former movie star turned California governor who had emerged over the years as a conservative hero, touting the motto "Peace Through Strength."

Reagan entered the White House with an entourage bent not merely on deterring and containing the Soviet Union but on weakening and rolling back its empire. Thirty-two members of his administration, including Reagan himself, were members of Paul Nitze's Committee on the Present Danger. In his opening months in office, Secretary of Defense Caspar Weinberger boosted military spending by 13 percent. He revived every nuclear weapons program that Carter had killed (notably the B-1 bomber) and accelerated all the others. The Joint Chiefs of Staff, the National Security Agency, and the new CIA director, William Casey, took Reagan's rhetoric as a green light for a more aggressive posture worldwide—funding covert programs to overthrow Communist regimes and repel leftist insurgencies, sending spy ships into Soviet waters and spy planes into Soviet airspace, even disrupting and shutting off the Soviet military's command-control networks.

In October 1981, Reagan signed a new guidance for the use of nuclear weapons, a National Security Decision Directive called NSDD-13, which cut and pasted various concepts from Carter's PD-59—especially the idea of waging protracted nuclear warfare—then took them a few steps further. For instance, while the Carter doctrine's main goal was to convince the Kremlin's leaders that they could not win a nuclear war (mainly because it was unwinnable), NSDD-13 stated, up front, that, if deterrence failed and nuclear war erupted, "the United States and its Allies must prevail"—must win.

This idea was nothing new. Throughout the 1950s and 1960s, the Joint Chiefs of Staff maintained that, in a general nuclear war with the Soviet Union, U.S. policy was "to prevail." But no president in all those years had taken this language seriously. Even Eisenhower allowed that the best hope in a nuclear war was not "to lose any worse than we have to." And, in 1969, the first year of the Nixon administration, Henry Kissinger issued a directive formally rescinding the Chiefs' policy.

Now, though, under Reagan, the idea enjoyed a revival, endorsed by the administration's top civilians. Nitze's committee had done much to propagate the idea during Carter's years in the White House, and Reagan named Nitze to be his chief arms negotiator. The chief Soviet affairs specialist on the National Security Council now was Richard Pipes, a Russian history professor at Harvard who had recently written a widely read essay in *Commentary* magazine called "Why the Soviet Union Thinks It Could Fight and Win a Nuclear War," which implied that the United States should start thinking along the same lines. A young scholar named Keith Payne, who had coauthored an article in *Foreign Policy* called "Victory Is Possible" (referring explicitly to victory in a nuclear war), was now a consultant for the Arms Control and Disarmament Agency, where Eugene Rostow, Walt Rostow's brother, a longtime friend of Nitze's and cofounder of the Committee on the Present Danger, was director. Richard Perle, the combative defense policy aide to Henry "Scoop" Jackson, the Senate's leading anti-détente Democrat, was now the assistant secretary of defense for global strategic policy.

To the extent that Reagan and his aides thought at all about nuclear arms control, they viewed it mainly as a vehicle for propaganda. President Carter's 1979 agreement with NATO, to deploy new missiles in Europe, was falling apart, as the continent's left-wing political parties and disarmament activists were pushing hard to reverse the decision, viewing the Pershing II in particular as a first-strike weapon. Allied leaders told Reagan that the missiles could not be deployed, as a practical matter, unless the United States also put forth an arms control proposal. Richard Perle suggested that Reagan propose a ban on all nuclear weapons in Europe. This would require the Russians to dismantle hundreds of their SS-4, SS-5, and SS-20 missiles—in exchange for which the United States would cancel the Pershing II and Ground-Launched Cruise Missiles, which had not yet been deployed. In other words, the Soviets get rid of a lot of weapons; the U.S. gets rid of nothing. Perle knew full well that the Soviets would reject such a trade, and he wanted them to. Years earlier, as a student at Hollywood High School, Perle had been friends with the daughter of Albert Wohlstetter, the RAND strategist and, later, chairman of the European-American Workshop, which lobbied strenuously for the Euro-missiles. The two discussed nuclear issues in detail, and when young Richard ventured into the professional world, Wohlstetter helped him land his first key jobs, including that of Senator Jackson's defense aide.

Weinberger liked Perle's idea—which came to be called the "zero option"—and brought it up at an NSC meeting on October 13. Reagan's secretary of state, Alexander Haig, a former Army general, didn't like the idea at all. Haig asked what would happen in a year or two, when it came time to deploy the missiles and we had this zero option on the table. Surely the Europeans wouldn't let them be deployed.

Don't worry, Weinberger assured him. The Soviets will reject the idea, and we will be seen as "the White Hats" for having proposed it.

At heart, though, and dating back several decades, Ronald Reagan detested nuclear weapons and, as passionately as Jimmy Carter, wanted to see them abolished—a fact that some of his aides, once they learned of it, worked hard to keep hidden. On March 23, 1982, Reagan let the secret slip. He was in New York, delivering a speech to the National Conference of Christians and Jews, and decided to give an interview to the *New York Post*. As a final question, an editor at the paper asked him about the Soviet arms buildup.

Reagan began his answer by lamenting that the Soviet leaders were impoverishing their own people to pay for their armaments, a policy that was succeeding, as they were now a military superpower. "This is one of the reasons why we can't retreat on what we're doing," he went on, "because I believe we've come to the point that we must go at the matter of realistically reducing"—and here he paused for a moment, as if weighing his words—"if not totally eliminating the nuclear weapons, the threat to the world."

Some were stunned by the remark, so at odds with his hawkish words and actions as president till then—though, for the same reason, they didn't take it seriously, dismissed it as clichéd rhetoric.

What may have impelled Reagan to go public was that, a month earlier, on February 26, he received his briefing on the SIOP. He had agreed, a few weeks before then, to observe a high-level exercise at the Pentagon's Nuclear Military Command Center, scheduled for early March. Thomas Reed, a former secretary of the Air Force and long-time friend of Reagan's who was now working nuclear issues on the NSC staff, was surprised that Reagan had agreed to take part at all, "given," as he later wrote, "his personal distaste for the subject." But Reed was concerned that, without a SIOP briefing ahead of time, Reagan wouldn't understand what he was watching. So, more than a year into his presidency, later than any of his Cold War predecessors, Reagan consented to hear that briefing too.

The SIOP was still a "horror strategy," as Kissinger had called it after his exposure. In fact, it had grown deadlier still, since, under Carter's PD-59, the plan now also targeted Soviet "leadership," which SAC interpreted as firing nuclear weapons at the offices, residences, summer dachas, and relocation bunkers of every Soviet commissar, minister, regional governor, and oblast chief.

Sitting in the White House Situation Room, Reagan heard the briefers from the Joint Staff calmly tell him that, in a Soviet attack, about 5,700 nuclear weapons would explode on American soil, destroying three quarters of the U.S. strategic nuclear forces and killing 80 million Americans.

The briefers spelled out the Major Attack Options and Selective Attack Options from PD-59, as well as an option for Launch Under Attack: firing the missiles, especially the land-based ICBMs, before they were hit by the incoming Soviet warheads. (Most of SAC's officers had figured, from the time of the first centralized war plan, that this is what any president would want them to do.) Nothing was said about the small-scale Limited Nuclear Options, which Nixon and Carter had called for and which SAC had never taken seriously. Very little was said about "withholds" (sparing certain categories of targets from attack) or a "reserve force" (holding back certain missiles as a signal of restraint), neither of which SAC had ever thought plausible if the Soviets struck first.

Around the same time, Caspar Weinberger and his staff were writing their own detailed guidance for nuclear targeting, which reversed the Carter administration's priorities. PD-59, and the SIOP as it stood at the time of Reagan's briefing, called for hitting the Soviets' leadership, nuclear weapons, conventional military forces, and urban industries—in that order of priorities. Weinberger's guidance placed nuclear weapons and conventional military forces at the top of the list, followed by leadership, then urban industries—though it also contained an option for not attacking senior Soviet leaders, so that they could negotiate an end to the war. In short, the guidance was a revival of the idea of nuclear weapons as warfighting tools. It was also an attempt at fleshing out NSDD-13, Reagan's directive of a year earlier, mandating that, if a nuclear war happened, the United States "must prevail."

SAC's officers had no idea how to prevail, nor did anyone tell them how to go about doing so, although the document's aggressive tone restored some legitimacy to their long-standing preference for an all-out attack. However, by the time the planning got to that stage, Reagan was no longer paying attention to the nuances, realizing, from the SIOP briefing, that nuclear war left little room for nuance.

Clearly, Reagan was no dove. His aversion to nuclear weapons was more than matched by his anathema toward Communism, and the latter restrained him from taking action on the former; in fact, it put him in the same camp as those calling for more nuclear weapons.

Then, on February 11, 1983, Reagan experienced an epiphany—saw a way to fuse his two, seemingly contradictory positions. The moment came after a nearly two-hour lunch with the Joint Chiefs of Staff, where they discussed the MX missile and the various proposals for a mobile basing scheme. Reagan supported the MX, but he also recognized the difficulties involved in making the missile mobile and, therefore, less vulnerable to a Soviet first strike. At some point during the meeting, he hit upon what he thought was a way out—"a super idea," as he called it in his diary. He wrote:

> So far the only policy worldwide on nuclear weapons is to have a deterrent. What if we tell the world we want to protect our people not avenge them; that we're going to embark on a program of research to come up with a defensive weapon that could make nuclear weapons obsolete? I would call upon the scientific community to volunteer in bringing such a thing about.

The diary entry didn't come out of nowhere. A year earlier, Reagan had met with Edward Teller, the co-designer of the hydrogen bomb, co-founder of the Lawrence Livermore Laboratory, and now an advocate of a laser weapon to shoot down Soviet missiles in outer space as they streaked across the heavens toward American territory. Most people, including other physicists, regarded Teller's notion as a pipe dream; but Reagan was intrigued, and he would consult with Teller several times as his "super idea" took form.

On March 23, 1983, not quite six weeks after his revelatory meeting with the Chiefs, Reagan delivered a prime-time speech on nationwide television. It started out as a pitch to spend more money, on top of an already boosted defense budget, to counter the Soviet military threat. Then he turned to what he previewed, at the start of his speech, as "a very big decision" that he had recently made. "I've become more and more deeply convinced," he said, "that the human spirit must be capable of rising above dealing with other nations and human beings by threatening their existence," adding, "Let me share with you a vision of the future which offers hope."

He then unfurled the idea from his diary jottings: "What if free people could live secure in the knowledge that their security did not rest upon the threat of instant U.S. retaliation to deter a Soviet attack, that we could intercept and destroy strategic ballistic missiles before they reached our own soil or that of our allies?"

Finally, he made what he saw as his historic proclamation: "I call upon the scientific community in our country, those who gave us nuclear weapons, to turn their great talents now to the cause of mankind and world peace, to give us the means of rendering these nuclear weapons impotent and obsolete."

Reagan had written this part of the speech, with the help of only a handful of White House advisers working, at his direction, in total secrecy. His cabinet secretaries—including Caspar Weinberger and the new secretary of state, George Shultz—had reviewed a draft of the speech that left out this section. They learned about it only when they watched Reagan reading it aloud on television. They were surprised—and not in a good way.

They knew that the president was spinning fantasies. Reagan acknowledged in the speech that his vision was "a formidable, technical task," which "may not be accomplished before the end of the century." But, he went on, "current technology has attained a level of sophistication where it's reasonable for us to begin this effort." Anyone who knew anything about the state of anti-ballistic-missile technology knew that this was simply not true.

When Teller was revealed as the chief inspiration for the speech, and when Teller himself began to brief lawmakers and reporters on his ideas for a space-based laser weapon, Senator Edward Kennedy lambasted the idea as "a reckless 'Star Wars' scheme," a reference to the blockbuster movie that featured Jedi fighters shooting laser beams at intergalactic spaceships. By this time, the Pentagon had officially titled the project the Strategic Defense Initiative (SDI, for short), but everyone called it "Star Wars" and dubbed Reagan's TV address "the 'Star Wars' speech."

Reagan's science adviser told him that the project, as outlined, had little if any technical validity at the moment. State Department officials wrote memos explaining that, if such a weapon got to the testing stage, it would violate the ABM Treaty. Many arms control advocates objected that the Soviets would view it as part of a first-strike threat. They weren't off the mark. From the onset of ABM research, dating back to the 1950s, many advocates—within the U.S. military and its scientific annexes—viewed missile defenses as an adjunct to a nuclear-war-winning strategy. The scenario went like this: the president launches a nuclear first strike against Soviet missiles; the Soviets retaliate with their surviving missiles, but they would be so few in number that our ABM system would shoot them down with little trouble. Victory is possible indeed.

When Robert McNamara was secretary of defense, he and his whiz kids analyzed the ABM systems on the drawing board and found them wanting: the interceptors had failed their tests or, to the extent they seemed to pass them, it was because the tests were rigged. A few years into his tenure, McNamara came to a more profound realization: even if the ABM system worked flawlessly, the Soviets could overwhelm it by building—and launching—a few extra missiles, and they could keep building more offensive missiles, more quickly and cheaply than the U.S. could keep building defensive interceptors. At best, then, ABMs would spawn an offense-defense arms race, which the offense—the Soviets—would win.

It was this realization that impelled Nixon and Kissinger to negotiate the ABM Treaty with the Soviet Union. McNamara first proposed limits on defensive as well as offensive arms at a 1967 summit in Glassboro, New Jersey, with Soviet prime minister Alexei Kosygin. Initially Kosygin was puzzled, finding the notion of limiting defensive weapons as not only absurd but "immoral." Over time, though, he and others on the Politburo came to grasp McNamara's logic and, by the time Nixon entered office, consented to pursuing a treaty.

Senior officials in Reagan's Pentagon soon liked Star Wars. Neither Weinberger nor Perle believed for a minute that such a weapon would work; but they figured the Soviets might think it would work, and in that case SDI could add another pound of pressure to push the Kremlin's regime over the edge. And so they—and, after a while, other administration officials—touted the program as avidly as their straight faces allowed. The more exotic branches of the military also jumped on the bandwagon, slapping the "SDI" label on as many projects as possible, in order to win them larger budgets. A special SDI Office was created, with a separate budget, amounting, soon enough, to several billion dollars a year.

Everyone had a reason to get with the program. Reagan was one of the very few who took it at face value, who really thought American ingenuity could make it work, who envisioned it as a shield that could protect the United States—and, as we shared the technology, the entire world—thus rendering nuclear weapons obsolete.

He could not have known it at the time, but his Star Wars speech kicked off the most intense year of the Cold War since the Cuban missile crisis two decades earlier.

Two weeks before the speech, on March 8, Reagan delivered an address to the National Association of Evangelicals, in which he referred to the Soviet Union as an "evil empire." Almost six months later, on September 1, Soviet air defense crews shot down Korean Air Lines Flight 007, mistaking it for an American spy plane, as it accidentally crossed into Soviet airspace, killing all 269 passengers on board, including a U.S. congressman.

On September 26, Soviet early warning radars sounded the alarms for what seemed to be an attack by American ICBMs. False alerts, in the United States and the Soviet Union, were more common than most people knew. In Jimmy Carter's final year as president, three "false missile warning incidents," as they were called, occurred in a two-week period from late May to early June, all caused by a computer error. In two of the incidents, senior officers ordered SAC pilots to board their planes and start their engines. In a separate incident, which took place the previous November, the error occurred when a test disc was mistakenly inserted into the North American Air Defense Command's computer. Worries grew so intense that Carter's national security adviser, Zbigniew Brzezinski, was awakened in the middle of the night and informed that the Soviets had launched 250 ICBMs against the United States; Brzezinski and the officers at NORAD weren't entirely certain that the alert wasn't real until the radar indicated that the warheads had exploded on American targets, when, obviously, they had not.

None of these incidents prompted a presidential crisis, in part because the international climate was calm; few believed that the Soviets had really launched an attack. But the Soviet Union's false warning on September 26 came at a time of intense nervousness. As it happened, the chief air defense officer on duty, Lieutenant Colonel Stanislav Petrov, figured that the radars had to be mistaken and decided, entirely on his own judgment, not to notify his superiors. If Petrov had been less sure of himself and sent an emergency message alert to the next level—in other words, if he'd been more like his comrades who shot down KAL Flight 007 a month earlier under similar circumstances—World War III might have started that day.

In November, the Kremlin broke off negotiations on a Soviet-American nuclear arms control accord. The talks hadn't made much progress, but they provided the only forum where the two sides could talk about anything. With the suspension of those sessions, communications between the superpowers shut down.

At that point, Reagan decided that the Cold War was getting too hot, that he needed to soften the tone and substance of his policies toward Moscow.

To some degree, on some level, Reagan knew that the United States bore some of the blame for the tensions. Early on in his presidency, analysts at the CIA, NSA, and Naval Intelligence had briefed him on recent technological breakthroughs that allowed their spies, sensors, and satellites to probe more deeply than ever into the Soviet military's operations, to monitor and disrupt its movements. The upshot was that, contrary to what Reagan and his officials had been saying in public, the Russian Bear was not ten feet tall; in fact, he was quite vulnerable, and American secret sentries could exploit those vulnerabilities. Reagan didn't completely understand the technical details of these exploits, but he quickly grasped the implication: if the big war came, the United States could win. He urged the directors of the agencies to keep up the pressure. And they did.

Even a little before Reagan took office, the Navy and the NSA, in a joint program called Ivy Bells, were sending specially built mini-submarines into Russian harbors, where they tapped into the undersea transmission cables of Soviet nuclear subs returning to port. Air Force and CIA spy planes were routinely crossing into Soviet airspace on intelligence-gathering missions, to test the readiness of Soviet air defense crews, provoke them into turning on their radar, then record everything about the radar's emissions.

Under Reagan, these sorts of programs were stepped up. In August and September of 1981, an armada of eighty-three U.S., British, Canadian, and Norwegian ships sailed near Soviet waters, undetected. In April 1983, forty U.S. warships, including three aircraft carriers, approached Kamchatka Peninsula, off the USSR's eastern coast. As part of the operation, Navy combat planes simulated a bombing run over a military site twenty miles inside Soviet territory. The ships and the planes maintained radio silence, jammed Soviet radar, and transmitted false signals; as a result, they avoided detection, even by a new Soviet early-warning satellite orbiting directly overhead. An internal NSA history noted, "These actions were calculated to induce paranoia, and they did."

The simulated bombing run, in particular, incited Yuri Andropov—the former KGB director who had ascended to the Kremlin's top post after Leonid Brezhnev died toward the end of 1982—to issue an order authorizing air defense units to "shoot to kill" any foreign aircraft intruding into Soviet airspace. Though neither Reagan nor any other senior U.S. official made the connection at the time, this order set the stage for the shoot-down of KAL 007 four months later. In fact, just hours before the Boeing passenger plane mistakenly flew across the border, an American spy plane, sporting a similar radar profile, had been spotted in the same area. (Of course, even if Flight 007 had been a spy plane, shooting it down would have been an extreme reaction.)

The KAL shoot-down was one of three events in the fall of 1983 that inspired Reagan to shift his thinking. The others were a blockbuster TV movie and a NATO war game that nearly turned real.

On Sunday night, November 20, ABC aired a two-hour made-for-TV film called *The Day After*, a drama depicting the effects of a nuclear war on the people in and around Lawrence, Kansas, not far from a Minuteman ICBM complex. In one of the show's most haunting scenes, a dozen or so missiles are seen blasting off from their silos and streaking up through the sky. An estimated 100 million Americans watched the broadcast. The network and its local affiliates set up 1-800 hotlines staffed with counselors to answer questions and allay anxieties. Many viewers even stayed tuned for the post-show discussion by a panel including Robert McNamara, Henry Kissinger, conservative columnist William F. Buckley, and astronomer Carl Sagan, who, in a particularly memorable line, likened the nuclear arms race to "a room awash in gasoline" with "two implacable enemies. . . . One of them has nine thousand matches, the other seven thousand matches; each of them is concerned about who's ahead, who's stronger." For weeks after, discussions were held about the movie at hundreds of churches and schools across the nation.

Reagan watched the movie at Camp David a month before the broadcast. (The network had sent him a videotape in advance.) He wrote in his diary: "It's very effective & left me greatly depressed." Still, it did not turn him away from his arms buildup. Quite the contrary, it made him all the more determined "to do all we can to have a deterrent & to see there is never a nuclear war." At the moment, he saw no choice.

But between the president's private screening and the nationwide telecast came the third big event that fall, and it may have turned his head around most decisively. A NATO war game, called Able Archer 83, took place November 7–11. It was a command-post exercise to test the procedures that officers and their troops would follow if a ground conflict against the Warsaw Pact escalated from conventional war to nuclear. In one sense, it was a routine exercise, the latest episode of a game that took place every autumn; but in another sense, it was something new.

It was an unusually large exercise and unusually realistic too. A fleet of military cargo transport planes flew 19,000 soldiers, in 170 sorties, from the United States to bases in Europe, all the while maintaining radio silence. The commanders moved from a "permanent war head-quarters" to an "alternate war headquarters." B-52 bomber crews taxied the planes to their runways and loaded them with dummy bombs that looked remarkably real. SAC raised its nuclear alert levels gradually through the five DEFCON settings all the way to "general alert"—that is, to the final stage before war.

The Soviets were monitoring all of this, as they generally did (and as the U.S. commanders knew they would), but they reacted in ways that they never had during any previous exercise—in ways similar to how they might have acted if the U.S. were gearing up for a real attack. Marshal Nikolai Ogarkov, the chief of the general staff of the Soviet armed forces, ran the response from a bunker just outside Moscow. Strategic nuclear forces were put on alert. Nuclear-capable aircraft in East Germany, Poland, and Czechoslovakia—the Warsaw Pact's frontline countries in a war against NATO—were also placed on high alert. Helicopters transported nuclear warheads from storage sites to missile launchers.

American intelligence agencies were watching these Soviet moves, just as Soviet agencies were watching the Americans. Ordinarily, when the Soviets took such actions, the agencies would notify the Joint Chiefs or the secretary of defense or, if things looked particularly dicey, the president—and onward and upward the escalation might spiral. But a three-star general named Leonard Perroots, the deputy chief of staff for intelligence at the U.S. Air Force's European headquarters in Germany, decided to do nothing. He'd been apprehensive about Able Archer 83, viewed it as needlessly provocative, and so interpreted the Soviets' actions not as a threat but as a rational, defensive response to what *they* saw as an *American* threat.

Six weeks earlier, Lieutenant Colonel Petrov, the Soviet air defense officer who decided not to report the detection of an apparent U.S. missile attack, might have averted war by violating protocol. Now Lieutenant General Perroots, the American intelligence officer monitoring Able Archer, may well have done the same.

While Able Archer was unfolding, Oleg Gordievsky, a London-based KGB colonel who had turned double agent, was providing his

British handlers in MI6 with documents revealing that Soviet officials were viewing the exercise as a prelude to an attack by the United States and NATO—and responding to it with their own nuclear alert. The British, as was customary, shared the intelligence with their American cousins.

At first, and for more than a year after, the CIA's top officials were skeptical, dismissing the Soviets' "war scare" as "propaganda," designed to inflame anti-American sentiment in Western Europe. In a Special National Intelligence Estimate on the subject, issued the following May, analysts "strongly" concluded that, both in the context of Able Archer and in general, "Soviet actions are not inspired by, and Soviet leaders do not perceive, a genuine danger of imminent conflict or confrontation with the United States."

However, six years later, the President's Foreign Intelligence Advisory Board—a panel of experts with insiders' experience and outsiders' disinterest—disputed this judgment categorically. In a ninety-four-page report stamped Top Secret and six other classification labels (Wnintel, NoForn, NoContract, Orcon, Umbra, Gamma), the board members concluded precisely the opposite: "There is little doubt in our minds that the Soviets were genuinely worried by Able Archer" and feared that NATO was about to launch an attack "under cover" of the exercise. "At least some Soviet forces," the report added, "were preparing to preempt or counterattack" what they saw as an imminent strike.

The report made a still broader point. From the late 1970s to the mid-1980s, it concluded, Soviet military and intelligence forces had been "redirected" in a way that suggested the Kremlin leadership "was seriously concerned about the possibility of a sudden strike launched by the U.S. and its NATO allies." Jimmy Carter's PD-59, with its talk of protracted nuclear warfare, was interpreted as preparations "for a preemptive strike"—a view reinforced by the development of the MX and Trident II missiles, which the Soviets saw as "highly lethal" weapons aimed at "their silos and other hardened targets." More alarming still was the European-based Pershing II missile, which, with its pin-point accuracy and mere five-minute flight time to Moscow, was seen not as a counter to the Soviet SS-20 but as "yet another step toward a first-strike capability," specifically as a weapon to "decapitate" the Soviet leadership, to prevent the Kremlin from responding to a larger American first strike, which would follow. These conclusions, the report noted, were based on "sensitive reporting"—an intelligence-world euphemism for communications intercepts or well-placed spies. It was the deployment of the Pershing II that provoked the Soviets into walking out of the arms control talks near the end of 1983. It also prompted them to create a device, known as the "dead hand," which would detect a nuclear explosion on Soviet soil and, in case it was an American first strike that killed the Kremlin leaders, would send a signal that launched a Soviet retaliatory strike automatically.

On the day that Able Archer began, Grigory Romanov, the Politburo member in charge of the Soviet military-industrial complex, exclaimed at a meeting of his comrades, "The international situation at present is white hot, thoroughly white hot!"

Reagan had no idea these things were going on at the time. Still, just days after the wrap-up of Able Archer, Robert "Bud" McFarlane, his national security adviser, showed him Oleg Gordievsky's reports of Soviet activities during the exercise, suggesting that Soviet leaders really thought the United States was getting ready to launch a nuclear first strike under the cover of an exercise—a report that Reagan received with "genuine anxiety," McFarlane later recalled. Reagan had been pushing hard against the Kremlin, in hopes that the pressure might bring down the system; but "it did bother him" that the Soviets could seriously entertain "the very idea" that he would launch a first strike. In his memoir, Reagan wrote about "some people in the Pentagon who claimed a nuclear war was 'winnable,'" adding, "I thought they were crazy." He may have forgotten by then that he had signed a National Security Decision Directive, declaring that, if nuclear war broke out, the United States "must prevail." He may not have known that American generals had pushed and planned for a first-strike capability ever since the dawn of the nuclear age.

On November 18, one week after Able Archer, Reagan met with Secretary of State George Shultz to discuss setting up a back channel of communication with Moscow. He wrote in his diary that day: "I feel the Soviets are so defense minded, so paranoid about being attacked that without being in any way soft on them we ought to tell them no one here has any intention of doing anything like that."

The next morning, at seven-thirty, a group of twelve senior officials—including Shultz, McFarlane, Vice President George H. W. Bush, and CIA deputy director Robert Gates—met for breakfast in Shultz's dining room at the State Department. The very topic of reopening talks with Moscow was extremely sensitive; Shultz told the group not to tell anyone else that the meeting had even taken place. For two hours, they discussed possible courses of action. Bush made the central point—that the public was uneasy about the lack of communication with Russia. All the participants agreed that high-level contact should resume. Some endorsed the move to keep tensions from escalating; others thought the moment was ripe because America's recent actions had ratcheted up tensions just enough. McFarlane, who was among the latter faction, advised starting talks again, "now that we are in a position of strength in dealing with the Soviets." In the end, the group decided that Reagan should try to shift perceptions, both at home and abroad, by doing what he did best—delivering a speech.

McFarlane set about writing the address with Jack Matlock, a former State Department official who had taken part in every Soviet-American summit during the era of détente and who now ran the Soviet affairs desk at the NSC. Reagan was set to deliver it on December 20, until his wife, Nancy, urged him, on the advice of her astrologer, to push the date back to January 16. (Matlock shrugged and said the postponement would do no harm.) The speech, televised from the

East Room of the White House, was a dramatic contrast from Reagan's earlier pronouncements on the Soviet Union. There was no talk of an "evil empire" or the irreconcilable conflict between freedom and Communism. The key line was this: "If the Soviet government wants peace, then there will be peace. Together we can strengthen peace, reduce the level of arms, and know in doing so that we have helped fulfill the hopes and dreams of those we represent and, indeed, of people everywhere. Let us begin now."

He had to wait a while for a response. Andropov died of kidney failure on February 9. Four months later, CIA analysts, after more fully absorbing the Gordievsky reports, took the first steps toward changing their minds on the effects of Able Archer, even acknowledging the possibility that the Soviets might genuinely be fearful of an American first strike. William Casey, the agency's director, spelled out the full details of the Soviet war scare in a memo to Reagan, who described it to his aides as "really scary." In mid-June, Reagan talked with McFarlane and Shultz about a possible meeting with Andropov's replacement, Konstantin Chernenko. "I have a gut feeling we should do this," Reagan wrote in his diary shortly afterward. The one exchange of letters that he'd had with the new Kremlin leader bolstered his view "that the Soviets are plotting against us & mean us harm." But, he added, "maybe they are scared of us & think we are a threat." Either way, he concluded, "I'd like to go face to face & explore this with them."

Nine months later, on March 10, 1985, Chernenko—who'd been old and ill when he took the helm—died of heart congestion. A few months earlier, during his election campaign for a second term, a reporter asked Reagan why, unlike every other president since Herbert Hoover, he hadn't met with the Soviet leader. Reagan replied, with a grin, "How can I? They keep dying on me." And now here went another one.

Then, almost immediately after the Kremlin's spokesmen announced Chernenko's death, they also declared that his replacement would be Mikhail Gorbachev.

Gorbachev was a true reformer, the first to rise to the top since Khrushchev, and Gorbachev's vision of reform went far beyond what any Party leader had ever proposed, at least in public. He recognized, and maneuvered to act on, the fact that the Soviet Union was in shambles: its ideology was moribund, its economy dysfunctional. He wanted to restructure everything, open up the country to the world; but that would require slashing the military budget, which consumed nearly all of the government's resources—and that would require assurances that the United States and NATO no longer posed a threat to the USSR's existence, a threat that he and his comrades felt in their bones was very real.

In his first months in power, Gorbachev talked a good game, but few senior officials in Washington took him seriously. Gorbachev too was less than certain that all the pieces of his plan would fall into place. Though he differed from his comrades in many ways, he shared their dread of the United States as an imperialist power, fueled by the military-industrial complex and bent on world domination. Still, to get his reforms under way, he needed to take a chance; he needed to meet with the leader of this power—another high risk, since he viewed Reagan as a "class enemy" with a "caveman outlook"—and so, a summit was arranged between the two men for November 19–20, at a château on Lake Geneva.

The meeting started out tense. The two men argued over the Strategic Defense Initiative, which Gorbachev viewed as a threat and Reagan still saw as a shield for peace; Reagan complained about Soviet support of socialist revolutions in the Third World; Gorbachev complained about the influence of the military-industrial complex over American policy. After a few of these rounds, Reagan suggested that they go for a stroll along the lake, outside the château, just the two of them and their translators. A few minutes into the walk, they ducked into a nearby cabin.

When they sat down next to a roaring fireplace, Reagan suddenly asked Gorbachev what he would do if the United States were attacked by aliens from outer space. "Would you help us?" Reagan inquired.

Gorbachev replied, "No doubt about it."

Reagan said he felt the same way; he too would help the Soviets if aliens invaded them.

This was an age-old obsession of Reagan's, dating back at least to a 1951 Hollywood movie called *The Day the Earth Stood Still*, about an enlightened scientist from outer space who visits earth to warn its leaders that they need to halt their dangerous games with nuclear weapons. Two years after the Geneva summit, well into his new détente with the Russians, Reagan raised the theme again, this time in his speech to the United Nations General Assembly. "I occasionally think how quickly our differences worldwide would vanish," he told the gathered heads of state, "if we were facing an alien threat from outside this world." As the speech was being drafted, the Joint Chiefs excised this line, finding it too mawkish and, frankly, loony. Reagan put it back in. They took it out one more time. Reagan put it back in. This was how he viewed the world.

From the moment in Geneva when Gorbachev told Reagan that the Soviets would aid America if the aliens attacked, the atmosphere between the two men lightened, turned cordial. When they came back to the château for more talks, Shultz noticed that they seemed like old friends, in a good mood, engaged in animated conversation.

When the summit ended, the two leaders released a joint statement declaring that a nuclear war "cannot be won and must never be fought"—a rebuke of Reagan's national security directive, NSDD-13, four years earlier—and directing their diplomats to negotiate a treaty cutting both sides' nuclear arsenals by half.

For the next ten months, Shultz and his Soviet counterpart, Eduard Shevardnadze, kept in touch and developed their own good relationship—Shultz was the sole member of Reagan's cabinet who took Gorbachev's reformist rhetoric seriously—but the arms negotiations stalled.

Gorbachev was getting desperate. In February 1986, three months after the Geneva summit, he gave a speech to the Communist Party Congress, calling for new policies of *perestroika* (restructuring the economy, specifically loosening the government's controls) and *glasnost* (openness, free speech, and the relaxation of censorship). But he needed that arms treaty—some concrete steps toward relaxing international tensions—before his comrades and rivals would accept such radical measures.

In mid-September, he asked Reagan for "a quick one-on-one meeting" to break the logjam. The meeting took place just one month later, over the weekend of October 11–12, in Reykjavik, Iceland. In the run-up to Geneva, Reagan had subjected himself to an intense tutorial on the Soviet Union, reading more than a hundred single-spaced pages of materials prepared by the CIA and the State Department's intelligence bureau as well as listening to weekly two-hour briefings. He headed to Reykjavik with no preparation, not even a set of proposals; it wasn't billed as that sort of summit.

Gorbachev, on the other hand, arrived with a full-blown agenda to jump-start dramatic cuts in nuclear armaments. Just before this second summit, he outlined the agenda at a meeting of the Politburo, warning his comrades that, if the cuts weren't made, the Soviet Union "will be pulled into an arms race that is beyond our capabilities, and we will lose it because we are at the limit of our capabilities." The "pressure on our economy will be unbelievable."

At their first meeting, on Saturday morning, after talking broadly on the need to eliminate not just weapons but the sources of mutual distrust, Gorbachev unfurled a proposal for a comprehensive arms treaty—not just cutting strategic nuclear weapons by 50 percent but also eliminating all medium-range missiles in Europe (the "zero option" that the Pentagon had put forth as a propaganda ruse at the start of Reagan's presidency) as well as freezing the number of short-range missiles, committing to a ten-year period when neither side would withdraw from the ABM Treaty, and, during that same ten years, banning tests of SDI weapons except in a laboratory. As a bonus, Gorbachev would exempt the British and French from the zero option; they could keep their independent nuclear arsenals.

The two leaders took a break, so Reagan could take the surprise offer to Shultz and his other advisers. After three hours, he came back with a counter. The 50 percent reduction should apply not only to the number of strategic weapons but also to the throw-weight of long-range missiles, since the U.S. viewed the Soviets' heavy, MIRV'ed missiles as a first-strike threat. In exchange, the U.S. would include its new air-launched cruise missiles—which were being placed on B-52 bombers—in the numerical limits on strategic weapons. He also said the elimination of medium-range missiles had to be global, otherwise the Soviets could take the SS-20s that they had in Asia—which were aimed at China—and move them across the Urals to Europe. However, Reagan added, as a compromise, he would agree to a limit of 100 missiles in Europe and 100 in Asia. Finally, he rejected any limit on SDI, noting that if the two sides got rid of all their ballistic missiles (which he considered the ultimate goal), a defensive system would be vital to guard against cheating.

Gorbachev took Reagan's concessions a step further, proposing that both sides cut not just ballistic missiles but all strategic offensive weapons—the bombs and warheads—by 50 percent.

Reagan said he was fine with that.

Gorbachev was excited. These are bold steps, he said, and we need bold steps. "Otherwise," he sneered, "it goes back to Karpov and Kampelman"—referring to Viktor Karpov and Max Kampelman, the chief Soviet and American arms negotiators—spooning out the "porridge we have eaten for years."

First, though, Gorbachev wanted some clarity. If the experts on both sides worked out some kind of deal on medium-range missiles in Asia, would Reagan accept zero missiles (again, excepting the French and British weapons) in Europe? Reagan said that he would.

Gorbachev then returned to the issue of SDI. If both sides slashed the number of strategic weapons, he argued, we would need to *strengthen* the ABM Treaty. Reagan replied that there was no need to worry about the U.S. gaining an upper hand in some offense-defense arms race because he planned to share the SDI technology with Russia and any other country that wanted it. Gorbachev scoffed at the notion. The United States, he pointed out, had refused to share technology for oil drilling equipment or even for milk factories. "Giving us the products of high technology," he said, "would be a second American Revolution," and he didn't expect that to happen.

Reagan insisted he was sincere. "If I thought the benefits wouldn't be shared," he said, "I would give it up." The session ended in frustration.

Their conversation resumed the next morning, this time with Shultz and Shevardnadze joining in. Gorbachev emphasized that they were entering uncharted territory, which they might never have a chance to explore again. "I wasn't in a position to make this proposal two years ago, and I may not be one year from now," he said.

Shultz asked if the 50 percent reduction applied to ballistic missiles or to all strategic nuclear weapons.

Gorbachev said it could apply to all weapons, but only if SDI research was confined to the laboratory. Reagan insisted that he harbored no hostile intent toward the Soviet Union, but Gorbachev countered that no one in the Soviet leadership could accept a deal permitting the United States to revoke the ABM Treaty and test defensive weapons in outer space.

They took a break. When they returned in mid-afternoon, Gorbachev outlined a still more drastic proposal. It included, as before, a ten-year nonwithdrawal clause in the ABM Treaty and a 50 percent cut in strategic offensive weapons, but with the following new spin: a 50 percent cut in each side's ballistic missiles over the next five years, then the elimination of all ballistic missiles after an additional five years. At that point, since neither side would have any ballistic missiles, there would be no need for ballistic missile defenses—no need for SDI.

Reagan took the proposal to his team. When he returned less than an hour later, things took a wild turn. Reagan accepted Gorbachev's proposal of halving, then eliminating offensive ballistic missiles. Gorbachev took the idea a step further: what about the bombs on aircraft?

Reagan said he was fine with including those weapons in the formula.

"Then let's cut the whole Triad," Gorbachev said—all three legs of the nuclear arsenals: land-based ICBMs, submarine-launched missiles, and bombers. Let's eliminate all strategic offensive weapons.

Shultz caught the spirit. "Let's do it!" he said.

But then Gorbachev repeated the catch: there must be no testing of ballistic missile defenses—SDI—in outer space.

Reagan wouldn't go that far. He allowed that the United States might end up not building SDI; it might turn out to be too expensive. But, he went on, he'd promised the American people that he wouldn't give up the program just yet. If he went back on that pledge, he confided, the "right wing" politicians back home "would kick my brains in." Reagan then appealed to the personal chemistry that the two men had clearly struck up. "I'm asking you for a favor," he pleaded.

Gorbachev said that he had promised his political comrades that he wouldn't allow SDI testing in space. "This is a last opportunity, at least for now," he said. If he and Reagan could agree to ban testing defensive weapons in outer space, he would sign the deal for zero offensive weapons "in two minutes."

Reagan said he couldn't do that, and the talks ground to a halt. Reagan was bitter, mumbling to the Russian leader, "I think you didn't want to achieve an agreement anyway."

It was a tragicomic denouement to ten hours of substantive conversation, in which the leaders of the two superpowers came so close to ending the nuclear arms race, obstructed only by their fantasies and fears—Reagan's fantasies, Gorbachev's fears—about a high-tech super-dome that hadn't yet been conceived, much less developed, tested, built, or deployed.

When he first came to power, Gorbachev had asked his chief science adviser, Yevgeny Velikhov, whether SDI would pose a threat. Velikhov replied—just as American science advisers had concluded through the decades—that the notion was fanciful and that the Soviets could design countermeasures, or build additional offensive missiles to saturate the system, more quickly and cheaply than the U.S. could augment its defenses. However, perhaps succumbing to pressures from his own military-industrial complex, Velikhov advised Gorbachev that it might be wise to build more missiles, just in case. But Gorbachev knew he couldn't afford another round of an arms race. At a Politburo meeting in March 1986, Gorbachev said, "Maybe we should just stop being afraid of SDI." The Americans were "betting precisely on the fact that the USSR is afraid of SDI." That was "why they are putting pressure on us—to exhaust us." Yet clearly, when Gorbachev met Reagan at Reykjavik, he and his comrades were still sufficiently afraid of SDI that any grand disarmament scheme would be unacceptable if the program weren't halted.

Still, Gorbachev came away from this summit elated. He now knew that this American president, though peculiar in some respects, had no intention of launching a first strike against the Soviet Union—a point he made fervently to the Politburo upon returning to Moscow. And so he turned up the throttle on *glasnost* and *perestroika*, which required not just economic reforms but—as a precondition—massive cuts in defense spending and a transformation of East-West relations. He needed assurances of external security in order to move forward with his domestic upheaval. Reagan gave him those reassurances. Subsequent conversations between Shultz and Shevardnadze bolstered his confidence.

In December 1987, Gorbachev came to Washington, where he and Reagan signed the Intermediate-Range Nuclear Forces Treaty, banning all U.S. and Soviet missiles of that type, not just in Europe but worldwide: in short, dismantling all the SS-4s, SS-5s, and SS-20s, even those aimed at China, as well as the Ground-Launched Cruise Missiles and Pershing IIs—2,600 nuclear-armed missiles in all.

The following May, Reagan flew again to Moscow, where he hoped to conclude a new strategic arms treaty but wound up making a bigger breakthrough still. In the early evening of Sunday, May 29, not long after their arrival, he and Nancy took a walk along the Arbat, a pedestrian thoroughfare near the U.S. embassy, and found themselves greeted warmly, even cheered, by a crowd of Muscovites out enjoying the balmy weather. Reagan was struck by how friendly, how normal, the Russian people seemed. The next day, strolling through Red Square after a meeting inside the Kremlin, he was asked by a reporter about his speech in 1983, five years earlier, in which he referred to the Soviet Union as an "evil empire." Reagan replied, "I was talking about another time, another era."

Many in Reagan's entourage were not so sure things had changed so dramatically. They didn't yet quite trust Gorbachev or the people around him. And they were alarmed by the apparent flip of their president—from Cold Warrior in his first term to nuclear disarmer in his second term. During the Reykjavik summit, when word got around that Reagan might trade away the entire U.S. arsenal, some of the NATO allies, especially the West Germans, panicked. The nuclear umbrella—America's guarantee to launch nuclear weapons at the Soviet Union in response to a Soviet invasion of Western Europe—still formed the centerpiece of transatlantic security. Was Reagan folding it up?

Soon after Reykjavik, Reagan's national security adviser, Admiral John Poindexter, wrote Reagan a six-page Top Secret/Sensitive memo titled "Why We Can't Commit to Eliminating All Nuclear Weapons Within 10 Years." In it, he argued that such a treaty could not be verified, that the other nuclear powers might not follow suit and would thus achieve supremacy, and that the security of Western Europe would deteriorate, given the Soviet Union's advantage in conventional forces. In short, Poindexter concluded, "neither our military experts [n]or our allies would support the idea of moving to the total elimination of all nuclear weapons until the world conditions change so that such weapons are unnecessary—and certainly not within 10 years."

Five months later, amid fears that Reagan and Gorbachev might resume their pitch for zero nuclear weapons at a summit in the near future, Poindexter's successor, Frank Carlucci, sent a slightly revised version of the memo to the new White House chief of staff, Howard Baker, along with a cover note acknowledging that "the President has long believed" in nuclear "abolition" but stressing that "it is the unanimous judgment of the national security community that such abolition would not be in our interest."

Around the same time, Carlucci sent Baker another memo arguing that a treaty banning medium-range missiles, which was in serious negotiation, would also be unwise. He acknowledged that the Defense Department had first put forth the "zero option" back in 1981, but only "as a ploy" to make the Soviets look bad when they rejected it. Withdrawing the Pershing IIs and Ground-Launched Cruise Missiles from Europe, even if it also meant the dismantlement of SS-20s, would return NATO to a time when a Soviet invasion could be halted or deterred only by nuclear weapons fired from inside the United States, thus reviving the question of whether an American president would "risk New York for Paris."

Reagan and Gorbachev signed the treaty for zero medium-range missiles anyway, but the prospects for a new *strategic* arms treaty were fading away, as negotiators failed to resolve disputes over such recondite matters as how to count bomber aircraft (which could carry between one and a dozen nuclear bombs) and whether to limit air- and sea-launched cruise missiles at all.

What these officials—American and Soviet—missed in their critiques and hesitations was that Reagan and Gorbachev were aiming not for some optimal refinement of the military balance but for the end of the Cold War, a goal that the officials viewed as naive fantasy but that, in fact, the two leaders had begun to bring about.

In the decades since, partisans have debated whether to credit the Cold War's end to Reagan's hostile rhetoric and arms buildup in his first term or to his turn toward détente and disarmament in his second term. In fact, it took both—Reagan the super-hawk and Reagan the nuclear abolitionist—and, at least as important, the rise of Gorbachev as his collaborator.

They were the most improbable leaders of their respective nations, and the great change could not have happened without the doubly improbable convergence of their reigns. Gorbachev needed to move swiftly if his reforms were to take hold; Reagan exerted the pressure that forced him to move swiftly and offered the rewards that persuaded his Kremlin rivals and skeptics to take the risks.

History sometimes moves in serendipitous patterns. If Yuri Andropov's kidneys hadn't given out, or if Konstantin Chernenko's heart had kept ticking a few years longer, Reagan's bluster would have come to naught and might even have exacerbated tensions; the Cold War could have raged on for years. Similarly, if Reagan hadn't been president in 1985—if Jimmy Carter or Walter Mondale had defeated him, or if Reagan had died and his vice president, George H. W. Bush, had taken his place—Gorbachev would not have received the push that he needed; those other American politicians were too traditional, too cautious, too sensible, to have pushed for such radical arms reductions or to take Gorbachev's radicalism at face value.

The Reagan years marked a time when the superpowers came closest to both a catastrophic war and a grand peace. The years also produced the first Cold War arms accord that reduced the number of nuclear weapons. But the big cuts would come in the years immediately following Reagan's time in office—and for reasons having little to do with any treaty or president.

CHAPTER 8

Pulling Back the Curtain

The pivotal moment in the arms race arrived—the ceaseless, forty-year buildup of the U.S. nuclear arsenal took a turn, then drew down sharply—when a civil servant named Franklin Miller took a close look at the SIOP.

Miller, a Phi Beta Kappa from Williams with a graduate degree from Princeton, came to the Pentagon in 1979 after a two-year stint in the State Department's politico-military bureau. When he first arrived, he worked on policy toward nuclear weapons based in Europe. In October 1981, he was promoted to director of strategic forces policy, just as President Reagan signed his national security directive, NSDD-13, ordering the rapid modernization of all three legs of the Triad—the land-based ICBMs, the submarine-launched missiles, and the bombers—a milestone that coincided with Miller's thirty-first birthday. Owing to a bureaucratic quirk, Miller's job gave him a role in coordinating policy on nuclear doctrine and arms control, but not on nuclear targeting—not on how many weapons the Strategic Air Command should have or how it should use them in a nuclear war.

Still, Miller detected a serious anomaly. When he took the job, he read all the Top Secret nuclear guidance documents signed not only by Caspar Weinberger, the current secretary of defense, but also by his predecessors under all the presidents dating back to John F. Kennedy.

Miller knew about the Limited Nuclear Options and Selective Attack Options, the orders to hold back a reserve force in the early phase of a war, the policies of controlling escalation and limiting damage in case deterrence failed. And yet, when he sat in on the annual SIOP briefing, which the SAC commander delivered at the Pentagon, he heard nothing about these options or policies.

A Navy friend introduced him to a young commander named Ed Ohlert, who was working in OP-65, the Navy's nuclear policy shop. Ohlert confirmed Miller's concerns about the disconnect between Washington's directives and Omaha's plans. Essentially, he said, all those interesting documents that Miller had been reading—the directives on strategic doctrine by Harold Brown, James Schlesinger, Robert McNamara, and their aides—were fiction; the officers in the Joint Strategic Target Planning Staff, the branch of SAC that actually wrote the war plans, ignored the documents. Sometimes the Joint Chiefs helped the officers cover their tracks: in negotiations with the defense secretary, they inserted caveats—noting, for instance, that the JSTPS would execute a limited attack, or spare Soviet cities from destruction, "to the extent that military necessity permits" or "to the degree practicable." The Chiefs understood that, in drawing up the war plan, JSTPS would decide that these ideas were not practicable or consistent with military necessity. But none of the earlier defense secretaries had noticed the fine print; they'd never followed up to make sure their directives were reflected in the war plan's final draft

For all practical purposes, Ohlert told Miller, the war plan contained only one option that was thoroughly conceived and rehearsed: MAO-4, the ultimate Major Attack Option—the option to destroy as many targets, with as many nuclear weapons, as quickly as possible. To the extent some smaller attacks were written into the plan, they weren't "limited" by any reasonable definition of the word: the Soviets would interpret it as an all-out attack and retaliate accordingly.

Sometimes JSTPS would play word games to protect the plan. Since McNamara's first revision to the SIOP, in 1962, every defense secretary had ordered an option that let the president refrain from attacking Soviet or Chinese cities. But, Ohlert told Miller, if a nuclear war happened and if the president selected that option, he would wind up bombing cities anyway. There were two reasons for this. First, the actual "no-cities" option, as devised by JSTPS, excluded just twenty-four "urban areas"—described as Soviet and Warsaw Pact "regional political centers"—from the target list. That meant lots of other, very large cities, besides those twenty-four, would still get hit. Second, even those exempted cities would get hit to some extent because the JSTPS defined an "urban area" as a circle within which 95 percent of a city's population *lived*. However, in many cities, the factories, military facilities, and government buildings—the prime targets—were located away from most residences; so the bombs and warheads could pummel those targets without hitting "urban areas."

There was another semantic sleight of hand that allowed the JSTPS to understate the damage done by the war plan. When the officers calculated how many people would be killed and how many buildings would be destroyed, they took into account only the *blast* of the bombs. They ignored the other effects of a nuclear explosion—heat, fire, smoke, radioactive fallout—rationalizing that those effects couldn't be measured precisely, since they depended on wind, weather, and other variables. Tens of millions of civilians would die from those effects, even if the president had expressly ordered that their lives be spared.

In the course of gathering evidence of these massive discrepancies, Miller came across Wayne Lumsden, a computer whiz in the Office of Program Analysis and Evaluation, the successor to the Office of Systems Analysis created by McNamara's whiz kids. Lumsden was as low-profile as they came: he worked literally in the Pentagon's basement, monitoring the JSTPS database for software errors and mishaps, a purely technical task—but it gave him full access to the database itself, including all the targets in the SIOP and a rundown of which U.S. weapons would hit them. Miller had Lumsden transferred to his directorate, thus giving him the same access without Omaha's knowledge.

The database revealed that the disparity between Washington's orders and Omaha's plans was even wider than Miller had thought. One of the most blatant instances turned out to be the planning for Limited Nuclear Options. Miller asked an analyst in the Defense Intelligence Agency, the Pentagon's own intelligence bureaucracy, how many discrete objects the Soviets' early warning systems could track—how many incoming missiles it could detect as individual missiles—before they all merged into a vague blob on the radar screens. The answer was 200. In other words, on the Soviets' radar screens, 200 missiles and 2,000 missiles looked exactly the same. And yet in SIOP's smallest "limited" attack option, the United States would launch nearly 1,000 missiles. To Soviet air defense officers, this would look like an all-out attack.

Worse still, in every limited option, SAC would launch weapons from all three legs of the Triad—ICBMs, submarine-launched missiles, and bombs dropped by B-52 airplanes. It was a case of bureaucratic politics run amuck: the missile commanders, the submariners, and the bombardiers had all demanded a piece of every attack option—and they each got their piece. As a result, if there were a war, the missiles would land a half-hour after the president's order, while the much slower airplanes wouldn't start dropping bombs until several hours later. Even if the Soviet leaders were inclined and able to distinguish between a limited and an all-out attack, they would interpret such a prolonged series of strikes—from the air, land, and sea, over a stretch of many hours—as an all-out campaign.

After compiling several similar examples of this trait, Miller put together a briefing to present to his superiors. By this time, Ed Ohlert had been called back to the Navy. To replace him, Miller hired a brash, bright twenty-eight-year-old named Gil Klinger. The two had met in 1983, when Klinger, still a graduate student at Harvard's John F. Kennedy School of Government, had a summer job working for the Navy on the highly accurate warhead for the Trident II missile. Two years later, he won a slot in the Presidential Management Internship Program, and Miller arranged for him to intern in his office, working with

Ohlert on the strategy-mismatch project. After earning his degree at Harvard, Klinger spent six months working in the Pentagon's Joint Staff, reviewing Annex C of the Joint Strategic Capabilities Plan, the JCS guidance for the SIOP—perfect preparation for returning to Miller's office in 1987.

Miller was not a dove or an advocate of disarmament. He agreed with the idea of Limited Nuclear Options laid down by Kaufmann, McNamara, Kissinger, Schlesinger, and the others. His goal was to translate their abstract idea into actual policy and plans—to make limited options truly limited.

With Weinberger's full backing, he and Klinger rewrote the guidance for the war plan. They redefined "urban areas" so the phrase meant what most people thought it meant; they inserted an option allowing the president to "ride out" a Soviet first strike rather than launching on warning of an attack; and they cut down all the nuclear options in size and intensity.

The Selective Attack Options, which had once involved launching thousands of weapons against all sorts of targets across the entire Soviet Union, were now limited to no more than 100 weapons for each option, and they would be aimed only at Soviet military targets. A new category, called Basic Attack Options, would launch fewer than twenty nuclear weapons—again, only at military targets—in a single, compact geographical area. Even the Major Attack Options were not quite as destructive as they had once been. As in previous war plans, MAO-1 involved hitting only Soviet nuclear sites, MAO-2 added conventional military targets, MAO-3 combined the first two options as well as "leadership" targets, and MAO-4 included all of those sites plus "war-supporting industries"—but those industries, many of them in cities, could be hit only by bombers, not by ballistic missiles, which is to say they couldn't be hit right away. The point was to let some time pass, to see if the war could be halted and the bombers called back to their base, before inflicting the most devastating damage. The old all-out attack option, which unleashed every weapon against every target, was removed from the SIOP. Nor were factories and other structures to be destroyed per se, unless they directly supported the Soviet war effort.

The key phrase, of course, was "per se." Nuclear weapons were so powerful—the effects of blast, fire, smoke, and radiation would spread so widely—that many millions of people would die, and many thousands of buildings would collapse, regardless of the fine-tuning.

Miller and Klinger sometimes talked about this fact. They knew that, if a nuclear war broke out, the pressures to escalate would be immense. Klinger once told Miller, "If (God forbid) there's a nuclear war, and if (God forbid) you and I survive it, and if (God forbid) the Russians win, we're going to be put on trial at Nuremberg."

Miller was not amused at the thought of being tagged a war criminal.

Still, both of them also thought—as did the nuclear strategists before them—that, if there was a chance, even a small one, that all-out war could be averted and the damage even somewhat limited, then they were obligated to give it a try; and that meant devising war plans—giving the president options—that made the aversion possible.

⸻ ❧ ⸻

In November 1988, Reagan's number two, George H. W. Bush, won the presidential election, and at first it seemed as if Miller would soon be on the outs. Some of the generals who were fed up with Miller's intrusions on their turf advised some of Bush's incoming advisers—especially Paul Wolfowitz, who would be the undersecretary of defense for policy—to take him down a few notches. But then Bush chose Dick Cheney to be secretary of defense, and Miller was in the clear.

Miller was on friendly terms with Cheney. Each year, as part of a program created during Jimmy Carter's presidency, a group of officials from the State Department, the Pentagon, and the intelligence agencies, as well as select members of Congress, took part in a beyond-Top-Secret exercise testing the procedures for "continuity of government" in case of a nuclear attack. The team was flown all over the country, from one obscure military base to another, where they actually would be taken during a nuclear war, and rehearsed running a regime under emergency powers. Cheney was chairman of the Republican Conference in the House of Representatives, and he'd been the White House chief of staff under President Ford, so he was seen as an ideal pick for the group's chief of staff. Miller was one of the Pentagon staffers on the team, and, during their leisure hours, he got to know Cheney and told him about his work on the SIOP. Cheney was interested.

The two kept talking periodically, so, by the time he was sworn in as defense secretary, Cheney was up to speed on what Miller had been doing. In the fall, the SAC commander, General John Chain, brought his aides in to brief him and the Joint Chiefs of Staff in the Tank—the Chiefs' conference room on the third floor of the Pentagon—on the latest revisions to the SIOP. Cheney asked Miller to sit in.

Conversations with Miller had primed Cheney to notice peculiarities in the war plan, and he was particularly struck by one slide showing that the SIOP's main attack plan hit the Soviet transportation network with 725 nuclear weapons.

Cheney asked Chain why.

Chain looked at the colonel who had been running the briefing's slideshow and reading the script. The colonel shrugged. Chain told Cheney he'd get back to him on that.

Afterward, Cheney brought Miller into his office and asked him what was going on. Miller said he didn't know: Weinberger and Carlucci had given him a mandate to investigate whether the SIOP reflected the president's policies, but the Joint Staff had barred him from examining targets—either the individual targets themselves or the way JSTPS calculated how many weapons to hit them with.

Cheney told Miller that the bar was hereby lifted and had him write a memo, which Cheney then signed, ordering the SAC commander to give Miller and his staff access to all documents that they requested. Cheney also promoted Miller to the rank of deputy assistant secretary of defense for nuclear forces and arms control policy and stated explicitly that one of his jobs was to lead a "SIOP Review," which would be conducted jointly by Miller (acting on Cheney's behalf), the Joint Staff, and the JSTPS. Miller in turn promoted Gil Klinger to take over his old job as director for strategic forces—and made him his agent in the review's sessions at SAC's Omaha headquarters.

Then came a moment of serendipity. A lieutenant colonel from JSTPS, who'd been given a two-year assignment to Miller's office (as much, it was suspected, to keep an eye on Miller as to assist him in his work), handed him a copy of the Blue Book. The Blue Book was very different from the Black Book, the thin binder that the president would use to review his attack options in case of nuclear war. The Blue Book, which was as thick as an epic Russian novel, was essentially the owners' manual for the SIOP, laying out the formulas and the premises of the calculations for what kinds of weapons would be aimed at which targets, how many were needed to inflict various levels of damage—everything that SAC's war planners needed to know and, more to the point, everything that Cheney wanted Miller to find out. This was SAC's secret treasure map, shown to no one outside SAC's inner sanctum, not even to the Joint Chiefs or the secretary of defense, and certainly not to some deputy assistant secretary.

At this point in their study, the Blue Book only confirmed and fleshed out what Miller and Klinger had discovered. More illuminating was the process that the book revealed—the specific way that a group of colonels in Omaha had been calculating how to allocate SAC's nuclear weapons to Soviet targets. Through the SIOP Review, Miller and Klinger would be commandeering the jobs of those colonels.

Armed with Cheney's mandate and the Blue Book's insights, they could now do what no one outside SAC—and no civilians anywhere—had ever done. They would conduct a zero-based, bottom-up, target-by-target review of the SIOP—then construct an all-new SIOP, indicating which targets really needed to be destroyed, and how many weapons were really needed to destroy them, under the guidelines set in the nuclear policy documents signed by the secretary of defense and approved by the president.

In December 1989, Miller sent Klinger and a few other aides to Omaha to begin the deconstruction. On their first day, they walked into the Air Room—the workspace of the JSTPS, a vast open auditorium three stories beneath Building 500 of SAC headquarters, filled with whiteboards, mainframe computers, and big maps of the Soviet Union, Eastern Europe, and China—and they could feel the gust of hostility. Klinger was barely thirty years old; everyone in the room was older and more senior. Officers who had been around for a while were wearily reminded of McNamara's whiz kids; those too young to recall those days had heard the stories and absorbed the resentments. Klinger was tempted to say something snide but knew that he needed these officers' help, so he pumped his capacity for politeness to unprecedented levels, telling them that he looked forward to working with them, so he could better understand the important work they were doing.

An Air Force colonel, who was having a hard time restraining himself from committing violence, growled at Klinger, "What difference does your *review* make?"

Klinger replied, with as mature a calm as he could muster, "If you're telling me that it doesn't matter how much the official nuclear war plan differs from what the president thinks it is, then I don't think anything matters."

The colonel said nothing in return, and the frost receded, a bit.

Work began the next morning. Klinger and his aides asked to see a few targets. One of the first, which they'd noticed ahead of time in the SIOP's National Strategic Target List, was a Soviet bomber base in Tiksi, inside the Arctic Circle. It wasn't even a primary base; it was a dispersal base, where Soviet planes would land *after* dropping their bombs on American targets, and the climate was so forbiddingly cold and windy that the base couldn't be used for more than half the year. And yet, it turned out, the SIOP called for firing seventeen nuclear weapons at a five-mile radius around the base—regardless of the season—including three Minuteman II ICBMs, each carrying a 1.2-megaton warhead.

Klinger noticed redundancy throughout the calculations in the Blue Book, and, now that he was in the belly of the beast, he searched for more examples. He had no trouble finding them.

He was especially struck by the way the plan went after the Soviet army's tanks. The SIOP aimed a lot of weapons not only at the tanks themselves, but also at the factory that produced the tanks, the steel mill that supplied the factory, the ore-processing facility that supplied the steel mill, and the mine that furnished the ore.

Klinger asked why they needed to destroy the entire production chain. His liaison officer told him that, if they left any part of the chain intact, the Soviets could reconstruct the factory and rebuild tanks. Though Klinger didn't know it, this was the same unfathomable frame of mind that, back in the early 1960s, led General Curtis LeMay to insist on destroying not just the repair depot at a Soviet air base but also the factory that built the spare parts supplying the repair depot because, otherwise, the Soviets could reconstruct their air force—never mind that thousands of American bombs and warheads would have just reduced the entire country to a smoldering radioactive ruin. Much at SAC had changed in the thirty years since LeMay's command; but in the bowels of the building, in its most mechanical and secretive compartment, where the flight paths of doom were plotted, the old cylinders were roaring full blast on autopilot.

Back at the Pentagon, specialists at the Defense Intelligence Agency had briefed Klinger and Miller on the art and science of "nodal analysis." As applied to warfare, nodal analysis examined a system or network with an eye toward identifying the central links—the nodes—so that the commanders could allocate their weapons most cost-effectively: destroy the nodes, which in some cases would take only a few weapons, and the whole system falls apart. There were some officers in the SAC Air Room who specialized in this sort of analysis; they were among the few people who welcomed Klinger's visits, since, as he discovered when he came across them one day, the leadership of the Joint Strategic Target Planning Staff had never paid attention to their advice.

One of these analysts told Klinger, when they first met, "We've been waiting for you for a long time."

From talking with these analysts and perusing the Blue Book, Klinger unraveled the mystery of why the SIOP laid down 725 nuclear weapons on the Soviet transportation network. It turned out that JSTPS had decided, for unclear reasons, to launch nuclear weapons against all railroad yards above a certain metric capacity and all railway bridges that stretched for longer than a certain distance. But, as the Defense Intelligence Agency's logistics specialists told them, this standard was completely arbitrary; it had no bearing on the military value of a target. Some long bridges and large railroad yards weren't used by the military at all; some very short bridges and small rail yards were militarily vital. There were other absurdities. For instance, the loading zones on the Russia-Poland border were clearly vital military targets: Russian and Polish rail tracks had different gauges; the loading zones were where Soviet armored vehicles would be switched from one track to the other before proceeding to the front lines of a war with NATO. The SIOP did target those loading zones—but it left unscathed some road bridges a couple miles up the river, because the JSTPS had called for attacking the Soviet "rail system," not the "transportation system." Bridges on roads weren't targeted at all.

Klinger pointed this out at one of his sessions with the target planning staff at SAC headquarters. "You're throwing all these weapons, and you're not even destroying the transit system," he told them. "What's going on?"

Silence filled the room for a few seconds. Then a major spoke up. "Sir, I've got to tell you," he said, "we've got nothing." A few of his fellow officers laughed.

"Okay, then," Klinger said, taking advantage of the opening, "let's fix this problem." It was at this point that some of the officers with JSTPS realized that they had a problem.

Another source of excess was the complicity of SAC's Intelligence office, whose job was to justify as many weapons for SAC as possible.

The poster child for this phenomenon was the Soviets' anti-ballistic-missile site near Sheremetyevo Airport on the outskirts of Moscow. The SIOP called for pummeling all the elements of the site—the control center, the radars, and the interceptors—with a total of sixty-nine nuclear warheads and bombs.

The rationale, it turned out, was that the guidance called for destroying the site with near-total certainty. SAC Intelligence estimated that each of the Soviet interceptors had a high probability of shooting down an incoming warhead. Therefore, SAC had to send in sixty-nine warheads to make sure that at least one of them got through.

This was insane. No defensive system in the history of warfare had been so effective. But Klinger couldn't press his challenge very far. He and Miller had no authority to challenge intelligence estimates. So at the end of their work, after drastically paring down the SIOP's requirements, there were still sixty-nine warheads aimed at this complex. (After the Cold War was over and Western inspectors got a look, they discovered that the ABM system at Sheremetyevo was worthless; it couldn't have shot down a single warhead coming straight at it.)

As he delved more deeply into the war plan, Klinger saw that much of it made no sense on any grounds. At one point, he had Wayne Lumsden print out the latitude and longitude of all the targets in the SIOP database. He then asked the graphics department to plot all those points on a huge map of the Soviet Union and draw circles around each point, signifying the area that would be destroyed by the specific weapon aimed at each target.

The result was a vivid, color-coded display of massive death and destruction. It showed a staggering number of bombs and warheads hitting nearly every city in overlapping density. Hundreds of targets were so close to one another that, in many cases, one weapon would hit more than one target, and one target would get hit by three, five, as many as seven nuclear weapons.

Klinger wondered how many weapons were aimed at Moscow and its environs. On the map, he drew a fifty-mile circle around the capital and counted the number of weapons that were aimed at targets within the circle. There were 689 of them, many releasing more than a megaton of explosive power.

"Overkill" was a severe understatement for what had gone on for decades.

The SIOP was a broken machine, the discombobulated aggregate of compartmentalized calculations. One analyst was instructed to aim a missile at a ball-bearing factory; another plotted the flight path for a bomber to destroy the Ministry of Defense headquarters; still another programmed a cruise missile to ravage a major railroad yard. Nobody took the broader look; nobody saw that the three targets were within a short hike of one another—and that, therefore, just one of those weapons would be enough to demolish them all. And, because the Blue Book specified that those targets had to be destroyed with high confidence, more than one weapon had to be aimed at each, meaning that all these structures would get clobbered by a half-dozen weapons, in some cases more.

Moscow was hardly unique. The same thing would happen in Leningrad, Vladivostok, Novosibirsk, Omsk, Tomsk—any city that housed military targets or war-supporting industries or political-relocation sites.

Few officers, even inside JSTPS, had known the full scope of their war plan's bloat. The colonels and generals in the Pentagon's Joint Staff, who had so fiercely resisted Miller's intrusions, were stunned; they hadn't realized how much they didn't know—how much their brother officers at SAC, whose shroud they'd been protecting, had misled them.

Then came a revelation that put everything in perspective. By this time, the Bush administration and the Soviet Union were negotiating the Strategic Arms Reduction Treaty. During one of his early trips to Omaha, Klinger asked one of the officers at JSTPS to analyze whether the treaty's prospective cuts would affect their ability to fulfill their mission—whether they could continue to deter nuclear war and limit damage if deterrence failed.

The officer replied that he didn't do that sort of analysis.

Klinger, thinking he wasn't making himself clear, rephrased the question.

The officer said that he understood the question perfectly well. He explained that JSTPS was prohibited from setting requirements or analyzing whether a certain kind of attack, with a certain number of weapons, would be militarily effective. This prohibition had been laid down in 1960, with the first SIOP, when Navy admirals feared that Air Force generals would use the war plan as a tool for controlling the Navy's arsenal and budget.

Klinger was astonished. The officers who drew up the war plan didn't know—weren't allowed to figure out—how many weapons they needed to protect the nation? What did they do then?

The officer replied that they take all the weapons that are assigned to SAC and aim them at all the targets on their list.

Finally, after all these months of trying to unscramble the oddities of the SIOP, Klinger decoded the mystery: the United States' nuclear war plan was based on supply, not demand—on how many weapons the warriors happened to have, not on how many they needed.

SAC's commander, General Jack Chain, had recently testified before Congress that he needed 10,000 nuclear weapons because he had 10,000 targets. Many people, including Klinger, had thought that Chain was joking or that he was cynical or stupid. But no, this was the mentality of the nuclear targeteers; this was what they did.

The implication was stunning. Back in McNamara's time, the whiz kids had famously asked, "How much is enough?" The chief whiz kid, Alain Enthoven, later coauthored a book, a combination treatise and memoir, with that question as its title. Now, it turned out that nobody had ever asked the question in a way, or from a position, that mattered. The authors of the Defense Department's directives on how to use (and not use) nuclear weapons may have thought they were asking the question; but they'd lacked access to the machinery of the SIOP—they hadn't known how to ask the question in a way that the JSTPS officers could translate into their operational plan. Meanwhile, the JSTPS officers were barred from asking, or trying to answer, the question on their own. Washington and Omaha were running on parallel, sometimes wildly divergent tracks—which had been Curtis LeMay's intention all along: he didn't want civilians, or even rival branches of the military, meddling with his war plan, and he designed SAC explicitly to keep them out.

Back in Washington, Cheney and the chairman of the Joint Chiefs, General Colin Powell, were about to meet with Vice Admiral Ron Eytchison, the vice director of JSTPS. Miller prepped Cheney to ask the three-star admiral the same question that Klinger had asked the aide out in Omaha: Would the limits negotiated at the Strategic Arms Reduction Talks affect SAC's ability to execute U.S. policy? Eytchison supplied the same answer: he didn't know; that's not a question that JSTPS asks or answers.

The reaction from Powell and Cheney was the same as Klinger's had been when the reality hit him: a disbelieving stare, eyes unblinking, jaw slightly agape. The problem, they all realized, was deeper than they'd ever suspected; the pathologies were embedded in the organization—the very existence—of the SAC bureaucracy.

From that point on, roughly every two months over the course of their review, usually on a Friday afternoon from three o'clock until five, Miller and Klinger briefed their latest findings to Cheney and Powell in the secretary's third-floor conference room.

Powell had risen through the Army's ranks as an infantry soldier, a grunt fighting in the rice paddies of Vietnam—and, like most grunts of his generation, he had little interest in the nuclear enterprise. In the mid-1980s, as commander of the Army's V Corps in Europe, Powell took part in a tabletop war game, in which the Soviets invade West Germany. His armored divisions shot up the invaders, but then the Soviets sent in reinforcements, overwhelming the corps. At that point, under the rules of the game, he was supposed to ask permission to fire nuclear weapons. But Powell thought that made no sense: the Soviet troops were in West German territory; clobbering them with nukes would kill millions of West German citizens.

Powell pointed this out to the game manager, who assured him that the civilians had all been evacuated.

Oh? Powell asked. Where did they go?

The manager replied that he didn't know, he was only reciting what was in the plan.

Powell then asked what the Soviets were likely to do after he launched the nuclear weapons.

They'll probably fire their nuclear weapons, the manager responded.

"Does this make any sense at all?" Powell asked the manager, who didn't know what to say.

Powell concluded from the exercise that war with the Soviet Union probably would trigger nuclear war; that nuclear weapons, once used, couldn't be controlled; and that, therefore, war had to be prevented at all cost.

This was one problem Powell had with the whole business of Limited Nuclear Options. He told Miller, during one of their sessions, that there was nothing to support the idea that we could drop a few nukes on Soviet territory and say, "Let's stop here." There was nothing in the intelligence reports to suggest that the Soviets would play the same game—that they would do anything but retaliate, and with more than just a few nukes of their own.

Still, Powell thought that, as long as we had nuclear weapons, and as long as there was a chance they might be used, there might as well be some way of controlling the damage, if at all possible. And so he supported Miller and Klinger in their work—and ordered the officers of the Joint Staff to support the work too.

By the early spring of 1991, Miller, Klinger, and their increasingly sympathetic—though, in some cases, still resistant—collaborators in JSTPS and the Joint Staff were finishing up the SIOP Review. They'd gone back over every target, debating whether it needed to be a target and, if it did, whether just one weapon should be launched at it or whether it was a sufficiently important target to justify two or more weapons, and what kinds of weapons: did the target need to be destroyed right away, in which case a missile should cover it; or was the need less urgent, in which case a bomber, taking several hours to reach its goal, would be sufficient.

Miller and Klinger, with the support of Cheney and Powell, were the first two outsiders to breach the wall. At the end of the process, their team wound up cutting the "required" number of U.S. strategic nuclear weapons by half—from about 12,000 to 5,888—and even that was after several compromises; a more stringent review could have cut more. Even so, it was the steepest reduction in Cold War history, and it stemmed not from an arms control treaty or the relaxation of international tensions, but rather from a purely technical, deep-dive analysis of how many weapons U.S. policy required. (In a bit of whimsy, Klinger considered getting a custom license plate for his car reading "5888," but decided that his superiors wouldn't be amused seeing it on display in the Pentagon parking lot, much less tooling around the nation's capital.)

In the fall of 1991, SAC's commander, General George Lee Butler, who had replaced Jack Chain at the start of the year, came to Washington and briefed Cheney, Powell, and their staffs on the new SIOP—the first SIOP to reflect all of the Miller-Klinger changes. Butler had been the Joint Staff's director of strategic plans and policy during the final phase of their work and had thoroughly absorbed its lessons. In his first months at SAC, he'd conducted his own review of the SIOP, while it was still in transition, and came away appalled by the degree of overkill. During his briefing in the Pentagon, Butler not only presented the new plan, he took credit for it. Miller and Klinger smiled at each other. Success in bureaucratic politics comes when those in charge claim a once-unpopular idea as their own. By this measure, the two civil servants had achieved a remarkable success.

Finally, around the same time Miller and Klinger were breaching walls in Omaha, another, literal wall was toppled—the Berlin Wall separating East and West Berlin—followed quickly by the collapse of the border between East and West Germany and, with that, the end of the Cold War. Miller and Klinger leapt back into the SIOP and—with Cheney's orders, Powell's endorsement, and cooperation from the JSTPS—removed all the targets that lay inside Eastern Europe. Those countries, once under Soviet rule but now independent, had housed hundreds of targets—mainly air defense sites, which American nuclear missiles would destroy in order to pave a "corridor," allowing American bombers to fly toward their targets inside the USSR without getting shot down on the way. While they were at it, Miller and Klinger examined how many targets should be removed if, as seemed possible, the Soviet Union fell apart and, therefore, only the republics possessing nuclear weapons—Russia, Ukraine, Kazakhstan, and Belarus—remained on the list.

In the end, they cut the requirements for another couple thousand bombs and warheads, leaving the number of strategic weapons at 3,500—the lowest number since 1962, when the nuclear arms race began.

———⊗⊗⊗———

George H. W. Bush didn't pay a lot of attention to the nuclear war plan. For one thing, he trusted his national security team to do that. For another, he had more urgent tasks on his plate: maneuvering through the end of the Cold War and the crumbling of the Soviet Union without setting off new tensions; invading Panama and arresting its drug-dealing dictator, Manuel Noriega, while minimizing strife in its capital; and, perhaps most delicately and forcefully, mobilizing a half-million troops and an alliance of Western, Muslim, and Arab nations to oust Iraqi dictator Saddam Hussein's invading army from Kuwait.

On November 8, 1990, the day Bush announced a doubling of troops for that operation, he received a briefing on the new, more flexible options for the nuclear war plan. The top players were in the room—Cheney, Powell, and Vice President Dan Quayle—as were some staffers, including Miller and Klinger.

When the briefers displayed the chart showing the distinctions among the major attack options—MAO-1, MAO-2, MAO-3, and MAO-4—Bush turned to Cheney and asked, in a calm, no-nonsense tone, "Tell me the difference in the number of people I'm going to kill."

Klinger was impressed but also shaken. He had never before heard that question asked in the first person. For more than a year, he'd been immersed in the bubble of the SIOP, thinking about nuclear war day and night, to the point where he'd honed it into an abstraction. That was the only way to stay sane while pondering megatons and mega-deaths—to focus on the calculations and the scenarios, which, after a while, loomed in the mind as more palpable, certainly more controllable, than the catastrophic chaos that would ensue if the war games played out in real life. Mordant humor was another way of keeping sane: hence the special appeal of *Dr. Strangelove* to many nuclear strategists, doubly so to Klinger, a young man with a mordant streak, who, when asked at cocktail parties what he did for a living, would sometimes reply, "I plan the deaths of millions of Soviet citizens." Yet here was Bush, the man who would actually make that decision—who would select the option and push the button—facing up to the consequences of his actions. Suddenly, nuclear war seemed not so abstract.

Meanwhile, the Soviet Union, its empire, the raison d'être for the SIOP and the Cold War, was falling apart. On March 31, 1991, the Warsaw Pact formally dissolved. On August 18, a cabal of hard-liners in the Kremlin arrested Mikhail Gorbachev, held him captive in Crimea, and seized power. Boris Yeltsin, who had been elected president of the Russian Federation a few months earlier, led protests outside the White House, the stately headquarters of the parliament. On August 21, the military took the protesters' side, the coup ended, and Gorbachev returned—but to a very different Moscow. The Communist Party, to which he still pledged fealty, was kaput. On the last day of the year, the Soviet Union was formally dissolved, replaced by a confederation of independent states, and Yeltsin took Gorbachev's place in the Kremlin, which was now the governing center of a new democratic Russian Republic.

It had taken nearly a year for Bush and his security advisers to drop their skepticism about Gorbachev's reforms and intentions. They were even more leery of Yeltsin when he first mounted his challenge to Gorbachev; but after he led the revolt against the coup plotters, Bush aligned himself completely with the new Russian leader and sought ways to signal America's support for this new revolution. He saw clearly that Russia posed no threat to the West, and he wanted the Russians to know that the West posed no threat to them. The whole premise of the nuclear standoff was now shattered; having been briefed on the revised SIOP, Bush knew that massive cuts in nuclear weapons were not merely feasible but under way, and he wanted to make deeper cuts still. But he was frustrated with the bureaucratized arms control process; the latest round of negotiations, the Strategic Arms Reduction Talks, had been going on for nine years, since Reagan's second year in office.

So, on Friday night, September 27, in a televised speech, he announced that he was taking a series of unilateral steps, which would "make the world a less dangerous place than ever before in the nuclear age." For thirty-six years, SAC had kept some of its bomber aircraft on runway alert, fully loaded, pilots in or near the cockpit, ready to take off in minutes; Bush was now ordering them to stand down and to taxi off the runways. He also ordered all nuclear weapons to be removed from surface ships, conventional subs, and tactical aircraft.

Four months later, in his State of the Union Address, he went further and announced the withdrawal of all short-range nuclear weapons from Europe (and from South Korea, while he was at it). In the September 27 speech, he'd said that, in the face of all these cuts, the United States must "vigorously" continue the "strategic modernization program," including the B-2 bomber and the Strategic Defense Initiative.

Now, he announced the shutdown of SAC itself, renaming it the U.S. Strategic Command and rotating its chiefs between Air Force generals and Navy admirals, so it would no longer be dominated by the vested interests of one service.

In outlining each step, Bush invited the Russians to reciprocate— which they did, in some cases, at least for a while—but he stressed that, even if they didn't, his actions were in America's interests.

Bush had planned his actions and written his speech in consultation with only a handful of officials and aides in the White House, the Pentagon, and the State Department, alerting his wider cabinet and U.S. allies, as well as Yeltsin, just hours before the broadcast. Cheney made the case that Bush should put more emphasis on urging the Russians to reciprocate. Ultimately, though, he too had no complaints, and neither did anyone else in a position of power. Navy surface ship commanders had long been weary of carrying nuclear weapons on board, telling their superiors that the bombs and missiles hindered their mobility— made them think twice about entering contested waters—and barred them from docking at the ports of several allies. Army commanders in Europe had long despaired of having to maintain nuclear missiles and artillery rockets, seeing them as security burdens in peacetime and useless weapons of terror—sure to incite retaliation—in a conflict. Colin Powell, who as chairman of the Joint Chiefs would expedite Bush's commands, felt that way more than most.

By this time, in a separate series of moves, the United States had started to dismantle the MIRV'ed ICBMs unilaterally, canceling the ten-warhead MX missile and stripping the three-warhead Minuteman III so that its nosecone carried just one. The officers of Strategic Command assented to these moves, in part because Miller's SIOP Review revealed that they had far more weapons than they needed.

Without the SIOP Review and its drawdown of "required" U.S. weapons, the commanders in Omaha might not have adjusted to the end of the Cold War, or followed Bush's orders, as unperturbedly as they did.

Bush proved to be a victim of his own success. He'd made his reputation as a manager of international crises, but with the Cold War won and the nuclear arms race over, at least for now, this specialty seemed unimportant to a majority of American voters, and he lost his bid for reelection to the Democratic candidate, Bill Clinton, the governor of Arkansas, who promised to rev up the sagging domestic economy. Across the river, in the Pentagon, shortly before his retirement ceremony, Cheney turned to Frank Miller, exchanged a few words over the demise of the Soviet Union, the unanticipated evaporation of the era's existential foe, and said, "Just when we got the SIOP right, the bastards gave up on us."

But in fact the SIOP wasn't quite right yet: it would still make the Russian rubble bounce; and "the bastards"—the Russians—weren't quite yet ready to give up. This became clear when the twin ghosts of Ronald Reagan's fantasy and the Russians' paranoia came back to haunt this brief respite from history.

On January 3, 1993, two and a half weeks before the end of Bush's presidency, he and Boris Yeltsin signed the START II treaty, which prohibited land-based ICBMs from carrying more than one warhead apiece. The accord reversed the most destabilizing action in the history of the arms race. ICBMs loaded with MIRVs—multiple warheads, each of which could strike widely separated targets—were at once the most potent and the most vulnerable weapons in both sides' arsenals. In a crisis, a desperate or risk-prone leader might be tempted to launch a first strike, if just to preempt the enemy from launching a first strike. In short, the very existence of MIRVs on ICBMs created a hair-trigger situation, in which both sides might feel an incentive to strike first. START II would remove that incentive.

Cheney advised Bush that he could make this deal without any sacrifice in U.S. power because the MIRVs on the Trident II missiles were accurate enough to destroy hardened targets, such as Russian missile silos; and, since the Trident IIs were on submarines, prowling beneath the ocean's surface, undetectable, they were not vulnerable to a first strike. If the Russians ever again believed an American president wanted to launch a first strike, the Trident IIs would bolster their fear; but the chances of a first strike, to preempt the other side's first strike, would dim to zero; there would be no hair trigger, no incentive to make such a desperate move.

But this dream was not to be. Some Russians, it turned out, were still distrustful. After several years of debate and delay, the Russian parliament ratified the treaty only on the condition that the United States formally reaffirm its adherence to the ABM Treaty—in short, only if Washington promised not to move ahead with the Strategic Defense Initiative. By this time, support for SDI had hardened as a shibboleth among Republicans and some hawkish Democrats as well. They refused the Russians' demand, and the treaty—along with the ban on MIRV'ed ICBMs—collapsed.

The nuclear arms race was not over after all.

CHAPTER 9

"A Shrimp Among Whales"

William Jefferson Clinton entered the White House on January 20, 1993, caring little about foreign policy. The Cold War was over; hot wars and body bags seemed a plague of the past. In his early days as president, he often skipped his daily intelligence briefing, letting his national security adviser, Tony Lake, hear it instead. But eventually, as Trotsky said of those who take no interest in war, war takes an interest in them, and, just weeks into Clinton's term, Kim Il-sung, the dictator of North Korea, roused that interest.

No country on earth was more intractable than North Korea. Since its founding in the wake of the Second World War, the leader of this hermetically sealed nation—the first and last of Josef Stalin's idolaters—had brutalized his own people, threatened his neighbors, and stymied all outside overtures. Within a year of taking office, Bill Clinton, hardly a hawk, would nearly clash arms with this country, even knowing that the conflict might escalate to nuclear war.

Five years earlier, in 1989, during the presidency of George H. W. Bush, the CIA had spotted the North Koreans building a reprocessing facility near their nuclear reactor at Yongbyon. When finished, this reactor would enable them to convert fuel rods into weapons-grade plutonium. Bush launched a policy of "comprehensive engagement" with North Korea, an all-fronts diplomatic campaign to keep this threat contained, pledging economic assistance and, finally, in September 1991, announcing that he was unilaterally withdrawing all U.S. tactical nuclear weapons from South Korea. (He was doing the same in Western Europe, as part of his nuclear initiatives with post-Soviet Russia, so figured he might as well expand the gambit.) This set off a flurry of diplomacy from the North Korean leaders. They had signed the Non-Proliferation Treaty in 1985; now they also initialed the NPT's Safeguards Agreement, which allowed the International Atomic Energy Agency to send inspectors, install cameras inside the reactors, and place the fuel rods under lock and key.

Now, though, the North Koreans were preparing to remove the fuel rods from their storage site, expel the inspectors, and withdraw from the NPT.

In response, Clinton urged the United Nations Security Council and America's allies in the region, notably South Korea and Japan, to impose economic sanctions. North Korea's spokesmen declared that sanctions would trigger war. For nearly a year, tensions built, then abated, then built once more, as U.S. officials met with North Korean emissaries in talks that went nowhere. Finally, at Clinton's direction, as the reprocessing churned on and crisis neared, the Joint Chiefs of Staff drew up plans to send 50,000 troops to South Korea—bolstering the 37,000 that had been there for decades—along with more than 400 combat jets, 50 warships, and extra battalions of Apache helicopters, Bradley fighting vehicles, multiple-launch rockets, and Patriot air defense missiles. Beyond mere plans, Clinton ordered an advance team of 250 soldiers to set up a logistical headquarters, which could manage this massive influx of firepower if it was mobilized. These moves sent a signal that the United States was willing to go to war to keep North Korea's fuel rods under lock.

Clinton's secretary of defense, William Perry, a veteran weapons scientist, asked the Joint Chiefs and General Gary Luck, the commander of U.S. Forces in Korea, to game how a war would play out. On May 19, Clinton and his top aides met in the Cabinet Room to hear the results. Perry, who had been briefed ahead of time, delivered the news. The U.S. forces could strike the Yongbyon reactor and set back Kim's nuclear program by several years, he began. But the North Koreans—whom he likened to "adolescents with guns"—possessed a large army and thousands of artillery rockets, some tipped with chemical shells, many of them within firing range of Seoul, South Korea's capital, with a population of 10 million, just thirty-five miles south of the border. If they struck back, which the intelligence community believed they would, the assault could kill or injure 30,000 Americans—nearly as many casualties as produced in the three years of the first Korean War—in addition to a half-million South Korean soldiers and as many as a million civilians. And this estimate assumed that the North Koreans used no atomic bombs—though a minority view within the CIA considered it possible that they had built two bombs before the reprocessing was discovered during the Bush administration.

After Perry's briefing, everyone in the room agreed that war was too risky to contemplate. Yet they kept mobilizing military forces and pressing for sanctions, hoping that the pressure would push the North Koreans into dropping their plans to reprocess the fuel rods—but knowing that it might push them over the edge into war.

Clinton was hardly the first president to grapple with the dilemmas of trying to stop a less powerful but restless nation from joining the nuclear club. In the earliest days of the nuclear age, the challenge was to block America's *allies* from getting a bomb. Great Britain was the third nation to build an atom bomb, after the United States and the Soviet Union, but this feat raised little concern: the Manhattan Project, during World War II, had been in some ways a joint American-British endeavor; and though, after the war, Washington banned the sharing of atomic secrets, London was well enough along to test its own A-bomb in 1952 and its first H-bomb not long after, with little disturbance to the two nations' special relationship.

France was another matter. In 1954, President Eisenhower's secretary of state, John Foster Dulles, proposed sending the French two tactical nuclear weapons to stave off the North Vietnamese army at Dien Bien Phu. Three years later, he suggested at least letting, if not helping, the French build their own atomic arsenal. But Eisenhower wavered, and, in 1961, his successor, John Kennedy, fervently opposed the idea. In a telegram to British prime minister Harold Macmillan, Kennedy cited two reasons for rejecting France's request for atomic assistance. First, the Germans, whose relations with Paris were still tense, might react by building their own bomb, a move that, just fifteen years after the defeat of the Third Reich, would "shake NATO to its foundations."

Second, Kennedy opposed "Nth-country" nuclear programs generally, a phrase referring to the theoretically countless number of countries, beyond the first three (the 4th, 5th, 6th . . .), that might develop their own bombs. In conversations with some of his aides, Kennedy called the problem his "private nightmare." The bilateral face-off with the Soviet Union, frightening enough, was at least manageable; throw in a half-dozen other nations, each with their own interests, allies, and enemies, and not only would chaos reign, but the two big powers might get sucked into a nuclear war not of their making. For the same reason, Kennedy opposed Israel's nuclear program, for fear that it would push the Arab countries into building their own bomb, possibly with Soviet help, thus fanning the flames of superpower conflict into the already-turbulent Middle East. He pressured Israel's prime minister, David Ben-Gurion, to let American scientists inspect the country's Dimona nuclear reactor, which the CIA suspected was not entirely civilian in nature. Indeed it was not: by 1963, with covert aid from France, the Israelis were generating enough plutonium to make an atom bomb.

This was the other reason Kennedy opposed helping the French get a bomb: he didn't trust Charles de Gaulle, the former Resistance hero who'd risen to the presidency on a pledge to restore the centrality of *la France*, independent of NATO, meaning independent of American hegemony. As a State Department official put it in an internal memo, reflecting a broad consensus in Washington, "When we and the British differ, the British align themselves with us. When we and the French differ, the French go their own way." Kennedy assured de Gaulle that the United States would continue to station some nuclear weapons on the European continent, as a guarantee of retaliation to a Soviet attack. He made these assurances during the Berlin crisis, when many Western Europeans wondered whether an American president would really "risk New York for Paris." De Gaulle concluded that some future president might not, and in 1964 fielded the first weapons of the *force de frappe*, the French atomic arsenal.

By then, Kennedy had been assassinated and Lyndon Johnson had succeeded him as president, but McGeorge Bundy remained the national security adviser, and he wrote—and signed—National Security Action Memorandum No. 294, which stated, "It is the policy of this government to oppose the development of nuclear forces by other states, other than those whose forces would be assigned as part of a NATO nuclear force, targeted in accordance with NATO plans, and, except when supreme national interests were at stake, used only for the defense purposes of the Alliance." Since de Gaulle's *force de frappe* was entirely independent of NATO, Bundy declared that the United States would not assist the French nuclear program in any way.

But 1964 saw a potentially more disturbing development: the first test of an atom bomb by a Communist country other than the Soviet Union—namely, China. The specter of a Red Chinese bomb set off alarms similar to that of a North Korean bomb thirty years later. Mao Zedong, China's leader and father of its Communist revolution, was a wild card, vying for supremacy within the worldwide Communist movement by lambasting Moscow's sclerotic Kremlin leaders as insufficiently aggressive in the struggle against American-led imperialism. Some, especially in the Pentagon, feared that, once Mao assembled an arsenal of atomic weapons, he might use them or, short of that, brandish them as cover to pursue conventional aggression against Taiwan, Japan, or South Korea—which an American president might be hesitant to fight off, lest the effort trigger a Chinese nuclear response. Taiwan's president, Chiang Kai-shek, was particularly nervous about this Asian variant on the scenario that worried many in Europe—would the president risk Los Angeles for Tokyo or Taipei?

In anticipation of a nuclear test, William Bundy, McGeorge's brother, who was the assistant secretary of defense for international security affairs, wrote a memo asking General Earle Wheeler, chairman of the Joint Chiefs of Staff, to "prepare an operational plan for an air attack" against China's nuclear production facilities. Wheeler replied that the plan should allow the use of U.S. nuclear weapons, to make sure the Chinese targets were destroyed.

However, most officials were less panicked. A study by the State Department's Policy Planning Staff, coordinated with the Pentagon and the CIA, concluded that a "ChiCom" bomb (ChiCom being the common shorthand for "Chinese Communist") did not justify "actions which would involve great political costs or high military risks." The intelligence agencies weren't certain where some of the Chinese nuclear sites were located, so a preemptive strike might not take out all the targets. It might also inflame radical movements worldwide and help mend the growing rift between Beijing and Moscow. Finally, within a few years, the sites could be rebuilt. In any case, the study and other memos concluded, the Chinese could build only a few "crude" A-bombs in the coming few years, so they were unlikely to pose a threat to the United States or its allies.

At a meeting with congressional leaders, called by President Johnson on October 19, three days after China's nuclear test, Secretary of Defense Robert McNamara noted that, after a *Soviet* first strike, the United States would still have 2,700 nuclear weapons. Of those, 800 would be enough to inflict unacceptable damage on the USSR—leaving plenty of warheads and bombs to attack other targets, including those in China.

However, McNamara added, the Chinese test did highlight a broader problem: a half-dozen countries now had the technical ability to build atom bombs quickly and relatively cheaply, if they made a political decision to do so. China's new nuclear status might compel some of them, notably Japan and India, to go that route. It was important, McNamara said, to figure out a way to limit the global spread of nuclear weapons—the Nth-country problem that had worried Kennedy when the French were building their bomb.

Since the summer, interagency meetings had been called to discuss the feasibility and wisdom of an international treaty to ban the spread of nuclear weapons. The Chinese test lent the topic new urgency. On October 29, President Johnson asked McGeorge Bundy to assemble a special task force to take a hard look at the problem. Bundy quickly appointed ten scientists and former officials to the committee. The chairman would be Roswell Gilpatric, who had been deputy secretary of defense until just after Kennedy's assassination. The staff director would be Spurgeon Keeny, the National Security Council's chief arms control specialist.

The members met five times, in great secrecy, between December 1 and January 8. They began their work, in the Old Executive Office Building, with few preconceptions. At an NSC meeting a few months earlier, Secretary of State Dean Rusk had suggested that the selective spread of nuclear weapons could be a *good* thing: for instance, the United States might *want* to help India build a nuclear arsenal, as a deterrent to Chinese aggression. In their meetings, the members of the Gilpatric Committee vigorously discussed Rusk's idea. But in their report, which was issued January 25, they rejected the notion, concluding unanimously that an expanded roster of nuclear powers—even if some of them were currently American allies—would "add complexity and instability to the deterrent balance between the United States and the Soviet Union, aggravate suspicions and hostility among states neighboring new nuclear powers, place a wasteful economic burden on the aspirations of developing nations, impede the vital task of controlling and reducing weapons around the world, and eventually constitute direct military threats to the United States."

The report's recommendations were ambitious: a multilateral treaty, written and enforced jointly with the Soviet Union, to ban the further spread of nuclear weapons, impose sanctions against countries that didn't sign the treaty, and offer security guarantees or economic assistance—including technology for nuclear-powered electricity—to those that did sign. It also urged negotiation of an additional accord to cut the arsenals of those nations that already had the bomb. Such an accord would serve as a signal that the nuclear powers were reducing the role that these weapons played in their security policies—and, possibly, as an incentive for other countries to follow suit.

In response to the report, the NSC worked up a draft of a Non-Proliferation Treaty, which, in August, President Johnson submitted to the United Nations' Disarmament Commission. This was done in cooperation with Soviet officials, who feared proliferation—and the threat it might pose to their own empire—even more than their American counterparts. In September, the Soviets presented a similar document to the U.N. General Assembly. In November, the General Assembly adopted a resolution endorsing the same goals. On January 1, 1968, after several rounds of diplomacy, tightening some clauses and loosening others, the two superpowers put the final touches on a joint treaty. They formally signed it on July 1, along with sixty other countries.

Its text reflected most of the Gilpatric group's suggestions. Nuclear states—the United States, the Soviet Union, Great Britain, France, and China—were barred from transferring nuclear weapons or technology to others. Nonnuclear states were barred from receiving or developing nuclear weapons. In exchange for this restraint, these nations were granted an "inalienable right" to obtain materials for the peaceful use of nuclear energy, which the nuclear states would provide at reasonable cost.

The Gilpatric Committee had also recommended that the United States and the Soviet Union call an eighteen- to twenty-four-month moratorium on the construction of new ICBMs and negotiate a treaty reducing their strategic bombs and warheads by 30 percent. Had they done this, the two superpowers might have preempted the next, and most destabilizing, round of the nuclear arms race. The United States was two years away from deploying the Minuteman III, the first ICBM carrying multiple warheads; the Soviet Union wouldn't match that feat until five years after that. But General Wheeler, the chairman of the Joint Chiefs, opposed the idea. And Spurgeon Keeny, the committee's staff director and its most ardent disarmament advocate, conceded that a moratorium on construction "might be difficult to get out of and would complicate our subsequent bargaining position" on further arms control talks. The Russians were also unlikely to freeze production of their missiles, as they were just beginning to catch up with the Americans.

In the final draft of the Non-Proliferation Treaty, the nuclear states agreed merely "to pursue negotiations in good faith on effective measures relating to cessation of the nuclear arms race at an early date." The language was vague to the point of evasive: "to *pursue* negotiations" did not require them to *hold* negotiations; measures "*relating* to cessation" of the arms race would not necessarily end it. The NPT did inspire the two superpowers to begin strategic arms limitation talks, which led to the nuclear treaties that followed. But in the twenty-three years between the signing of the treaty and the end of the Cold War, the Americans doubled—and the Soviets sextupled—the number of warheads on their ICBMs.

There was also a loophole in the clause granting nonnuclear states the inalienable right to pursue "peaceful nuclear energy." The technology for nuclear energy and nuclear weapons was the same. The only difference was the degree of uranium enrichment: below a certain level, it remained peaceful; above that level, it was weapons-grade. A nation could advance well along the spectrum of legally permitted "peaceful" enrichment, then, with no warning, cross the line to "weapons-grade," abrogate the treaty, and declare itself a nuclear power.

In short, the NPT could legitimize the arms race of the nuclear nations and facilitate the arming of nuclear wannabes.

Still, by the time Bill Clinton faced off against Kim Il-sung, the Non-Proliferation Treaty was more than a quarter-century old and had been signed—and faithfully followed—by 188 nation-states: all of the world's states except India, Israel, Pakistan, and Sudan. And now North Korea was threatening to become the first of those 188 to sign out.

Like previous presidents confronting nascent nuclear powers, Clinton found himself in a hard spot: if he did nothing, North Korea—the most isolated, madcap, threat-spewing country in the world—would get its hands on an atomic bomb; yet if he followed through on his threats and ordered sanctions, followed by a military mobilization, he might ratchet up the tensions, exacerbate Kim Il-sung's paranoia, and incite a war. The dilemma seemed irresolvable.

Watching the crisis unfold from his farm in Plains, Georgia, former president Jimmy Carter thought that he could, and should, step in to save the day.

At one point during his presidency, Carter had announced the imminent withdrawal of all U.S. troops from South Korea. His advisers in the White House, the State Department, and the Pentagon, as well as fellow Democrats on Capitol Hill, talked him out of the idea; but his near-effort endeared Carter to Kim Il-sung. In the thirteen years since he'd left office, the North Korean government had invited him to Pyongyang three times. Each time, Carter asked senior U.S. officials for permission, but they always discouraged him, noting either that relations with North Korea were too tense or that negotiations were going too well and that, in either case, his unavoidably high-profile presence—no American president, sitting or otherwise, had ever before visited the country—would get in the way.

Now, though, Carter thought that war was looming too large and that Clinton's approach was aggravating the situation, a view bolstered by conversations he had with a few Chinese officials, with whom he'd stayed in touch, and with James Laney, the U.S. ambassador to South

Korea, who was sounding similar alarms to his colleagues in the State Department. Carter decided that it was time to take the North Koreans up on their standing invitation: to go to Pyongyang and talk with Kim, whatever the authorities in Washington had to say about it.

On June 6, Carter sent Clinton a letter, notifying him of his plans. Clinton was traveling in Europe when the letter arrived, so Vice President Al Gore, a former U.S. senator from Tennessee who had a cordial relationship with Carter, read it instead and asked the national security team for advice on what to do. The team was divided over whether to let Carter make the trip. Those who had served under President Carter—notably Tony Lake and Clinton's secretary of state, Warren Christopher—were leery: Carter, they warned, was a loose cannon who would ignore instructions and possibly freelance a deal. Gore took their point but thought it was a risk worth taking. Whatever else might be said about him, Carter had a sterling record when it came to personal diplomacy, having prodded Menachem Begin and Anwar Sadat, the recalcitrant leaders of Israel and Egypt, to sign a peace treaty, which was still in effect. Clinton and Kim had both painted themselves into a corner and needed an escape hatch, a clear path to back away from the brink without appearing to buckle under pressure. Carter might provide that hatch; even if he just reduced tensions, that would be better than nothing.

Gore called Carter and suggested one change in his letter to Clinton. In the sentence about the North Koreans' renewed invitation, Carter had written, "This time, I have accepted." Gore advised him to change it to read, "I am inclined to accept." If he made that revision, Gore said he would urge Clinton to approve the trip. Carter, seeing the point, made the change.

Although the White House portrayed Carter's venture as a purely private trip, Clinton did send a team of State Department officials and CIA analysts down to Georgia ahead of time to brief the former president on the full scope of the crisis, the military balance, and the political calculations. Before flying to Seoul, Carter sat for a second meeting with senior officials in the Delta lounge at Washington's National Airport. That meeting included Bob Gallucci, the assistant secretary of state who oversaw Clinton's Korea policy and who'd led the earlier briefing in Plains; Carter had admired that briefing and liked Gallucci. Also present was Tony Lake, Clinton's national security adviser. Lake had directed the State Department's Policy Planning Staff during the Carter administration; Carter remembered him and didn't much like him. Lake gently cautioned his former boss not to undercut the current U.S. negotiating position, which stated that sanctions would remain in place until a deal was struck and that, as part of any deal, North Korea would have to halt reprocessing. Lake also reminded Carter to tell the North Koreans that he was representing only himself—standard protocol when former presidents visited foreign countries, but, Lake noticed, Carter didn't take well to the command.

Carter arrived in Seoul on June 13, crossed the Demilitarized Zone into North Korea soon after, and spent the next three days locked in conversation with Pyongyang's leaders, including Chairman Kim Il-sung, eighty-two years old but still alert.

As it turned out, both sides in the White House debate over whether Carter should make the trip had been right. After the long hours of meetings, meals, and a ride on Kim's yacht, the North Korean leader backed down from his threats. *And* Carter went way beyond his instructions, negotiating the outlines of a twelve-point treaty without any authorization from—in fact, against the express directives of—the Clinton administration. Not only that, but as his trip was wrapping up, Carter called Gallucci, who happened to be at an NSC meeting in the White House Cabinet Room, to tell him that he'd reached an accord with Kim and would be announcing some of its terms in five minutes on CNN. (This was another surprise to Clinton's people: Carter had brought along a camera crew from the cable news network.)

The officials—including Gore, Lake, and Gallucci—gathered around a TV and watched the live broadcast, stunned and fuming.

They had told Carter, as had President Clinton in their single, some-what chilly conversation, not to negotiate anything. At the same time, Carter did break the deadlock. Kim agreed to stop reprocessing plutonium and to let the international inspectors stay in place. (The inspectors hadn't yet been kicked out, but before Carter's trip, they were about to get the boot.)

Four months later, on October 21, after grueling negotiations, the United States and North Korea signed an accord, called the Agreed Framework, which followed some of Carter's provisions. North Korea renewed its commitment to the Non-Proliferation Treaty and locked up the reactor's fuel rods. In exchange, the United States, with financial backing from South Korea and Japan, agreed to provide fuel oil and two light-water nuclear reactors, a type of reactor that could provide only electricity and was explicitly allowed under the NPT. The Agreed Framework also specified that, upon delivery of the first light-water reactor (the target date was 2003), international agents would begin intrusive inspections of suspected North Korean nuclear sites—not just the one at Yongbyon but others as well. After the second reactor arrived, North Korea would ship its fuel rods out of the country, essentially giving up the ability to build nuclear weapons.

Other articles of the accord called for both sides to "move toward full normalization of political and economic relations." Within three months of its signing, the two countries were to lower trade barriers and install ambassadors in each other's capitals. The United States was also to "provide formal assurances" that it would neither invade nor use—or even threaten to use—nuclear weapons against North Korea.

Initially, North Korea kept its side of the bargain. The same could not be said of the United States. Because the Agreed Framework was not a formal treaty, it did not require Senate ratification. But Congress balked on the financial commitments, as did South Korea. The light-water reactors were never fully funded. Steps toward normalization were never taken, though here, both sides were at fault. In 1996, a North Korean spy submarine shored up on South Korean soil; in reaction, Seoul suspended its share of energy assistance; Pyongyang retaliated with typically inflammatory rhetoric, threatening to turn the South Korean coast into a "sea of fire."

By the middle of 2000, relations started to warm somewhat. Kim Il-sung had died a few months before the signing of the Agreed Framework. Now his son and successor, Kim Jong-il, invited President Clinton to Pyongyang, promising to sign a treaty banning the production and export of long-range missiles. Secretary of State Madeleine Albright and a team of specialists made the advance trip in October.

Kim Jong-il was one of the world's battier leaders. Tales were legion of his egomaniacal extravagance and his weird ambitions. He consumed exotic cuisines and high-end cognacs, while his people starved. A cinephile with a library of some 15,000 movies, he once abducted a notable South Korean director and actress, imprisoned them, then forced them to make films of his own creation, to fulfill his dream of turning Pyongyang into the Hollywood of the Far East. (After eight years, the director and actress escaped.)

Yet, in his negotiations with Albright, Kim appeared serious, rational, and knowledgeable. At one point, fourteen issues remained unresolved, and he sat with Albright and her aides, going over each one, delving into details on those that he wanted to resolve and feigning vagueness on those that he didn't. For example, when Albright asked if he proposed to ban the export of all missiles or just those of long range, he replied that he meant all missiles—and not just missiles, but the technology to develop them.

When Albright returned to Washington, her team stayed behind, working at a frantic pace with their North Korean counterparts, trying to hammer out a deal. But time was running out, and Clinton devoted the final weeks of his second term, futilely as it turned out, to pursuing a peace treaty with the Middle East—the fantasy of every president of the previous quarter-century. The unsettled nature of the 2000 presidential election, with a prolonged recount of ballots in Florida, suspended all other diplomatic activity. Differences were still pending between Albright's team and Kim's over a missile ban. However, as Clinton left the White House, the stage was set for diplomatic progress—and, meanwhile, the fuel rods remained under closely monitored lock and key.

———— ∞∞∞ ————

George W. Bush defeated Al Gore in the race for the presidency after the U.S. Supreme Court halted the recount in Florida. A few days before Bush took office, a half-dozen members of Clinton's national security team crossed the Potomac River to the Northern Virginia home of Colin Powell, the retired general and former JCS chairman who was tapped to be the new secretary of state, a choice widely viewed, and praised, as a sign that Bush might pursue a moderate, internationalist foreign policy. The Clinton team briefed Powell for two hours on the status of the North Korean talks. Halfway into the briefing, Condoleezza Rice, the new national security adviser, showed up, having just flown in from Texas, where she'd been meeting with Bush. Powell had been listening to the briefers with enthusiasm, leaning forward in his chair. Rice was pointedly skeptical, leaning backward.

In early March 2001, barely a month into Bush's term, Kim Dae-jung, South Korea's president, came to Washington for a state visit. On the eve of his arrival, Powell told reporters that, on Korean policy, Bush would pick up where Clinton had left off. After reading this remark in the next morning's newspapers, Rice phoned the secretary of state, on the president's orders, to make clear that this was not going to happen. Powell had to eat his words, later admitting that he had leaned "too forward in my skis." It was the first of many times Powell would find himself out of step with the rest of the Bush team—the lone diplomat in a sea of hard-liners.

If Powell was embarrassed by Bush's stance, Kim Dae-jung was humiliated. KDJ, as Korea-watchers called him, was a new type of South Korean leader, a democratic activist who, during his country's authoritarian period, had spent years in prison for his political beliefs and had run for president promising a "sunshine policy" of opening up relations to the North. During the Clinton years, South Korea's ruling party had been implacably hostile to the North; efforts to hold serious disarmament talks were obstructed at least as much by Seoul's sabotage as by Pyongyang's manipulations. Now South Korea had a leader who could be a partner in negotiations—but the United States had a leader who was uninterested in negotiating.

In Bush's view, articulated openly by his vice president, Dick Cheney, to negotiate with an evil regime was to recognize that regime, legitimize it, and—if the talks led to a treaty—prolong its reign. Bush told a reporter, on the record, "I loathe Kim Jong-il." He held Kim Dae-jung in contempt as a naïf. KDJ had also committed what Bush took as a personal insult: before his Washington trip, he'd met with Russian president Vladimir Putin and issued a joint statement endorsing the preservation of the Anti-Ballistic-Missile Treaty. Everyone knew that Bush placed a high priority on scuttling that treaty, in order to build a comprehensive missile-defense system. So when KDJ arrived in Washington, Bush publicly criticized him and his sunshine policy. He, Cheney, and Secretary of Defense Donald Rumsfeld had already decided not only to isolate North Korea, in the hope that its regime would crumble, but also to ignore South Korea, in the hope that its next election would restore a conservative to power.

Bush turned out to be the naive one. Kim Jong-il survived U.S. pressure, and KDJ was replaced by Roh Moo-hyun, a populist who ran on a campaign that was not only pro-sunshine but anti-American. Relations were further soured by Bush's 2002 State of the Union Address, in which he tagged North Korea, Iran, and Iraq as an "axis of evil."

By this time, the Agreed Framework was unraveling. Even before Clinton left office, signs were clear that the North Koreans were enriching uranium, an alternative way to build an atom bomb. Specifically, they were supplying missile technology to Pakistan, and, in exchange, Pakistan was providing them with the devices to enrich uranium. Abdul Qadeer Khan, a Pakistani nuclear physicist and the father of his country's enriched-uranium program, was hawking the ingredients for such a bomb to various tyrants, and U.S. intelligence agencies noticed that North Korea was shopping for everything on the list. In retrospect, it seemed Kim's scientists had commenced their buying spree in 1997, three years after the Agreed Framework was signed—well after it was clear to them that the United States would not be providing the light-water reactors. Strictly speaking, they weren't violating the Agreed Framework, which banned only the reprocessing of plutonium and said nothing about enriched uranium.* However, in a joint declaration in 1992, North and South Korea had agreed not to "test, manufacture, produce, receive, possess, store, deploy or use nuclear weapons"—any sort of nuclear weapons—and, explicitly, not to "possess nuclear reprocessing and uranium enrichment facilities." And the Agreed Framework stated that North Korea would "consistently take steps to implement" this declaration. Certainly the North Koreans were at least skirting the accord. When Clinton's aides found out about the shopping spree, they expected that when Gore became president, he would confront the North Koreans and tighten the Agreed Framework, maybe promise more economic aid in exchange for the North's abandonment of enriched uranium. Intelligence analysts were divided, and uncertain, over whether Kim was seeking to violate the accord, hedging with a backup plan in case the light-water reactors didn't come through, or building a bargaining chip for more aid.

In any case, by the early fall of 2002, signs of an impending enrichment program were unambiguous. On October 4, James Kelly, the assistant secretary of state for East Asian and Pacific affairs, flew to

---

* One of the U.S. diplomats at these talks, Wendy Sherman, absorbed this lesson twenty years later, when she became President Barack Obama's negotiator in the nuclear talks with Iran. The resulting deal blocked all the paths by which Iran might pursue a bomb, including enriched uranium *and* plutonium.

Pyongyang to confront officials with the evidence. To his surprise, they admitted the charge was true. But then, to the North Koreans' surprise, for the next two weeks the Bush administration kept the meeting—and the evidence—secret. The Senate was debating a resolution to give Bush the authority to go to war against Iraq. The public rationale for war was that Iraq's dictator, Saddam Hussein, possessed weapons of mass destruction. If it was known that North Korea was also making WMDs—and nuclear weapons, at that, not chemical or biological weapons, as was asserted (mistakenly, it turned out) about Saddam—it would have muddied the debate. Some would have asked why Bush saw a need to go to war against Iraq but not against North Korea.

The Senate passed the Iraq war resolution on October 11. The Bush administration publicly revealed what it had known for months about North Korea's enriched-uranium program six days later, on October 17.

On October 20, Bush formally withdrew from the Agreed Framework. He halted oil supplies to North Korea and urged other countries to cut off all economic relations with Pyongyang. The North Koreans, realizing that they'd once again boxed themselves into a corner, decided to replay the crisis of 1994: in late December, they expelled the international inspectors (this time for real—eight years earlier, they'd only threatened to do that), restarted the nuclear reactor at Yongbyon, and unlocked the container holding the fuel rods. On January 10, 2003, they withdrew from the NPT—but also said they would retract the withdrawal, and reverse all their actions, if the United States resumed its obligations under the Agreed Framework, including the signing of a nonaggression pact.

Another sign that Pyongyang was looking for a diplomatic way out appeared the same day, when delegates from its U.N. Mission paid a visit to Bill Richardson, the governor of New Mexico, who had served as U.N. ambassador during the Clinton administration. Richardson had negotiated with North Korea before. As a congressman, he once traveled to Pyongyang to retrieve the body of a constituent whose

Army helicopter had been shot down after drifting across the DMZ. He later arranged the release and return of an American hiker who was arrested as a spy after inadvertently crossing the North Korean border.

Since Jimmy Carter had served as an "unofficial" intermediary to jump-start nuclear talks in 1994, North Korean officials may have inferred that this was the Americans' way of saving face in dealing with out-of-favor regimes—to have middlemen do, behind the scenes, what presidents could not do in public. Richardson was willing to serve as intermediary; during his two days of talks, he stayed in touch with the State Department. But nothing came of the North Koreans' overture. They didn't understand American politics: Bush wasn't going to let a Democrat, much less a former Clinton appointee, handle his diplomacy; and, in any case, he wasn't interested in saving the accord.

On January 13, two days after the Richardson meetings, Jim Kelly tried to keep a line open. At a press conference in Seoul, he signaled that he understood what the North Koreans were doing and that a negotiated settlement was possible. "Once we get beyond nuclear weapons," he told reporters, "there may be opportunities—with the United States, with private investors, with other countries—to help North Korea in the energy area." But Kelly, like Powell two years earlier, was speaking out of turn. No subsequent overtures came from Washington. To the extent there was any debate within the administration, the revelation of North Korea's secret enriched-uranium program strengthened the hands of those opposed to diplomacy in principle.

When their approach to Richardson led nowhere, the North Koreans escalated the pressure. Over the next two weeks, U.S. spy satellites detected trucks pulling up to the site where the fuel rods were stored, then driving away toward the reprocessing facility. When Kim Il-sung *threatened* to take this step in 1994, Clinton warned that it would cross a "red line." When Kim Jong-il actually *did* it in 2003, George W. Bush said and did nothing.

Specialists inside the State Department and the Pentagon were flabbergasted. Once those fuel rods left the storage site, once reprocessing began, once plutonium was manufactured, the strategic situation would change: even if the North Koreans could be lured back to the bargaining table, even if they agreed to drive the fuel rods back to the storage site, no one on the outside could be certain that they'd completely disarmed; no one could ever know if they'd manufactured some plutonium and hidden it in a bunker.

In March, President Bush dispatched several fighter jets, as well as some B-1 and B-52 bombers, to the U.S. Air Force base in Guam, within range of North Korea. The clear intent was to signal a possible impending air strike on the reactor. But it was a feeble threat: by this time, the fuel rods had left the building. Bush made no moves to support, or otherwise prepare for, an air strike; he mobilized no ground or naval forces to deter or beat back North Korean forces if they retaliated to an air strike. Nor did he couple the movement of bombers with any diplomatic offers.

One reason for Bush's inaction, besides the inherent complications of an attack, was his invasion of Iraq, which also got under way in March; it would have been a stretch—in money, matériel, mental focus, and political support—to start preparing for a war in Northeast Asia too. In short, Bush took no military action because he couldn't. And he took no diplomatic action because he didn't want to.

In April, in the flush of the U.S. military's lightning victory over the Iraqi army and the toppling of Saddam Hussein, Secretary of Defense Donald Rumsfeld wrote Bush a memo, calling for "regime change" as a policy toward North Korea. In May, the commander of U.S. Forces in Korea held an officers' conference on how to adapt the tactics of the Iraq War to a possible conflict in his theater. The Pentagon began revising OPLAN 5027, its long-standing war plan against North Korea. In the new version, air strikes—using highly accurate "smart bombs," which proved to be an effective substitute for artillery in Iraq—would take place well before the arrival of U.S. ground forces. Finally, that same month, Bush all but threatened war, saying in a speech, as if he were addressing Kim Jong-il, "You're hungry, and you can't eat plutonium."

The miscalculation was that, though the North Korean people were hungry (a famine in the mid-1990s had killed as many as two million), Kim and the rest of the ruling elite were eating quite well. And since the Kim dynasty had sealed off the country as hermetically as the twenty-first century allowed, he could sustain a crisis far longer than other leaders might.

His father, Kim Il-sung, the founder of the North Korean state, had risen to power through guerrilla warfare—and governed in the same style. North Korea, as he'd put it, was "a shrimp among whales," and both Kims mastered the art of playing their large neighbors off one another, fostering an atmosphere of "drama and catastrophe." In the game of highway chicken, North Korea was the shrewd lunatic who very visibly throws his steering wheel out the window, forcing the other, more responsible driver to veer off the road.

Bush was disinclined to play the game, but even he came to realize he had no choice. In May, he recalled the bombers that he'd sent to Guam, and, finally, opened a diplomatic track, involving the major powers of the region. He sent Jim Kelly to Beijing for preparatory talks. At this meeting, Li Gun, North Korea's experienced deputy foreign minister, announced that his country now had nuclear weapons—he referred to them as a "deterrent"—and said that they would not be dismantled unless the United States dropped its "hostile attitude" toward his country. In Washington, Kelly phrased the statement in a positive light, telling his superiors that the North Koreans had put forth a "bold, new proposal": they would drop their nuclear weapons program if Washington signed a nonaggression pact. But Bush was in no mood, telling one reporter that the North Koreans were "back to the old blackmail game."

This was the Bush-Cheney-Rumsfeld line: as long as the North Koreans were pursuing nuclear weapons, even to sit down with them would be an act of appeasement, succumbing to blackmail, rewarding bad behavior. Cheney once put it this way: "We don't negotiate with evil; we defeat it."

Cheney was the prime mover in all these campaigns for regime change and for the resistance to diplomacy. Those who knew him from his days as secretary of defense, during the presidency of Bush's father, were puzzled by his evolution from conservative but competent manager to blazing ideologue. Some attributed his tectonic shift in views to the 9/11 attacks; others thought the end of the Cold War, leaving America as "the sole superpower," galvanized his imperial ambitions; still others wondered whether his heart attack shortly after the 2000 election—his fourth—might have finally done some slight damage to the flow of oxygen to his brain. Colin Powell, who had worked alongside him in the Pentagon, told friends that Cheney hadn't changed at all: the difference was that, in his former job, he'd had "adult supervision"; now, with George W. ceding him authority on national security matters, he was in charge.

In any case, by August, it was becoming clear that Cheney's efforts to destabilize North Korea were not succeeding. Nor were the North Koreans' efforts to lure the United States into bilateral negotiations. In a compromise, both sides agreed to attend what came to be called "Six-Party Talks," to take place in Beijing, involving the United States, China, Russia, Japan, and the two Koreas. At these talks, the White House allowed Kelly, for the first time, to meet, one on one, with his North Korean counterpart—but only for twenty minutes and only if delegates from the other four powers were in the same room. Kelly was also barred from making any offers or suggesting the possibility of direct negotiations. Even then, he was instructed to begin any private chat with these words: "This is not a negotiating session. This is not an official meeting."

For the previous year and a half, Colin Powell's State Department had favored a diplomatic solution to the Korea crisis, while Donald Rumsfeld's Pentagon and key players in the White House—most fervently, Cheney and his staff—opposed it. The August meeting in Beijing was President Bush's idea of a compromise—but it was a middle path that paved no path at all: he let Kelly talk, but didn't let him say anything meaningful; Kelly went to the table, but had nothing to put on it.

Even so, the bureaucratic warring persisted. Just before the talks took place, John Bolton—the undersecretary of state for arms control, who had been serving as Cheney's mole at Foggy Bottom, letting the vice president know whenever Powell leaned too forward on arms control—gave a speech in which he called North Korea "a hellish nightmare" and Kim Jong-il "a tyrannical dictator." True enough, but not the sort of invective that senior officials tend to blurt out on the eve of a diplomatic session.

Around this time, Charles "Jack" Pritchard, the administration's North Korea envoy, resigned in protest. He told one reporter, "My position was the State Department's envoy for North Korean negotiations, yet we were prohibited from having negotiations. I asked myself, 'What am I doing in government?'"

Bush, Cheney, and Rumsfeld viewed their unwillingness to negotiate as a virtuous contrast to the Clinton administration's keenness for diplomacy. Early on in the Bush term, an NSC memo stated the rationale for a no-talks policy: to preserve "moral clarity."

However, Clinton's Agreed Framework had kept North Korea from acquiring a bomb for nearly a decade. Intelligence officials estimated that, without the accord, North Korea could have built dozens of atom bombs by the time Bush took office—to store as a deterrent, rattle for intimidation, sell to the highest bidder for much needed hard currency, or all three.

In October 2003, the North Koreans announced that they had reprocessed all 8,000 of their fuel rods and had solved the technical problem of converting the plutonium into weapons. Three months later, a private delegation—which included Jack Pritchard and Siegfried Hecker, a former director of the Los Alamos nuclear weapons lab—flew to North Korea for a private tour of the Yongbyon reactor. It was the first time since the crisis began that a Westerner had been inside. Hecker came away convinced that the North Koreans had indeed reprocessed the fuel rods; he saw the plutonium, though he wasn't shown enough to infer whether they'd built any bombs.

On October 9, 2006, the ambiguity was clarified: the North Koreans set off their first nuclear explosive at an underground test site. It was a small explosion, as far as nuclear bombs go: around 1 kiloton; it may have been a partial dud. But it swung the door wide open; North Korea was now a nuclear weapons state.

A year and a half earlier, on May Day 2005, they had successfully fired a ballistic missile into the Sea of Japan, crashing that barrier too and raising the good chance that, sometime in the future, North Korea could put the two triumphs together—they could deploy nuclear-armed missiles.

Soon after the nuclear explosion, Bush got serious about arms control talks with Pyongyang, largely at the urging of Condoleezza Rice, who was now his secretary of state. In the past, Cheney and Rumsfeld would have joined forces to quash such a move, but around this time Bush forced Rumsfeld to resign—for many reasons, most of them having to do with his failed policy in Iraq, which was now consumed by a sectarian civil war and an anti-American insurgency. As a result, Cheney found himself increasingly isolated. In early 2007, Bush let an assistant secretary of state, Christopher Hill, hold bilateral talks with North Korea in Berlin—the sort of talks that he had prohibited back when Kim Jong-il was merely threatening to detonate an atom bomb. Hill and his counterpart even signed a disarmament accord, but it was shot through with so many loopholes as to be meaningless.

The restraints that Bill Clinton had imposed with the Agreed Framework, and had come close to nailing down in the talks on a missile ban, snapped off and blew away, perhaps forever. For the first time in nearly forty years, nuclear proliferation was a front-burner threat.

CHAPTER 10

"Let's Stipulate That This Is All Insane"

When Barack Obama entered the White House at the age of forty-seven, the first black president in the nation's history, he confronted a wall-to-wall disaster zone: two aimless unpopular wars, the worst financial crisis since the Great Depression, and the impending collapse of the auto industry. Yet, beyond dealing with those emergencies and passing a bill for universal health care, he found room on his plate for another grand task: the abolition of nuclear weapons.

He offered it up on April 5, 2009, ten weeks after his inauguration, in his first major speech in a foreign country, during a European Union summit in Prague. "I'm not naïve," he assured the crowd of thousands in Hradcany Square after declaring his ambition. "The goal will not be reached quickly, perhaps not in my lifetime." And, he said, "as long as these weapons exist," he would "maintain a safe, secure and effective arsenal to deter any adversary and guarantee that defense to our allies." But in the meantime, he proclaimed, "the United States will take concrete steps toward a world without nuclear weapons."

The speech didn't come out of nowhere. As an undergraduate at Columbia University, Obama had written a thesis on nuclear disarmament. After winning a seat in the U.S. Senate, just five years before winning the presidency, he nabbed a spot on the Foreign Relations Committee and threw himself into the work; often, as a hearing rambled on beyond its first hour, Obama and the chairman, Richard Lugar, would be the only senators in the room. Lugar, a moderate Republican, almost thirty years Obama's senior, was impressed and took to mentoring the up-and-comer on policy and process.

Lugar had developed a passion for keeping loose nukes locked up. His interest took hold back in 1991, as the Soviet Union was collapsing and some of its consulate officials, whom he'd met in discussions at nuclear arms control talks, came to warn him and Senator Sam Nunn—the ranking Democrat on the Senate Armed Services Committee—that the world was in trouble. The officers guarding the Soviet nuclear stockpile were deserting in droves, leaving fissile materials and even the weapons themselves open to rogue elements and terrorists. The new Russian government, which was broke, needed Western money to pay the guards and Western technicians to build new locks.

Nunn and Lugar joined forces—bipartisan projects were the norm in Congress at the time—to sponsor an amendment to the defense appropriations bill, adding $100 million to help protect Soviet nukes from scavengers, domestic and foreign. "Nunn-Lugar" soon became the trademark for the cause that the amendment was promoting, and, over the next several years, its sponsors traveled frequently to Russia, Ukraine, Kazakhstan, and Belarus—the former Soviet republics where nuclear weapons were based—to witness the dangers, and observe the dismantlement, of missiles, warheads, and bombs.

Prior to all this, Lugar hadn't followed the nuclear debates very closely, and when he was briefed on the basics, he was horrified by the destructiveness of these weapons. On one of his first inspection trips, to the Pervomaisk missile base in Ukraine, he watched an enormous ICBM, capped with multiple warheads, being pulled out of its silo. He asked his hosts if he could go into the tube to see the launch facility. They took the long elevator ride down. The first thing he saw was a guard's desk, and on the wall behind it were photographs of major

American cities. It suddenly occurred to him: those cities had been the targets of that missile. He shivered a little.

After one Foreign Relations hearing in 2005, a few months into his Senate term, Obama asked Lugar if he could go with him on one of these trips. They went that August, on a weeklong tour of nuclear, chemical, and biological weapons sites in the former Soviet republics. It was an eventful trip: Russian border guards detained the senators for three hours at the airport in the Siberian city of Perm, demanding to search their aircraft, which they suspected was a spy plane. Top Kremlin officials, alerted by the U.S. embassy, eventually prevailed upon the guards to let the plane leave for their next stop, in Ukraine, and apologized to the senators. During their holdup, Obama and Lugar discussed the issues, and the politics of the issues, more deeply than they had before.

When he launched his campaign for the White House, Obama talked a bit about nuclear weapons, but, to the extent he discussed foreign policy at all, he focused more on the wars in Iraq and Afghanistan—the need to end the former and to delve more deeply into the latter.

Then, on January 4, 2007, four gray eminences of the national security establishment—Henry Kissinger, George Shultz, William Perry, and Sam Nunn (the "Four Horsemen," they came to be called)—wrote an op-ed for the *Wall Street Journal* titled "A World Free of Nuclear Weapons." Humanity, they wrote, was "on the precipice of a new and dangerous nuclear era," with terrorists and rogue states, such as Iran and North Korea, clamoring to get their hands on a pocketful of bombs. These upstarts hadn't spent years installing the "step-by-step safeguards" that the established nuclear powers had put in place during the Cold War in order "to prevent nuclear accidents, misjudgments or unauthorized launches." As a result, it would be hard, maybe impossible, to replicate the old Soviet-American balance of terror "without dramatically increasing the risk that nuclear weapons will be used." Citing the near-miss effort by Reagan and Gorbachev to eliminate U.S. and Soviet nuclear weapons at Reykjavik (where one of the Four

Horsemen, George Shultz, had been a prodder), the authors urged the next American president to revive that summit's agenda as a "joint enterprise" with the world's other nuclear powers.

With the possible exception of Shultz, none of the authors really foresaw the possibility, or much wanted, a world with zero nuclear weapons; when pressed, they acknowledged preferring that the existing nuclear powers—certainly the United States—retain a few warheads for deterrence. Their intent was to lend theatrical urgency to a series of risk-reducing steps that they viewed as practical for the short term: sharply reducing the number of nuclear weapons, especially the hair-trigger land-based ICBMs; eliminating short-range nuclear weapons situated near tense borders; improving the security of nuclear stockpiles worldwide; halting the production of fissile material; banning nuclear tests; and helping to resolve regional conflicts that could escalate to nuclear war.

Obama saw the *Journal* piece as legitimizing his own views, which might have been dismissed as starry-eyed if he'd expressed them prior to its publication. The following October, Obama would be celebrating the fifth anniversary of the speech that put him on the map—his address, at a rally in his hometown of Chicago, opposing the then-impending invasion of Iraq. ("I don't oppose all wars," he'd famously said at that rally. "What I am opposed to is a dumb war . . . a rash war.") Now he would give another speech, which he hoped would put him over the top in the presidential primaries against the Democratic Party's favorite, Hillary Clinton. The former first lady, now the junior U.S. senator from New York, had voted for the Iraq War, a vote that Obama would cite in his speech as the decisive contrast between them. For he was running not just against Senator Clinton but, more broadly, against "Washington's conventional thinking," the "groupthink that led us to war in Iraq."

While writing the anniversary speech, he told his staff that he did not want simply to criticize the Iraq War and those politicians who'd voted to fund it; he also wanted to present a positive agenda—an example of his policies, which, as he put it in the speech, would "leave the world a better place than our generation has found it." He found the example in his work on loose nukes under Lugar's tutelage and in the Four Horsemen's op-ed in the *Journal*. He began the wind-up toward that portion of the speech with an assurance. "We will not pursue unilateral disarmament," he said. "As long as nuclear weapons exist, we'll retain a strong nuclear deterrent. But," he added, throwing the pitch, "we'll keep our commitment under the Nuclear Non-Proliferation Treaty on the long road toward eliminating nuclear weapons."

Soon after taking office, he and his staff—many of whom had also worked on his campaign—discussed what topic to address at his upcoming speech in Prague. "A world without nuclear weapons," and a pledge to "take concrete steps" toward that goal, seemed a natural choice.

As for those concrete steps, Obama was already in the tangled process of deciding what they would be.

—————∞∞∞—————

Near the start of every president's term since Bill Clinton's, Congress had required the Defense Department to submit a Nuclear Posture Review, a document laying out the rationales behind its policies, deployments, and budgets on nuclear weapons. The bulk of these documents read like boilerplate, but each edition contained a few bold passages that signaled a change by the new administration—though often more in aspiration and attitude than in policy.

In 2002, President George W. Bush's review declared that nuclear weapons "provide credible military options to deter a wide range of threats." It also called for "greater flexibility" in nuclear-attack options and new types of weapons, including earth-penetrating nuclear warheads and very-low-yield battlefield nukes, which could "complement other military capabilities."

Those new weapons never got off the drawing board, much less onto any battlefields, but Obama wanted to make clear that, under his presidency, the United States no longer harbored such goals or entertained such thoughts. Bush and his team had wanted to increase the role of nuclear weapons ("to deter a *wide* range of military threats" and to "*complement*" other military forces); Obama, in his Prague speech, had called for reducing the role of the bomb.

In the journals and seminars of many arms control activists and scholars, one long-proposed way of doing this was to declare a policy of "no-first-use"—a pledge that the United States would never be the first country in a conflict to use nuclear weapons. This would mark a reversal of American policy dating back to the dawn of the nuclear age. Ever since then, military doctrine had stated, and every president had affirmed, that, if an enemy (especially the Soviet Union) attacked the United States or its allies, even if just with conventional weapons, the president reserved the right to respond with nuclear weapons. This was the essence of "extended deterrence" and the "nuclear umbrella"; it was the centerpiece of America's treaty obligations, especially to the allies in NATO. The advocates of no-first-use argued that the Cold War was over, the Soviet Union was gone, the new Russia wasn't going to invade Europe; and if some unforeseen conflict did take place, the new generation of high-tech conventional munitions—the GPS-guided drones and smart bombs, which exploded with pinpoint accuracy—would destroy targets that only nuclear weapons could have leveled in decades past. In short, it was hard to imagine a scenario in which the United States would *need* to use nuclear weapons first—and, given these changes in technology and geopolitics, still harder to imagine an American president *deciding* to use them first. Finally, if the United States, the inventor of the atom bomb and the only country that had ever dropped one in anger, told the world that it no longer found the bomb useful, except to deter an attack by others, then maybe other countries—especially those that hadn't yet built their own bombs—would steer clear of the nuclear genie.

Several of Obama's White House aides were advocates of no-first-use, and, as drafts of the Posture Review circulated among senior and midlevel officials in the national security bureaucracy, these advocates pushed to include a statement that the "*sole* purpose" of nuclear weapons was to deter (or retaliate against) a nuclear attack on the U.S. or its allies. But there were many, in the State Department and the Pentagon, who opposed a no-first-use policy, and they suggested a slight but significant change in wording—a statement that, at most, retaliation against a nuclear attack was the "*primary* purpose" of these weapons.

The most persuasive critic of the no-first-use advocates was Secretary of Defense Robert Gates. At sixty-five, Gates was the oldest of the president's cabinet chiefs; more significant, he was the sole holdover from George W. Bush's cabinet. Obama had asked him to stay on: in part, to co-opt his esteem and credibility; in part because, after a conversation, they both realized they shared a pragmatic bent. Gates had served under nearly every president since Nixon (the one exception being Clinton, during whose two terms he retreated to academia and corporate boards). He'd worked his way up from a lowly CIA analyst to the agency's directorship, with a side stint as deputy national security adviser in the White House of Bush's father, where he polished his skills in bureaucratic politics, especially the craft of how to run a meeting so that most of the participants agreed with his solution to a problem while believing that they'd devised it on their own. Gates was above all a cautious man: as the CIA's deputy director, in the Reagan administration, he'd been the most persistent skeptic of Gorbachev's reforms, railing against—and, fortunately, losing to—George Shultz's pleas to take up the new Soviet leader's call for disarmament. As defense secretary in the final two years of George W. Bush's term, determined to stave off the prospect of another American war against another Muslim nation, Gates stymied Vice President Dick Cheney's push to bomb the nascent nuclear sites in Iran.

This same caution colored his view of no-first-use. In the mid-to-late 1960s, he had been an intelligence officer at an ICBM base, but he never developed a penchant for the nuclear subculture; he didn't quite buy the intricacies of nuclear deterrence theory. He did, however, believe in the basics: he viewed the nuclear standoff as an essentially stabilizing force, which had kept the peace for more than a half-century, through myriad crises; and he saw no point in tampering with what seemed to work.

In the late fall and early winter of 2009, the National Security Council held a few sessions on the subject, some of them including President Obama. Gates rarely spoke at these meetings, choosing his moments shrewdly, to maximize their impact. At one of these moments, he raised three points of caution about upending this longtime policy. First, he wondered why the United States would want to box itself in unilaterally. Second, he warned that the allies would view no-first-use as an abandonment of America's prime security guarantee, a folding up of the nuclear umbrella. His concern wasn't so much the NATO allies—no one was worrying any longer about a Russian invasion of Western Europe—but rather Japan and South Korea, whose leaders were worried about aggression from China and North Korea.

Gates's third point, which he raised in the chillingly even tone that he often mustered to close a deal, was that North Korea and a few other hostile countries possessed biological weapons; intelligence agencies were reporting that Russia had plans to load anthrax in some of the warheads on its SS-18 ICBMs. A large-scale biological attack could kill hundreds of thousands, even millions, of Americans. The United States had given up bio weapons long ago, so it couldn't "retaliate in kind." Certainly any president would at least want to consider responding to such a hideous attack with nuclear weapons, so shouldn't we make that possibility clear to all potential aggressors from the outset—to deter them from contemplating such an attack?

No one in the room offered a rebuttal to this final point. Gates had spelled it out beforehand to James Miller, his deputy undersecretary for nuclear issues. Miller, who had studied nuclear strategy in graduate school at Harvard, came to the Pentagon determined to push for no-first-use as policy, as a way of reducing the role of nuclear weapons and to dissuade other states from going nuclear. But Gates's argument struck him as sound; it made him change his mind.

Obama thought it was crazy for any American president to use nuclear weapons first, under any circumstances. For one thing, given the U.S. military's conventional superiority, it wasn't necessary. For another, he had read enough history to know that the "nuclear taboo," as some called it, was real: the destructiveness of the bomb was too enormous; the risk of escalation to global catastrophe was too high. Still, Obama recognized the distinction between believing in no-first-use and declaring it as national policy, and, in that context, he saw that Gates had a point.

Still, Obama was seeking some way to tell the rest of the world—and his own generals—that he really did mean to reduce the role of nuclear weapons. He had been a professor at the University of Chicago Law School, and so, he put Gates's argument to the grill. Which nations, he asked, are we talking about when we talk about a biological weapons threat? He went through the list—Russia, China, North Korea, Iran, maybe Syria—analyzing which of those countries, if they used biological weapons, might compel a nuclear response, perhaps because no other military response was available. The only ones that stood out, in that sense, were Russia and North Korea. The U.S. already had a well-defined security arrangement—an acknowledged state of mutual deterrence—with Russia. That left North Korea, and the one distinctive thing about North Korea was that, several years earlier, it had withdrawn from the Non-Proliferation Treaty.

Obama suggested this for a policy: the United States will not use, or threaten to use, nuclear weapons against countries that had no nuclear weapons and that were abiding by the NPT.

Neither he nor the others in the room knew or remembered, but thirty years earlier, during Jimmy Carter's presidency, Paul Warnke, director of the Arms Control and Disarmament Agency, and his deputy, Spurgeon Keeny, had come up with the same idea and summarized it in a speech for Secretary of State Cyrus Vance. (A decade before then, back in 1965, Keeny had been staff director of the Gilpatric Committee, which first proposed an international treaty to stop the spread of nuclear weapons.) But the name they gave the idea—"negative security assurances"—was the opposite of catchy, and it went nowhere.

Obama thought his formula might placate the allies while still conveying the message that he was not going to use these weapons except in the direst circumstances. First, his language would not exclude the option of first use against North Korea and possibly Iran, if the mullahs enriched their uranium into weapons. Second, it would further isolate those countries and possibly prod them to change their ways. Third, it supplied another incentive for countries that had signed the NPT to remain compliant.

Gates had no problem with this wording. Jim Miller, who was drafting the Posture Review, still had to resolve the debate over whether second-strike deterrence should be the "sole" or the "primary" purpose of nuclear weapons. Neither fit into Obama's new language. He came up with a compromise: the *"fundamental* role."

Some of the White House staffers weren't pleased with this resolution. Ben Rhodes, one of Obama's closest advisers since early in the campaign and now his communications director for national security affairs, was particularly dismayed. Rhodes had written the Prague speech and, in private meetings, had argued strongly for no-first-use as the centerpiece of a policy to "reduce the role of nuclear weapons." Obama's twist—essentially no-first-use, with a few exceptions—brought the country closer to the Prague agenda but, to his mind, fell short.

While this debate was going on, Ivo Daalder, Obama's new ambassador to NATO, came up with another way to get at the main goal. A former scholar at the Brookings Institution, Daalder had worked on nuclear issues during Obama's campaign and was set to work in the White House until the president offered him the more appealing post overseas. The United States still had 180 nuclear weapons in Western Europe—all of them bombs to be carried by tactical fighter planes—a small fraction of the Cold War peak but far more than could be justified on security grounds; in fact, as almost everyone conceded, the bombs served no military purpose whatsoever. So Daalder suggested cutting the number by half and persuaded the NSC Deputies Committee to take up the proposal. The deputies—the second-tier officials in the various departments who managed day-to-day security matters and teed up big issues for the cabinet secretaries in the Principals Committee—liked the idea. But the Principals did not. Obama's diplomats were in the thick of negotiations with the Russians to update the Strategic Arms Reduction Treaty, which was about to expire, and Hillary Clinton—Obama's erstwhile opponent who was now his secretary of state—thought that unilateral cuts would diminish her bargaining leverage. She and others around the table also feared that such a move would upset the NATO allies; the fact that the weapons had little, if any, military utility only bolstered the case that they were needed to cement the transatlantic political ties. Daalder's idea was dismissed with little discussion.

The question was never brought to Obama personally, but some of the Principals and their aides knew it didn't have to be. One thing that Gates, Clinton, Rhodes, and others were beginning to realize—to their relief or dismay—was that the new president wasn't keen on *unilateral* arms cuts. Like Clinton, he thought they might blunt his leverage in nuclear talks with Russia; and, like Gates, he didn't see what the United States would gain for its trouble. Obama was a genuine intellectual, a purveyor of ideas, a voracious reader of history and philosophy. But his first foray into politics had been as a community organizer on the South Side of Chicago, bringing factions together by finding common ground. Obama had lofty ideals but a pragmatic style. As Rhodes put it to his colleagues, "He paints within the lines."

⸎

The negotiations with Russia, which kept Hillary Clinton and other senior officials from taking Daalder's proposal seriously, were the follow-on talks to START—President George H. W. Bush's Strategic

Arms Reduction Treaty—and, so, were called New START. Like most nuclear arms accords of the previous forty years, it would prove to be as troublesome as it was beneficial.

The talks were emerging as the centerpiece of Obama's policy to "reset" Russian-American relations, which had deteriorated during the eight tense years of George W. Bush's presidency. Obama would have rather focused more on locking up loose nukes—the issue that he'd worked on with Dick Lugar—and halting the spread of nuclear weapons to other countries, especially Iran and North Korea. Having first studied nuclear issues during the Reagan years, the baroque era of the arms race, he saw the abstract calculations of "nuclear exchange" scenarios as an absurd sideshow. But he had no choice but to put the bilateral nuclear game on the front burner: START was set to expire at the end of 2010; maybe the precise balance of nuclear arms wasn't the most important thing to settle in Russian-American relations, but it was important to keep a lid on what might otherwise be an upwardly spiraling arms race, and so he had to wrap up New START before the clock ran out.

Having declared the treaty to be the centerpiece of his reset policy, the prerequisite to progress on other, more vital issues, Obama raised the stakes in getting it ratified by the U.S. Senate. It was a treaty of modest accomplishment—so modest as to be unassailable, by any serious critic, on substantive grounds. But the most consequential critic was Republican senator Jon Kyl, who publicly acknowledged that the treaty was "relatively benign" but told the White House that he would vote it down unless Obama agreed to spend a lot more money on nuclear weapons.

Kyl wasn't just one senator; he was the Senate's Republican Whip, the man responsible for counting and corralling his party's votes. He had also cultivated a reputation, over the previous decade, as the party's leading expert on nuclear weapons, and so his opinion—his vote—on such matters swayed the votes of other, less-informed Republicans. The Democrats held fifty-nine of the Senate's 100 seats, a solid majority;

but motions to ratify a treaty required sixty-seven votes—a two-thirds majority. In other words, Obama needed eight Republicans to vote with him on New START. If Kyl opposed the treaty, those eight would be very hard to come by: the treaty could collapse, and the Russian reset with it.

Obama and Russian president Dmitry Medvedev signed the treaty on April 8, 2010. In May, anticipating Kyl's demands, Obama approved a ten-year, $80 billion program to sustain and revamp the Department of Energy's nuclear weapons complex—the labs and other facilities where plutonium was processed, tritium was stored, and warheads were assembled. This amounted to an increase of $10 billion over President Bush's final budget. Obama also promised to spend $100 billion, over the same ten-year period, to modernize the missiles, bombers, and submarines carrying those warheads.

These concessions seemed to do the trick. On September 16, the Senate Foreign Relations Committee voted, by a margin of 14 to 4, to recommend ratifying the treaty. The motion was favored not just by all of the panel's Democrats but also by three of its seven Republicans. Ratification by the full Senate seemed likely.

Vice President Joe Biden, who well knew the workings of Congress, having spent thirty-five years in the Senate before signing on as Obama's running mate, was convinced that trying to appease Kyl was a waste of time. Shortly after the committee vote, at a meeting in his West Wing office with a few of his staffers, Biden said Kyl would never vote for New START—or any other nuclear arms control deal—no matter how many concessions the president made.

"Here," he said, "I'll prove it to you." He picked up his phone, called Kyl directly, and asked him if there was any way he might be persuaded to vote for the treaty. Kyl said there was not.

But then came the Republicans' power play. Kyl's vote might not have been needed, but he could block a vote from taking place. Obama had hoped to get the treaty ratified by the full Senate before the midterm elections in November, but this now seemed improbable. The

Senate would adjourn on September 29, not quite two weeks after the Foreign Relations Committee voted in favor of the treaty. Kyl was close to Senate minority leader Mitch McConnell, who had long declared that his party's main goal was to make Obama a one-term president. Kyl advised McConnell to make sure that no motion to vote on ratification would come to the floor in that two-week span. The treaty was still holed up by the day of the midterms, which resulted in the triumph of the Tea Party movement, a faction of Republican voters and insurgent candidates who were disgruntled with "big government," which they saw as embodied by Obama's health care plan and his $800 billion economic-stimulus bill. The election dealt the Democrats a "shellacking," in Obama's words. Besides capturing a majority in the House of Representatives, Republicans picked up six seats in the Senate.

The only way Obama could get the treaty ratified now would be to hold a vote before the newly elected Senate convened in January, and the Republican leaders drummed up one excuse after another for holding off action until then.

After a few more rounds of talks with Kyl, Obama tossed in another $5.5 billion for the nuclear weapons complex. At this point, though he wouldn't admit it, Kyl too had a vested interest in seeing New START ratified. Without the lavish nuclear budget, almost no Republicans would vote for New START; but without New START, few Democrats would vote for a lavish nuclear budget—and when it came to normal Senate business, the Democrats still had a majority. Kyl instructed McConnell to schedule the vote before the New Year. It took place on December 22, just before the Christmas break, as one of the session's final acts.

For all of Obama's concessions, Kyl wound up, as Biden predicted, voting against the treaty. But he loosened his grip on his fellow party members, and New START was ratified by a margin of 71 to 26, with thirteen Republicans joining the unanimous bloc of Democrats to vote in favor. (Had the ratification vote been postponed till after the New Year, the treaty probably would have been rejected.)

Obama got the nuclear arms control treaty. Kyl got a down payment on the next round of the nuclear arms race.

⊗≫⊗

With New START behind him, Obama was eager to explore broader realms of cooperative arms control, hoping to persuade Medvedev to help keep Iran and North Korea from building nuclear weapons and to lock up more loose nuclear materials in the former Soviet republics and elsewhere. He succeeded at these efforts, to some extent, for a while.

But Obama also wanted to push ahead with deeper cuts in Russian and American nuclear armaments. The question he faced was how deep the cuts could go, and that meant plowing into the question that previous presidents had asked, with varying degrees of intensity and resolution: how many nuclear weapons did the United States really need—how much was enough, and what did "enough" mean: enough to do what?

Frank Miller had forced this question toward the end of the Cold War. The Joint Chiefs and the generals in Omaha wound up agreeing to 5,888 as the necessary number of U.S. strategic nuclear weapons—a 50 percent cut from before the probe—and then slashing the number further, to 2,200, after the Soviet Union collapsed. George H. W. Bush and Boris Yeltsin set that as the maximum number of weapons that each side could deploy under the Strategic Arms Reduction Treaty. Under the Obama-Medvedev New START, the generals put up no resistance to cutting that number further, to 1,550—and that was without changing George W. Bush's nuclear weapons guidance in the slightest. This absence of a protest suggested that there was still a lot of slack in the nuclear war plan's "requirements"—still a lot of overkill, even after Frank Miller's belt-tightening. With a change in guidance, the numbers might be brought down lower still.

And so Obama ordered a detailed review of the SIOP. The idea was to delve into the nuclear war plan at least as deeply as Miller had—with one difference: this time, the civilians faced little resistance from the four-star general who led what was now called Strategic Command.

The commander was Robert Kehler, and the difference between him and Jack Chain, the general who tried to block Frank Miller's intrusions (and who said he needed ten thousand weapons because he had ten thousand targets), was enormous. They were a vast generation apart: Chain, rising through the ranks as a fighter pilot in Korea and Vietnam; Kehler, twenty years younger, coming up as a missile officer, then as a senior officer in the Air Force's Space Command, and picking up political skills as a legislative liaison in the interim. More relevant, Kehler had served in the Joint Staff's nuclear and chemical directorate when Frank Miller was waging his assault on the SIOP; and so he saw, in greater detail than most of his fellow officers, the full scope of bloat in the nuclear plan and thus in the nuclear arsenal. When he arrived as head of StratCom in 2011, two years into Obama's term, he recognized that, while the bloat had thinned out considerably, there was still a lot of overkill; there was room for deeper cuts.

The civilian official who, for all practical purposes, ran the new SIOP review—who set the agenda, asked most of the questions, issued the challenges, ran the numbers—was Jim Miller (no relation to Frank, though they knew each other), who had played the lead role in drafting the Nuclear Posture Review. In the early to mid-1990s, Jim Miller had worked on the House Armed Services Committee and was picked by its chairman, Les Aspin, to be one of just two staffers—the other was a Republican—to get full briefings on the SIOP. The head of StratCom at the time was General George Lee Butler, who had previously worked on the Joint Staff as director of strategic plans and policy, while Frank Miller did his deep dive. Butler took command at Omaha as the subsequent reforms were being implemented; much of the excess was still in place, and he was appalled, doing little to conceal his disgust while briefing the young House staffer, showing him slide after slide of crowded cities and hollow structures, shaking his head, and gasping, "Can you believe this is a *target*?"

So Kehler and Jim Miller went into Obama's review with a full grasp of the issues and a mutual awareness of what they each knew. Before the first meeting, Miller told the general, "If you say we need more weapons, we'll be skeptical." Kehler understood. He said he'd let Miller know if he and the other civilians were cutting "too close to the bone."

Obama had ordered a "90-day review" of the war plans, but it took much longer. Kehler and a few of his staff traveled to Washington from StratCom headquarters in Omaha every couple of weeks, over a span of four months, to meet with the group of second-tier officials and officers who made up the NSC's Deputies Committee. The sessions, held sometimes in the White House Situation Room, sometimes in the Pentagon, were grueling marathons, Kehler guiding the others through a rundown of all the targets and all the options for attacking them.

At one point, they broke down the review into target categories and sub-categories—for instance, Russian strategic nuclear forces and, within that category, ICBM silos, ICBM launch control centers, and the warheads' storage sites. Even after Frank Miller's reforms, the SIOP was aiming redundant layers of nuclear weapons at all of these targets. So Jim Miller and others around the table asked whether StratCom needed to hit all of the targets or whether hitting just some—say, the silos but not the control center, or the other way around—would do the job.

The SIOP also called for firing two warheads at each of these targets—three at some of the blast-resistant ICBM silos. Was that necessary? Would one less warhead per target be sufficient?

Kehler explained that the existing guidance, signed in the early years of George W. Bush's presidency, specified that those targets be destroyed with very high confidence. To do that, StratCom needed to launch two or three warheads at each, in case one strayed off course or failed to explode. This was an old pattern, dating back to the rancorous rivalries at the first SIOP conference in 1960: high "damage-expectancy" numbers justified a "requirement" for more weapons; more weapons opened a wedge for more targets, and on and on the cycle spiraled. When Kehler was on the Joint Staff, working with Frank Miller on his SIOP Review, he saw that the generals at Omaha had been ratcheting up the cycle in this manner for decades; and when Jim Miller was briefed on the SIOP as a congressional staffer, he saw the same game.

It didn't need to be this way, Kehler told the deputies. If they wanted to change the guidance—to reduce the chance of damaging a target from, say, 90 percent to 75 percent—then he could revise the SIOP, so that it aimed just one weapon at that target instead of two or three, and the excess weapons could be eliminated.

The guidance had been inflating the requirement for weapons in other ways. One day, when Jim Miller was going through the SIOP's list of Russian targets, he found that the latitude and longitude of several targets corresponded to empty fields. It turned out that, according to Air Force Intelligence, these fields were to be used as backup air bases, where Russian bombers could land after dropping their bombs, in case their primary bases had been destroyed. Since the guidance required destroying "secondary bomber bases," the SIOP called for launching several weapons at these empty fields. This was insane. Kehler allowed that the fields were, at the very least, over-targeted.

This led to a deeper debate over just what the point of the arsenal was. If the "sole" or "fundamental" purpose of nuclear weapons was to deter an adversary from launching a nuclear attack on the United States and its allies, then there was plenty of leeway for miscalculation and error; you could pass up a lot of Russian targets, and therefore cut a lot of American weapons, without degrading deterrence. But if you were concerned about what happened if deterrence failed, if nuclear war erupted, then there might be less leeway; and, in that case, you had to figure out what you wanted to do—how you wanted to fight this nuclear war. If you wanted to destroy the enemy's remaining nuclear weapons and other military sites, then you would have less room for error.

Tell me what you want to do, Kehler said to the group on a few occasions. Then we can figure out how many weapons we need.

Much of the ensuing discussion proceeded from Kehler's premises; it played out within the lines that had been drawn in the early days of nuclear strategy, at least in its highly classified forums, beginning with Robert McNamara's adoption of the counterforce doctrine. No one in the decades since had figured out how to translate the theory into practice—how to fight and win a limited nuclear war along military principles. At the same time, even many skeptics figured that they might as well try; if nuclear war came (and during much of the Cold War, many assumed that it would), better to try limiting the damage and ending the war quickly.

A few officials around the table during this latest review dissented from this premise, most outspokenly Vice President Biden's chief adviser on nuclear issues, Jon Wolfsthal. When Biden interviewed him for the job two weeks into Obama's first term, Wolfsthal was up front in his opinions and ambitions: he was a firm advocate of nonproliferation—several years earlier, he'd worked for the Department of Energy as an on-site inspector of the Yongbyon reactor in North Korea—and an equally firm believer in "minimum deterrence." This was the idea that only a small number of nuclear weapons were needed to deter a nuclear attack; that those weapons should be aimed at the enemy's cities, or its main economic resources, because they were what the Russians valued most. Trying to destroy the enemy's military forces, by contrast, would require an enormous arsenal, spark an arms race, and send a futile signal in any case because, once nuclear missiles start flying, escalation to all-out war is all but inevitable. The idea—which had once been enshrined as doctrine by Navy admirals in their battle to stave off Air Force dominance and was still advocated by many arms control activists—had long been out of favor in official circles: most of America's nuclear weapons had really been aimed at military targets all along. But Wolfsthal saw himself as a gadfly and wanted to push for the idea of sharp cuts and minimum deterrence within policymaking circles, at least as a restraint against a revitalized arms race. Biden, who saw his own role as a devil's advocate—a check against groupthink—in President Obama's inner circle, encouraged Wolfsthal to keep pushing.

Wolfsthal was fascinated by the sessions with General Kehler and the national security team: he'd been studying these issues for years but mainly in academic settings, never at such an intricately detailed, or highly classified, level; and he greatly respected Kehler for his intelligence and candor, even if he disagreed with many of his views. But he also found the sessions constraining: he was pleased that the deputies were making headway in finding rationales for cutting the nuclear arsenal, but they were snipping at the margins, not blowing out the core— executing the same old war plan, just more efficiently.

To shake things up, Wolfsthal brought in a fifty-seven-page study, recently published by the Federation of American Scientists, a prominent arms control group, calling for a shift in nuclear war policy to "infrastructure targeting"—threatening to destroy neither the Russians' military sites (the targets of a counterforce strategy) nor their cities (the targets of minimum deterrence in the 1960s) but rather their oil refineries, iron and steel works, aluminum plants, nickel plants, power plants, and transportation hubs. These comprised "the sinews of modern societies," the study's authors observed, and the prospect of their destruction would deter any Kremlin chief—any national leader— from launching a nuclear attack.

Kehler took up the proposal with his best rendition of an open mind—as he'd said at the outset, it was up to the political leaders to decide what to do with nuclear weapons—but it was clear that Wolfsthal's plea was going nowhere. Kehler's staff officers were annoyed that this civilian was messing with the war plan. Midlevel officials from the Pentagon and the State Department waved away Wolfsthal's notion as a nightmare for the allies.

At the start of these sessions, Kehler had suggested that the group focus on what to do if deterrence failed. Once that premise was accepted, the rest—the whole logic of long-standing nuclear policy, with its counterforce strategy and limited options—followed like a row of tumbling dominoes. It was reminiscent (though no one in the room could have known it, since the transcripts of the secret tapes wouldn't be published for a few more years) of President Kennedy's conversation with Robert McNamara and Maxwell Taylor near the end of 1962, when Kennedy mused that "40 missiles" would be enough to deter the Russians—but then allowed that, "as a practical matter, if the deterrent fails and they attack, what we want to do is be firing at their missile sites," and he would need more than forty missiles to do that.

If deterrence failed, would the American president, whoever he or she might be, want some options other than attacking Russia's cities or—as in Wolfsthal's proposal—their "infrastructure targets"? The consensus preferred more options.

After all the paring down of the excess and overkill, Kehler and the other officers in the room agreed that the United States could safely eliminate one third of its nuclear arsenal—that the New START limits of 1,550 warheads could be further reduced to 1,000.

To Jim Miller, this was a good start, but not much more. It meant only that, in the event of a nuclear war, the United States would hit some Russian targets with one warhead instead of two, or two instead of three—it meant that the rubble would bounce one less time.

But then Kehler and the Chiefs added a caveat that would likely nullify even that bit of progress: they would not endorse this reduction unless the Russians cut their arsenal by roughly the same amount in a follow-on treaty to New START. They made the point clearer still in a subsequent conversation with President Obama, saying they would publicly oppose unilateral cuts of this magnitude.

On the basis of the SIOP Review and this strong warning, a group of officers and officials—led by Jim Miller, General Kehler, and Kehler's operations deputy at StratCom, a civilian analyst named Greg Weaver—drafted a classified document guiding the "employment," meaning the use, of nuclear weapons. Its rhetoric was, in one sense, loftier than earlier documents of this sort, in that it expressed, up front, the goal and feasibility of dramatic nuclear arms reductions in the near future. It was also less delusional, in that it made no mention of "prevailing" in a nuclear war or suffering "acceptable losses," which no one had ever defined.

But otherwise, in its recitation of the core principles of nuclear deterrence and nuclear warfighting, the document was much the same as those produced by previous administrations. All three legs of the Triad would be maintained, as would some nuclear weapons in Europe. It called for the United States "to maintain significant counterforce capabilities against potential adversaries." To rub the point in, and to rebut any notion—stemming from rumors or press leaks—that Jon Wolfsthal's proposal had made a dent in official policy, the document stated that the United States "does not rely" on a "'minimum deterrence' strategy."

The guidance did declare that U.S. policy was "to achieve a credible deterrent, with the lowest possible number of nuclear weapons"—but this directive was blunted by its concept of what was "possible." Specifically, it stated that, if America's arsenal was much smaller than Russia's, the disparity "could raise concerns" among the allies "and may not be conducive to maintaining a stable, long-term strategic relationship."

Therefore, though the SIOP Review had concluded that security requirements "would allow" reductions "by up to one-third" from the limits set by New START, the document stated that the Obama administration would be ordering no such cut.

Obama was personally inclined to make those cuts; he understood the logic of the SIOP Review; he saw—he knew from the outset of his presidency, and had assumed before then—that the United States had more nuclear weapons than it needed for any plausible purpose. He proclaimed in a speech in Berlin, in June, the same month that the classified guidance was published, that the United States could "maintain a strong and credible strategic deterrent, while reducing our deployed strategic nuclear weapons by up to one-third."

Around this time, in an NSC meeting to discuss the new nuclear guidance, Obama, at one point, grew impatient with the otherworldliness of the scenarios and calculations. "Let's stipulate that this is all insane," he said. Then he added, "*But . . .*" and proceeded to plunge down the logical rabbit hole. He kept the numbers where they were: in part because he wanted to negotiate deeper cuts with the Russians, who might see no need to reciprocate if he cut his arsenal unilaterally; in part because he knew he would get no support for the move from the Chiefs, the Congress, or anyone in his cabinet. It would be a fight, and the stakes weren't worth the effort: the difference between 1,550 warheads and 1,000 wasn't that huge, especially if 1,000 marked the end of the road—if an insistent cut now precluded deeper cuts in the future.

For several reasons, then, stemming from his pragmatic bent and from his preference for sustainable change that might trigger more change, Obama decided, again, to paint within the lines.

The Defense Department printed its Nuclear Employment Strategy (the administration's new term for what used to be called the Nuclear Weapons Employment Policy) in June 2013, almost two years after President Obama ordered the SIOP Review. That same month, Obama's attention was drawn to a more urgent matter when it came to nuclear weapons: the election of Hassan Rouhani as president of Iran on a platform of political and economic reform. Soon after, Rouhani's Western-leaning foreign minister, Mohammad Javad Zarif, met with John Kerry, Obama's second-term secretary of state. They were the first high-level talks between the two countries since the Islamic Revolution thirty-four years earlier; and Kerry described them as productive and cordial.

In his first campaign for president, Obama had said he'd be willing to hold talks with any dictator, including the leaders of Iran and North Korea, a statement that outraged many in the foreign policy establishment, including his rival, Hillary Clinton. After taking office, he sent out feelers to North Korea, to no effect, but kept trying. In February 2012, two months after the death of the Dear Leader, Kim Jong-il, Obama offered his successor—Kim's twenty-eight-year-old son, Kim

Jong-un—substantial food and energy aid in exchange for a moratorium on testing nuclear devices and missiles. Two months later, North Korea test-fired a rocket, then unleashed the usual barrage of fiery rhetoric, and it was clear that talking with the new Kim was useless. Obama piled on more sanctions, convinced the members of the U.N. Security Council to follow suit, and tried, less successfully, to prod the Chinese government to crack down on its ally to the east. Some called Obama's policy "strategic patience," but he knew the wait for progress would be long.

Iran was working out very differently. Talks between Iran and the P5+1 group—the five permanent members of the Security Council (the United States, Russia, China, Britain, and France) plus Germany—were making slow but substantial progress. After two years of negotiations, they signed a meticulously detailed, 159-page accord with the most intrusive inspection procedures of any nuclear arms control pact in history, blocking all of Iran's possible paths to a nuclear weapon. In exchange for dismantling its nuclear programs, the P5+1 nations would lift economic sanctions that they'd imposed on Iran after discovering its covert uranium enrichment plants, which were illegal under the Non-Proliferation Treaty. (Other sanctions, which the U.N Security Council had passed to penalize Iran for testing ballistic missiles and supporting terrorists, remained in place.)

On August 5, 2015, as part of his campaign to promote the deal against strenuous opposition from the Israeli government (though not most Israeli security officers), from Sunni Arab leaders (who, like the Israeli political leaders, wanted to wage war on the Shiite government of Iran), and from most Republicans in the U.S. Congress (who opposed any diplomatic triumph for the young, black Democratic president), Obama delivered a speech at American University in Washington, D.C., drawing parallels with President Kennedy's speech there fifty-two years earlier. Obama portrayed the Test Ban Treaty, which grew out of that earlier speech, and his own Iran nuclear deal as examples of what Kennedy had called a "practical" and "attainable peace"—a peace "based not on a sudden revolution in human nature but on a gradual evolution in human institutions, on a series of concrete actions and effective agreements"—words that Obama quoted in his own address.

Obama always saw this sort of accord—barring nuclear weapons from a hostile country that was on the verge of building them—as a bigger step toward world peace than some Russian-American nuclear treaty, which might help preserve a balance of power that was steady to begin with. But he also considered it important to keep the Russian-American contest from heating up, to keep that balance from spinning out of whack—and once he refocused his attention on what was happening in that contest, he saw trouble.

First (and this required no special attention, it absorbed Obama's time as much as the talks with Iran), the reset with Russia was short-circuiting and tensions were flaring to levels unseen since the Cold War. Vladimir Putin, the former KGB officer who succeeded Boris Yeltsin as president in 2000, had demoted himself to prime minister in 2008 and was replaced in that year's election by his former deputy, Dmitry Medvedev. It was a stroke of luck for Obama, who entered the White House eight months later, because Medvedev was genuinely keen to reform Russia's economy, reducing its dependence on oil and gas, and reaching out to the West for investment and trade. For a while, Obama's reset policy bore considerable fruit—until Medvedev went too far.

The turning point came in March 2011, when Russia declined to veto a U.S.-sponsored resolution in the United Nations Security Council calling for military intervention in Libya—a move that ended in the ouster and assassination of Russia's ally, Muammar Qaddafi. Putin had been chafing at America's dominance and swagger since the implosion of the Soviet Union, an event that he later decried as "the greatest geopolitical catastrophe" of the twentieth century. He and many others of the old school also shuddered at President Bill Clinton's "enlargement" of the NATO military alliance and its absorption of onetime members of the Warsaw Pact—even the Baltic states abutting Russia's border.

In 2012, Putin—who had never completely ceded control to

Medvedev—ran for president again and won. He and his foreign minister, Sergei Lavrov, were full partners with the United States in the Iran nuclear talks and in imposing sanctions on North Korea; Russian leaders, dating back to Stalin, had always blocked neighbors, even their closest allies, from laying their hands on an atom bomb. But otherwise, Putin began reversing some of Medvedev's more accommodating policies. As the Russian economy revived to some degree, he began rebuilding the military and modernizing his nuclear missiles. In February 2014, he annexed Crimea, which Nikita Khrushchev had given to Ukraine sixty years earlier, and, in August, Russian tank columns and Special Forces rolled into eastern Ukraine.

Obama and several of the NATO allies sent aid to Kiev and imposed sanctions on Moscow. In the larger scheme of Russian-American relations, Obama knew what he had feared for some time—that there would be no follow-on to New START.

The SIOP Review of his first term assumed there would be negotiations toward a treaty; he'd joined his generals in rejecting the idea of unilateral nuclear arms cuts, in part, to retain leverage in those talks— to prod the Russians into cutting their arms too. Now, with his second term as president half-over, Obama felt it was a good time to take a second look at the nuclear issues, to assess what the United States could and should do—how many weapons it needed, whether all three legs of the Triad needed to be upgraded, and whether it should move closer still to a no-first-use policy—on objective grounds of national security, quite apart from what the Russians were doing and what he'd previously promised Congress as part of the deal to ratify New START.

This was the second trouble spot that Obama saw when he came up for air from the fight for the Iran nuclear deal: he realized that Jon Kyl and the other Republican leaders in the Senate had taken him for a ride. Back in 2010, when they threatened to block ratification unless he pledged to modernize the full Triad (and also make a fairly substantial down payment), Obama wrote them a carefully worded letter. He pledged to request funds to "modernize *or* replace" all three legs of the

Triad. He did not regard this as a promise to buy any new weapons. To "modernize" a missile might mean upgrading its software or installing new communications gear. Nor did he—in his letter or any other exchange with Republicans—attach a dollar figure to the pledge.

Now, all of a sudden, the hawks in Congress were rolling out a grand list of new weapons—new ICBMs, bombers, submarines, air-launched cruise missiles, and a few different models of new warheads—carrying a total price tag of $1.3 trillion over the next thirty years. No one had mentioned these weapons back when Obama and Kyl reached their deal: the technical specifications for these weapons hadn't yet been drawn up; no contracts had been issued. Yet the Senate Republicans were saying that Obama had signed on to the whole package, as part of the deal for New START.

Obama was agitated. Even if he were inclined to green-light a new generation of weapons for all three legs of the Triad, the sticker shock would hold him back. Pentagon officials had recently outlined an array of conventional weapons, cyber war programs, and defenses against exotic but plausible threats that needed to be funded in the coming years. Now the generals and their allies in Congress wanted another $1.3 trillion as insurance against nuclear war, which Obama regarded as the least likely threat—and a threat for which the country was already amply prepared.

Here was another reason to revisit the questions that Obama had posed, but ultimately skirted, during his first term as president.

Maintaining the nuclear Triad didn't have to mean preserving the present size of each leg. So the National Security Council considered once again whether the United States needed all of its land-based ICBMs. There were 450 of them—fewer than half the number that the Air Force had kept on alert for decades before the reductions spurred by Frank Miller's SIOP Review and formalized by START, the arms treaty signed by George H. W. Bush and Boris Yeltsin—and each missile held just one warhead. The military had signed on to those reductions; were further cuts really out of bounds?

In the early days of Obama's first term, during the drafting of the Nuclear Posture Review, some on the White House staff proposed getting rid of the ICBMs altogether. These missiles had once been the only nuclear weapons possessing the range, speed, and accuracy to destroy blast-hardened targets, such as Russian or Chinese missile silos, within minutes of launching. But now the Trident II missiles could pose the same threat, and they were loaded on Trident submarines, which roamed beneath the ocean's surface, undetectable—whereas ICBMs sat in fixed silos, which were vulnerable to an adversary's first strike. Secretary Gates, General Kehler, and the Joint Chiefs persuaded Obama that the land-based missiles were useful as a hedge against a technological breakthrough in antisubmarine warfare or in case communications with the subs—inherently a bit tenuous—broke down.

Still, Obama and his staff were skeptical that a hedge required 450 ICBMs. The missile silos were scattered across three widely separated Air Force bases—150 each, in Montana, Wyoming, and North Dakota—and, during his first term, Obama was disposed to shut down one of them. The base in North Dakota also housed a wing of B-52 bombers, so removing just the missiles wouldn't save much money. He asked if the base in Wyoming could be closed before 2012, when he would face reelection. He was told it couldn't be, so he dropped that idea as well: in case he lost, he didn't want to saddle his successor with such a big decision. That left the base in Montana, and the state's Democratic senator, Jon Tester, was waging an uphill battle for reelection. Losing the base would lose Montana a huge chunk of its revenue, so Obama dropped that idea too.

Now, though, in the summer of 2016, approaching the end of his presidency, Obama took another look at the possibilities. On June 6, Ben Rhodes, his longtime adviser, who had written the Prague address, gave a heads-up to the impending second look in a speech to the Arms Control Association. He acknowledged that many in the audience would have liked the president to do more to cut the nuclear arsenal—and then reminded them that his term wasn't over yet. The modernization deal that he'd made with Jon Kyl, Rhodes said, "was put together in a different budget environment, with a different Congress," amid different "expectations about our future arms control efforts." As the president prepared "to hand the baton off to his successor," he would "review" the modernization plans once again.

Obama had bought the arguments that some ICBMs were necessary and that, at some point, they would have to be replaced or modernized. The missiles—Minuteman IIIs—had been in their silos for forty-five years; they, or the systems wired up to their launch sites, were showing signs of alarming decrepitude.

In October 2010, at the base in Wyoming, a whole squadron of Minutemen—fifty nuclear-armed missiles—went dark for an hour, and the officers at Strategic Command didn't tell the president, the secretary of defense, or even the Joint Chiefs of Staff until afterward. Bob Gates feared that terrorists might have gained access to the launch sites. Obama wondered if the incident suggested the missiles might be disabled—or launched—by a cyber attack. (He ordered the National Security Agency to conduct a yearlong investigation, which resulted in an overhaul of the system's software.) In his letter to Senator Kyl, pledging to "replace or modernize" the Triad, this sort of overhaul fell into the category of "modernize," and there might be more work of that sort to do. But now, almost five years later, Obama wondered how long he could stretch out modernizing the missiles before replacing them— and, once they were replaced, whether the nation needed to replace all of them. What adjustments, if any, would the military have to make if there were only 300 ICBMs, or 150, or 50?

He posed the question to Susan Rice, his national security adviser, a former State Department official in Bill Clinton's administration who had been one of Obama's early supporters in his run for the White House and had served as U.N. ambassador in his first term. Rice passed the query on to Ashton Carter, who had recently been confirmed as Obama's fourth secretary of defense.

Carter ignored the message.

Rice phoned him to ask what was going on.

Carter replied that the questions were a waste of time, the issues had been settled, and he wasn't going to deal with them.

Rice, famously intolerant of guff, told him that this was a request from the president and he couldn't brush it off.

Carter agreed to assign some staff to work the problem, but for the final eighteen months of Obama's presidency, he stood out as the main bulwark against any efforts from the White House to meddle with the war plan.

Ash Carter would have once been an unlikely candidate for that distinction. He graduated from Yale with majors in physics and medieval history, followed by a Rhodes Scholarship at Oxford and a postdoc at Rockefeller University. After that, he took a job at the Office of Technology Assessment, a research branch of Congress, where he analyzed mobile basing schemes for the MX missile. Then he moved on to MIT, where he coauthored a critical study of President Reagan's space-based missile defense program; then joined the Harvard faculty, following the path, paved by many physicists from an earlier generation, of applying scientific principles to the pursuit of nuclear arms control.

When Bill Clinton became president and named Congressman Les Aspin, a former McNamara whiz kid, as his secretary of defense, Carter became Aspin's assistant secretary for global strategic affairs. From that post, Carter ran the first Nuclear Posture Review, with an eye toward upending the strategic establishment. In an early draft of the document, he called for eliminating ICBMs and sharply reducing the fleet of bombers—in short, for relying almost entirely on submarine-launched missiles and a strategy of minimum deterrence. The operations chiefs of all three services—a three-star general, a two-star, and a vice admiral—wrote a letter to the director of the Joint Staff, protesting the very existence of the study. When John Deutch, the deputy secretary of defense, heard a briefing of the draft, he stopped it after just a few minutes and ordered the vu-graph slides destroyed.

The Cold War may have been over, but the nuclear Triad was still holy, and memories—dating back to McNamara's time—of young civilians meddling with the magic still set off shudders.

Carter returned to Harvard after one term and wrote a few books and articles on national defense. In Obama's first term, he reentered the Pentagon, rising from undersecretary of defense for acquisition to deputy secretary and finally—after waiting impatiently through the brief tenures of two successors to Robert Gates—ascending to the helm. But by this time, he was a changed man: he'd latched on to the central premises of the nuclear enterprise.

The question of missile modernization came up at a meeting of the National Security Council in the summer of 2016. John Holdren, Obama's science adviser, had devised several ideas for extending the scheduled lifetime of the Minuteman ICBMs and thus delaying the purchase of new missiles. Jon Wolfsthal, now Obama's chief arms control staffer, revived the idea of doing away with land-based ICBMs, this time with a twist—proposing to put more MIRV warheads on the submarine-launched missiles, in order to maintain the same total number of nuclear weapons.

Carter and some of the military officers in the room were annoyed: to them, the staff was playing games. Besides, ICBMs were fairly cheap to buy and maintain, especially compared with submarines, which everyone supported replacing at some point, since subs were invulnerable to a first strike and, therefore, a stable deterrent to war.

Wolfsthal had suggested, through Susan Rice, that Obama issue a memo, stating what he wanted to do before the NSC took up the question. But Rice, very much reflecting Obama's view, insisted on putting the issue through the normal process. And in this process, the Principals Committee—the interagency group of cabinet secretaries and military chiefs—predictably rejected the idea of reducing, much less eliminating, the ICBM force.

—⊷∞∞⊶—

The rehashing of no-first-use was more rancorous still. Right out of the box, Ash Carter tried to cut off all discussion. This was a dangerous idea, he proclaimed. The allies relied on the nuclear option for their security; the Japanese were especially nervous about the notion, given their proximity to China and North Korea.

John Holdren disagreed. He and Carter had been colleagues at Harvard, fellow physicists and public policy scholars who had ambled down the career path of scientists pitching for nuclear arms control, though Holdren—a decade older than Carter—had never veered off course. Holdren told the room that he and Ash had argued about no-first-use for twenty years. To his mind, it was simply not credible that the United States would launch nuclear weapons in response to a conventional or biological attack. For one thing, there really was a nuclear taboo, and we weren't going to be the ones to cross that line. For another, we didn't need to cross that line, as we could repel any nonnuclear attack with modern conventional arms.

Carter snapped back, red-faced, yelling. Obama stepped in, telling the combatants to calm down. "We're all friends here," he said in his preternaturally cool tone.

Holdren added his own calming words: "We're all physicists here."

Ernest Moniz, the secretary of energy, a nuclear physicist and former chairman of the physics department at MIT, turned to Holdren, a plasma physicist, and scoffed, "You're *sort of* a physicist."

Obama laughed. "Is this nerd-shaming?" he asked.

At its core, Obama sympathized with Holdren's side of the argument; he thought the whole debate was as absurd as this exchange. He turned to General Joseph Dunford, the chairman of the Joint Chiefs of Staff, and asked whether he could imagine any president ordering the first use of nuclear weapons—whether he could imagine *advising* a president to use nuclear weapons first in a conflict.

The way Obama framed the question put Dunford in a spot: to say he could imagine such a thing would be tantamount to disagreeing with the president in front of the cabinet. But Obama also knew that, as a four-star general in the Marine Corps, which hadn't fielded nuclear weapons in decades and had never possessed long-range nuclear weapons, Dunford had no deep attachment to this branch of warfare. And so, the general said, No, he couldn't imagine such a thing.

But Obama also knew that this wasn't quite the same thing as endorsing a formal declaration of no-first-use, and he didn't ask the chairman where he stood on that question. In any case, Wolfsthal and Holdren were outflanked. Carter, Moniz, and John Kerry opposed changing policy. Moniz had played a crucial role in negotiating the Iran nuclear deal, but half of his department's budget went to the U.S. nuclear weapons enterprise, and, in various forums, he vigorously protected its interests. He was also concerned about giving the Russians any room to think they could get away with an act of aggression. Kerry was concerned about the allies, and even the champions of no-first-use conceded the concern was serious, particularly among the Asian allies. Soon after the meeting, the *Wall Street Journal* reported, based on a leak, that Obama was contemplating a no-first-use policy. The article prompted panicked phone calls from the Japanese and South Korean foreign ministers.

In Obama's mind, no-first-use was the commonsense reality, but he understood it was also, still, the third rail of nuclear deterrence politics: it set off too many shocks and jitters to be discussed out loud, much less enshrined as policy.

———— ∞ ————

In the late summer, toward the tail end of these second takes on the nuclear questions, the National Security Council held a war game that probed a still more fundamental question, so provocative that it had never been asked in such a high-level forum: Are there circumstances in which the United States should not use nuclear weapons even in response to an adversary's *nuclear* attack?

The game didn't start out asking that question. U.S. intelligence agencies had recently reported that the Russians were modernizing their nuclear arsenal, including their tactical nuclear weapons—short-range missiles, artillery rockets, even nuclear torpedoes and depth charges. The United States had junked these sorts of weapons in the 1980s and 1990s, finding them unnecessary and dangerous, but the Russians—who already had 2,000 tactical nukes in Europe—were building more. Their officers had written doctrinal manuals spelling out scenarios in which these weapons might be used on the battlefield; and in military exercises, they'd simulated using them in just those ways. These exercises began with NATO invading Russian territory; Russia fires a very low-yield nuclear weapon to stave off the attack; the NATO armies, fearing escalation to all-out war, halt their invasion. The Russians referred to this tactic as "escalate to de-escalate"—they escalate the conflict in order to compel NATO to back down.

Avril Haines, Obama's deputy national security adviser, had come across these intelligence reports in her previous job as deputy director of the Central Intelligence Agency. Among Obama's national security aides, Haines had the most unusual background. Born and raised on the Upper East Side of Manhattan, she was a lawyer with a degree in theoretical physics, a pilot's license, and a brown belt from an elite judo institute in Japan. She was the first woman to hold the number-two jobs at either the NSC or the CIA, and she made little mention of the fact that she'd attained both.

Haines called a Deputies Meeting of the NSC to play a game testing how the United States might act in an "escalate to de-escalate" scenario—testing whether Russia's new nuclear strategy might thwart America's ability to project power in the region. The scenario started out a bit differently: the Russians invade one of the Baltic countries; NATO fights back effectively; to reverse the tide, Russia fires a low-yield nuclear weapon at the NATO troops or at a base in Germany where drones, combat planes, and smart bombs were deployed. The question: What do U.S. decision makers do next?

Initially, the generals in the room—Paul Selva, the vice chairman of the Joint Chiefs, and Philip Breedlove, the allied commander in

Europe—steered the discussion toward operational issues: how many of which nuclear weapons should be launched at what targets?

Then Colin Kahl, Vice President Biden's national security adviser, raised his hand. Kahl wasn't a specialist on nuclear matters; in Obama's first term, he'd worked in the Pentagon as the chief civilian official on Middle East affairs, and before then, he'd taught at Georgetown University's School of Foreign Service. But Kahl thought the generals were missing the big picture. The minute the Russians drop a nuclear bomb, he said, we would face a world-defining moment—the first time an atom bomb had been used since 1945. It would be an opportunity to rally the entire world against Russia. If we restricted our response to conventional combat and diplomatic ventures, we could isolate and weaken the Russian leaders, policies, and military forces. However, if we responded by shooting off some nukes of our own, we would forfeit that advantage and, more than that, normalize the use of nuclear weapons.

Breedlove seemed confused. He understood the debate over whether the United States should be the first to use nuclear weapons in response to a conventional attack; but it seemed perverse to consider using conventional weapons in response to a nuclear attack.

Still, after a few hours of discussion, examining Kahl's broader political challenge, NATO's conventional military strength, the puzzle of which targets to hit with nuclear weapons, and whether a nuclear response would end the war any sooner or more successfully than a conventional response, a consensus formed in the room—among the civilians and, though with mixed feelings, the military officers—that, at least as a first step, the United States should respond with conventional military operations.

A month later, the NSC's Principals Committee—the group of cabinet secretaries and military chiefs, chaired by Susan Rice—played the same game, to a different outcome. The session began the same way as the Deputies meeting. The generals discussed operational details. Then a civilian challenged the premise that they should respond with nuclear weapons at all. In this case, the challenger was Adam Szubin, the acting undersecretary of the treasury, sitting in for his boss. Szubin's specialty was counterterrorism and other national security matters, most of which involved blocking financial transactions and imposing sanctions. If the Russians used nuclear weapons, Szubin said, we could rally the entire globe against them—with sanctions, shutdowns, trade blockades, travel bans: the impact would be more devastating than any tit-for-tat nuclear response.

Ash Carter fired back with the same temper that he'd unleashed against John Holdren in the meeting on no-first-use. It was *crucial* to meet a nuclear attack with a nuclear response, the allies would *expect* us to do this, and if we didn't, that would be *disastrous* for NATO, the end of *all* our alliances, the end of America's *credibility* worldwide.

General Dunford agreed with Carter, though in a more measured tone. So did Ernest Moniz, the energy secretary. Antony Blinken, the deputy secretary of state, sitting in for John Kerry, was undecided, saying he saw the logic on both sides.

The question then turned back to operational matters, specifically: where to aim the nuclear response? Someone suggested Kaliningrad, but it was noted that Kaliningrad was part of Russia; if the United States hit it with nuclear weapons, Russia might fire back at the United States. As for aiming a few nuclear weapons at the Baltics, to hit the Russian invaders, well, the bombs would also kill a lot of Baltic—which is to say, allied—civilians. Finally, the generals settled on firing a few nuclear weapons at the former Soviet republic of Belarus, even though, in the game, it had played no role in Russia's incursion into the Baltics or in the nuclear strike.

The game didn't last beyond the first two moves. The majority of officials agreed with Carter that the crucial point was to demonstrate America's will and ability to uphold the alliance and retaliate in kind. The military purpose of the retaliation seemed not to matter.

When Avril Haines heard that the Principals had ended the game by using nuclear weapons, even knowing that doing so wouldn't do anything to win or halt the war, she suggested printing up T-shirts reading, "Deputies should run the world."

— ∞ —

In this season of second looks, Avril Haines, Jon Wolfsthal, and Ben Rhodes asked Obama if he would like to make a speech—perhaps his Farewell Address—assessing the status of the Prague agenda, his pledge at the start of his presidency to take "concrete steps toward a world without nuclear weapons." Such an address could also serve to tee up the issues of the reviews on nuclear policy—the reexaminations of no-first-use and modernization—for his successor, who seemed certain to be the Democratic candidate, Hillary Clinton.

Then came the election and the shocker: Clinton lost to Donald Trump. It was uncertain whether Clinton would have taken the second looks seriously, in any event; as secretary of state in Obama's first term, she'd sided with Bob Gates and the generals on almost every issue. But with Trump in the White House, the chances of change dropped to near zero. And, for a Farewell Speech, Obama now had much larger hopes to rekindle—not least concerning the future of American democracy.

Still, the White House staffers wanted to put some of the reassessment on the public record, so the speech that they'd started to draft for Obama was passed instead to Vice President Biden, who delivered it on January 11, nine days before the end of their term, at the Carnegie Endowment for International Peace.

The speech celebrated those aspects of the Prague agenda that he and Obama had fulfilled: New START, the Iran nuclear deal, and additional steps to lock up loose nukes. And then came this assertion:

> Given our non-nuclear capabilities and the nature of today's threats, it's hard to envision a plausible scenario in which the first use of nuclear weapons by the United States would be necessary—or make sense. President Obama and I are confident

we can deter—and defend ourselves, and our Allies, against—non-nuclear threats through other means. The next administration will put forward its own policies. But, seven years after the Nuclear Posture Review, the President and I strongly believe we have made enough progress that deterring—and, if necessary, retaliating against—a nuclear attack should be the sole purpose of the U.S. nuclear arsenal.

Obama read and approved the speech in advance. He had always believed the line about "sole purpose"—he had never strayed from the view that no president, in his or her right mind, would use nuclear weapons except in response to a nuclear attack. He saw the merits of the opposition's arguments just enough to hold back from declaring no-first-use as U.S. policy or declaring second-strike deterrence to be "the sole purpose" of nuclear weapons. Now, though, he let Biden, who had floated trial balloons on a number of issues through the eight years of his presidency, hoist this one in clear view. It was good to get his true thoughts on the record. The next administration, as the speech noted, would "put forward its own policies."

CHAPTER 11

"Fire and Fury"

S oon after George H. W. Bush was elected president, in November 1988, Donald Trump put out the word that he would like to be the chief U.S. negotiator at the Strategic Arms Reduction Talks. No one took the notion seriously. Trump was famous, mainly from the gossip columns of the New York tabloids, as a self-promoting real estate magnate with a frenetic nightlife. Two weeks into his term, Bush nominated Richard Burt, who had served as assistant secretary of state for politico-military affairs and as ambassador to West Germany.

Not long after, Trump ran into Burt at a Manhattan reception, introduced himself, and offered some advice on how to get a "terrific deal" at the arms talks.

Burt feigned interest.

Trump, who was also known as the author of a ghostwritten best-selling book called *The Art of the Deal*, leaned in and shared his magic. Arrive late at the first session, he told Burt. Walk up to the main guy on the Russian side of the table, stick your finger in his chest, and say, "Fuck you!"

Just over two years later, in July 1991, Burt managed to get a treaty signed, reducing each side's nuclear arsenals by one third, without following Trump's suggestion. That same month, Trump filed for bankruptcy—his third, this one on his Taj Mahal hotel-casino in Atlantic City.

And yet, a quarter-century later, through an unlikely convergence of events, including a successful reality-television show, an alienated electorate, a poorly run campaign by his Democratic opponent, Hillary Clinton, and some help on social media from WikiLeaks and the Kremlin, Donald Trump took the oath of office as president of the United States.

He hadn't changed a bit: still boastful, querulous, preposterously self-confident, even in realms far out of his element—including the realm of nuclear weapons. Several times, during his presidential campaign and his tenure in the White House, Trump claimed expertise on the subject, stemming from his late uncle, Dr. John Trump, an engineering professor at MIT, who had worked on radar during World War II and later designed X-ray generators for cancer therapy. "I used to discuss nuclear with him all the time," Trump claimed.

The depths of the new president's cluelessness were most thoroughly unveiled on July 20, at a meeting in the Tank—the Joint Chiefs' conference room on the third floor of the Pentagon—where the top brass gave him a slideshow-briefing on America's military strength and operations throughout the world. His secretary of defense, James Mattis, a retired Marine four-star general, had proposed the briefing to Gary Cohn, the White House economic adviser, who welcomed the opportunity. Both men, along with several other officials, were disturbed by just how little Trump understood about the role of diplomacy and the world economy in shaping American power. A survey of the international situation—the role of troops abroad, the importance of allies, the balance of power, the array of threats and opportunities—might do him good.

Trump, Cohn, and some of the other White House staffers crossed the Potomac at ten o'clock on the designated morning. Mattis, Secretary of State Rex Tillerson, and General Joseph Dunford, the chairman of the Joint Chiefs, delivered separate portions of the briefing. Trump grew noticeably impatient, as did his chief strategist, Steve Bannon, who despised the whole roomful of "globalists"—his expletive for the denizens of the "swamp" that he and Trump had said they would drain in their term of office. During the question period, both of them spewed complaints, asking why we weren't winning in Afghanistan, why we still needed to support those freeloaders in NATO, what was so important about keeping troops in South Korea.

The big-gulp moment came when one of Dunford's aides displayed a chart showing the dramatic reduction in American and Russian nuclear weapons over the decades. It was presented as a success story about arms control, stability, and the declining dependence on weapons of catastrophic destruction.

But Trump viewed the chart from a different perspective, telling the group that he wanted *more* nuclear weapons. He pointed to the graph's peak year, 1969, when the United States had 32,000. (Most of them were tactical weapons—short-range missiles, artillery shells, or bombs based on naval warships—that had long ago been dismantled, to the military's relief.) Trump asked why he didn't have that many weapons now.

Mattis and Tillerson talked him down, noting the legal restrictions, the practical obstacles, the enormous cost, and the fact that the roughly 2,500 nuclear weapons in the active U.S. arsenal today were better suited to perform their missions than the much larger force of a half-century earlier.

After a few more raucous exchanges, Trump and his entourage left the room. Seconds later, Tillerson sighed and said, under his breath but loudly enough for many who'd stayed behind to hear, that the president of the United States was a "fucking moron."

Trump seemed to have grasped, momentarily, why the nation didn't need 30,000 nuclear weapons. But a few weeks later, at a meeting in the Oval Office with his national security adviser, Lieutenant General H. R. McMaster, Trump brought up that chart again. McMaster hadn't been at the session in the Tank, due to a family obligation, but he knew the arguments well enough. As long as we have enough nuclear weapons to inflict unacceptable damage on our adversaries, we're fine, he assured the president. If we build too many weapons, our enemies might think we were amassing a first-strike capability, which, in a crisis, might prompt them to launch a preemptive strike against us.

Again, Trump seemed to understand. But a month or so later, he asked, still again, why he couldn't have a nuclear arsenal as big as what previous presidents had.

———— ∞∞∞ ————

Trump's cavalier attitude toward nuclear weapons raised eyebrows and rang alarm bells, because it looked as if his words might spill over into actions. Trump was eager to get out of Obama's Iran nuclear deal—against the advice of all his advisers, who argued that it at least reduced the chance of another war with another Muslim nation in the Middle East. And he was directly, swaggeringly, threatening to go to war against North Korea.

In 2016, North Korea had test-launched twelve ballistic missiles, half of them successfully, and detonated two nuclear devices. On the campaign trail, Trump said that he would persuade Chinese president Xi Jinping to overthrow Kim Jong-un's regime. In April 2017, shortly before his first meeting with Xi, Kim launched three more missiles. Trump warned, "If China is not going to solve North Korea, we will." In June, after realizing that China was not so willing or able to take care of the problem, Trump admitted that his original plan "has not worked out"—thus implying, as he'd stated before, that he would "solve North Korea" his way.

On the Fourth of July, in what he called an Independence Day "gift to American bastards," Kim launched a missile that, had it followed a different flight path, could have hit the West Coast of the United States. Three weeks later, he followed up with tests of another potential ICBM as well as four short-range missiles, which landed in the Sea of Japan.

On August 8, ten days after those tests, Trump told reporters outside the clubhouse of his golf course in Bedminster, New Jersey, "North

Korea best not make any more threats to the United States," or else "they will be met with fire and fury like the world has never seen." Kim Jong-un, he said, "has been very threatening, beyond a normal state, and, as I said, they will be met with fire, fury and, frankly, power, the likes of which the world has never seen before"—repeating the line, almost word for word, as if he'd rehearsed it after being told that this was how President Harry Truman described the effects of the atomic bomb that leveled Hiroshima.

It was a message far different from America's policies of deterrence dating back to President Eisenhower. Trump wasn't saying that he would rain fire and fury on North Korea, should Kim dare to launch an attack on the United States or its allies. He was saying that he would attack North Korea if Kim were merely to "make any more threats." Nor was Trump saying that he would launch a preemptive strike, responding to warnings that North Korea was about to attack. Rather, Trump was threatening to launch a *preventive* strike, to prevent North Korea from so much as developing the *ability* to attack the United States.

Five days later, H. R. McMaster said on a Sunday news show that "classical deterrence theory" did not apply to Kim Jong-un because he'd committed "unspeakable brutality" against his own people and imprisoned or murdered anyone who seemed to oppose his regime, including members of his own family. This was an odd statement: monstrous behavior for the sake of self-preservation was a clear sign that deterrence theory—the idea that a threat to an adversary's survival will deter him from aggression—very much did apply to Kim. (Two months later, the CIA's top Korea analyst would say at an agency-sponsored conference that Kim was a "very rational actor" who "wants what all authoritarian rulers want"—to "rule for a very long time and die peacefully in his own bed." For that reason, the analyst said, in a tacit rebuke to McMaster, Kim had "no interest in going toe to toe" with the U.S. military.) Still, if McMaster believed what he said, and if Trump believed it too, the implication was that, once North Korea built a nuclear-armed missile that could attack the United States,

Trump might well launch a preventive attack. If deterrence didn't work on Kim, Trump would have no other choice.

On September 19, Trump went further, using his address before the United Nations General Assembly to berate Kim as "Rocket Man" (in later speeches and tweets, he expanded the putdown to "Little Rocket Man"), adding that, if America were "forced to defend itself or its allies," it would "have no choice but to totally destroy North Korea." This was another departure from U.S. deterrence policy, which no longer threatened to annihilate entire populations—especially one, like North Korea's, enslaved by a dictatorial regime and in no way accountable for its actions.

Kim answered the taunt in a press release, denouncing Trump as a "mentally deranged U.S. dotard." This was standard rhetoric for Kim and his predecessors, but never had any Western leader dipped to the same level of crudeness. To an extent unseen in sixty-four years, millions of people shook in fear that—as a result of miscommunication, out-of-control escalation, or deliberate provocation—war might actually erupt on the Korean Peninsula.

Some of the worriers worked in the Trump administration. By the time of the U.N. speech, the Joint Chiefs of Staff and the officers of U.S. Pacific Command had devised a concrete plan for attacking North Korea. Previous war plans for the region had assumed that North Korea would start the war with an invasion or some other act of aggression against South Korea or Japan. The Trump-ordered plan assumed the United States would strike the first blow.

It was a plan covering what officers call "the full array of military options," different options for different scenarios—including, ultimately, if necessary, a nuclear option. The scenarios began with North Korea *preparing* to launch a missile. If intelligence indicated that the missile was armed with a nuclear warhead, one set of actions would be recommended; if the missile was headed toward Japan, the plan would suggest a different set of actions; if it was headed toward the United States, a different set still.

Under the plan, the first phase of the U.S. attack was to strike the launch pad with Army Tactical Missiles, known as ATACMs—ballistic missiles tipped with highly accurate conventional munitions, deployed on U.S. Army bases in South Korea, having sufficient range to hit targets throughout North Korea. Under this scenario, if the North Koreans hadn't yet launched their missile, the ATACM would destroy it on the launch pad; if they had launched the missile, the ATACM would hit the launch pad anyway, demonstrating what the United States was willing to do—and possibly injuring or killing some of the North Korean leaders, maybe even Kim himself, who often observed missile tests in person. (Assassinating foreign leaders was banned by law, but a loophole allowed killing someone as "collateral damage"—the by-product of an attack on a military target.)

Some on the White House staff believed, or at least hoped out loud in private conversations, that the North Koreans would not retaliate: the strike would have been too small, too clearly confined to one target, for them to expand the confrontation; Kim and his entourage would be so shocked by the strike—by the sheer, unprecedented act of an American attack—that they would have to step back. When vague details about the plan were leaked to the press, it became known as the "bloody nose" plan—the idea being that a single punch would make Kim wobble and bring the fight to an end: a politico-military TKO.

But military officers, including those who wrote the plan, were not so confident that Kim would simply reel. They thought it more likely that he would retaliate, against South Korea or Japan, possibly against American military units in either or both of those countries—forcing the president to hit back, and so the conflict would spiral upward, eventually escalating to all-out war.

The Joint Staff's OPLAN—the long-standing, regularly updated operational plan for a large-scale conflict in the region—contained an option to launch nuclear weapons at eighty targets, mostly military and leadership sites, across North Korea. The OPLAN was not the starting point for the plan that Trump ordered; the new plan laid out a series of more limited strikes, with several stages of escalation, which, at some point, might force Kim to alter his calculus and back down. But the officers had no illusions that they knew where Kim's cracking point was; most of them figured he probably *wouldn't* crack. The OPLAN was what would be put in motion if the Trump-ordered plan didn't produce the desired effects. So the military commanders and the Joint Chiefs urged the president to take no action unless and until he was ready to go the full distance, H-bombs included.

When a reporter asked Mattis if there were military options that the U.S. could take without putting South Korea at risk, he replied, "Yes, there are, but I will not go into details." The telling point was that he did not claim the options were realistic.

At first, Mattis ignored the request from the White House to work up a new war plan. The request came early on in Trump's term, after intelligence revealed that the North Koreans were about to test an intercontinental ballistic missile. Mattis wasn't keen on preventive war; nor was he confident that the first blow in such a war would be the final blow. He'd read the war plans on the shelf, and he'd seen—just as his predecessors under Presidents Carter, Clinton, Obama, and the two Bushes had seen—that, if the North Koreans retaliated (and there was every reason to think they would), hundreds of thousands, maybe millions, of civilians would die in South Korea and Japan, including American citizens in Seoul and elsewhere, who couldn't be evacuated quickly enough. In short, Mattis didn't think there were any good military options in Korea, and he didn't want to foster the illusion that there were.

Mattis's resistance infuriated McMaster, who was Trump's point man on the task. The two officers did not get along. As the president's national security adviser, McMaster thought he should be regarded as an equal by the secretary of defense, but he felt that Mattis treated him the way a four-star general treats a three-star—as a subordinate. McMaster too had been a decorated wartime commander—the leader of

a tank squadron in the first Gulf War, a master counterinsurgency tac-
tician in the Iraq War—but he never commanded a unit larger than an
armored cavalry regiment, which consisted of about 3,500 troops. By
contrast, Mattis had been commander-in-chief of U.S. Central Command, overseeing 200,000 personnel from all the services in military
operations across the Middle East, North Africa, and South Asia. Mattis had also been senior military adviser to a secretary of defense, while
McMaster had no prior Washington experience.

Finally, McMaster, who did not retire from the Army before taking his White House job (contrary to the urgings of friends and colleagues), felt an obligation to salute the president's orders—to serve
his agenda and provide him with options to accomplish it. He dispar-
aged the entourage around Mattis—"sycophants," he privately called
them—who saw their job as, in their own behind-the-scenes character-
izations, protecting the nation from Donald Trump.

In the end, McMaster got his—and Trump's—way. Mattis could
slow-roll his disobedience for only so long. Before the end of spring, a
new war plan was in place. Once written, it wasn't stuffed inside a dusty
vault; it was rehearsed at all levels of command. And there were times
when the top officials and officers thought they might have to play out
the plan for real.

Starting on March 6 and continuing through November 29, every
time the North Koreans launched a ballistic missile—fifteen launches
in all, involving twenty-two missiles—the National Military Command Center, inside the Pentagon, coordinated a "national event"
conference call with the relevant four-star generals, including the
chairman of the Joint Chiefs of Staff and the commanders of Strategic
Command, Pacific Command, Northern Command, and U.S. Forces
Korea. Early warning radars, installed in South Korea, detected the
launch—and usually preparations for the launch—in real time. The
officers were plugged into the conference call within a few minutes of
the alert.

General John Hyten, the commander of StratCom, had stepped

up the rehearsals of these conference calls since arriving at the Omaha headquarters the previous November, toward the end of Obama's presidency. The conference calls in 2017 had an air of urgency, not only because they weren't drills, but also because, until a North Korean missile was launched, and sometimes not until it touched down, the American generals did not know for sure whether it carried a warhead—didn't know whether the launch was a test or the onset of an attack.

On at least five of those fifteen occasions, when a different type of missile was launched (for instance, a missile with three stages, suggesting it might be an ICBM) or when it seemed headed toward Japan, the National Military Command Center brought cabinet secretaries into the conference call—Mattis, McMaster, Tillerson, and sometimes Secretary of the Treasury Steven Mnuchin.

The crises never got to the point where Trump was called in; by the time when he might have been, the nature of the launch—the fact that it was a test—had been established. But if these officers and officials had decided to take military action, Mattis possessed the legal authority to fire ATACMs at the North Korean launch site—to take the first step in what he and others thought would probably spiral into a major war. And starting with North Korea's missile launch in March, its second launch of the year, the ATACMs were moved into position and kept in a constant state of readiness.

On two occasions, just after the North Koreans launched their missile, Mattis ordered the U.S. commander in South Korea to fire an ATACM—not at the launch pad or at any other target inside North Korea, but rather into the Sea of Japan, along a path running parallel to the North-South Korean border. On those two occasions, South Korean officers, who were brought into the consultations, fired Hyunmoo-2 missiles—their version of ATACMs—at the same time, along a similar path. The South Koreans fired their missiles on three additional occasions when Mattis decided not to.

Both of the ATACM firings took place between June and early August—before Trump's bellicose remarks of August 8. In other words, when Trump threatened to inflame North Korea in "fire and fury like the world has never seen," he wasn't pulling words out of thin air. The war plan that he'd ordered was in place. The U.S. military had launched "demonstration attacks," using the same missiles that it would fire in the first round of the war. On the inside, just as much as on the outside, the fear of war had foundation.

There was another reason for nervousness about war. On October 11, while appearing on his favorite Fox News show, hosted by Sean Hannity, Trump said, "We have missiles that can knock out a missile in the air ninety-seven percent of the time, and if you can send two of them, it's going to get knocked down."

No one knew where Trump got this figure. Not even the most fervid supporter of the U.S. missile defense program would have made such an extravagant claim. The most recent report by the Pentagon's Office of Testing and Evaluation concluded that the program had demonstrated "a limited capability" to defend against "small numbers" of medium- to intermediate-range missiles and only "a fair capability" against short-range missiles. The one system designed to shoot down intercontinental missiles, aimed at the United States, had worked in only ten out of nineteen tries.

But if Trump believed what he was saying, he might believe that he could get away with launching an attack on Kim's regime, basking in the unfounded confidence that, if Rocket Man fired back, America's missile defenses would work miracles.

———— ⬗ ————

Amid this spiraling war rhetoric, the draft of a new Nuclear Posture Review was leaked to the press. The document declared, as a "bedrock truth," that nuclear weapons play "a critical role" in deterring not only a nuclear attack but other kinds of aggression too—an explicit reversal of the Obama review, which asserted that deterring a nuclear attack was the "fundamental" (if not quite the "sole") purpose of nuclear weapons. The Trump administration's Posture Review also called for "a flexible, tailored nuclear deterrent strategy," in which all the military services and combatant commands would "plan, train, and exercise to integrate U.S. nuclear and non-nuclear forces." And, although the authors denied that this was intended to enable "nuclear war-fighting," that was precisely what it did.

Finally, the document laid out plans "to replace" the current Triad of strategic weapons with new nuclear-armed ICBMs, submarines, bombers, and cruise missiles. These plans were said to "affirm" programs "initiated during the previous administration," though in fact they marked a major expansion. (Obama had pledged to "modernize *or* replace" the current Triad of nuclear weapons, leaving open the question of whether new weapons were necessary or whether simply modifying existing ones would be adequate.)

Many commentators linked the language of the review to Trump's rants against North Korea as part and parcel of the same phenomenon—a reckless, headlong gallop by the current president to the brink of nuclear war and possibly beyond. But Trump had nothing to do with the Nuclear Posture Review; it was written almost entirely inside the Pentagon, as previous reviews had been, with still less direction or input than usual from the White House.

The new review reflected a resurgence of the nuclear establishment, a decades-long style of thinking, which Obama had tried, but not quite managed, to push aside. But the timing of this revival, its convergence with the rise of Trump, put a dangerous new spin on the game.

At the start of his term, it was far from inevitable that Trump would usher in such a revival. In fact, it seemed as if the opposite might occur.

Trump chose Jim Mattis as his secretary of defense because he'd heard that Mattis's nickname, as a Marine commander, was "Mad Dog." Trump thought that America wasn't winning wars because the people in charge were too soft. To him, wars were about killing bad guys; therefore, a general named Mad Dog would pour the heat on mercilessly. At one rally during the transition between the election and inauguration, Trump announced that "Mad Dog Mattis" would be his

defense secretary—prompting whoops and cheers from the crowd—
and boasted that he was loading his cabinet with "the greatest killers."

He was surprised, then, to learn that Mattis opposed torture as a
way to get detainees to talk, telling Trump that, in his experience, he
could eke out more information with "a pack of cigarettes and a couple of beers." Mattis, it turned out, was a soldier-scholar, an intellectual
bachelor with a library of some 7,000 volumes, who, while in combat,
carried a copy of Marcus Aurelius's *Meditations* in his rucksack. Mattis
had famously told his troops in Iraq, "Be polite, be professional, but
have a plan to kill everybody you meet." The key, though, was that he
believed the directive's first clause was as important as the second. He
was fine with turning up the violence in the thick of combat; but, like
most modern generals, he was loath to start a war that couldn't be won
or wasn't necessary.

As a Marine, he hadn't thought much about nuclear weapons; the
Corps had rid itself of nukes decades before he entered its ranks. But
after retiring from the military in 2013, he took a visiting fellowship
at Stanford University's Hoover Institution, where he came under the
tutelage of Bill Perry and George Shultz, the former secretaries of defense and state, respectively, who had coauthored the "Four Horsemen"
op-ed in the *Wall Street Journal*, calling for a world without nuclear
weapons. Mattis wasn't inclined to go that far, but he was open to per-
suasion that the nuclear arsenal could be substantially cut.

In January 2015, Mattis testified before the Senate Armed Services
Committee and raised questions about a wide range of national security issues, including nuclear weapons. "Do they serve solely to deter
nuclear war?" he asked. "If so, we should say so, and the resulting clarity
will help determine the number we need." Another question he posed:
"Is it time to reduce the Triad to a Dyad, removing the land-based missiles? This would reduce the false-alarm danger."

Mattis was raising questions, not answering them, but his leanings
were clear. They were so clear that, the week before Trump's inauguration, eight of the previous nine commanders of U.S. strategic nuclear

forces signed a letter to the *Wall Street Journal*, urging the retention and upgrading of all three legs of the Triad as vital for national security. (The one commander who didn't sign the letter was General George Lee Butler, who had been so appalled by the excesses revealed in Frank Miller's SIOP Review that, not long after retiring, he publicly called for the gradual elimination of not only the ICBMs but all nuclear weapons.)

On January 27, one week after his inauguration, Trump signed a memo to Mattis, ordering an updated Nuclear Posture Review. Over the next five months, Mattis toured the nuclear weapons complex—missile silos, bomber bases, submarine pens, and, of course, StratCom headquarters, where he got the full SIOP briefing. It didn't take long for him to absorb the arguments for retaining the Triad, including the land-based missiles. Most of the arguments had been around for decades, ever since the unplanned creation of three types of nuclear weapons—corresponding to the three branches of the armed forces—had transmogrified into strategic doctrine, then dogma.* The three legs of the Triad, the arguments went, would complicate an enemy attack and provide a hedge against technical mishaps or unexpected vulnerabilities.

But Mattis also heard two new arguments. One was floated by retired General Bob Kehler, the former head of StratCom who had helped Obama's security team plumb the nuclear war plan and who had been the main author of the letter to the *Wall Street Journal* defending the Triad. Kehler pointed out that, since President George

---

* Initially, the Army was going to build ICBMs, but the Air Force, which already had the bombers, won the contract to build the missiles. The Army was instead given the anti-ballistic-missile projects (which never took off) and already had the ground-launched tactical nuclear weapons in Europe and South Korea (which were eventually all dismantled). Over time, Army soldiers joined Marines in their indifference, at best, toward nukes.

H. W. Bush's unilateral initiatives, none of America's bombers had been on runway alert and few were loaded with nuclear bombs. If there were a nuclear war, it would probably be preceded by spiraling tensions, which would give the president time to put the planes on alert—though it was possible he wouldn't take that step, knowing it might escalate tensions. In any case, on a day-to-day basis, the United States already had a dyad; eliminating the ICBMs would leave just one leg, the submarines, and if some technological breakthrough made the submarines vulnerable, the entire nuclear arsenal would be obsolete. Kehler's argument—which he had outlined to a few previous defense secretaries from his perch at StratCom—had appeal to senior officials whose jobs swayed them toward extreme caution about security.

The second argument, which had germinated inside the Pentagon's Joint Staff, was known as the "sponge theory." The idea was that, without the ICBMs, there would be only five "strategic" targets in the continental United States—three bomber bases (in North Dakota, Missouri, and Louisiana) and two submarine ports (in Bangor, Washington, and Kings Bay, Georgia). The Russians could launch an attack on those five targets with just one or two MIRV'ed missiles—and, in a crisis they might think they could pull it off. StratCom would be left with only the half-dozen or so submarines at sea; and the president might not launch their missiles, knowing that if he did, the Russians could strike back with much more. On the other hand, the theory continued, if the U.S. kept its 400 ICBMs, the Russians would have to fire at least 400 (probably more like 800) warheads to destroy them—and that would constitute, by any measure, a "major attack." Any American president would have to retaliate, and the certainty of that prospect would deter the Russians from attacking in the first place.

During his tour of the nuclear sites, Mattis stayed in touch now and then with Bill Perry, his former mentor on these matters. During one of their phone conversations, Mattis asked him about the sponge theory. Perry had never heard the argument before, and it took him a while to process its logic. In the 1970s, when Perry was the Pentagon's chief scientist, hawks had warned that the Soviets might launch 2,000 nuclear warheads, in order to destroy the 1,000 ICBMs that the U.S. had at the time, on the premise that the president wouldn't retaliate because this was a "limited" attack and because, if he did, the Soviets would strike again. Now people very similar to the hawks of forty years before were arguing that the Russians would not launch warheads against 400 ICBMs because the president would see that as a *large* attack. To Perry, the two positions—mutually exclusive, across generations—had one thing in common: they were both contrived to justify the perpetuation of land-based missiles. Perry objected to three other aspects of the theory. First, even if there were something to the logic, 400 ICBMs seemed excessive; a couple dozen would probably serve as a sufficiently daunting sponge. Second, whatever the scenario, the U.S. would still have more than 1,000 warheads on submarines at sea; no Russian leader could casually assume that the American president wouldn't launch them. Finally, Perry dismissed the premise that the Russians would be eager, however desperate the circumstances, to launch a nuclear first strike at the United States.

Mattis, however, found the theory compelling—enough so to dissuade him from getting rid of land-based missiles. As for cutting the number of those missiles, his aides offered two arguments against that idea. First, Obama had left the White House with 400 ICBMs in place, and there was no appetite to go below what some in the Joint Staff were cleverly calling "the Obama program of record." Second, as Obama himself had reasoned, there would be no strategic gain, and plenty of political resistance, to ordering cuts of this sort unilaterally.

By midsummer, Mattis was phoning Perry less and less frequently. Perry sighed that his friend and former assistant had "gone over to the dark side," succumbing to the "nuclear mafia."

This wasn't entirely true, yet. Mattis still harbored doubts about some of their notions. Unlike conventional warfare, which he'd studied and fought, learning lessons from his books and from his experiences on the battlefield, there were no chronicles, no empirical evidence, of how a nuclear war might unfold. He wanted to check the conclusions that he was tentatively reaching.

So he assembled a group of seven longtime experts—he called them the "Graybeards"—to hash out ideas with him. It was not a balanced group. Five of them were retired four-star officers, including four former StratCom commanders—Bob Kehler, Kevin Chilton, Larry Welch (all Air Force generals), and Henry Chiles (a Navy admiral). The other two were civilians. One was Rose Gottemoeller, the deputy secretary general of NATO and Obama's New START negotiator, who had met Mattis when the two were at Stanford. The other civilian was Frank Miller.

Miller had met Mattis when he was a colonel in the Pentagon, and the two continued to talk from time to time. In the final years of the Cold War, Miller had done more than any single official in history to revise the nuclear war plan, pushing the officers in Omaha to cut the number of nuclear weapons by half and then, as the Soviet Union dissolved, by another three fifths. But he was not a disarmer for its own sake. He firmly believed in the value of "limited nuclear options." His main motive in slashing the arsenal and reshaping the SIOP was to make limited options more limited and more feasible.

After leaving government in 2005, Miller became a defense consultant, remaining very much an insider on several classified projects. Midway into Barack Obama's presidency, he saw the intelligence reports that the Russians were modernizing their tactical nuclear weapons and publishing new doctrinal documents spelling out the "escalate to de-escalate" strategy, which envisioned staving off a NATO invasion by firing a small number of low-yield nuclear weapons, which they hoped would compel NATO to back down. He also noticed that certain Russian military units were rehearsing this strategy in exercises.

This was the scenario that the National Security Council had tested in a war game toward the end of Obama's presidency, except that the game began with the Russians attacking a Baltic nation and resorting to nuclear weapons when they found themselves overwhelmed by

NATO's conventional counterattack. The deputies concluded that the United States should push ahead with its superior conventional arms and not respond with nukes. The Principals—the cabinet secretaries—concluded that the U.S. had to meet a nuclear attack with a nuclear response, in order to preserve the credibility of American "extended deterrence."

Miller hadn't heard about this game. But he did note that Obama had talked about "reducing the role of nuclear weapons in national-security policy"—while the Russian military seemed to be doing the opposite.

In any case, Miller was puzzled. The United States had junked tactical nuclear weapons long ago, for good reason. Why were the Russians reviving theirs? He figured that they must be detecting some weak spot in the U.S. deterrent, a gap that their new low-yield nukes could exploit. Back in the late 1970s, Miller had worked on NATO nuclear issues in the State Department and the Pentagon. This was when the Soviets were building SS-20 missiles, which could hit targets in Western Europe from launch pads inside the USSR. The U.S. had lots of nuclear weapons in Western Europe at the time, but none of them had the range to hit the USSR. To retaliate against an SS-20 attack, the president would have to launch weapons from the United States—which could prompt the Soviets to fire back at American territory, and that prospect might deter the president from retaliating at all. (It was a reprise of the old French concern: "Would the president risk New York for Paris?") German strategists especially talked about a "gap in the escalation spectrum." In order to fill that gap, President Carter was pressured, and finally agreed, to build new weapons—the Pershing II ballistic missile and the Ground-Launched Cruise Missile—which could hit Soviet targets from bases in Western Europe.

All these years later, Miller still believed that, for every move the Russians made in the nuclear arms competition, the United States needed to make a credible blocking move. The Pershing IIs and GLCMs were needed to counter the SS-20. Now, he thought, the U.S.

needed something to block the advantage that the Russians seemed to think they could gain from their new low-yield weapons.

This was the problem weighing most heavily on Miller's mind when Mattis asked him to join the Graybeards. The group wound up meeting three times—on June 20, August 15, and November 1—in the secretary's conference room on the third floor of the Pentagon, usually with Mattis in attendance, along with his deputy, some of the Chiefs, and a few of the civilian and military staffers who were assembling the Nuclear Posture Review.

The first two sessions consisted mainly of introductions, presentations, and only quick snatches of discussion about controversies that would be taken up later. Mattis did make two noteworthy remarks at the August meeting. The first concerned reports of Trump's tirade at the July 20 briefing in the Tank, where he angrily asked why the military couldn't build back the 30,000 nuclear weapons that it had in the late 1960s. Mattis told the group not to worry, there was not going to be a nuclear arms buildup. As secretary of defense, he had no intention of expanding the arsenal; he would make that point explicitly in the Nuclear Posture Review, and he would highlight it personally to the president.

Second, Mattis invited the Graybeards to take part, if they desired, in the process of drafting the Posture Review. Miller, ever the bureaucratic operator, was the only one in the group who took Mattis up on the offer. Over the next few months, he came to the Pentagon once a week to meet with the directors of the review's working group, to discuss the draft, and to advance his views.

At the third and final Graybeards session, on November 1, Miller pressed those views hard, arguing for the urgency of the "escalate to de-escalate" threat and for what he and some of the staffers had come to view as a solution—an American low-yield nuclear warhead to match the Russians': specifically a modification of the warhead on some of the Trident II submarine-launched ballistic missiles.

Initially, none of the other Graybeards, and few of the officials in the room, were keen on the idea. Larry Welch, one of the retired generals, who'd commanded SAC in the mid-1980s, saw no point in the tit-for-tat exchanges that Miller envisioned.

"When they go low, we go high," Welch said, in a play on the phrase coined by Michelle Obama, the former first lady, to describe how Democrats should respond to the Republicans' rhetorical assaults during the recent presidential election.

Miller, who had known Welch for years, was nonplussed. Was Welch advocating massive retaliation? We could already go high, so why were the Russians spending so much money on nuclear weapons, unless they thought that the threat to go high—to retaliate with high-yield nukes—wouldn't deter them?

At this point, Kevin Chilton, another of the retired StratCom commanders, started whistling "Off We Go into the Wild Blue Yonder." He told Miller that this low-yield Trident II warhead would be a *strategic* weapon. If the Russians saw it launched from a Trident submarine and hurtling their way, they would view it as a strategic attack—maybe the first volley of a much larger attack—and respond accordingly. If you wanted to send a message, an air-launched cruise missile, fired from a single bomber, would do it more clearly. (The cruise missile was also a strategic weapon; the fact that Welch and Chilton were both retired Air Force officers may have colored their views toward a Navy weapon.)

Mattis leapt in and, picking up on these points, raised a larger question. "Does anybody here believe nuclear war can be controlled?" he asked.

Everyone in the room, including Miller and the generals, shook their heads no, except for Elbridge Colby, the deputy undersecretary of defense for strategy and, as it happened, grandson of former CIA director William Colby. A denizen of various think tank panels and government commissions over the past decade, but new to the Pentagon and fairly low on its totem pole, Colby raised his hand and, after being recognized, said, "Mr. Secretary, strategic thinkers of my generation do think there are opportunities to limit nuclear conflict," adding that the side which prepares for the possibility of limited conflict has an advantage over the side that doesn't.

Mattis's eyes seemed to glaze over, but General Dunford, the JCS chairman, rephrased what he saw as Colby's point—that it didn't matter whether *we* think nuclear war can be controlled; what mattered was whether *the Russians* think it can be. Miller followed through on that point, contending that the Russians did think they could control nuclear war (why else would they be building all those tactical nuclear weapons?) and that, therefore, we had to convince them that they couldn't.

At this point, Rose Gottemoeller, the NATO deputy and former arms control negotiator, spoke up through a remote link from Brussels and challenged the whole premise of the debate. From what she'd read in CIA and State Department intelligence reports, Miller was misinterpreting Russian strategy. First, the Russian officers who wrote the new doctrine, and who tested it in exercises, had said explicitly that they would use nuclear weapons—would "escalate to de-escalate"—only if NATO invaded their territory, only if the Russian republic was endangered. Second, their renewed focus on tactical nuclear weapons was driven by fear of America's superiority in highly accurate long-range conventional weapons. *We* had created a "gap in the escalation spectrum," and they were trying to fill it with tactical nuclear weapons. Yes, they had a lot of them—about 2,000, in various forms—but a half-century earlier, *we* had fielded an even larger number of tactical nuclear weapons in Europe to counter the Soviet Union's conventional superiority. What the Russians were doing now gave them no new capability—nothing that required us to build a new type of nuclear weapon. Instead, Gottemoeller said, we should "declare victory" in this competition and stay focused on maintaining NATO's conventional strength, which is where our advantage lay.

Miller countered with a broadside slam. Don't pay attention to what the Russians say about what they're doing. They've violated nearly every arms control accord they've signed—and here, Miller recited the list of breaches: the Intermediate-Range Nuclear Forces

Treaty, the Biological Weapons Convention, the Chemical Weapons Convention, a half-dozen more—some of them trivial or technical, but violations nonetheless. It was a list that Miller had run down countless times in speeches and congressional testimony. It didn't quite pertain to Gottemoeller's point or to the generals' hesitation about deploying a new low-yield weapon; and Gottemoeller noted that the Russians were in full compliance on New START, the treaty most relevant to this discussion. But Miller's theme—that the Russians were cheats and liars, that Putin was a sneaky bastard longing for the Soviet empire—resonated in the room. Beyond that, the solution he put forth—the low-yield Trident II warhead—didn't violate any treaties and cost almost nothing. And given the scenario that Miller had spun, the Navy would need to modify just a few dozen of its warheads to a low-yield version.

In this light, Miller was trying to shift the question from "Why produce these weapons?" to "Why *not*?"

Gottemoeller's objections were hardly radical. The previous March, in hearings before the House Armed Services Committee, General Hyten, the head of StratCom, was asked whether he needed new low-yield nuclear weapons to deal with the Russians' "escalate to de-escalate" threat. Hyten replied that his arsenal, as it stood, had "a number of capabilities" that would provide the president with "a variety of options to respond to any number of threats." He went further a few weeks later, at a speech to military reporters, assuring them that he was "very comfortable with the flexibility of our response options." At the same House hearing, General Paul Selva, vice chairman of the JCS, noted, in answer to the same question, that the U.S. already had nuclear-capable aircraft in Europe, fitted with low-yield bombs, which would also "deter the Russians from escalating to nuclear warfare" if they found themselves losing a conventional war.

Nonetheless, in the end, Miller won the debate, in part because he helped write the document. The Nuclear Posture Review, which the Defense Department published in January 2018, described plans to "modify a small number" of existing Trident II warheads to "provide a low-yield option." It also called for "expanding flexible U.S. nuclear options," including "low-yield options," in order to preserve "credible deterrence against regional aggression"—citing, in particular, Russia's growing arsenal of low-yield tactical nuclear weapons.

The generals read the document, saluted, and got on board. In March, at a hearing before the Senate Armed Services Committee, General Hyten reversed his earlier stance and endorsed the Posture Review's call for a low-yield warhead, saying, "We felt strongly that we needed another delivery option." He added that, if the Russians fired a low-yield warhead at a NATO ally and the United States lacked low-yield warheads of its own, the president would face a choice of "surrender or suicide." In separate hearings, Mattis too invoked this dilemma—"surrender or suicide"—to justify the low-yield warhead.

Both Mattis and Hyten cited Henry Kissinger as having coined the phrase. Kissinger may have had a point when he wrote (and Nixon uttered) those words back in 1969, when the SIOP—SAC's nuclear war plan—called for firing thousands of nuclear missiles at the Soviet Union, China, and Eastern Europe in response to a small-scale attack. But it was a stretch to paint such a stark picture nearly a half-century later, when, even without a low-yield Trident II warhead, the president could choose from a wide range of small-scale options—with which General Hyten had pronounced himself "very comfortable" just a year earlier. The irony was that this wide array of options existed in large part because of the SIOP Review, in the late 1980s, led by Frank Miller.

The nuclear age was entering another phase of abstraction. How many "options" were necessary to deter a nuclear attack? Was the balance of power as delicate as these scenarios portrayed it to be? Was Putin, or any other leader, so keen to find an opening, some gap in the escalation spectrum, that allowed him to launch a nuclear attack—that made nuclear war seem more tempting than an alternative course of action? And if he was disposed to play the extremely refined form of limited nuclear war that this scenario laid out, how would he know that the American low-yield nuclear warhead was, in fact, low-yield?

The language of this discourse also obscured the fact that the "low-yield" Trident II warhead wasn't, in the scheme of world history, so low. In fact, it would wreak more destruction than most people alive had ever witnessed from a single explosion. The conventional bombs that leveled buildings in Iraq, Afghanistan, and elsewhere in the first two decades of the twenty-first century had the explosive power of 2,000 *pounds* of TNT. The low-yield Trident II warhead would explode with the blast power of 8 *kilotons*—meaning 8,000 tons, or 16,000,000 pounds—plus the heat, smoke, and radiation that would spread like toxic wildfire.*

In July 2018, Frank Miller appeared on a panel at the Aspen Security Forum, in Aspen, Colorado, to discuss nuclear deterrence in the twenty-first century. After he spelled out his case for a low-yield Trident II, the panel's moderator, Michael Gordon, a longtime defense reporter for the *New York Times* and the *Wall Street Journal*, raised a question.

"Just to put a little specificity here," Gordon asked, "what is a low-yield Trident's yield, approximate?"

"Single digits," Miller replied.

"Digits of what?" Gordon asked.

"Well, kilotons," Miller answered.

"OK, so it's like the size of the Hiroshima bomb," said Gordon, who'd studied history and knew that the Hiroshima bomb had a yield of about 12 kilotons.

---

* Like all hydrogen bombs, the standard Trident II warhead was designed to detonate in two stages: the "primary" (a fission weapon similar to the bombs dropped in 1945), which triggers the "secondary" (the fusion implosion). The secondary is what boosts the explosive power of the weapon, which in the case of the Trident II amounts to 150 kilotons. The primary, by itself, would release a much smaller blast—about 8 kilotons.

"Well," Miller said, a bit annoyed, "if you want to be pejorative, you can say that."

"I'm not being pejorative," Gordon said. "I'm just saying . . . this is not like a firecracker."

⎯⎯⎯∞⎯⎯⎯

When Jim Mattis went up on Capitol Hill to request funding for the low-yield Trident II, he was met with apprehension. Not because of the cost—the price tag for modifying a few dozen warheads was $65 million, a pittance in a defense budget exceeding $700 *billion*. Nor were many lawmakers concerned about this new weapon per se. Rather, they were concerned about the man who had the power to launch it.

Arms control advocates had long argued that low-yield nuclear weapons were destabilizing because they lowered the threshold between conventional and nuclear war. They seemed to be—they were designed to be—more usable as weapons of war, and, therefore, some president, in a crisis, might feel more tempted to use them. The human factor was key: some presidents might resist the temptation; others might risk all.

Donald Trump wasn't the first president who inspired mistrust on this score. In 2003, after the invasion of Iraq, some Air Force generals proposed building a new low-yield nuclear warhead that burrowed underground before exploding, seeing it as an ideal weapon for killing some future Saddam Hussein in his bunker. But many on the House and Senate Armed Services Committees did not trust President George W. Bush with such a weapon, so they tacked on an amendment to that year's defense budget, prohibiting the "testing, acquisition, or deployment of a low-yield nuclear weapon"—and barring the Department of Energy from even conducting research or development for such a weapon—without the advance approval of Congress.

Now, fifteen years later, Mattis was running into similar problems with Trump. It wasn't the first time he'd heard this concern.

On October 30, two and a half months after Trump's "fire and fury" fusillade at North Korea, Senator Edward Markey—a Massachusetts Democrat, the fourth-longest-serving member of Congress (mainly in the House), and a firm advocate of nuclear arms reduction—sat on the dais of the Foreign Relations Committee, listening to Mattis and Rex Tillerson testify at a hearing on whether the president needed new congressional authorization to use military force against terrorists around the world.

When his turn came to ask questions, Markey expanded the inquiry. Could Trump launch a nuclear first strike, he asked, without consulting any members of Congress?

Mattis hesitated, called the question "hypothetical," and noted that the process for launching nuclear weapons was "extremely rigorous." When Markey repeated the question, Mattis allowed that he could imagine the president ordering a first strike if an adversary was seen "preparing" to launch an attack and if the threat was "imminent." Tillerson added that no president had forsworn first use as an option and that the policy had "served us for seventy years."

None of this was news to Markey. He was long aware of the president's exclusive power to destroy the planet. At the start of Trump's term, he had drafted a bill to prohibit a nuclear first strike without congressional consent. But few of Markey's colleagues, even those on the Senate Foreign Relations Committee, knew just how unchecked the president's powers on this front were.

Among those senators was Bob Corker, the committee's Republican chairman. Corker, a businessman from Tennessee, was deeply conservative, but he was also agitated by stories he'd been hearing about Trump's mental state. Recently Corker had made a stir by tweeting that the White House was like an "adult day care center" and telling a reporter that Trump's reckless threats toward other countries were paving a "path to World War III." After the hearing, with the Mattis-Markey exchange in mind, Corker told his staff that he was "riled up" by the issue of nuclear command-control and wanted to hold a separate hearing on the subject as soon as possible—"something real sober," as he put it, "pointing out that the President has the power to basically destroy the world."

The hearing was held just two weeks later, on November 14. In the interim, the Congressional Research Service prepared a memo, noting, among other facts, that it would be the first hearing on the subject in forty-one years.

In his opening statement, the committee's ranking Democrat, Benjamin Cardin of Maryland, said that he didn't usually get questions about foreign policy at town hall meetings, but ever since Trump's warning to North Korea, a lot of constituents had been asking, "Can the President really order a nuclear attack without any controls?"

The committee staff had assembled three witnesses—one retired four-star general, one Democrat, and one Republican. The first to testify was the general—Robert Kehler, the former StratCom commander who had guided President Obama's security team through the SIOP and, just before Trump's inauguration, had signed the letter to the *Wall Street Journal* calling for the retention of the Triad.

Kehler's main point was that the president did not have a completely free hand. "The United States military does not blindly follow orders," Kehler said. "A presidential order to employ U.S. nuclear weapons must be legal. The basic legal principles of military necessity, distinction, and proportionality apply to nuclear weapons, just as they do to every other weapon."

Cardin asked who would decide whether the order was illegal.

"Well," Kehler replied, "that is one of the things that would be on the plate of the commander of Strategic Command."

"So," Cardin said, "let me just drill down on this." If Kehler were still head of StratCom, and if the president ordered a first strike that did not meet the legal test of proportionality, could he decide "to disobey the Commander in Chief?"

"Yes," Kehler replied. "If there is an illegal order presented to the military, the military is obligated to refuse to follow it."

Some of the senators and their staff raised their eyebrows a few notches. Ordinarily, someone in Kehler's position would avoid answering such a question, pleading—as Mattis had, when Markey posed a similar question—that it was "hypothetical."

But upon further questioning, Kehler's bold assurance turned wobbly. Republican senator Ron Johnson of Wisconsin asked him how he would have gone about refusing to follow an illegal order.

Kehler replied, "I would have said, 'I have a question about this,' and I would have said, 'I'm not ready to proceed.'"

"And then what happens?" Johnson asked.

"Well," Kehler said. He paused, and nervous laughter flitted through the chamber. "As I say," he went on, with a slight grin, "I don't know exactly. Fortunately, we've never—these are all hypothetical scenarios. I mean, they're real, in terms of—"

Johnson interrupted, "We are holding a hearing on this, so—"

"Exactly," Kehler replied. "This is the human factor in our system. The human factor kicks in."

And that opened the door to the question of what happens to all the legal principles when the human is Donald Trump.

Senator Chris Murphy, Democrat of Connecticut, raised the point in the starkest terms. "Let me just pull back the cover for a minute from this hearing," he began. "We are concerned that the President of the United States is so unstable, is so volatile, has a decision-making process that is so quixotic, that he might order a nuclear-weapons strike that is wildly out of step with U.S. national security interests. Let's just recognize the exceptional nature of this moment in the discussion that we are having today."

Murphy then asked the Republican witness, Peter Feaver, who had worked as a special adviser to President George W. Bush, whether an enemy power's mere possession of a nuclear weapon, with the range to reach the United States, would constitute an "imminent attack" and thus put the president on solid legal ground in ordering a first strike.

Feaver, while noting that he wasn't a lawyer, replied that it probably did pass the legal test. "I think it would, in most people's minds, constitute a grave threat to U.S. national security, particularly if it was a North Korean nuclear warhead atop a North Korean missile that was capable of reaching the United States," he elaborated

Brian McKeon, the Democratic witness, who had worked in the NSC and the Pentagon under President Obama, disagreed. "Senator," he said, "the mere possession of a nuclear weapon, I do not think would meet that test." The North Koreans "have a nuclear weapon today, we know that much." If the president considered it sufficiently threatening to warrant a first strike, there would be plenty of time to seek congressional authorization.

As the hearing went on, it became clear that the debate was ultimately beside the point. Kehler noted that "nuclear decision-making at the highest level" is "a consultative process," involving many people—the head of StratCom, the secretary of defense, and other advisers—any one of whom could say, as he put it, "Wait, stop, we need to resolve these issues." But, he also acknowledged, if the president wanted to launch one of the many pre-set attack options that were listed in the nuclear war plan, the fact that the option was in the plan meant that the military lawyers had already vetted it. Ultimately, he acknowledged, the "decision authority"—the legal power to launch nuclear weapons—"resides with the President."

Senator Markey, who had prompted the hearing, then made what he considered the central point:

> Absent a nuclear attack upon the United States or our allies, no one human being should have the power to unilaterally unleash the most destructive forces ever devised by humankind. Yet, under existing law, the President of the United States can start a nuclear war without provocation, without consultation, and without warning. It boggles the rational mind. I fear that, in the age of Trump, the cooler heads and strategic doctrine that we once relied upon as our last best hope against the unthinkable seem less reassuring than ever.

The hearing came to a close after a few hours—by contrast, the 1976 hearing on the same subject had lasted four days—with no consequences. Markey's legislation had no more chance of passing than similar bills put forth in the past. (In 1972, Senator William Fulbright proposed an amendment to the War Powers Act, prohibiting the president from launching a nuclear first strike without congressional approval. It was voted down, 10 to 68.) Few in Congress had ever wanted the responsibility of making weighty decisions on war and peace. Few Republicans at this hearing even took much interest in exploring the dilemmas. Most of them used their time not to ask probing questions but to warn against the dangers of letting—as Florida senator Marco Rubio put it—"a bunch of bunker lawyers decide that they are going to disobey any order that they disagree with."

It was sobering to some senior officers who watched the hearing that not a single senator, not even any of the Republicans, bothered to dispute the claim, openly expressed by some of the Democrats, that President Trump was "unstable" or that his very presence in the Oval Office—his everyday access to the button—made nuclear war more possible.

General Kehler, sitting as a witness, may have been most flustered of all. It was up to Congress to set the rules on the procedures and safeguards for the use of nuclear weapons. If the members of Congress thought the president was unfit to command, then they needed to take responsibility and change the procedures; they couldn't just toss it in the laps of the military. Worse still would be if they raised provocative questions about the president's fitness, then did nothing, leaving the generals with a chain of command that no one could trust. Yet, he thought to himself, that is what this committee was doing.

There was a history of senior officials and underlings maneuvering around an untrustworthy chain of command. Back in the summer of 1974, amid reports of President Nixon's frequent drunkenness under the pressures of Watergate and his imminent impeachment, Secretary of Defense James Schlesinger quietly asked the Joint Chiefs of Staff to call him if they received any "unusual orders" from the commander-in-chief (neither the secretary of defense nor the Chiefs were, then or now, in the chain of command for nuclear orders). In late 1973, Major Harold Hering, a Minuteman launch officer in training, asked his instructors, "How can I know that an order I receive to launch my missiles came from a sane President?" And, more broadly: "What checks and balances exist to verify that an unlawful order does not get in to the missile men?" Hering, a proud Air Force officer, had served multiple tours as a helicopter pilot in Vietnam. He simply wanted assurances that, if he ever got the signal to launch nuclear missiles against a foreign country, he would be following legal orders, as military law required. He was instantly yanked out of missile crewman class, given a desk job, and, after a review board hearing, drummed out of the military.

Nobody wanted to answer Hering's questions, in part because they couldn't be answered without raising doubts about the whole system of command and control over nuclear weapons. They aroused suspicions that the elaborate process of consultation over the decision to launch nuclear weapons might be fragile. "The human factor kicks in," as General Kehler testified. There was no safety switch in place, no circuit breaker that someone could throw, if the human turned out to be crazy.

Donald Trump wound up not going to war with North Korea after all. Instead, on New Year's Day 2018, Kim Jong-un launched a peace offensive, offering to send a delegation to the upcoming Winter Olympics in Seoul and calling for warmer relations with South Korea, including "bilateral contact, travel, cooperation and exchange on a broad scale." South Korean president Moon Jae-in, eager for détente, embraced the offer, forming a joint North-South team at the Olympics and scheduling a summit in which both leaders would cross the Demilitarized Zone together. On April 20, six days before this summit, Kim announced that he would cease testing nuclear weapons or medium- to long-range missiles. On June 12, Kim and Trump held their own summit, in Singapore—the first time a North Korean leader and a sitting American president had ever met face-to-face.

How did this happen? Did Trump's campaign of "maximum pressure" work? Did his intensification of sanctions, his threat of raining "fire and fury" on North Korea, and the ATACM "demonstration attacks" frighten Kim to the bargaining table? Was Trump, perhaps unwittingly, testing Richard Nixon's "Madman Theory"? Nixon had told Henry Kissinger to warn the North Vietnamese that he was crazy and might use nuclear weapons if they didn't end the war. The ploy failed, possibly because the North Vietnamese didn't believe Nixon was mad in quite that way. Did Kim fear that Trump might really be a madman?

President Moon certainly feared he might be. American officials put out the word—this time without pretending—that Trump was erratic, unpredictable, different from previous presidents, though all this was clear without these messages. This was what led Moon to accept Kim's overtures at once, to schedule a summit, to urge Kim to ask for a separate meeting with Trump, and to urge Trump to accept the invitation.

Kim too may have been shaken by the strange American president's pressure; no previous administration had fired missiles in response to a North Korean action. But the chronology called this theory into question. Trump issued his "fire and fury" warning on August 8. Three weeks later, on August 28, Kim test-fired an intermediate-range ballistic missile over Japan. On September 3, he detonated a nuclear device at a test site for the sixth time, this one the most powerful explosion to date, so powerful that he declared it to be—and several Western analysts concluded that it probably was—a hydrogen bomb. On September 14, he test-launched another intermediate-range missile. Finally, on November 28, he fired a missile having the range to strike U.S. territory.

In other words, after Trump's most bellicose remarks, Kim conducted four tests honing his ability to strike America and its allies. Far from appearing intimidated by Trump's threats, Kim seemed to be moving steadily along his path to acquiring a nuclear arsenal. In his New Year's Day address, Kim said he could now move for peace because, in the past year, he had satisfied the "great historic cause of perfecting the national nuclear forces" and now possessed "a powerful and reliable war deterrent, which no force and no thing can reverse." Three months later, he justified his announcement of a test moratorium on the grounds that he had "verified the completion of nuclear weapons" and, therefore, "we no longer need" to keep testing.

It may never be known whether Kim pivoted because of Trump's pressure or because North Korea now had a nuclear deterrent, fulfilling the atomic dreams of his father and grandfather. Both factors may have played a role. Daniel Ellsberg, the nuclear war planner turned antiwar activist, counts twenty-five instances—before Trump entered office— of American presidents threatening to use nuclear weapons since the end of World War II. Ellsberg deplores these threats as reckless—regards them as synonymous with using nuclear weapons, "in the precise way that a gun is used when you point it at someone's head in a direct confrontation." Yet, even he acknowledges that "several" of these threats may have been effective in deterring war or in damping down a conflict and that, either way, in "most" of these cases, senior U.S. officials believed the threats were effective—meaning that, in future crises, they or their successors might issue similar threats again, though it may be only a matter of time before one of these bluffs is called, with catastrophic consequences.

Whatever pushed Kim to the bargaining table, Trump proved incapable of exploiting any leverage he might have gained. In previous meetings with foreign leaders, especially with autocrats (Russia's Vladimir Putin, China's Xi Jinping, Saudi Arabia's King Salman), Trump had purred and rolled over when they treated him with respect (feigned or real), and Kim pushed those same buttons masterfully. At their June summit in Singapore, Trump gave away more than he got, canceling an upcoming U.S.–South Korea military exercise, while Kim pledged only "to work *toward* complete denuclearization of the Korean Peninsula," without setting a timetable or defining "denuclearization." Yet on that basis, Trump declared, after the summit, that there was "no longer a nuclear threat from North Korea" and hailed Kim as a "good friend" and "great leader." For more than a year afterward, he touted his relationship with Chairman Kim. "He wrote me beautiful letters," Trump gushed at one rally. "We fell in love."

The rest of the world, including many American officials and experts, gasped in dismay and puzzlement. Months before his summit with Kim, Trump had withdrawn from the Iran nuclear deal, a highly detailed accord that blocked the mullahs of Tehran from every possible path toward acquiring a nuclear weapon, calling it "the worst deal ever," even though Jim Mattis, after reading the text three times, characterized its verification protocols as "robust" and even though the International Atomic Energy Agency attested, repeatedly, after several inspections, that Iran was abiding by its terms.

Not long after junking that deal, Trump pulled out of the Intermediate-Range Nuclear Forces Treaty, which Ronald Reagan and Mikhail Gorbachev had signed, as a Cold War coda, in 1987. Trump accused the Russians of cheating, as had President Obama. The treaty barred both countries from testing ground-launched missiles having a range of 500 to 5,000 kilometers; the Russians *had* tested a cruise missile within the prohibited range. But withdrawing from the treaty gave the Russians what they wanted. The Russian military had abhorred the INF Treaty from the moment Gorbachev signed it. When George W. Bush was president, Russia's defense minister, Sergei Ivanov, implored Secretary of Defense Donald Rumsfeld three times to make a deal allowing both sides to get out of the treaty. Rumsfeld ignored the request, knowing that there was no appetite, in the U.S. or Western Europe, for bringing back these sorts of missiles. Killing the treaty would help only the Russians, giving them free rein to build as many of these weapons as they liked and to blame the breakdown on the Americans, while doing nothing for the West. Trump was falling in the trap that Rumsfeld had skirted.

New START, the treaty signed by Obama and Dmitry Medvedev, will expire in 2021, and neither Trump nor Putin has taken a single step toward negotiating an extension or a sequel. New START placed limits on Russian and American strategic nuclear weapons—the missiles and bombers aimed at each other's territory. Both countries have abided by this treaty's terms; not even implacable foes of arms control have claimed otherwise. It was a modest treaty ("relatively benign," as Jon Kyl, its leading critic in the Senate, described it). But if it disappeared, the lid would blow off: generals on both sides could press for more weapons, to satisfy more "requirements" and to fill "gaps" in fanciful scenarios; if East-West relations remained tense, the nuclear arms race, after decades of winding down, could rev up for another brutal round.

Trump was not solely to blame for these tensions or breakdowns. He came to the White House two decades into the post–Cold War disorder, amid a diffusion of global power, the crumbling of power blocs, the shifting of borders, the diminishing authority of institutions. Yet he certainly accelerated these trends, sometimes willfully, ripping up treaties, shrugging off alliances, scrambling the arrangements of the global system that the United States had created and helped lead, to its benefit, since the end of World War II.

He came to the White House believing that the world was a mess because his predecessors didn't know how to make good deals—and that he would clean things up because making deals was his specialty. In June 2018, shortly before his first summit with Kim Jong-un, Trump met in the White House with Shinzo Abe, Japan's prime minister. Abe proposed that he and Trump get their respective national security teams to work out a joint negotiating strategy. H. R. McMaster, who'd heard the suggestion ahead of time, was enthusiastic about the idea, as was much of his staff: the two teams had similar views; the two countries had common interests.

But Trump waved away the idea. There are two things you need to know, he told Abe. First, he said, "I am the greatest negotiator in the history of the White House." Second, when he was about to make a big deal, he went on, he didn't prepare with a lot of documents; he went into the room and let his gut take a reading of the guy across the table.

For Abe, this was a turning point; he suddenly realized that, as long as Trump remained president, Japan could no longer count on the United States as a reliable ally.

And so, just minutes after the Singapore summit began, Trump's gut told him that Kim Jong-un was his friend and, after it was over, it told him that a vague pledge about "denuclearization" was tantamount to an ironclad bond of peace. When they held their second summit in Hanoi, eight months later, both men approached it with misconceptions: Kim believed that Trump was so desperate for a deal, he'd agree to anything; Trump believed that he and Kim could settle all their disputes in one grand bargain—Trump lifting all economic sanctions if Kim dismantled his entire nuclear program—strictly on the strength of what he saw as their deep friendship. The summit ended disastrously, without a closing lunch, much less a signing ceremony. If anyone still believed that Trump was a master in the art of the deal, Hanoi shattered the illusion.

Most presidents come to realize that nothing in their lives has quite prepared them for the weighty rigors of the Oval Office. Most react to the shock by hunkering down with their briefing books, listening to experts, convening their top advisers, consulting their predecessors, asking questions, balancing options, and developing a keen awareness of their own styles of thinking: their strengths and limits. Trump seemed never to reach that moment of awakening. He never thought he needed to learn much beyond what he already knew. To Trump, everything was a deal, deals depended on personal relations, and he navigated the nexus between the two through the finely tuned nerve endings of his gut.

The bomb—the weapon of fire and fury that Trump threatened to rain down on North Korea to punish its leader and obliterate the entire nation—has coexisted with humanity for three quarters of a century with no catastrophes, as yet, since the two explosions, over Hiroshima and Nagasaki, that set the nuclear age in motion. Still, all along, the generals and their aides have kept churning out war plans and calculating the consequences on our side versus their side—the targets destroyed, the cities ravaged, the millions of people killed—spinning them in a way that might yield some kind of victory. They have seen this as their job: to seek ways to make these weapons usable, in case the commander-in-chief wanted to use them.

Yet throughout this history, when crises occur and the generals haul out their war plans and serious men and women discuss their options, weighing the costs and benefits of going nuclear, every president has decided that the risks are too enormous. Dwight Eisenhower blithely likened nuclear weapons to bullets; John Kennedy mused that he'd have no choice but to go nuclear if the Soviets tried to grab West Berlin; Lyndon Johnson mulled a nuclear option in Vietnam (where generals had figured, a decade earlier, that they'd have to go nuclear if more than a few thousand troops were thrown into battle); Richard Nixon issued nuclear threats over Vietnam and a few Middle East hot spots; Ronald Reagan signed documents touting the goal of fighting and winning a nuclear war; Bill Clinton came close to attacking North Korea (which, if Kim Il-sung had retaliated, might have escalated to nuclear war)—and yet, when these presidents reached their "moment of thermonuclear truth" (as McGeorge Bundy put it during the Berlin crisis of 1961), they backed away from that option. They decided that they would not push the button, unless it was absolutely, unavoidably necessary, if then.

One fear during the Cold War was that a "clever briefer," in Washington or Moscow, might persuade the American president or the Soviet premier that the calculations and scenarios in their nuclear war plans were grounded in something real—that the balance of power and the alignment of circumstances made it possible to pull off a nuclear first strike, to fight and win a nuclear war—and that, in a desperate crisis, one leader or another might give it a go. One concern about Donald

Trump, a man who believed he knew a lot but in fact knew very little, and who lacked the impulse or curiosity to learn more, was that he seemed more susceptible to the wiles of a clever briefer than any of his dozen predecessors in the age of the bomb. This was why the fear of nuclear war resurfaced with his rise to power.

But Trump was a symptom, not the cause, of our common nuclear problem. At the dawn of the Republic, James Madison wrote in *The Federalist No. 10*, "Enlightened statesmen will not always be at the helm," which is why he and the other Founders devised checks and balances to a potential autocrat's power—a legislature, judiciary, free press, and (they hoped) an educated public.

At the dawn of the nuclear age, Harry Truman wrested control of the bomb away from the generals, entrusting it to the top civilian authority, because he understood that, as he put it, "this isn't a military weapon." But neither Truman nor anyone since devised checks or balances to the fears, whims, or impulses of the unenlightened statesman whose rise Madison feared as inevitable.

Just months after Hiroshima, Bernard Brodie, one of the pioneering nuclear strategists at the RAND Corporation, a scholar who lacked the ambition or temperament to move into official circles, wrote, "Everything about the atomic bomb is overshadowed by the twin facts that it exists and that its destructive power is fantastically great." The story of the bomb ever since has been—and will continue to be—the story of presidents and generals grappling with these twin facts, figuring out the best way to maneuver around them or to reconcile with them.

With the spread of the bomb came a logic—a stab at a strategy—on how to deter its use in warfare. The logic involved convincing adversaries that you really would use the bomb in response to aggression; part of that involved convincing yourself that you would use it, which required building certain types of missiles, and devising certain plans, that would enable you to use them—and, before you knew it, a strategy to deter nuclear war became synonymous with a strategy to fight nuclear war. And when crises arose, the logic encouraged, almost required, escalating the cycle of threats and counterthreats, just up to the point where deterrence and war converged, in order to maintain credibility. The compelling, and frightening, thing about the logic was that, once you bought into its premises, you fell into the rabbit hole; there seemed no exit. The presidents who fell deep into this hole, who faced the abyss where the logic led, avoided its end point—avoided war—by scrambling out of the hole, snapping out of the logic, like snapping out of a bad dream.

William Kaufmann, who developed the counterforce strategy, spent twenty years in the hothouse it built, toiling as a special assistant to every secretary of defense under every president from John Kennedy to Jimmy Carter. He explored every crevice of the logic—the scenarios, doctrines, and plans for nuclear war—as deeply as anyone. Then he got out, looked at the edifice from a distance, and thought, "God, that's a crazy world."

It is crazy, and it is our world, and there is no escaping it. Absent some transformation in global politics, an upheaval so immense that it can hardly be imagined, the bomb will always be with us, looming over everything. Sometimes it has loomed as a restraining force: probably a few wars have not occurred because of the fear that, once started, they might escalate to nuclear war. But past is not precedence. Some incalculable mix of shrewdness and sheer luck has kept the holocaust at bay; who knows how many wars we can dodge before an alignment of slow-wittedness and misfortune tips the balance the other way.

The trick is to stay aware that, out of sight as it seems, the bomb is still here. The presidents who managed to keep it locked up, in the gravest of crises, did so not through ignorance or innocence but rather by immersing themselves in the bomb's logic, scoping out the full depths of the rabbit hole, and comprehending, with calm urgency, the need to find a way out.

Acknowledgments

At the start of Donald Trump's presidency, I thought it might be time to write another book about nuclear war. At first I considered updating my first book, *The Wizards of Armageddon*, which was published in 1983. But as I undertook some preliminary research, I realized an entirely different book was now necessary.

Wizards told the story of the "defense intellectuals" who devised the theories of nuclear deterrence and nuclear warfighting, then helped weave those ideas into national policy. *The Bomb* focuses on the policymakers—the pressures and dilemmas they faced, the options they considered, the decisions they made.

It is now possible to tell this story because, in the last few decades, thousands of once Secret and Top Secret documents have been released—beyond the thousands that I managed to get declassified in the early 1980s through the Freedom of Information Act and Mandatory Declassification Reviews. More important, the nature of those documents has transformed the picture. When I wrote *Wizards*, for example, almost nothing in the open archives revealed what President John F. Kennedy thought or said about nuclear issues; nor had his secretly recorded tapes been released. Now there are mountains of material—about Kennedy, Johnson, Nixon, Carter, Reagan, Clinton, and some new, revelatory documents about Truman and Eisenhower, as well—and these treasures, which haven't been plowed much by others, form the core of this book.

I have also drawn on recollections of key players in the story: several of the 160 people that I interviewed while researching *Wizards*, forty-seven people that I interviewed expressly for this new book, and dozens more that I've tapped as sources for articles and columns I've written for various publications in the past few decades. I thank all of these people—officials and officers, past and present, living and dead—who cooperated with me back then, recently, and in the times in between.

I thank two scholars, both longtime friends, whose work has greatly influenced me: David Alan Rosenberg, the dean of American nuclear history, who has been poring through boxes, folders, and files for even longer than I have; and William Burr of the National Security Archive, who, through shrewd and patient use of FOIA and MDR, has pried more classified documents from an increasingly resistant bureaucracy than anyone out there. Conversations that I've had with David and Bill these past couple of years—discussions about the documents and about the underlying issues—have been enlightening and enjoyable.

Other scholars, some of them friends, have also been helpful: Steven Aftergood, Bruce Blair, Joshua Epstein, Gordon Goldstein, Matt Korda, Hans Kristensen, Timothy Naftali, Olga Oliker, John Pike, Daniel Sneider, and Marc Trachtenberg.

I must also thank the four professors at the Massachusetts Institute of Technology, where I attended graduate school many years ago, who first guided me through the bizarre world of nuclear strategy: William Kaufmann, George Rathjens, Jack Ruina, and (still among the living) Kosta Tsipis. I would not have made any headway in this field without them.

I thank the archivists at the various presidential libraries, especially those of John F. Kennedy, Ronald Reagan, and Jimmy Carter. These institutions are invaluable for the preservation of our history and democracy, and their underfunding in recent years is shameful.

I have been the "War Stories" columnist at *Slate* since the end of 2002. This book is in no way a compilation or extension of those columns, but my reporting on the national-security beat has informed my perspective and kept me up to date. I thank my *Slate* editors (past and present) over this time: Jacob Weisberg, Julia Turner, Will Dobson, June Thomas, David Plotz, Joshua Keating, Lowen Liu, and Jared Hohlt.

It is a great pleasure and honor, once again, to thank Alice Mayhew, the legendary editor at Simon & Schuster. This is the fourth book I've written under her supervision. The first was *Wizards*, which, along with the next two—*The Insurgents* (on the revival of counterinsurgency doctrine) and *Dark Territory* (on the emergence of cyber war)—form a trilogy about the interplay of war, ideas, and politics in post–World War II America. It is fitting, and satisfying, that we've come full circle, together, with *The Bomb*.

I thank the entire team at Simon & Schuster: Jonathan Karp, Stephen Bedford, Sara Kitchen, Lewelin Polanco, Lisa Erwin, Lana Roff, Larry Hughes, Amar Deol, Kimberly Goldstein, and Annie Craig. I also thank Julie Tate, who fastidiously fact-checked the manuscript, though I'm entirely to blame for any remaining errors, and Fred Chase, who did the scrupulous copyediting.

I thank Rafe Sagalyn, who has been my literary agent for all six of my books as well as a trusted friend and counselor. I also thank his energetic assistant, Brendan Coward.

I thank the warm hospitality of Edward and Paula Hughes, Leonard Gordon, and Lori Lefkovitz.

Finally, I thank my family: my mother, Ruth Kaplan Pollock, a source of moral support all these years; my wife, Brooke Gladstone, best friend, love of my life, compass of my conscience; and our daughters, Maxine and Sophie, who continue to inspire and astonish me.

NOTES

The material in this book is based on documents—many of them once classified—and interviews with the story's key players and participants. Some of the interviews for the first three chapters were conducted in the 1980s while I was researching *The Wizards of Armageddon*, for which I obtained thousands of once classified documents through the Freedom of Information Act and Mandatory Declassification Reviews, and interviewed 160 participants. In that book, I listed all the people that I interviewed (many of whom are no longer living) but did not attribute specific information to them. To the extent that what they told me has since been declassified, I identify them here. Some of Chapter 9 is based on an article that I wrote for *Washington Monthly* ("Rolling Blunder: How the Bush Administration Let North Korea Get Nukes," May 2004), for which I interviewed several officials on the record; I identified them in the article and here. For later chapters, except where otherwise specified, interviews were conducted on "deep background," and I am not listing their names. In general, if material is based entirely on those interviews, I say nothing in these source notes. If it's based on documents and those interviews, I cite the document, then add "and interviews."

INTRODUCTION

1   *"they will be met":* Peter Baker and Choe Sang-Hun, "Trump Threatens 'Fire and Fury' Against North Korea if It Threatens U.S.," *New York Times*, Aug. 8, 2017.

1   *"a rain of ruin":* "Statement by the President Announcing the Use of the A-Bomb at Hiroshima, Aug. 6, 1945," Public Papers, Harry Truman, 1945–1953, Document 93.

CHAPTER 1: *"Killing a Nation"*

4   *"The war will be over":* LeMay told me this story in a 1981 interview. It is also quoted in Fred Kaplan, *The Wizards of Armageddon* (New York: Simon & Schuster, 1983), 43.

5   *The generation of Army airmen:* Perry McCoy Smith, *The Air Force Plans for Peace, 1943–45* (Baltimore: Johns Hopkins University Press, 1970), 8.

6   *Soon after Hiroshima:* David Alan Rosenberg, "American Atomic Strategy and the Hydrogen Bomb Decision," *Journal of American History*, June 1979.

6   *"I don't think":* David Lilienthal, *The Journals of David E. Lilienthal*, Vol. 2: *The Atomic Energy Years* (New York: Harper & Row, 1964), 391.

6   *In 1949:* Warner R. Schilling, "The Politics of National Defense: Fiscal

1950," in Warner R. Schilling, Paul Y. Hammond, and Glenn H. Snyder, *Strategy, Politics, and Defense Budgets* (New York: Columbia University Press, 1962).

7   *"random mass slaughter":* Hearings, House Armed Services Committee, The National Defense Program: Unification and Strategy, Oct. 1945, 183–89.

7   *"without serious injury":* "Clothes and the Bomb," *New York Times,* Oct. 12, 1949.

7   *By 1952: History of the Joint Strategic Target Planning Staff: Background and Preparation of SIOP-62* (U.S. Strategic Air Command, History and Research Division), 2 [hereinafter: *History of JSTPS: SIOP-62*].

8   *"In a general war":* JCS 2101/244, Appendix A to Enclosure A, "Strategic Concept for General War" (attached to NSC 5410/1, "U.S. Objectives in the Event of General War with the Soviet Bloc"), March 29, 1954, NA/MMB.

8   *The term "general war":* Cited in memo, U.S.G. Sharp to Secretary, JCS, on changes in CINCEUR Plan 100-1 through 100-4, Aug. 21, 1958, CCS 381 (11-15-48), Sec. 19, NA/MMB.

9   *"great equation":* Robert J. Donovan, *Eisenhower: The Inside Story* (New York: Harper & Row, 1956), 17–18.

9   *Throughout his presidency:* E.g., Memo of Conference with the President, Nov. 21, 1959, Box 2, White House Office, Office of Staff Secretary, Subject Series, DoD, Vol. 4 (1), DDEL.

10   *"maximum protection":* Speech of Secretary of State John Foster Dulles, "The Strategy of Massive Retaliation," Council on Foreign Relations, Jan. 12, 1954.

10   *"It is the policy":* JCS 2101/244, op. cit.

11   *"is not just calling for":* Memo, Dec. 10, 1955, Box 355, Senate, Committee on Armed Services (SAC Ops) folder, LBJL.

11   *Ridgway resigned:* Ridgway letter to Secretary of Defense Charles Wilson, leaked to *New York Times,* July 15, 1955.

11   *"a radical departure":* Memo, Radford to Generals Twining, Taylor, Pate, and Adm. Burke, "Strategic Concept and the Use of U.S. Military Forces," March 28, 1956, Records of JCS, Chairman's File, 301 Military Strategy (Posture), NA/MMB.

11   *Radford met with Eisenhower:* Memo of Conference with the President, May 14, 1956, Box 15, Ann Whitman File, Eisenhower Diary Series, DDEL.

12   *"fatuous":* Ibid. Taylor told me in a 1981 interview that he was shocked; part of the story appears in Kaplan, op. cit., 196.

13   *"The only possible":* "Net Evaluation of Damage Anticipated in Initial Stages of US-USSR Nuclear War," Box 12, Ann Whitman File, Eisenhower Diary Series (January 1956 Diary), DDEL.

13   *Kenney had run:* Melvin Deaile, "The SAC Mentality: The Origins of Strategic Air Command's Organizational Culture, 1948–51," *Air & Space Power Journal*, March–April, 2015.

14   *LeMay ordered a drill:* Col. Phillip S. Meilinger, "How LeMay Transformed Strategic Air Command," *Air & Space Power Journal*, March–April, 2014.

14   *When LeMay had been:* Robert McNamara told this story in Errol Morris's documentary, *The Fog of War* (2003). McNamara worked as a statistical analyst for LeMay during World War II. The two would be at frequent loggerheads with each other twenty years later, when McNamara was secretary of defense and LeMay was Air Force chief of staff.

15   *"killing a nation":* Robert Frank Futrell, *Ideas, Concepts, Doctrine: A History of Basic Thinking in the United States Air Force, 1907–64* (Maxwell AFB, AL: Air University Press, 1971), 122.

15   *"Delta-Bravo-Romeo":* JCS-2056/7, Aug. 12, 1950, Records of JCS, CCS-37311 (12-14-45), Sec. 2, NA/MMB.

15   *LeMay thought:* Kaplan, op. cit., 41–44.

15   *On this point:* JCS-2056/13, March 28, 1951, JCS File List, 1951–53, CCS 373.11 (12-14-48), Sec. 4, NA/MMB.

15   *"the entire stockpile":* Rosenberg, "American Atomic Strategy and the Hydrogen Bomb Decision," 70.

15   *In preparation for LeMay's plan:* "Target Systems," SAC Progress Analysis, Nov. 1, 1948–Dec. 31, 1955, Nathan F. Twining Papers, Box 84, LoC.*

16   *From 1949:* Ibid.*

16   *Around this time:* Kaplan, op. cit., chapters 6, 8, 9.

17   *NAVWAG's main thesis:* "Unclassified Summary of NAVWAG Study No. 5," Jan. 22, 1958, White House Office files, Office of Staff Secretary, Subject Series, Alpha Subseries, Box 21, Nuclear Exchange (1) folder, Box 21, DDEL.

18 *In the summer of 1957:* "War and Peace in the Nuclear Age; Bigger Bang for the Buck: An Interview with John Coyle," *Open Vault*, WGBH, March 26, 1986; and 1981 interview with Coyle, who had been NAVWAG's director.

18 *"inroads":* Lt. Col. William Draper, memo to White, 1957 White House files, Nathan Twining Papers, Box 97, LoC.*

19 *"through the over-use":* White testimony, attached to memo, deputy chief of staff to all major commanders, Feb. 28, 1959, Thomas White Papers, Box 26, Chief of Staff memos, LoC.*

19 *A few years earlier:* Kaufmann, "The Requirements of Deterrence," Memorandum #7, Princeton Center of International Studies (1954), reprinted in William Kaufmann, ed., *Military Policy and National Security* (Princeton: Princeton University Press, 1956).

20 *He titled one:* W. W. Kaufmann, "The Puzzle of Polaris," Feb. 1, 1960, att. to memo, Roscoe Wilson to White, Feb. 17, 1960, Thomas White Papers, Box 36, Missiles/Space/Nuclear folder, LoC.* For more on Kaufmann, the origins of counterforce, and its partial adoption by the Air Force, see Kaplan, op. cit., Chapters 13, 15.

20 *"bonus":* Letter, Cpt. John H. Morse to Lewis Strauss, chairman, Atomic Energy Commission, Feb. 14, 1957, Records of Special Asst. for National Security Affairs, NSC Series, Briefing Notes Subseries, Box 17, Target Systems (1957–61), DDEL.

21 *"the most important segment":* Letter, White to Power, May 11, 1959, Thomas White Papers, Box 29, 1959 Top Secret File, LoC.*

21 *"sadist":* Richard Rhodes, *Dark Sun: The Making of the Hydrogen Bomb* (New York: Simon & Schuster, 1995), 451.

21 *"Why do you want":* Interview with Kaufmann, 1980; Kaplan op. cit., 246.

22 *"a wider range":* Memo, White to Power, Feb. 27, 1961, Thomas White Papers, Box 48, 1961 Top Secret File, LoC.*

22 *The Joint Chiefs: History of JSTPS: SIOP-62,* 4.

22 *"fallback position":* Letter, White to Gates, June 10, 1960, Thomas White Papers, Box 41, 1960 Top Secret File, LoC.*

23 *"Unity in the Strategic Offensive":* I obtained the briefing in the early 1980s through a FOIA request.* For more on the SIOP's contents and politics, see Kaplan, *The Wizards of Armageddon*, Chapter 18; the briefing is mentioned on 264.

23 *White and his staff:* Memo, White to Power, "Recommended Actions for Increasing Capabilities and Readiness Posture of SAC Forces," July 19, 1960, Thomas White Papers, op. cit.*

23 *On July 6:* Memo of conference with the President, July 6, 1960, White House Office file, Office of Staff Secretary Subject Series, DD Subseries, Box 2, DoD, Vol. 4 (5), DDEL.

23 *Nearly a year earlier:* "18 Questions," JCS-2056/134, Sept. 4, 1959, with enclosure CM-386-59, Aug. 24, 1959 (FOIA)*; Kaplan, op. cit., 264.

23 *On August 16: History of JSTPS: SIOP-62.*

24 *"This is just like Communism":* Transcript, "Adm. Burke's Conversation with Secretary Franke, 12 August 1960," Arleigh Burke Papers, SIOP/ NSTL Briefing Folder, Navy Yard, Washington, DC*; Kaplan, op. cit. 265-67.

24 *"You're more generous":* "Minutes, CNO Deputies' Conference, 18 August 1960," Arleigh Burke Papers, Transcripts & Phonecons (NSTL).*

24 *More than half: History of JSTPS: SIOP-62.*

25 *This did not include:* Message, "CincPacFlt to CNO, Feb. 1, 1961," Arleigh Burke Papers, NSTL/SIOP Messages, Exclusives & Personals.*

25 *Just twenty-nine officers: History of JSTPS: SIOP-62.*

25 *Burke well understood:* E.g., Burke's notes on conversation with Eisenhower, Cable, Burke to CincPacFlt, LantFlt, USNavEur, Part 3, Aug. 12, 1960, Arleigh Burke Papers, SIOP/NSTL Briefing folder.*

25 *At the first SIOP:* Memo for Record, "Report on Planning Conference at SAC Hq, Omaha, 24–26 Aug. 1960, on Strategic Planning for a National Strategic Target List (NSTL) and a Single Integrated Operational Plan (SIOP)," Aug. 27, 1960, Arleigh Burke Papers, Memos & Letters (NSTL).*

25 *As it turned out: History of JSTPS: SIOP-62.*

25 *All told:* Kaplan, op. cit., 269. This figure comes from handwritten notes of SIOP-62, provided to the author.

26 *That meant 500 extra targets:* Cited in memo, CincLantFlt to CNO, "Minutes of the 21st Mtg. of JSTPS Policy Committee," March 22, 1961, Arleigh Burke Papers, NSTL/SIOP Messages, Exclusives & Personals.*

26 *"at least":* Cited in memo, Op-06 to Op-00, "JCS 2056/189, "The Initial NSTL & SIOP (Nov. 1960)," Arleigh Burke Papers, Memos & Letters (NSTL).*

26   *In the first round:* Message, CincLant to CNO, Nov. 22, 1960, Arleigh Burke Papers, NSTL Messages, Exclusives & Personals.*

26   *Still, the final draft:* Memo, CincLantFlt to CNO, April 27, 1961, Arleigh Burke Papers, NSTL Messages, Exclusives & Personals.*

27   *The SIOP, it turned out:* Memo, Navrestracomd to CNO, Nov. 3, 1960, ibid.*

27   *Calculating the ratios:* Message, CNO to CincPacFlt, CincLantFlt, USNavEur, Nov. 24, 1960, ibid.*

27   *If a war started with short notice:* Memo, Op-06 to Op-00, op. cit.*; 3,423 weapons and 7,847 megatons, from Kaplan, op. cit., 269; 1,043 targets from *History of JSTPS: SIOP-62.*

27   *The objective: History of JSTPS: SIOP-62.*

28   *The answer came:* Kaplan, op. cit.; confirmed in Daniel Ellsberg, *The Doomsday Machine: Confessions of a Nuclear War Planner* (New York: Bloomsbury, 2017), Prologue.

28   *On December 1: History of JSTPS: SIOP-62.*

28   *In the discussion:* Ibid.

29   *At Eisenhower's request, Kistiakowsky:* Memos, Eisenhower to Kistiakowsky, Oct. 19, 1960, and Kistiakowsky to Andrew Goodpaster, Nov. 7, 1960, White House Office files, Office of Staff Secretary, Subject Series, Alpha Subseries, Box 16, Dr. Kistiakowsky (6), DDEL; interview with Kistiakowsky, 1980.

29   *Before the trip:* Interview with Rathjens, 1980.

29   *"Do we have any options":* Kaplan, op. cit., 270.

29   *The next day: History of JSTPS: SIOP-62.*

CHAPTER 2: *The Race Begins*

31   *"missile gap":* John F. Kennedy, *The Strategy of Peace*, ed. Allan Nevins (New York: Harper & Row, 1960), 33–38.

32   *"pay any price":* Kennedy, Inaugural Address, Jan. 20, 1961, Historic Speeches, JFKL.

32   *At his first meeting:* Memorandum of Conference with the President, Jan. 25, 1961, National Security Files, Box 345, Conferences with JCS, 1–2/61, JFKL.

32   *Toward the end:* Eugene Zuckert, Oral History Interview, p. 2, JFKL.

32   *"whiz kids":* Elie Abel, "The Thinking Man's Business Executive," in
      The Kennedy Circle, Lester Tanzer, ed. (Washington, DC: Luce, 1961).

33   *He found them:* Fred Kaplan, *The Wizards of Armageddon* (New York:
      Simon & Schuster, 1983), esp. Chapter 16.

33   *It was the briefing:* Ibid., 270–72. I based this account on sources below
      and on my interviews in the early 1980s with McNamara and those
      who went with him: Gen. Lyman Lemnitzer, Roswell Gilpatric, Mar-
      vin Stern, and Herbert York.

34   *"fantastic":* Memo, Navrestracomd-Omaha to CNO, "JSTPS Briefing
      for McNamara on 4 February," Feb. 6, 1961, Arleigh Burke Papers,
      NSTL/SIOP Messages, Exchanges & Personals.*

34   *"urban-industrial":* McNamara, Draft Presidential Memorandum to
      JFK, "Recommended Long-Range Nuclear Delivery Forces 1963–
      1967," National Security Files, Departments & Agencies Series, De-
      fense Budget 63, 1/61–10/61, JFKL.*

34   *"Mr. Secretary":* Kaplan, op. cit., 272. In *Doomsday Delayed* (New York:
      Hamilton Books, 2008, p. 26), the late John Rubel, an assistant secre-
      tary of defense at the time, wrote that Power cracked the same "joke" at
      the briefing in December 1960.

35   *The briefing took place:* Kaplan, ibid., 260-62, based on interviews with
      Kaufmann, McNamara, Ellsberg, Charles Hitch, Alain Enthoven,
      Frank Trinkl, and others.

36   *"96 Trombones":* McNamara, Memo, March 1, 1961, Presidential Of-
      fice Files, Box 77, DoD Defense Budget, Jan.–March 1961, JFKL;
      McNamara, "Assignment of Projects within the DoD," March 8, 1961
      (FOIA).*

36   *"Prepare a draft memorandum":* Kaplan, op. cit., 274–75, based on the
      McNamara memo above and interviews with all the officials named
      here.

36   *Ellsberg had conducted:* Ellsberg writes about this at great length in *The
      Doomsday Machine: Confessions of a Nuclear War Planner* (New York:
      Bloomsbury, 2017), esp. Chapter 2.

37   *A few years earlier:* Kaplan, op. cit, 124.

37   *"spasm":* As far as I can tell, this memo has not been declassified.
      Ellsberg told me about it in interviews for *Wizards*. He also discusses it
      in *The Doomsday Machine*, Chapter 8. It is summarized in Carl Kaysen,

Memorandum of conversation with Harry Rowen, May 25, 1961 (drafted May 27), National Security Files, Carl Kaysen Series, BNSP 1–5/61, JFKL; Memo, Kaysen to McGeorge Bundy, June 8, 1961, National Security Files, Box 320, Memorandums, Kaysen, 6–8/61, JFKL. In both, Ellsberg is cited as the main author of the paper's nuclear section.

38   *"General, I have fought":* Kaplan, op. cit. 254.

38   *"does not now":* Lemnitzer, memo to McNamara, " 'Doctrine' on Thermonuclear Attack," April 18, 1961* (obtained through FOIA, now in *FRUS, 1961–1963,* Vol. VIII, National Security Policy, Document 25).

38f   *There was another vulnerability: History of JSTPS, SIOP-63,* 28–29.

39   *"attack options":* Memo, Lemnitzer to McNamara, "Guidance for the Preparation of the Single Integrated Operational Plan, 1963 (SIOP-63)," Aug. 18, 1961, https://archive.org/stream/SingleIntegrated-OperationPlanSIOP63/Single%20Integrated%20Operation%20Plan_SIOP-63_djvu.txt); *History of the Joint Strategic Target Planning Staff: Preparation for SIOP-63* (U.S. Strategic Air Command, History and Research Division, 1964), NSA/EBB No. 236, Document 2 [hereinafter: *History of JSTPS: SIOP-63*]. I wrote about SIOP-63 in Kaplan, op. cit. 279, based on interviews with McNamara, Ellsberg, Rowen, Enthoven, et al., but my mistake was assuming—because my sources believed—that SAC carried out McNamara's guidance. Documents noted here, which were still highly classified at the time of my interviews, indicate this wasn't so. Ellsberg expresses his surprise at realizing this, years later, in *The Doomsday Machine,* 272, 338.

40   *"unacceptable risk":* Memo, Lemnitzer to McNamara, op. cit. Appendix D, Vice of the Chief of Staff, U.S. Air Force (LeMay).

41   *Option 3 in particular:* Ibid., 16.

42   *"to the extent":* Memo, Lemnitzer to McNamara, op. cit., Appendix C.

42   *"to the degree practicable":* Ibid. Similar caveats are scattered throughout the memo and its attachments.

42   *Finally, the "damage-expectancy":* Ibid., Appendix, Views of Army Chief of Staff, Chief of Naval Operations, Commandant Marine Corps.

42   *"far in excess": History of JSTPS: SIOP-63,* 16.

43   *The Air Force wanted:* McNamara, Draft Presidential Memorandum to JFK, op. cit.*

43   *But McNamara insisted:* Memo, Bundy to JFK, "Policies previously approved in NSC which need review," Jan. 30, 1961, National Security Files, Box 313, NSC Meetings, JFKL.

43   *"the old estimate":* The quotes come from Memo, Kaysen to Bundy, "Secretary McNamara's Requirements for Long-Range Nuclear Forces, 1963–67," Oct. 11, 1961; and Kaysen to JFK, "Force Structure and Defense Budget," Nov. 22, 1961; both in National Security Files, Box 275, DoD Defense Budget 1963, JFKL.

44   *In August 1960:* For more on the collapse of the missile gap, see Kaplan, op. cit. Chapter 19, which relied on Memo, Lawrence McQuade to Paul Nitze, "But Where Did the Missile Gap Go?," National Security Files, Box 298, Missile Gap, 2–5/63, JFKL, and on interviews with McNamara, Gilpatric, Ellsberg, Herbert Scoville, and Howard Stoertz.

44   *just four long-range missiles:* Kaysen, Memo to Gen. Maxwell Taylor, "Strategic Air Planning and Berlin," Sept. 5, 1961, Appendix B, "SIOP-62: An Appreciation,"* p. 3 (available at NSA/EBB No. 56, Document 1); and interviews noted above.

44   *Before Discoverer:* Memo, Kaysen to JFK, "Force Structure and Defense Budget," Nov. 22, 1961; National Security Files, Box 275, DoD Defense Budget 1963, JFKL.

45   *General Lemnitzer had recently told:* Memo, Lemnitzer to JFK, Oct. 5, 1961, *FRUS, 1961–1963,* Vol. VIII, National Security Policy, Document 49.

45   *"finite deterrence":* Memo, Kaysen to JFK, op. cit.

45   *At a meeting:* Carl Kaysen, Oral History, Vol. 1, 7/11/66, JFKL.

46   *"the whole spectrum":* Memo, Bundy to JFK, op. cit.

46   *"counter force deterrent":* Memo, Bell to JFK, Jan. 30, 1961, National Security Files, Box 313, NSC Meeting No. 475, JFKL.

46   *In his first substantive meeting:* Memorandum of Conference with President, Feb. 6, 1961, National Security Files, Charles Clifton Papers, Box 346, Conference with the President, JCS, 1–2/61, JFKL.

CHAPTER 3: *The Crises*

48   *The Berlin crisis:* For background, see Robert M. Slusser, *The Berlin Crisis of 1961* (Baltimore: Johns Hopkins University Press, 1973);

Frederick Kempe, *Berlin 1961: Kennedy, Khrushchev and the Most Dangerous Place on Earth* (New York: Putnam, 2011).

48　*"peaceful coexistence":* Robert M. Slusser, "The Berlin Crises of 1958–59 and 1961," in Barry M. Blechman and Stephen S. Kaplan, *Force Without War* (Washington, DC: Brookings Institution, 1978).

49　*Eisenhower had stressed:* Memorandum of Conversation, Eisenhower and Khrushchev, "Berlin and Germany," Camp David, Sept. 26, 1959, *FRUS*, 1958–1960, Vol. IX, Berlin Crisis, 1959–1960, Germany, Austria, Document 13.

49　*"a test of our nerve":* Theodore Sorensen, *Kennedy* (New York: Harper & Row, 1965), 657.

49　*"It will be a cold winter":* Arthur Schlesinger, Jr., *A Thousand Days* (Boston: Houghton Mifflin, 1965), 348.

49　*"will be prepared":* Memorandum, McNamara to JFK, May 5, 1961, reprinted in U.S. State Dept., *FRUS*, 1961–1963, Vol. XIV, Berlin Crisis, 1961–1962, Document 22.

50　*On June 28:* Acheson to JFK, "Berlin," June 28, 1961, National Security Files, Box 81a, Germany-Berlin-General-Acheson Report, 6/28/61, JFKL.

50　*"the whole position":* Memo for the Record, Discussion at NSC meeting, June 29, 1961, National Security Files, Box 313, NSC Meeting No. 486, JFKL.

51　*"The planning for":* Kaysen to Bundy, July 3, 1961, National Security Files, Box 320, Minutes & Memoranda, Staff Memoranda, Carl Kaysen, 6/61–8/61, JFKL.

51　*"should not be asked":* Kissinger to Bundy, "General War Aspect of Berlin Contingency Planning," 7/7/61, National Security Files, Box 81a, Germany-Berlin-General, 7/7–7/17/61, JFKL.

52　*"all agree":* Bundy, Covering Note on Henry Kissinger's Memo on Berlin, July 7, 1961, National Security File, Box 381, Germany-Berlin-General, 7/7/61, JFKL.

52　*"to prepare war plans":* Memo, Bundy to JFK, "Briefing for Thursday NSC Meeting," July 12, 1961, National Security File, Box 313, NSC Meeting No. 487, JFKL.

52　*"the various steps":* Memo, Taylor to JFK, "Suggested Remarks at close of NSC Meeting, 13 July 1961," National Security File, Box 313, NSC Meeting. No. 487, JFKL.

52   *Twelve days later:* Text of speech in National Security File, Box 82, Germany-Berlin-General, 7/23–7/26/61, JFKL.

53   *Rowen and Kaysen spent:* It's worth elaborating how the once Top Secret-Sensitive story of JFK's first-strike plan came to light. I wrote a piece of the story in *The Wizards of Armageddon* (pp. 294–301), based on interviews with nine participants and close observers: Kaysen, Rowen, Kaufmann, Bundy, Ellsberg, Marcus Raskin, Ted Sorensen, Air Staff General David Burchinal, and RAND analyst Frank Trinkl. Some readers doubted the story was true. Michael Beschloss, in *The Crisis Years: Kennedy and Khrushchev, 1960–63* (New York: HarperCollins, 1991), dismissed the first-strike plan as a "back-of-the-envelope calculation." During my research for *Wizards* at the JFK Library, I noticed several documents on Berlin in the index for the Carl Kaysen Papers, but they were all classified. I asked one of the curators when they were likely to be released. He replied, "As long as there's still a Berlin, probably never." After the Berlin Wall fell in 1989, I filed a Mandatory Declassification Review for the documents. Meanwhile, the National Security Archive also filed a FOIA request for the first-strike study and, after several years, pried it loose from the Maxwell Taylor Papers at the National Defense University. My request with the JFK Library yielded a more redacted version of the study as well as documentation of the JCS response, the meeting with General Power, and other records. Based on all these documents and my earlier interviews, I wrote an article titled "JFK's First Strike Plan" for the October 2001 issue of *The Atlantic.* It appeared a few days after the 9/11 terrorist attacks and so went pretty much unnoticed. Frederick Kempe, in his book *Berlin 1961*, devoted a few passages to the plan. As far as I know, what I've written here, which also includes material from documents declassified since the *Atlantic* piece, is, to my knowledge, the first detailed account.

53   *"Here is what":* Kaysen to Rowen, cover memo (Sept. 6, 1961) to Memo, Kaysen to Taylor, "Strategic Air Planning and Berlin," Sept. 5, 1961, Carl Kaysen File, Box 374, Military Policy-SAC, JFKL.*

53   *"Is this really":* Memo, Kaysen to Taylor, op. cit. This version of the document, in NSA/EBB No. 56, Document 1, is much more lightly redacted than the one in the JFK Library.

54   *"assumptions are reasonable"*: Memo, Maj. W. Y. Smith to Taylor, "Strategic Air Planning and Berlin," Sept. 7, 1961, Carl Kaysen File, Box 374, Military Policy-SAC, JFKL.*

56   *"You're crazy!"*: Kaplan, *The Wizards of Armageddon*, 299, based on interviews in 1981 with Kaysen and Sorensen.

56   *"How does this"*: Marcus G. Raskin, *Being and Doing* (New York: Random House, 1971), 62–63. This book of political philosophy is the first published mention of the first-strike study. Ellsberg (who was friends with Raskin, as was I) alerted me to the passage, which spurred me to interview Raskin and, after him, others.

56   *The first briefing*: President's schedule, Thursday, July 20, 1961, 10:00 a.m., NSA/EBB No. 480, Document 7-C.

56   *"hopelessly inadequate"*: 1961 Report of the Net Evaluation Subcommittee, National Security Council, ibid., Document 7-A.

57   *"And we call ourselves"*: Dean Rusk, *As I Saw It* (New York: W. W. Norton, 1990), 246–47.

57   *The second briefing*: The date comes from Scott D. Sagan, "SIOP-62: The Nuclear War Plan Briefing to President Kennedy," *International Security*, Summer 1987.

57   *"General, why are we hitting"*: This exchange and JFK's teeth-tapping come from Carl Kaysen, Oral History, Vol. 3, 11/21/02, JFKL. Sagan's list of the meeting's participants, drawn from a JFK Library document, doesn't include Kaysen, but Kaysen said in the Oral History—and to me, in my 1981 interview with him—that Rostow brought him along.

57   *"Berlin developments"*: Memo, Taylor to Lemnitzer, Sept. 19, 1961, RG 718, Chairman's Papers, Maxwell Taylor Records, Box 34, Memoranda for the President 1961, National Archives, NSA/EBB No. 56, Document 3.

58   *"the time of our greatest danger"*: Memo of Conference with Pres. Kennedy, Sept. 20, 1961, *FRUS*, 1961–1963, Vol. VIII, National Security Policy, Document 44.

59   *On October 3*: Memo of Conversation, Oct. 3, 1961 (doc. dated Oct. 4), National Security File, Box 317, Memos & Minutes, Meetings with the President—General—9/61–1/62, JFKL.

61   *One week later*: Minutes of Meeting with the President, Cabinet Room, Oct. 10, 1961, 11:00 p.m., National Security File, ibid. (also in National Security File, Box 83).

61   *"Preferred Sequence":* State-Defense Draft, "US Policy on Military Action in a Berlin Conflict," Oct. 18, 1961, National Security File, Box 83, Minutes of Meetings with the President, JFKL.

63   *As Bundy summarized:* Memo, Bundy to JFK, "Berlin meeting, 10 o'clock, Friday, October 20," 10/20/61, National Security File, ibid.

63   *"an ominous thing":* Memo of Meeting with the President, Oct. 20, 1961, 10:00 a.m., National Security File, ibid.

64   *"like sausages":* Aleksandr Fursenko and Timothy Naftali, *Khrushchev's Cold War* (New York: W. W. Norton, 2006), esp. Chapter 10.

64   *Bundy had a hand in writing it:* WGBH, "War and Peace in the Nuclear Age: At the Brink: Interview with Roswell Gilpatric," *Open Vault*, March 7, 1986.

64   *"While the Soviets":* Roswell Gilpatric, speech, Hot Springs, VA, Oct. 21, 1961, https://www.cia.gov/library/readingroom/docs/1961-10-21.pdf.

66   *at the group's first meeting:* All quotes are from transcripts of the secretly recorded tapes of the ExComm sessions. Copies of the tapes are available from JFKL. The best transcript overall is by the University of Virginia–Miller Center of Public Affairs, in *The Presidential Recordings, John F. Kennedy—The Great Crises*, Vols. 2 and 3, Timothy Naftali, Philip Zelikow, and Ernest May, eds. (New York: W. W. Norton, 2001). However, there are several well-known lapses in some of its transcripts, owing perhaps to the use of poor noise-reduction technology, which erased much more than just hiss. The most authoritative transcript of the session on the final day of the crisis is *Presidential Recordings: Cuban Missile Crisis, Oct. 26, 1962* (Boston: John F. Kennedy Library, 1987). I have also drawn on the transcriptions by Sheldon Stern, the Library's former chief historian, in his books, *Averting "The Final Failure": John F. Kennedy and the Secret Cuban Missile Crisis Meetings* (Stanford: Stanford University Press, 2003) and *The Cuban Missile Crisis in American Memory: Myths Versus Reality* (Stanford: Stanford University Press, 2012). Finally, I have listened to these tapes, and, where what I heard is clear and departs from the published versions, I've gone with my own ears.

69   *Meanwhile, the CIA informed Kennedy:* Memo from McCone, National Security Files, Box 313, Folder 40, NSC Mtgs., 1962, No. 507, 10/22/62, JFKL.

70   *By this time, the CIA was reporting:* CIA, Memorandum, "The Crisis USSR/Cuba," Oct. 27, 1962, https://nsarchive2.gwu.edu/nsa/cuba_mis_cri/621027%20The%20Crisis%20USSR-Cuba.pdf.

74   *Decades later:* Martin Tolchin, "US Underestimated Soviet Force in Cuba During '62 Missile Crisis," *New York Times,* Jan. 15, 1992.

74   *Kennedy told just six advisers:* McGeorge Bundy, *Danger and Survival: Choices About the Bomb in the First Fifty Years* (New York: Random House, 1988), 423–33.

74   *In a phone conversation:* Dictaphone record, phone conversation, JFK and Eisenhower, Oct. 28, 1962, JFKL.

74   *In his 1965 biography:* Sorensen admitted this in his recollections in *Back to the Brink: Proceedings of the Moscow Conference on the Cuban Missile Crisis, Jan. 27–28, 1989,* ed. Bruce J. Allyn, James G. Blight, and David A. Welch (Lanham, MD: University Press of America, 1992), 92–93. He also admitted it to me in a 1997 interview.

74   *"propaganda":* Sorensen, *Kennedy,* 714.

75   *The other palace historians:* Chiefly Schlesinger, *A Thousand Days.* The most prominent anti-Kennedy history is Garry Wills, *The Kennedy Imprisonment* (New York: Atlantic/Little Brown, 1982). It is striking how many otherwise excellent historians have continued to fall for the official history, despite the fact that the secret tape recordings—publicly available since 1987—prove it definitively false.

75   *"We misled":* Bundy, *Danger and Survival,* 434.

CHAPTER 4: *"This Goddamn Poker Game"*

76   *"It seems":* All quotes from this meeting are from Miller Center of Public Affairs, *The Presidential Recordings: John F. Kennedy,* Vol. 6, ed. David Coleman (Charlottesville: University of Virginia–Miller Center, 2016), 28ff, esp. 35, 42, 47–48.

78   *Would the president risk:* The "New York for Paris" formulation might first have been expressed in Memorandum of conversation, JFK and Congressional leaders, June 6, 1961, *FRUS,* 1961–1963, Vol. XIII, Western Europe and Canada, Document 231. The concern is expressed or cited in dozens of documents in the Kennedy Library's folders and files on the Berlin crisis.

78   *Even after the Berlin crisis settled:* Telegram, Rusk to Embassy in France, May 5, 1961, *FRUS*, ibid., Document 227.

79   *"The U.S. has come":* Address by McNamara at Ministerial Meeting of North Atlantic Council, May 5, 1962, *FRUS*, 1961–1963, Vol. VIII, Western Europe and Canada, Document 82. The backstory on the speech comes from Kaplan, op. cit., 283 (based on interviews with Kaufmann, Rowen, McNamara).

80   *"repeat to the point":* Bundy's handwriting on memo to McNamara citing JFK's view of the speech, quoted in ibid., 284 (provided to author).

80   *When Paul Nitze:* Ibid., 285, based on 1981 interview with Nitze.

80   *But McNamara insisted:* McNamara, " 'No Cities' Speech," June 9, 1962, http://www.atomicarchive.com/Docs/Deterrence/Nocities.shtml. Background from Kaplan, ibid., based on interviews with Kaufmann, Ellsberg, McNamara.

81   *"total war, total annihilation":* Ellsberg, *The Doomsday Machine*, 148–49. Ellsberg told me this story in a 1980 interview. McNamara publicly revealed his views on the subject in his memoir, *In Retrospect* (New York: Crown, 1995), 345.

82   *"We might try":* Memorandum, McNamara to JFK, "Recommended FY 1964–FY 1968 Strategic Retaliatory Forces," Nov. 21, 1962, National Security Files, Box 275, Defense Budget FY 1964, Vol. 1, JFKL.*

83   *"The Air Force has":* Memo, Taylor to McNamara, "Recommended FY 1964–FY 1968 Strategic Retaliatory Forces," Nov. 20, 1962, ibid.*

84   *In January 1963:* Richard Kugler, "The Politics of Restraint: Robert McNamara and the Strategic Nuclear Forces, 1963–69" (PhD diss., MIT, 1975), 82–83.

85   *"living in total dreamland":* Memo, Col. L.G. Legere, Feb. 4, 1962, *FRUS*, 1961–1963, Vol. VIII, Document 127.

85   *This evolution began:* David G. Coleman, *The Fourteenth Day: JFK and the Aftermath of the Cuban Missile Crisis* (New York: W. W. Norton, 2012), 124.

85   *the Chiefs advised him:* Memorandum of conversation, "Laos," April 29, 1961, FRUS, 1961–1963, Vol. XXIV, Laos Crisis, Document 67; Oral History Interview, Arleigh Burke, Jan. 20, 1967, 36–37, JFKL.

85   *"don't seem to have* cojones":* Miller Center of Public Affairs, *The*

Presidential Recordings, John F. Kennedy: The Great Crises, Vol. 1, ed. Timothy Naftali (New York: W. W. Norton, 1997), 47–50.

86   *Even more than McNamara:* Memorandum of conversation, W. Y. Smith to Taylor, Briefing for the President on Berlin, Aug. 9, 1962, *FRUS,* 1961–1963, Vol. XV, Berlin Crisis, 1962–1963, Document 93.

86   *At the moment, Khrushchev:* Arthur M. Schlesinger, Jr., *A Thousand Days* (Boston: Houghton Mifflin, 1965), 899.

86   *In December:* Letter, JFK to Khrushchev, on nuclear testing, Dec. 28, 1962, http://www.presidency.ucsb.edu/ws/index.php?pid=9308.

86   *The back-and-forth:* Ted Sorensen, *Counselor: A Life at the Edge of History* (New York: HarperCollins, 2008), 326; Arthur M. Schlesinger, Jr., *Journals, 1952–2000* (New York: Penguin, 2007), 194.

86   *"I speak of peace":* Transcript, JFK, Commencement Address, American University, June 10, 1963, JFKL.

88   *"sincere":* CIA Information Report, "Soviet Reaction to President Kennedy's US Foreign Policy Speech at American Univ., 15 June 1963," National Security Files, Box 305a, President's speech, JFKL.

88   *"were favorably surprised":* CIA Information Report, "Soviet Reaction to 10 June Speech of President Kennedy, 11 June 1963," ibid.

88   *Khrushchev, whom Kennedy:* Furscnko and Naftali, op. cit., 509. The same remark to Harriman: Telegram, Harriman to Rusk, July 27, 1963, *FRUS,* 1961–1963, Vol. VII, Arms Control and Disarmament, Document 354.

88   *The speech spurred Khrushchev:* Fursenko & Naftali, ibid.

88   *"hotline":* Memo of Understanding between the USA and the USSR Regarding the Establishment of a Direct Communications Link, June 20, 1963. (The line was teletype, not voice, as it was thought that inflections might be misinterpreted.)

88   *The U.S. Senate:* https://www.jfklibrary.org/JFK/JFK-in-History/Nuclear-Test-Ban-Treaty.aspx.

89   *"nuclear stalemate":* Bromley Smith, Summary Record of NSC Meeting, Sept. 12, 1963, 11:00 a.m.—Report of the Net Evaluation Subcommittee, National Security Files, Box 314, NSC Meeting, 9/12/63, JFKL. Other participants' notes are collected in an Attachment to the Summary Record, *FRUS,* 1961–1963, Volume VIII, National Security Policy, Document 141. The report itself can be found at NSA/EBB

No. 480, Document 10-A, the oral presentation to the NSC in Document 10-B.

91   *"Assured Destruction"*: Kaplan, op. cit., 317–19 (based on documents obtained through FOIA and interviews with McNamara, Enthoven, Kaufmann, and others). The first memo where the term and concept appear may be Kaysen to Bundy, "Comment on DOD Draft Memorandum, Strategic Striking Forces (August 31, 1963)," National Security Files, Box 5, DoD 1965, Sec. 2, LBJL.

91   *"Mutual Assured Destruction"*: Donald Brennan, "Strategic Alternatives: I," *New York Times*, May 24, 1971.

91   *To give the:* Memorandum, McNamara to LBJ, Recommended FY 1965–69 Strategic Retaliatory Forces, Dec. 6, 1963* (now at *FRUS*, 1961–1963, Volume VIII, National Security Policy, Document 151).

92   *"diminishing marginal returns"*: This point is made explicitly in Alain Enthoven and K. Wayne Smith, *How Much Is Enough?* (New York: Harper & Row, 1971), 207.

92   *"the destructive capacity"*: Memo, McNamara to LBJ, op. cit.*

92   *Enthoven would later:* Kaplan, op. cit., 317; Memo, McNamara to LBJ, Recommended FY 1966–70 Programs for Strategic Offensive Forces, Dec. 3, 1964* (now available as NSA/EBB No. 311, Document 2).

93   *A few hours before:* Memo, Bundy to LBJ, Dec. 5, 1963, *FRUS*, 1961–1963, Volume VIII, National Security Policy, Document 149.

93   *"greatest single requirement"*: Summary Record, NSC meeting, Dec. 5, 1963, *FRUS*, ibid., Document 150.

94   *"Damage Limiting: A Summary Study"*: I obtained this through FOIA*, summarized in *The Wizards of Armageddon*, 320–25. Kent describes the study in "Looking Back: Four Decades of Analysis," *Operations Research*, Jan.–Feb. 2002.

95   *Not long after:* Memo, McNamara to LBJ, Dec. 3, 1964* (now available as NSA/EBB No. 311, Document 2).

95   *"Would things be"*: LeMay said this to me in a 1981 interview and affirmed that he'd said it to several fellow officers at the time.

96   *The weapons labs had been developing:* Daniel Buchonnet, Lawrence Livermore laboratory, "MIRV: A Brief History of Minuteman and Multiple Reentry Vehicles," https://nsarchive2.gwu.edu /nsa/NC/mirv/mirv.html; Herbert York, "The Origins of MIRV,"

SIPRI Research Report #9 (Stockholm International Peace Research Institute, 1973).

96   *LeMay at first opposed:* Buchonnet, ibid.

97   *"development of":* Memo, McNamara to LBJ, Dec. 3, 1964* (now available as NSA/EBB No. 311, Document 2).

97   *In short, the MIRV:* Buchonnet, op. cit., acknowledges that Air Force proponents of MIRV viewed it as a first-strike weapon.

CHAPTER 5: *Madman Theories*

100   *One week:* JCS, "Joint Staff Briefing of the Single Integrated Operational Plan (SIOP)," January 27, 1969, NSA/EBB No. 173, Document 1.

101   *By the time Nixon:* Memo, Laurence Lynn, Jr., to Kissinger, "The SIOP," Nov. 8, 1969, NSA/EBB No. 173, Document 3.

101   *Nixon was visibly horrified:* Interview with Laurence Lynn, 2018.

101   *Kissinger had been:* See especially *Nuclear Weapons and Foreign Policy* (New York: Harper & Bros., 1957); *The Necessity for Choice* (New York: Doubleday, 1960).

101   *More pertinently:* Kissinger's term as a consultant in Kennedy's White House, which began on February 27, 1961, did not wear well. McGeorge Bundy, the national security adviser and his former Harvard colleague, fired him on September 14, 1962, citing concerns by many that his high-profile public views often differed from the administration's position and thus caused confusion at home and abroad. Others in the White House complained about his high expense submissions. As late as January 1963, Secretary of State Dean Rusk felt compelled to send a cable to all U.S. ambassadors, reminding them that Kissinger "has no official status whatsoever" and urging them "to take any appropriate occasion to discourage the impression, which appears to be prevalent in Europe, that Dr. Kissinger has any official responsibilities." Nor should they "seek appointments for him with people on whom he may wish to call." ("Dear Henry" Letter, Bundy to Kissinger, Sept. 14, 1962; Letter, David Klein, July 9, 1962; State Department Telegram, Eyes Only for Ambassadors, Jan. 17, 1963; all in National Security Files, Box 321, NSC Meetings & Memos, JFKL. The date of his appointment is in a memo by Bromley, in Box 320.)

101   *"Is this the best":* William Burr, "The Nixon Administration's 'Horror

Strategy' and the Search for Limited Nuclear Options, 1969–1972," *Journal of Cold War Studies*, Summer 2005.

102 *"We may have reached"*: "Notes on NSC Meeting, 13 Feb 1969," Feb. 14, 1969, NSA/EBB No. 173, Document 6.

102 *"The SIOP is a horror strategy"*: "President's Review of Defense Posture, San Clemente, July 28, 1970, Selected Comments, NSA/EBB No. 173, Document 14.

103 *"I call it the Madman Theory"*: Robert Haldeman with Joseph DiMona, *The Ends of Power* (New York: Times Books, 1968), 82–83.

103 *The idea had its roots*: Nina Tannenwald, *The Nuclear Taboo: The United States and the Non-Use of Nuclear Weapons Since 1945* (New York: Cambridge University Press, 2007), 228.

103 *"the most brilliant"*: William Burr and Jeffrey P. Kimball, *Nixon's Nuclear Specter: The Secret Alert of 1969, Madman Diplomacy, and the Vietnam War* (Lawrence: University Press of Kansas, 2015), 52.

104 *"is as much a psychological"*: Kissinger, "Editor's Introduction," *Problems in National Strategy* (New York: Praeger, 1965).

104 *"threats and counter-threats"*: Kissinger, *The Necessity for Choice*, 40–46.

104 *On his instructions*: Burr and Kimball, op. cit., 197.

104 *"I refuse to believe"*: Seymour M. Hersh, *The Price of Power: Kissinger in Nixon's White House* (New York: Summit, 1983), 126.

104 *"to demonstrate U.S. resolve"*: Report to Kissinger, "Vietnam Contingency Planning: Concept of Operations," Sept. 13, 1969, NSA/EBB No. 517, Document 11-A.

105 *"meanest"*: Hersh, op. cit., 128.

105 *"appalling"*: Burr and Kimball, op. cit., 222.

105 *Kissinger didn't bother*: Ibid., 223.

105 *He and Kissinger were hardly*: Ibid., 28.

105 *"We are not following"*: Tannenwald, op. cit., 203.

106 *In early 1968*: Ibid., 220–25.

106 *"exactly as you would"*: "President Says Atom Bomb Would Be Used Like 'Bullet,'" *New York Times*, March 17, 1955.

106 *He ordered nuclear-capable*: Burr and Kimball, op. cit., 36.

106 *Then again, even McNamara*: Tannenwald, op. cit., 198.

107 *"somewhat crazy"*: Leonard Garment, *Crazy Rhythm* (New York: Times Books, 1997), 174, 176–77.

107 *"discernible to the Soviets"*: Memo, Tab to Memo, Laird to Nixon, "Test of U.S. Military Readiness," Oct. 11, 1969, NSA/EBB No. 517, Document 16.

107 *For more than two weeks:* Burr and Kimball, op. cit., 254ff.

108 *"no significant reaction"*: Ibid., 281.

108 *"Americans put forces"*: Quoted in Richard Lebow and Janice Stein, *We All Lost the Cold War* (Princeton: Princeton University Press, 1994), 488.

108 *The Foster Panel:* Fred Kaplan, op. cit., 356–60, 368–70 (based on interviews in 1980–82 with Foster, Schlesinger, Yudkin, Schelling, Selin, Lynn, Martin, Wood, Seymour Weiss, Andrew Marshall, Gen. Russell Dougherty, Gen. Richard Ellis, Albert Wohlstetter).

110 *"Selective Attack Options"*: James Schlesinger, *Rationale for NU-OPTS,* RAND Report R-1608-PR (1968), quoted in Marc Trachtenberg, *History and Strategy* (Princeton: Princeton University Press, 1991), 40.

111 *"not that they are"*: Ibid.

112 *"a study reviewing"*: Memo, Kissinger to Rogers, Laird, Helms, "Military Posture and the Balance of Power," Jan. 21, 1969, *FRUS,* 1969–1976, Vol. XXXIV, National Security Policy, 1969–1972, Document 2.

112 *"Up to now"*: NSSM-3, May 8, 1969, quoted in Kaplan, op. cit., 366–67. (The study itself, which was provided to me by a source while I was researching *Wizards,* is oddly still classified.)

112 *After Selin left:* Ibid., 367–68.

113 *On July 27:* The briefing has not been declassified, but a memo from Odeen to Kissinger, written just prior to it, summarizes its points. Memo, "HAK Talking Points, DoD Strategic Targeting Study Briefing," July 27, 1972, NSA/EBB No. 173, Document 18.

114 *At a small interagency meeting:* State Department Information Memorandum, U. Alexis Johnson to Acting Secretary, "DPRC Meeting—June 27, 1972," ibid., Document 17.

114 *"an unprecedented opportunity"*: Memo, Kissinger to Nixon, "Secretary Laird's Recommendations on U.S. Strategic Policy," ibid., Document 19.

114 *"political, economic and military targets"*: "NSSM 169: Summary Report," June 8, 1973, ibid., Document 21.

115 *"We have been discussing"*: Memo, Jeanne W. Davis to Kissinger, "Minutes of the Verification Panel Meeting held Aug. 9, 1973," Aug. 15, 1973, ibid., Document 22.

116   *"pipe-smoking":* Gen. Thomas White, "Strategy and the Defense Intellectuals," *Saturday Evening Post,* May 4, 1963.

117   *"change in targeting strategy":* Remarks by Secretary of Defense James Schlesinger, Overseas Writers Association Luncheon, International Club, Washington, D.C., DoD Public Affairs Office; backstory comes from interviews with Schlesinger, Kaufmann.

118   *One week after his speech:* Memo, Nixon to Sec of State, Sec of Defense, Director CIA, Director, ACDA, "National Security Decision Memorandum 242: Policy for Planning the Employment of Nuclear Weapons," Jan. 17, 1974, NSA/EBB No. 173, Document 24-b.

118   *two and a half weeks later:* "Policy Guidance for the Employment of Nuclear Weapons," April 3, 1974, ibid., Document 25.

118   *General John Meyer:* Cited in Memorandum for the Record, Eric Anschutz, ACDA, "SIOP Expansion Studies," April 20, 1973, ibid., Document 20.

119   *"Are you out of your minds?":* Kaplan, op. cit., 370–71, based on interviews with Aaron and Lodal.

CHAPTER 6: *Bargaining Chips*

121   *Like many Navy veterans:* Brian Auten, *Carter's Conversion: The Hardening of American Defense Policy* (Columbia: University of Missouri Press, 2009), 61, 65; interview with President Carter, 2018.

122   *clenching his teeth:* On Carter's different types of smiles, see Zbigniew Brzezinski, *Power and Principle: Memoirs of the National Security Adviser, 1977–1981* (New York: Farrar, Straus & Giroux, 1983), 21–22.

122   *After the final slide:* Edward C. Keefer, *Secretaries of Defense Historical Series, Vol. 9: Harold Brown: Offsetting the Military Challenge, 1977–1981* (Washington, DC: Department of Defense Historical Office, 2017), 147–48; interview with President Carter.

122   *Brown, a nuclear physicist:* See esp. Harold Brown, "Strategic Force Structure and Strategic Deterrence," Speech to Soviet Academy of Sciences, March 1975, reprinted in Hearings, Joint Committee on Defense Production, *Civil Preparedness and Limited Nuclear War,* April 28, 1976, p. 130.

122   *Brown thought that whittling down:* Keefer, op. cit., 148.

122 *more than 1,300:* Robert S. Norris and Thomas B. Cochran, *US-USSR/ Russian Strategic Offensive Nuclear Forces, 1945–1996* (Washington, DC: Natural Resources Defense Council, 1997), Table 2.

122 *The last argument:* Interview with President Carter.

123 *Once in the White House:* Garrett M. Graff, *Raven Rock: The Story of the U.S. Government's Secret Plan to Save Itself—While the Rest of Us Die* (New York: Simon & Schuster, 2017), Chapter 13.

123 *In the first two:* William Odom, "The Origins and Design of Presidential Decision-59: A Memoir," in Henry D. Sokolski, *Getting MAD: Mutual Assured Destruction, Its Origins and Practice* (lulu.com, 2014), 180.

123 *"I'm pretty smart":* Ibid.; interview with President Carter.

123 *He ordered the first:* Interview with President Carter.

124 *He later learned:* Transcript, Zbigniew Brzezinski Oral History, University of Virginia–Miller Center, Feb. 18, 1982.

124 *"If, after the inauguration":* Quoted in Douglas Brinkley, "The Lives They Lived; Out of the Loop," *New York Times*, Dec. 29, 2002.

125 *During a trip to SAC headquarters:* Odom, op. cit., 180.

125 *"The SIOP, as you know":* Memo, Brzezinski to Carter, "Our Nuclear War Doctrine: Limited Nuclear Options and Regional Nuclear Options," March 31, 1977, NSA/EBB No. 390, Document 1.

125 *"comprehensive net assessment":* "Presidential Review Memorandum/ NSC-10: Comprehensive Net Assessment and Military Force Posture Review," Feb. 18, 1977, https://fas.org/irp/offdocs/prm/prm10.pdf.

125 *"essential equivalence":* Walter Slocombe, Memo, "Presidential Directive/NSC-18: U.S. National Strategy," Aug. 30, 1977, NSA/EBB No. 390, Document 2-A.

126 *Over the previous twenty years:* Keefer, op. cit., 458.

126 *they fielded something new:* Most of this section comes from my article "Warring Over New Missiles for NATO," *New York Times Magazine*, Dec. 9, 1979 (based on interviews with more than a dozen officials at the time).

127 *He saw Carter:* For more on the Carter-Schmidt animosity, see Brzezinski, *Power and Principle*, 25–26, 461–63.

130 *"killer warhead":* Walter Pincus, "Neutron Killer Warhead Buried in ERDA Budget," *Washington Post*, June 6, 1977.

130   *"gross oversimplification"*: Jimmy Carter, *White House Diary* (New York: Farrar, Straus & Giroux, 2010), 179.

131   *Yet, at the same time:* Brzezinski, op. cit., 304–5.

133   *"to create a vested interest"*: This section on the counterproductive consequences of nuclear arms control treaties is based on G. W. Rathjens, Abram Chayes, and J. P. Ruina, *Nuclear Arms Control Agreements: Process and Impact* (Washington, DC: Carnegie Endowment for International Peace, 1974); Fred Kaplan, "SALT: The End of Arms Control," *The Progressive*, Jan. 1978.

135   *Harold Brown's staff:* Keefer, op. cit., 172–73.

136   *"the year of maximum danger"*: For more, see Fred Kaplan, *The Wizards of Armageddon*, 136–41, 373–80.

136   *"a nuclear superiority:"* Paul Nitze, "Assuring Strategic Stability in an Era of Détente," *Foreign Affairs*, Jan. 1976.

136   *"Deterring Our Deterrent"*: Paul Nitze and T. K. Jones, "Deterring Our Deterrent," *Foreign Policy*, Winter 1976–77.

138   *Nitze and his wife:* Public Records, U.S. Federal Elections Commission, Washington, DC; cited in Kaplan, op. cit., 380.

139   *"I do not share"*: Letter from Brzezinski, July 16, 1979, Box 43, Missiles, 5–7/79, JCL. Copies of this letter were addressed to Sen. Mark Hatfield, Herbert York, George Kistiakowsky, and others.

139   *"We don't have prompt"*: Nuclear Targeting Policy Review, Nov. 1978, NSA/EBB No. 390, Document 3.

139   *"nauseating"*: Carter, *White House Diary*, 303.

139   *"not synonymous"*: Quoted in Keefer, 161–62.

140   *He and Smith:* Interview with Leslie Gelb, 2018.

140   *"the greatest threat"*: Edward Walsh, "Carter Sees No Early End to Crises," *Washington Post*, Jan. 9, 1980.

140   *"My opinion"*: Quoted in Editorial Note, *FRUS*, 1977–1980, Vol. 1, Foundations of Foreign Policy, Document 133.

140   *"the worst disappointment"*: Jimmy Carter, *Keeping Faith: Memoirs of a President* (Fayetteville: University of Arkansas Press, 1982), 482.

141   *Back in September 1977:* Memo, Slocombe, "Follow-On Studies for PD/NSC-18," Sept. 1, 1977, NSA/EBB No. 390, Document 2-B.

141   *Andrew Marshall:* For more on Marshall, see Kaplan, op. cit., Chapter 13 and 372, 387.

142 *His conclusion:* Nuclear Targeting Policy Review, op. cit.; and interviews.

143 *Odom took part:* Odom, op. cit.; and interviews.

144 *"endurance":* Detailed Minutes, Special Coordination Committee meeting, April 4, 1979, NSA/EBB No. 390, Document 4-A.

145 *Both documents:* Carter, PD/NSC-59, July 25, 1980, ibid., Document 12.

145 *"terminate the war":* Secretary of Defense, Policy Guidance for the Employment of Nuclear Weapons (NUWEP), Oct. 1980, ibid., Document 21.

145 *He didn't even attend:* Brzezinski, *Power and Principle,* 458.

145 *Still, on July 25:* His main reason for signing PD-59 comes from my 2018 interview with President Carter.

146 *"only on paper":* Odom, op. cit. This is confirmed by interviews with Gelb and others.

CHAPTER 7: *"A Super Idea"*

147 *Reagan entered:* This was stated often in the campaign and codified in NSDD-32, "U.S. National Security Strategy," May 20, 1982, https://fas.org/irp/offdocs/nsdd/nsdd-32.pdf.

147 *Thirty-two members:* Kaplan, op. cit., 386. Data obtained at the time from the Committee on the Present Danger.

147 *He revived every nuclear:* National Security Decision Directive (NSDD) 12, "Strategic Forces Modernization Program," Oct. 1, 1981, https://fas.org/irp/offdocs/nsdd/nsdd-12.pdf.

148 *"the United States and its Allies":* "Nuclear Weapons Employment Policy," https://fas.org/irp/offdocs/nsdd/nsdd-13.pdf.

148 *"to prevail":* See especially NSC 5904/1, "Statement of U.S. Policy in the Event of War," March 17, 1959, *FRUS,* 1958–1960, Vol. III, National Security Policy, Arms Control and Disarmament, Document 55.

148 *"to lose any worse":* Memo for Record, Conference of JCS with President, Feb. 10, 1956, Box 4, White House Office, Office of Staff Secretary, Subject Series, DoD Subject, JCS(2), DDEL.

148 *Kissinger issued a directive:* NSDM-27, "U.S. Military Posture," Oct. 11, 1969, https://fas.org/irp/offdocs/nsdd/nsdd-13.pdf. The last sentence,

before Kissinger's signature, reads: "NSC 5904/1—U.S. Policy in the Event of War—is hereby rescinded."

148 *Richard Pipes:* "Why the Soviet Union Thinks It Could Fight and Win a Nuclear War," *Commentary,* Sept. 1977.

148 *Keith Payne:* Colin Gray and Keith Payne, "Victory Is Possible," *Foreign Policy,* Summer 1980.

149 *Years earlier:* Robert Kaiser, "Senate Staffer Richard Perle: Behind-Scenes Power over Arms Policy," *Washington Post,* June 26, 1977.

150 *"the White Hats":* Minutes, NSC Meeting, Oct. 13, 1981, *FRUS,* 1981–1988, Vol. III, Soviet Union, Jan. 1981–Jan. 1983, Document 92.

150 *"This is one":* Quoted in Martin Anderson and Annelisse Anderson, *Reagan's Secret War: The Untold Story of His Fight to Save the World from Nuclear Disaster* (New York: Crown, 2009), 94.

150 *What may have impelled Reagan:* Daily Diary of President Reagan, Feb. 26, 1982, NSA/EBB No. 575, Document 13.

150 *"given . . . his personal distaste":* Thomas Reed, *At the Abyss: An Insider's History of the Cold War* (Novato, CA: Presidio Press, 2004), 244.

151 *Sitting in the White House Situation Room:* Notes of the briefing are unavailable, but a detailed outline, prepared in advance, can be found as an attachment to Memo, William Clark to Caspar Weinberger and Gen. David Jones, "National Defense/Security Briefings," Feb. 23, 1982, ibid., Document 12.

151 *Weinberger's guidance:* DoD, Policy Guidance for the Employment of Nuclear Weapons (NUWEP), June 1982, https://www.archives.gov/files/declassification/iscap/pdf/2013-111-doc01.pdf.

152 *"a super idea":* The Reagan Diaries Unabridged, Vol. 1, *January 1981–October 1985,* ed. Douglas Brinkley (New York: HarperCollins, 2009), 196.

153 *A year earlier:* Anderson and Anderson, op. cit. 113–14.

153 *"a very big decision":* Reagan, Address to the Nation on Defense and Security, March 23, 1983, http://www.atomicarchive.com/Docs/Missile/Starwars.shtml.

154 *"a reckless 'Star Wars' scheme":* Statement, Sen. Edward Kennedy, March 24, 1983.

155 *Initially Kosygin:* Memo of Conversation, Glassboro, N.J., June 23, 1967, *FRUS,* 1964–1968, Vol. XIV, Soviet Union, Document 231.

156   *"evil empire":* Reagan, speech, March 8, 1983, https://nationalcenter .org/ReaganEvilEmpire1983.html.

156   *Almost six months later:* Seymour M. Hersh, *"The Target Is Destroyed": What Really Happened to Flight 007 and What America Knew About It* (New York: Random House, 1986).

156   *"false missile warning":* Memo, Brown to Carter, "False Missile Alerts," June 13, 1980, Box 46, JCL.

156   *In a separate incident:* Robert Gates, *From the Shadows: The Ultimate Insider's Story of Five Presidents and How They Won the Cold War* (New York: Simon & Schuster, 1996), 114.

156   *As it happened:* David Hoffman, " 'I Had a Funny Feeling in My Gut,' " *Washington Post,* Feb. 10, 1999.

157   *Early on in his presidency:* Fred Kaplan, *Dark Territory: The Secret History of Cyber War* (New York: Simon & Schuster, 2016), 15; and interviews with senior intelligence officials.

157   *Ivy Bells:* Sherry Sontag and Christopher Drew, *Blind Man's Bluff: The Untold Story of American Submarine Espionage* (New York: Harper Collins, 1998).

158   *In August:* Benjamin Fisher, "The 1983 War Scare in U.S.-Soviet Relations," *Studies in Intelligence* (CIA, n.d.); and Benjamin Fisher, "A Cold War Conundrum: The 1983 War Scare" (CIA Intelligence Monograph, 1997), in NSA/EBB, No. 426, Documents 3, 4.

158   *"These actions":* Thomas R. Johnson, *American Cryptology During the Cold War, 1945–1989,* Book IV, *Cryptologic Rebirth, 1981–1989* (National Security Agency, Center for Cryptologic History, 1999), 318.

158   *"shoot to kill":* Fisher, "The 1983 War Scare," op. cit.

159   *An estimated 100 million Americans:* Robert D. McFadden, "Atomic War Film Spurs Nationwide Discussion," *New York Times,* Nov. 22, 1983.

159   *"a room awash in gasoline":* ABC News Viewpoint, " 'The Day After' Nuclear War/Deterrence Discussion," Nov. 20, 1983, https://www .youtube.com/watch?v=PcCLZwU2t34.

159   *"It's very effective":* The Reagan Diaries, Vol. 1, 273.

159   *It was an unusually large exercise:* Nate Jones, ed., *Able Archer 83: The Secret History of the NATO Exercise That Almost Triggered Nuclear War* (New York: The New Press, 2016), 28.

160 *The Soviets were monitoring:* President's Foreign Intelligence Advisory Board (PFIAB), "The Soviet 'War Scare,'" Feb. 15, 1990, vi; Jones, ibid., 34–37.

160 *But a three-star general:* Jones, ibid., 37; PFIAB, ibid., 27–28; Marc Ambinder, *The Brink: President Reagan and the Nuclear War Scare of 1983* (New York: Simon & Schuster, 2018), 224, 226, 249.

160 *While Able Archer was unfolding:* Fisher, "The 1983 War Scare," op. cit.; PFIAB, viii.

161 *"propaganda":* PFIAB, ibid., vi.

161 *"There is little doubt":* Ibid., 75.

161 *"redirected":* Ibid., 5.

161 *"for a preemptive strike":* Ibid., 2.

161 *"highly lethal":* Ibid., 47.

162 *"yet another step":* Ibid., 47, 66.

162 *"genuine anxiety":* Jones, op. cit., 45.

162 *"some people in":* Ronald Reagan, *An American Life* (New York: Simon & Schuster, 2011), 258.

163 *"I feel the Soviets":* *The Reagan Diaries*, Vol. 1, 290.

163 *"now that we are":* Memo of conversation, reprinted in Jones, op. cit., 285–88.

163 *McFarlane set about:* Ibid., 49.

163 *on the advice of her astrologer:* Ibid., 322fn.48.

164 *"If the Soviet government":* Reagan, Address to the Nation and Other Countries on United States-Soviet Relations, Jan. 16, 1984, RRL.

164 *"really scary":* Quoted in PFIAB, 17; the Casey memo is described on p. 11ff.

164 *"I have a gut feeling":* *The Reagan Diaries*, Vol. 1, 357.

164 *"They keep dying on me":* Reagan apparently cracked this line to several people, including his wife (Ronald Reagan, *An American Life*, 611), Canadian prime minister Pierre Trudeau (Oral History, Kenneth Adelman, University of Virginia–Miller Center, Sept. 30, 2013), Patrick Buchanan (Buchanan, "What Would Reagan Do?," *Utz Review*, April 11, 2014).

165 *"caveman outlook":* He viewed Reagan in this way even after the Reykjavik summit in 1986. See Session of the Politburo of the CC CPSU, Oct. 14, 1986, NSA/EBB No. 203, Document 21.

165 *The meeting started:* National Security Archive, Electronic Briefing Book No. 172, "To the Geneva Summit: Perestroika and the Transformation of U.S.-Soviet Relations," Documents 15–19.

165 *"Would you help us?":* Gorbachev, interview with Charlie Rose, March 26, 2009, https://www.youtube.com/watch?v=qyfdkw7wBW 0&list=PLY15F12IzJZ_ouvlRD7RI9mHJ0QxGZsWF.

166 *This was an age-old obsession:* Lou Cannon, *President Reagan: The Role of a Lifetime* (Washington, DC: PublicAffairs, 2000), 41.

166 *"I occasionally think":* Reagan, Address to U.N. General Assembly, Sept. 21, 1987, RRL.

166 *When they came*: Shultz, interview with Charlie Rose, March 26, 2009; George Shultz, *Turmoil and Triumph* (New York: Scribner, 1993), 606.

166 *"cannot be won":* Joint Soviet–United States Statement on the Summit Meeting in Geneva, Nov. 21, 1985, RRL.

166 *In February 1986:* "Excerpts from Gorbachev's Speech to the Congress," *New York Times*, Feb. 26, 1986.

167 *"a quick one-on-one meeting":* Letter, Gorbachev to Reagan, Sept. 15, 1986, NSA/EBB No. 203, Document 1.

167 *In the run-up to Geneva:* Ezgi Ustundag, "The Geneva Cold War Summit: 30 Years Later" (interview with Jack Matlock), *Duke Today*, Nov. 2015.

167 *"will be pulled":* Vladimir Zobok, "Gorbachev's Nuclear Learning," *Boston Review*, April 1, 2000.

167 *At their first meeting:* The official Soviet transcripts and U.S. memoranda of conversations, from all four sessions of the Reykjavik summit, are reproduced in NSA/EBB, No. 203, "The Reykjavik File," Documents 9–16.

170 *"I think you didn't want":* Ibid., Document 16. This remark is noted only in the Soviet transcript. Otherwise, the two sets are very similar in substance.

170 *Velikhov replied:* Zobok, op. cit.

171 *"Maybe we should":* Quoted in ibid.

171 *He now knew that:* Session of the Politburo, Oct. 16, 1986, op. cit.

171 *In December 1987:* INF Treaty, Dec. 8, 1987, https://www.state.gov/t /avc/trty/102360.htm.

172 *In the early evening of Sunday:* Helen Thomas, "A Spontaneous Stroll by President and Mrs. Reagan to . . ." UPI, May 29, 1988.

172 *"I was talking about":* Fred Kaplan, "'Evil Empire' Era Has Ended, Reagan Declares in Kremlin," *Boston Globe*, June 1, 1988.

172 *Soon after Reyjkavik:* Attached to Memo, Frank Carlucci to Chief of Staff (Howard Baker), "Nuclear Weapons Issues," March 18, 1987, Howard Baker Files, Box 4, Nuclear Weapons (3/19/1987) folder, RRL.

173 *"as a ploy":* Memo, "What Is Wrong with the Zero Option?," Howard Baker Files, Box 1, Arms Control (April–May 1987) folder, RRL. The document is unsigned, but it is in the same folder as other documents by Carlucci, and it bears the same style and tone as his cover note on nuclear abolitionism.

CHAPTER 8: *Pulling Back the Curtain*

Most of this chapter is based on interviews with the players involved in the story, though some information comes from retired General George Lee Butler's memoir, *An Uncommon Cause*, Vol. 2 (Denver: Outskirts Press, 2016), especially Chapter 23, which (he acknowledges in the book) was written by Frank Miller. There is also a brief mention of Miller and the SIOP Review in the University of Virginia–Miller Center's 2000 Oral History interview with Dick Cheney.

176 *"to the extent":* See Chapter 2.

188 *SAC's commander:* Lars-Erik Nelson, "Are 12,000 Warheads Enough? That Depends on Who's Counting," Tribune Media Services, April 16, 1990.

194 *"make the world":* Text reprinted in Susan J. Koch, *The Presidential Nuclear Initiatives of 1991–1992* (Washington, DC: National Defense University Press, 2012). This section is based largely on Koch's reporting and analysis of the initiatives.

CHAPTER 9: *"A Shrimp Among Whales"*

198 *Five years earlier:* Some of this chapter is based on my article "Rolling Blunder: How the Bush Administration Let North Korea Get Nukes," *Washington Monthly*, May 2004, which was based on many on-the-record interviews with key players in the Clinton and Bush administrations

(including Robert Einhorn, Robert Gallucci, Jack Pritchard, Wendy Sherman, and Joel Wit) as well as a few books, notably Joel Wit, Daniel Poneman, and Robert Gallucci, *Going Critical: The First North Korean Nuclear Crisis* (Washington, DC: Brookings Institution, 2004); and Scott Snyder, *Negotiating on the Edge: North Korean Negotiating Behavior* (Washington, DC: U.S. Institute of Peace, 1999). The chapter is also based on recent interviews with officials from that time, including (on the record) President Jimmy Carter; and also on some materials that weren't available at the time of my 2004 article, including Marion Creekmore, Jr., *A Moment of Crisis: Jimmy Carter, the Power of a Peacemaker, and North Korea's Nuclear Ambitions* (New York: PublicAffairs, 2006).

198 *"comprehensive engagement":* Wit, Poneman, and Gallucci, *Going Critical*, 79.

199 *Finally, at Clinton's direction:* Ibid., 24, 164, 205.

200 *If they struck back:* Ibid.; Creekmore, *A Moment of Crisis*, xx.

201 *Three years later:* Memorandum of conversation, U.S. Delegation to the Bermuda Meeting, March 23, 1957, "Atomic Energy Items: (1) French Request, (2) Test Limitation," https://digitalarchive.wilsoncenter.org /assets/media_files/000/000/028/28.pdf.

201 *"shake NATO":* Message, JFK to Macmillan, May 8, 1961, copied in Telegram, State Department of U.S. Embassy, London, NSA/EBB No. 617, Document 5.

201 *"private nightmare":* NSA/EBB No. 547, "Concerned About Nuclear Weapons Potential, John F. Kennedy Pushed for Inspection of Israel Nuclear Facilities."

201 *He pressured Israel's prime minister:* Avner Cohen and William Burr, "Kennedy, Dimona and the Nuclear Proliferation Problem: 1961– 1962," ibid.

202 *"When we and the British":* Memo, Edward Biegel, "WE [State Department Bureau of Western European Affairs] Answers to the [George] Ball Questionnaire," May 28, 1962, https://digitalarchive.wilsoncenter .org/document/110244.

202 *Kennedy assured de Gaulle:* Message, JFK to MacMillan, op. cit.

202 *"It is the policy":* Bundy, National Security Action Memorandum (NSAM) No. 294, April 20, 1964, https://fas.org/irp/offdocs/nsam -lbj/nsam-294.htm.

202 *Some, especially in the Pentagon:* See, for instance, Memo, Henry Rowen, "China As a Nuclear Power (Some Thoughts Prior to the Chinese Test)," Oct. 7, 1964, NSA/EBB No. 1, Document 4; Memo, Gen. L.L. Lemnitzer, CJCS, to McNamara, "A Strategic Analysis of the Impact of the Acquisition by Communist China of a Nuclear Capability," June 26, 1961, Box 410, National Security Files, Komer Files, China (CPR) Nuclear Explosion, JFKL.

203 *Taiwan's president:* Memorandum of conversation, President Chiang Kai-shek, Gen. Earle Wheeler, Taipei, Dec. 29, 1965, *FRUS, 1964–1968*, Vol. XXX, China, Document 115.

203 *"prepare an operational plan":* Cited in Memo, Maxwell Taylor to Director, Joint Staff, "Operational Air Plan (China)," Nov. 4, 1963, NSA/EBB No. 488, Document 13-A.

203 *Wheeler replied:* Footnote 7 to Memo, Robert Komer to McGeorge Bundy, Feb. 26, 1964, *FRUS, 1964–1968*, Vol. XXX, China, Document 20.

203 *"actions which would involve":* State Department Policy Planning Council, "An Exploration of the Possible Bases for Action Against the Chinese Communist Nuclear Facilities," April 14, 1964, *FRUS*, ibid., Document 25 (see Footnote 1 for the document's context); Memo, G.W. Rathjens, Arms Control and Disarmament Agency, "Destruction of Chinese Nuclear Weapons Capabilities," Dec. 14, 1964, NSA/EBB No. 1.

203 *At a meeting:* Memorandum for the Record, "President's Meeting with Congressional Leadership," Oct. 19, 1964, *FRUS*, ibid., Document 30.

204 *Since the summer:* See for example Memo, Klein and Rivkin to Bundy and Hornig, June 2, 1964, *FRUS, 1964–1968*, Vol. XI, Arms Control and Disarmament, Document 30; Summary of Actions, Principals Meeting, "Action Taken on the Non-Proliferation Paper," June 16, 1964, *FRUS*, ibid., Document 37.

204 *On October 29:* Phone conversation, Bundy and George Ball, Oct. 29, 1964, cited in Editor's Note, *FRUS*, ibid.

204 *Bundy quickly appointed:* Bundy, National Security Action Memorandum (NSAM) No. 320, "Task Force on Nuclear Proliferation," Nov. 25, 1964, *FRUS*, ibid., Document 51.

204 *The members met five times:* Draft Minutes of Discussion of the 2nd Meeting of the Committee on Nuclear Proliferation, Dec. 13–14,

1964; Secretary's Meeting with the Gilpatric Committee on Non-Proliferation, Jan. 7, 1965; Minutes of Discussion, Committee on Nuclear Proliferation, Jan. 7–8, 1964, in *FRUS*, ibid., Documents 56, 59, 60.

204   *Rusk had suggested:* Memorandum of conversation, "Summary of Actions," June 16, 1964, *FRUS*, ibid., Document 37.

204   *"add complexity":* "A Report to the President by the Committee on Nuclear Proliferation," Jan. 21, 1965, *FRUS*, ibid., Document 64.

205   *In response to the report:* Federation of American Scientists, "Nuclear Non-Proliferation Treaty (NPT) Chronology [1957–2000]," https://fas.org/nuke/control/npt/chron.htm.

205   *"inalienable right":* United Nations, "Treaty on the Non-Proliferation of Nuclear Weapons (NPT)," https://www.un.org/disarmament/wmd/nuclear/npt/text/.

205   *The Gilpatric Committee:* "A Report to the President by the Committee on Nuclear Proliferation," op. cit.

206   *"might be difficult":* Memo, Keeny to Bundy, "Arms Control Subjects to Be Explored with the USSR," Dec. 16, 1964, *FRUS*, ibid., Document 57.

206   *But in the twenty-three years:* Robert S. Norris and Thomas B. Cochran, *US-USSR/Russian Strategic Offensive Nuclear Forces, 1945–1996* (Washington, DC: Natural Resources Defense Council, 1997), Tables 1 and 2.

207   *Watching the crisis unfold:* Creekmore, op. cit.

208   *Whatever else might be said about him:* Lawrence Wright, *Thirteen Days in September: Carter, Begin, and Sadat at Camp David* (New York: Alfred A. Knopf, 1983).

208   *"This time":* Creekmore, op. cit., 70–71.

209   And *Carter went way beyond:* Kaplan, "Rolling Blunder," op. cit.; and interviews with President Carter and others.

210   *Four months later:* For details, see Wit, et al., op. cit., and Snyder, op. cit.

210   *"move toward":* "Agreed Framework between the United States of America and the Democratic People's Republic of Korea," Oct. 21, 1994, https://www.iaea.org/sites/default/files/publications/documents/infcircs/1994/infcirc457.pdf.

211   *He consumed:* Barbara Demick, "The Unpalatable Appetites of Kim Jong-il," *The Telegraph*, Oct. 8, 2011.

211 *A cinephile:* Paul Fischer, *A Kim Jong-il Production: The Extraordinary True Story of a Kidnapped Filmmaker, His Star Actress, and a Young Dictator's Rise to Power* (New York: Flatiron Books, 2015).

211 *Yet, in his negotiations:* Interviews for "Rolling Blunder" with Gallucci, Wit, Sherman, Einhorn.

212 *The Clinton team briefed Powell:* Ibid.

212 *Powell told reporters:* "Bush to Pick Up Clinton Talks on North Korea Missiles," *Washington Post*, March 7, 2003.

212 *"too forward":* Powell, interview with Andrea Koppel, CNN, March 14, 2003.

213 *"I loathe":* Bob Woodward, *Bush at War* (New York: Simon & Schuster, 2003), 340.

213 *"axis of evil":* President George W. Bush, State of the Union Address, Jan. 29, 2002.

213 *Abdul Qadeer Khan:* Catherine Collins and Douglas Frantz, "The Long Shadow of A.Q. Khan: How One Scientist Helped the World Go Nuclear," *Foreign Affairs*, Jan. 31, 2018.

214 *"test, manufacture":* "Joint Declaration of South and North Korea on the Denuclearization of the Korean Peninsula," Feb. 19, 1992, https://www.nti.org/media/documents/korea_denuclearization.pdf.

216 *"Once we get beyond":* Quoted in Michael Lev, "US Envoy Sees Cooperation with N. Korea if It Cools Off," *Chicago Tribune*, Jan. 13, 2003.

217 *"regime change":* "N. Korea 'Admits Having Nukes,'" CNN, April 25, 2003.

217 *In May, the commander:* GlobalSecurity.org, "OPLAN 527," https://www.globalsecurity.org/military/ops/oplan-5027.htm.

217 *The Pentagon began revising:* Ibid.

217 *"You're hungry":* David Sanger, "Aftereffects: The Asian Arena; Bush Shifts Focus to Nuclear Sales by North Korea," *New York Times*, May 5, 2003.

218 *"a shrimp among whales":* Snyder, op. cit., 20.

218 *"drama and catastrophe":* Ibid., 43.

218 *"hostile attitude":* "Bush Dismisses Kim's Nuclear 'Blackmail,'" *The Telegraph*, April 26, 2003.

218 *"We don't negotiate":* "Cheney's Tough Talk Derails Negotiations with North Korea," *Sydney Morning Herald*, Dec. 22, 2003.

219 *"This is not a negotiating session":* Kaplan, op. cit., from interview with Pritchard.

220 *"a hellish nightmare":* "U.S. Arms Diplomat Denounces North Korean Leader," *New York Times,* July 31, 2003.

220 *"My position was":* Kaplan, "Rolling Blunder," from interview with Pritchard.

220 *"moral clarity":* Ibid.

220 *It was the first time:* Siegfried Hecker, testimony, Senate Foreign Relations Committee, Jan. 21, 2004; and interviews with Hecker and Pritchard.

221 *On October 9, 2006:* Richard Garwin and Frank von Hippel, "A Technical Analysis: Deconstructing North Korea's October 9 Nuclear Test," *Arms Control Today,* Nov. 9, 2006; Fred Kaplan, "Korea Moves: How Did We Finally Get Back to the Negotiating Table?," *Slate,* July 13, 2005; Fred Kaplan, "Better Than Nothing: Decoding North Korea's Latest Moves," *Slate,* June 27, 2008.

CHAPTER 10: *"Let's Stipulate That This Is All Insane"*

Much of this chapter is based on interviews with twenty officials in the Obama administration, all conducted on a "deep background" basis.

222 *"I'm not naïve":* Remarks by President Barack Obama, Prague, April 9, 2009.

223 *Lugar had developed:* Interview with Richard Lugar, 2018.

224 *Russian border guards:* Peter Finn, "Delegation Led by U.S. Senators Detained Briefly at Russian Airport," *Washington Post,* Aug. 29, 2005; and interview with Lugar.

224 *"on the precipice":* George Shultz, William Perry, Henry Kissinger, and Sam Nunn, "A World Free of Nuclear Weapons," *Wall Street Journal,* Jan. 4, 2007; the background is based on interviews.

225 *"I don't oppose":* Transcript, Obama's speech against the Iraq War, Chicago, Oct. 2, 2002.

225 *"Washington's conventional thinking":* Ibid.; the background is based on interviews.

226 *"provide credible military":* Department of Defense, "Nuclear Posture

Review Report," Jan. 8, 2002, https://fas.org/wp-content/uploads
/media/Excerpts-of-Classified-Nuclear-Posture-Review.pdf.

228   *The most persuasive critic:* For more on Gates's background and style,
see Fred Kaplan, "The Professional," *New York Times Magazine*, Feb.
10, 2008; Fred Kaplan, "The Transformer," *Foreign Policy*, Sept.–Oct.
2010. His role in the debates comes from interviews.

231   *"negative security assurances":* Statement of Secretary of State Vance,
"U.S. Assurance on Non-Use of Nuclear Weapons, June 12, 1978,"
Department of State Bulletin, Aug. 1978, 52. For President Carter's
support of the idea, see Memorandum of conversation, June 12, 1978,
FRUS, 1977–1980, Vol. XXVI, Arms Control and Nonproliferation,
Document 499. The source of the idea comes from 2019 interview
with Leslie Gelb. For more on Keeny and the Gilpatric Committee, see
Chapter 9.

231   *"fundamental role":* Department of Defense, "Nuclear Posture Review
Report," April 2009, 15.

233   *"relatively benign":* Jon Kyl, "The New Start Treaty: Time for a Careful
Look," *Wall Street Journal*, July 8, 2010; and interviews.

234   *In May:* Barron Youngsmith, "START to Finish?," *New Republic*, Nov.
13, 2010; and interviews.

234   *On September 16:* Reuters, "Senate Panel OKs New Arms Treaty with
Russia," Sept. 16, 2010; and interviews.

235   *It took place on December 22:* Peter Baker, "Senate Passes Arms Control
Treaty with Russia, 71–26," *New York Times*, Dec. 22, 2010.

241   *"infrastructure targeting":* Hans M. Kristensen, Robert S. Norris, and
Ivan Oelrich, *From Counterforce to Minimal Deterrence: A New Nuclear Policy on the Path Toward Eliminating Nuclear Weapons* (Washington, DC: Federation of American Scientists, April 2009). That the
booklet was brought up at the meeting comes from interviews.

242   *"40 missiles":* See Chapter 4.

243   *"to maintain significant":* "Report on Nuclear Employment Strategy
of the United States," unclassified excerpts of the full report, delivered
to Congress, June 2013, https://fas.org/blogs/security/2013/06/nuke
guidance/.

243   *"maintain a strong":* President Obama, speech, Berlin, June 19, 2013;
Obama's reasoning comes from interviews.

244 *In his first campaign for president:* NBC News, "Clinton: Obama Is 'Naïve' on Foreign Policy," July 24, 2007.

245 *Two months later:* "Obama Engagement Policy 'in Tatters' After North Korean Rocket Defiance," *The Guardian*, April 13, 2012.

245 *Iran was working out:* Much has been written about the politics and substance of the Iran nuclear deal. The text of the Joint Comprehensive Plan of Action, as it was called, can be read at https://www.state.gov /documents/organization/245317.pdf. An inside account from the U.S. negotiating team is Wendy R. Sherman, *Not for the Faint of Heart: Lessons in Courage, Power, and Persistence* (New York: PublicAffairs, 2018). My view of the deal can be found in several (very favorable) columns I wrote in *Slate* on April 2, June 26, July 14, July 23, Aug. 6, Aug. 27, 2015.

245 *"attainable peace":* President Obama, speech, American University, Aug. 5, 2015.

246 *The turning point:* Michael McFaul, *From Cold War to Hot Peace: An American Ambassador in Putin's Russia* (New York: Houghton Mifflin, 2018); and interviews.

246 *"the greatest geopolitical catastrophe":* "Putin Deplores Collapse of USSR," BBC News, April 25, 2005.

246 *"enlargement":* President Bill Clinton's policy of expanding NATO was another turning point in the collapse of U.S.-Russian relations. See National Security Archive, Briefing Book No. 621, NATO Expansion: What Yeltsin Heard, March 16, 2018.

247 *"modernize or replace":* Message from the President on the New START Treaty, Feb. 2, 2011, https://obamawhitehouse.archives.gov/the-press -office/2011/02/02/message-president-new-start-treaty-0.

248 *$1.3 trillion:* Jon Wolfsthal, Jeffrey Lewis, and Marc Quint, *The Trillion Dollar Nuclear Triad* (Monterey, CA: The James Martin Center for Nonproliferation Studies, 2014).

250 *"was put together":* Ben Rhodes, speech, Arms Control Association, June 6, 2016, https://obamawhitehouse.archives.gov/the-press-office /2016/06/06/remarks-deputy-national-security-advisor-ben-rhodes -arms-control.

250 *In October 2010:* Marc Ambinder, "Failure Shuts Down Squadron of Nuclear Missiles," *The Atlantic*, Oct. 26, 2010; and interviews.

251 *After that, he took a job:* Office of Technology Assessment, MX Missile
     Basing, Sept. 1981; Ashton Carter and David N. Schwartz, *Ballistic
     Missile Defense* (Washington, DC: Brookings Institution, 1984).

251 *From that post.* Jannie E. Nolan, *An Elusive Consensus: Nuclear Weapons
     and American Security After the Cold War* (Washington, DC: Brook-
     ings Institution, 1999), Chapter 3; and interviews.

254 *Soon after the meeting:* Paul Sonne, Gordon Lubold, and Carol E.
     Lee, " 'No First Use' Nuclear Policy Proposal Assailed by U.S. Cabinet
     Officials, Allies," *Wall Street Journal*, Aug. 12, 2016. The article refers
     to a meeting in July. My account of the meeting comes from interviews.

258 *"Given our non-nuclear capabilities":* Vice President Biden, speech, Car-
     negie Endowment for International Peace, Jan. 11, 2017. Backstory of
     speech comes from interviews.

CHAPTER 11: *"Fire and Fury"*

260 *"terrific deal":* Bruce Blair, "What Exactly Would It Mean to Have
     Trump's Finger on the Nuclear Button?," *Politico*, June 11, 2016; story
     confirmed by Richard Burt in 2018 interview.

260 *That same month:* "Chapter 11 for Taj Mahal," Reuters, July 18, 1991.

261 *"I used to discuss":* BBC News, "Who Is Donald Trump's 'Brilliant Ge-
     nius' Nuclear Uncle John?," June 13, 2018.

261 *The depths:* Bob Woodward, *Fear: Trump in the White House* (New
     York: Simon & Schuster, 2018), 218–26.

262 *But Trump viewed the chart:* NBC News, "Trump Wanted Tenfold In-
     crease in Nuclear Arsenal, Surprising Military," Oct. 11, 2017.

262 *"fucking moron":* Shane Savitsky, "Tillerson Called Trump a 'Moron,'
     Almost Resigned," *Axios*, Oct. 4, 2017; and interviews.

263 *In 2016:* "North Korea's Missile Tests—A Timeline," CBS News, Sept.
     6, 2017.

263 *"If China is not":* "Trump Says US Will Act Alone on North Korea if
     China Fails to Help," *Financial Times*, April 3, 2017.

263 *"has not worked out":* @realDonaldTrump, tweet, June 20, 2017,
     11:38 a.m.

263 *"gift to American bastards":* "Kim Jong Un: Missile Launch a 4th of
     July 'Gift to American Bastards,' " *The Times* (London), July 5, 2017;

Timeline of North Korea Missile Launches in Trump's First Year, CNBC, March 14, 2018.

263 *"North Korea best not"*: Peter Baker and Choe Sang-Hun, "Trump Threatens 'Fire and Fury' Against North Korea if It Endangers U.S.," *New York Times*, Aug. 8, 2017.

264 *"classical deterrence U.S. theory"*: *This Week*, ABC News, Aug. 13, 2017.

264 *"very rational actor"*: Guy Taylor, "CIA: Kim Jong-un, North Korea Dictator, Is Not Crazy, but 'Very Rational Actor,'" *Washington Times*, Oct. 4, 2017.

265 *"Rocket Man"*: White House, Remarks by President Trump to the 72nd Session of the United Nations General Assembly, Sept. 19, 2017.

265 *"mentally deranged dotard"*: Choe Sang-Hun, "Kim's Rejoinder to Trump's Rocket Man: 'Mentally Deranged Dotard,'" *New York Times*, Sept. 21, 2017.

266 *"bloody nose" plan:* Ben Riley-Smith, "Exclusive: U.S. Making Plans for 'Bloody Nose' Military Attack on North Korea," *London Telegraph*, Dec. 20, 2017.

267 *"Yes, there are"*: Reuters, "Mattis Hints at Military Options on North Korea but Offers No Details," Sept. 18, 2017.

267 *The two officers did not get along:* Greg Jaffe and Josh Dawsey, "Trump and McMaster Have Seemed Anxious to Part but So Far Remain Together," *Washington Post*, March 1, 2018; and interviews. "Sycophants" comes from interview.

270 *"We have missiles"*: Quoted in Fred Kaplan, "The Worst Defense," *Slate*, Oct. 17, 2017.

270 *"a limited capability"*: Department of Defense, Office of Testing and Evaluation, "FY16 Ballistic Missile Defense Systems," https://www.dote.osd.mil/pub/reports/FY2016/pdf/bmds/2016bmds.pdf.

270 *The one system:* Missile Defense Agency, "Fact Sheet: Ballistic Missile Defense Intercept Flight Test Record," https://www.mda.mil/global/documents/pdf/testrecord.pdf.

270 *"bedrock truth"*: Department of Defense, Nuclear Posture Review, Feb. 2018, Secretary's Preface; other quotes from the review are on pages 2, viii, xii, ii.

272 *"the greatest killers"*: "Trump Says He 'Had a Lot of Fun Fighting' Hillary Clinton," ABC News, Dec. 1, 2016. That Trump hired Mattis on a misconception about his nickname comes from interviews.

272   *"a pack of cigarettes":* Eugene Scott, "Trump 'Surprised' by Mattis Wa-
       terboarding Comments," CNN, Nov. 23, 2016.

272   *Mattis, it turned out:* "Defense Secretary James Mattis' Extraordinary
       Reading Habits," CNBC, Sept. 15, 2018; Michael Doyle, "Advice
       Gen. Mattis' Favorite Philosopher Might Give to Donald Trump," Mc-
       Clatchy, Dec. 2, 2016.

272   *"Be polite":* Thomas E. Ricks, *Fiasco: The American Military Adventure
       in Iraq* (New York: Penguin, 2006), 313.

272   *"Do they serve solely":* Statement of James N. Mattis before the Sen-
       ate Armed Services Committee, Jan. 27, 2015, https://www.armed
       -services.senate.gov/imo/media/doc/Mattis_01-27-15.pdf.

272   *They were so clear:* Gen. C. Robert Kehler et al., letter, "The US Nu-
       clear Triad Needs an Upgrade," *Wall Street Journal*, Jan. 11, 2017. That
       the letter was written as an attempt to influence Mattis, and that Butler
       wasn't asked to sign, comes from interviews.

273   *On January 27:* Department of Defense, Nuclear Posture Review, Feb.
       2018, Secretary's Preface. The backstory on the review, and on Mattis's
       conversion, come from interviews.

276   *"Graybeards":* The group is mentioned, though not identified, in
       Cheryl Pellerin, Department of Defense News, "Mattis Begins Nuclear-
       Focused Trip," Sept. 13, 2017. The details here, about their meetings
       and debates, come from interviews in 2018–19.

281   *It was a list that Miller had recited:* For instance, Frank Miller, "Key-
       note, 2015 US StratCom Deterrence Symposium," July 29, 2015; "INF
       Treaty: The Problem with the Arms Control Community," *Defense
       News*, Oct. 24, 2018.

281   *"a number of capabilities":* Hearing, House Armed Services Committee,
       Military Assessment of Nuclear Deterrence Requirements, March 8,
       2017, 30.

281   *"very comfortable":* Gen. John E. Hyten, Military Reporters and Editors
       Association Conference, Keynote Speech, March 31, 2017.

281   *"deter the Russians":* Hearing, House Armed Services Committee, Mil-
       itary Assessment of Nuclear Deterrence Requirements, March 8, 2017,
       op. cit.

282   *"modify a small number":* Department of Defense, Nuclear Posture Re-
       view, Feb. 2018, xii.

282   *"We felt strongly":* Quoted in Joseph Morton, "StratCom Commander
      Backs Deployment of Low-Yield Nukes on Submarine-Launched Bal-
      listic Missiles," *Omaha World-Herald*, March 21, 2018.

282   *"surrender or suicide":* Ibid.; Rebecca Kheel, "Mattis Defends New Nu-
      clear Capability," *The Hill*, Feb. 6, 2018.

283   *"Just to put a little specificity here":* Transcript, "A New Nuclear Arms Race,"
      Aspen Security Forum, July 20, 2018, https://aspensecurityforum.org
      /wp-content/uploads/2018/07/ASF-2018-A-New-Nuclear-Arms-Race.pdf.

283f *Like all hydrogen bombs:* A clear technical description of the low-yield
      Trident II can be found in Stephen Young, "The Case of the 'Low-
      Yield' Trident Warhead," Union of Concerned Scientists, March 19,
      2018. That the yield is 8 kilotons comes from interviews.

284   *the price tag:* Paul Sonne, "Trump Poised to Get New Low-Yield Nu-
      clear Weapons," *Washington Post*, June 13, 2018.

284   *"testing, acquisition":* Congressional Research Service, "Nuclear
      Weapon Initiatives: Low-Yield R&D, Advanced Concepts, Earth
      Penetrators, Test Readiness," March 8, 2004, https://fas.org/sgp/crs
      /nuke/RL32130.pdf; and interviews.

285   *"extremely rigorous":* Hearing, Senate Foreign Relations Committee,
      *The Authorizations for the Use of Military Force: Administration Per-
      spective*, Oct. 30, 2017, 62–63, 70.

285   *At the start of Trump's term:* Ibid., 61.

285   *"adult day care center":* @SenBobCorker, tweet, Oct. 8, 2017, 8:13 a.m.

285   *"path to World War III":* Jonathan Martin and Mark Landler, "Bob
      Corker Says Trump's Recklessness Threatens 'World War III,'" *New
      York Times*, Oct. 8, 2017.

285   *"riled up":* E-mail, Algene Sajery [policy director, Senate Foreign Re-
      lations Committee] to staff, "11/7 Nuclear Hearing," Oct. 31, 2017,
      10:56 a.m. (provided to author). Sajery cites Corker's remarks, adding,
      "That's a direct quote."

286   *In the interim:* Cited in Hearing, Senate Foreign Relations Committee,
      Authority to Order the Use of Nuclear Weapons, Nov. 14, 2017, 1.

286   *"Can the President really":* Ibid., 2.

286   *"The United States military":* Ibid.

286   *"Well":* Ibid., 18. That senators and staff were stunned by Kehler's re-
      mark comes from interviews.

287 *"I would have said"*: Ibid., 20.

287 *"Let me just pull back"*: Ibid., 25.

287 *"imminent attack"*: Ibid., 26.

288 *"nuclear decision-making"*: Ibid., 25.

288 *"Wait, stop"*: Ibid., 20.

288 *"decision authority"*: Ibid., 25, 21.

288 *"Absent a nuclear attack"*: Ibid., 29.

289 *the 1976 hearing:* Hearing, House International Relations Committee, *First Use of Nuclear Weapons: Preserving Responsible Control*, March 16, 18, 23, 25, 1976.

289 *In 1972:* Cited in staff memo to Sen. Corker, "Hearing—Authority to Order the Use of Nuclear Weapons," Nov. 14, 2017 (provided to author).

289 *"a bunch of bunker lawyers"*: Senate Foreign Relations Committee, op. cit., 28.

290 *"unusual orders"*: This story is the subject of much controversy, but the weight of evidence indicates it is true. It first appeared in Bernard Gwertzman, "Pentagon Kept Tight Rein in Last Days of Nixon Rule," *New York Times*, Aug. 25, 1974. Details were elaborated in Seymour Hersh, "The Pardon," *The Atlantic*, Aug. 1983. Schlesinger confirmed the story to me in a February 1982 interview. However, in a 2008 Oral History interview with Timothy Naftali for the Nixon Library, he backpedaled, saying he was only trying to preserve "the integrity of the chain of command" in case some "hotheaded freelancer" gained control (which makes no sense whatever). Stanley Kutler, a respected Nixon historian, doubted the story ("The Imaginings of James R. Schlesinger," *Huffington Post*, April 1, 2014), but he mainly quotes officers at the time who were insulted by Schlesinger's memo, thereby suggesting it did exist. However, the key piece of evidence comes from Jeffrey Smith, former CIA general counsel, now the head of Arnold & Porter Kaye Scholer's National Security practice, who wrote the following in "Of Laws, Not Men," *Just Security*, June 9, 2017: "In 1974, I was an Army JAG lawyer assigned to the Office of the Deputy Undersecretary of the Army for International Affairs. . . . In the days before President Nixon resigned, [the deputy undersecretary] called me into his office, and said, 'I am not supposed to show you this, but

you should see it. It's important.' It was a message from the Chairman of the Joint Chiefs to the four-star Commanders-in-Chief . . . saying that if they received any 'execute orders' from the NCA (the National Command Authority, i.e. the President), they were not to carry them out unless the order was verified by the Chairman of the Joint Chiefs and the Secretary of Defense. This episode is now being recalled as an example of how our institutions responded in a responsible way at an extraordinary and critical time."

290   *"How can I know"*: Ron Rosenbaum, *How the End Begins: The Road to a Nuclear World War III* (New York: Simon & Schuster, 2011), Chapter 2.

290   *"bilateral contact"*: National Committee on North Korea, "Kim Jong Un's 2018 New Year's Address," National Committee on North Korea, Jan. 1, 2018, https://www.ncnk.org/node/1427.

290   *On April 20:* "North Korea Says It Will Suspend Nuclear and Missile Tests, Shut Down Test Site," *Washington Post*, April 20, 2018.

291   *On June 12:* Fred Kaplan, "A Win for Kim: This Was a Very Good Day for the Leader of North Korea," *Slate*, June 12, 2018.

291   *Kim too may have been shaken:* I assess whether Trump deserved credit for the summit, and the chronology of Kim's nuclear and missile tests, in Fred Kaplan, "A Nobel for Trump?," *Slate*, May 1, 2018.

292   *"great historic cause"*: "Kim Jong Un's 2018 New Year's Address," op. cit.

292   *"verified the completion"*: "Kim Jong Un's announcement falls short of dismantling nuclear weapons," *Nikkei Asian Review*, April 21, 2018.

292   *"in the precise way"*: Daniel Ellsberg, *The Doomsday Machine* (New York: Bloomsbury, 2017), 319–25.

293   *"no longer a nuclear threat"*: Peter Baker and Choe Sang-Hun, "Trump Sees End to North Korea Nuclear Threat Despite Unclear Path," *New York Times*, June 13, 2018.

293   *"good friend"*: Reuters, "Trump Likely to Meet 'Good Friend' Kim in Early 2019, Says He's Getting Along Well with North Korean Leader," Dec. 2, 2018.

293   *"great leader"*: CNN, "Kim Calls Second Summit a 'Courageous Political Decision' by Trump," Feb. 27, 2019.

293   *"We fell in love"*: John Bacon, "President Trump on Kim Jong-un: 'We Fell in Love' over 'Beautiful Letters,'" *USA Today*, Sept. 30, 2018.

293   *"the worst deal ever":* David Sanger and Steven Erlanger, "Trump Is Expected to Leave Iran Deal, Allies Say," *New York Times*, May 7, 2018.

293   *"robust":* Paul Sonne, "Mattis, Who Supported Staying in Iran Deal, Holds Out Hope for Curtailing Tehran," *Washington Post*, May 9, 2018.

293   *Trump accused the Russians:* Fred Kaplan, "Trump's Missile Misfire," *Slate*, Oct. 22, 2018.

296   *"clever briefer":* I don't know how long the phrase has been around. In Z. Antonino et al., *How to Avoid a Nuclear War: Proceedings of the 2nd International Seminar on Nuclear War* (Singapore: World Scientific, 1992), George Rathjens recalls concerns about a "clever briefer" scenario in the mid-1960s ABM debate (pp. 233–34). In "The Subterranean World of the Bomb" (*Harper's*, March 1978), Ron Rosenbaum describes Morton Halperin, who worked in the Pentagon in the mid-1960s, citing the scenario. William Kaufmann, who was special assistant to secretaries of defense under every president from John Kennedy to Jimmy Carter, described the syndrome in his MIT graduate school seminar on Strategic Nuclear Forces when I took the class in 1976.

297   *"Everything about":* Bernard Brodie, *The Absolute Weapon* (New York: Harcourt Brace, 1946), 52.

298   *"God, that's a crazy":* Interview with Kaufmann, 1980.

INDEX

ABOUT THE AUTHOR

Fred Kaplan is the national security columnist for *Slate* and author of five previous books, including *Dark Territory: The Secret History of Cyber War*, *The Insurgents: David Petraeus and the Plot to Change the American Way of War* (which was a Pulitzer Prize finalist), *1959: The Year Everything Changed*, *Daydream Believers: How a Few Grand Ideas Wrecked American Power*, and *The Wizards of Armageddon*. A former Pulitzer Prize–winning reporter for the *Boston Globe*, he has also written for the *New York Times*, the *Washington Post*, the *New Yorker*, *Foreign Affairs*, and many other publications. He has been a fellow at the Council on Foreign Relations and the New America Foundation. He has a PhD from MIT. He lives in Brooklyn with his wife, Brooke Gladstone.

CPSIA information can be obtained
at www.ICGtesting.com
Printed in the USA
BVHW051546170622
639741BV00002B/2

9 781982 107307